# EVER SINCE SINAI

# EVER SINCE

# Irving M. Bunim

# SINAI

*Essays on the valued, the vanishing,
and the everlasting in American Jewish life*

EDITED AND ANNOTATED BY

RABBI CHARLES WENGROV

FELDHEIM PUBLISHERS

Jerusalem • New York • 5738 / 1977

ISBN 0-87306-138-1

Published 1977

Philipp Feldheim Inc.
96 East Broadway
New York, NY 10002

Feldheim Publishers Ltd
POB 6525, Jerusalem, Israel

Printed in Israel

Dedicated
with love and profound appreciation
for the inspiration and loving companionship
for half a century,
to the memory of my dear wife
Blanche
ע״ה

במלא לבה ונפשה מדות החסד הוקירה

תורה שמרה באהבה וביראה

בשמירת הלשון היתה זהירה

בניה חנכה לתורה להאדירה

חזוק טהרת המשפחה לכל הזהירה

בשערי תורה יבכו וסספדו מכירייה

אשת חיל היתה בלומה

כל כבודה בת מלך פנימה

בלומה העענטשא בת ר׳ יוסף אפרים פישל ע״ה

שבקה חיים לכל חי כ״ב אדר תשל״ו

יהא זכרה ברוך

This book is based on a series of lectures that I delivered several years ago to students of the Rabbi Jacob Joseph Rabbinical Seminary who were preparing for ordination.

In editing the lectures and preparing them for publication, Rabbi Charles Wengrov has enhanced them by drawing on the timeless teachings of our heritage as well as the world's literature, to expand the significance and range of application of the lessons and insights that I have sought to express.

As in my previous work, *Ethics from Sinai* on Pirkey Avoth, there is little here that is really altogether original. In my own way I have tried to present some valuable thoughts that I gleaned from the rich classical heritage of our Sages, and from the great Torah scholars of our time whom I have been privileged to know. It is my hope and trust that it will be as rewarding an experience to read these pages as it has been for me to bring them into the light of day.

ABBREVIATIONS IN THE NOTES

b.          *ben*, the son of (used also in the text)

Deut.       Deuteronomy

MdRSbY      *Mechilta d'Rabbi Shim'on ben Yoḥai*

MhG         *Midrash haGadol*

MT          Rambam (Maimonides), *Mishneh Torah (Yad haḤazakah)*

R.          *Rav, Rabbi* (used also in the text)

Tan.        *Midrash Tanḥuma*

TB          *Talmud Bavli*, Babylonian Talmud

TJ          *Talmud Yerushalmi*, Jerusalem Talmud (TB and TJ are used also in the text)

---

Editor's note:

I should like to express my gratitude to the *Beth haS'farim haLe'umi* in Jerusalem. Without its resources and the unfailing courtesy of its staff, my work on this volume could not have been done.                                                                    CW

# contents

# 1

## With all your heart

וְאָהַבְתָּ אֵת ה׳ אֱ־לֹהֶיךָ בְּכָל לְבָבְךָ וּבְכָל נַפְשְׁךָ וּבְכָל מְאֹדֶךָ
(דברים ו, ה)

*And you shall love the Lord your God with all your heart and
with all your soul and with all your might*

(Deuteronomy 6:5)

THERE ARE MANY WAYS to serve the Almighty. We can
serve Him with our feet, going to the synagogue to join a congregation in
prayer. We can go to a wedding or a *b'rith*, to add to the cheer and joy. Or
we can go to the hospital to visit an ailing friend. . . . We can serve Him
with our hands, by doing a *mitzvah*: giving charity, putting on *t'fillin,*
taking up a *lulav* and *ethrog* at Sukkoth time, etc. We can serve Him with
our eyes and ears, studying Torah and listening as it is taught. Yet the main
element in serving Him remains the heart, the center of our thoughts and
emotions, intentions and hopes. The main thing remains to make His will
our own, to serve Him with all the energy and enthusiasm we show when
we pursue our own strong desires.

The supreme example in serving our Maker is of course our first
Patriarch, Abraham. When he was 100 and Sarah 90, she bore him a single
son, at last. Then the day came when the Almighty ordered him to take
the boy up Mount Moriah and (as Abraham understood it) to offer him up
as a human sacrifice. If this was His will, Abraham was ready to obey,
overcoming every natural instinct of a father's compassion and love. *So
Abraham rose early in the morning* (Genesis 22:3). He didn't flee, or even tarry,
staying in bed another half-hour, another hour. He carried through his
mission with determination, as he would have obeyed any other Divine
command — till at last his son lay bound on the altar, and he stood there
with his knife poised, ready to offer up the boy's life. *Then the angel of the
Lord called to him from heaven and said, "Abraham, Abraham!" And he said,
"Here am I." And he said, "Do not raise your hand against the lad or do anything*

9

*to him. For now I know that you fear God, since you have not withheld your son,
your only one, from me (Genesis 22:11–12).*

It is a familiar story in the Bible. Yet do we ever stop and look at those
last two words? Surely it is strange that the angel should say, "from me"!
What did *he* have to do with it?

The answer lies in *Pirkey Avoth* (iv 13) רבי אליעזר בן יעקב אומר : העוֹשֹה
מצוה אחת קוֹנה לוֹ פרקליט אחד. R. Eliezer b. Yaakov says: Whoever does
one mitzvah, one religious good deed, gains one defense attorney for himself. And one early commentary[1] explains: This means an angel, an advocate
or champion of uprightness and integrity — as Scripture says, *If there be for
him an angel, an advocate, one among a thousand, to vouch for a man's uprightness* (Job 33:23).

With his extraordinary obedience to the Almighty, Abraham created
an angel. By his acceptance of the Divine will as though it was his own
passionate wish, he created a strong, healthy angel, if you will. He did the
mitzvah with all his heart; so, as we might say, the angel he created was
full-blooded, hale and hearty. The angel acknowledged it: "you did not
withhold your son, your only one, from me" — from your obedience to
God that brought me into being me. Even if you had had to slay your
son for Him, and thus create me, you would not have withheld him.[2]

Well, we hear the story chanted from the Torah every year in the
synagogue, on the Sabbath of *parshath va-yéra*, and perhaps we muse and
think about it a while; and then we go home to eat the Sabbath meal. It
would be better to stop and think: How could *we* reach this level of serving
God?

The teaching of the Sages was quoted above, that "whoever does one
mitzvah gains one defense attorney for himself." The teaching has a sequel:
"and whoever does one sinful deed gains one accuser, one prosecuting
attorney for himself." With an *avérah*, a bad deed that disobeys the Torah,
you also create an angel — an evil one, a demon spirit that goes up to heaven
to accuse you before the Divine court of justice, and seeks to plague you
and harm you.

Think then of a man going to do a sinful thing. Consider for example
an American Jew who lives up to the Psalmist's baleful description, *but they
mingled with the nations and learned their activities* (Psalms 106:35). So, like
many a good American, he goes for his night of card playing "with the
boys." As the room becomes tinged with the interesting blue haze of heavy
tobacco smoke, he sits thoroughly absorbed and embroiled in his poker

10

game. His whole life is in the cards. Every fiber and nerve is concentrated, as he ponders and cogitates the cards that fate has dealt him. Heaven help his wife if she should try to interrupt him with some minor message like "Mendl, there's a small fire broke out in the kitchen."

From him, dear reader, we can learn how to do a mitzvah: with all your heart — because it is a way of showing a love of the God who gave us life and sustenance. A mitzvah should be done with every fiber of our being concentrated on it, with the absorption of the dedicated or addicted poker player.

The idea is not new. The noted ḥassidic sage R. Bunem of P'shis-cha said: We can learn three things from a thief: (1) He is not too lazy to go about his work even in the middle of the night. (2) If he does not succeed the first time, he tries again and again, until he gets what he is after. (3) He does not despise any article as not worth the trouble, but is willing to stake his life for trifles.[3]

The Baal Shem Tov himself (the immortal founder of ḥassiduth) taught: "If the evil inclination (Satan) is alert in his work to persuade a man to commit a wicked deed, because thus he (Satan) carries out his duty . . . let a man learn a lesson to be equally alert and diligent in *his* work, not to listen to the evil inclination." At another time he said, "From the strong desire of Haman learn how to do with enthusiasm and alacrity the will of Mordecai."[4] (Consider the Haman of our day, the infamous Adolf Hitler. When did we ever mobilize for a great mitzvah the energy, resources and efficiency that he mobilized for his plans of destruction?)

There is a story told about one illustrious rabbi in the Poland of a bygone year who had to travel about often to gather funds, to maintain his large, noted yeshivah for fine young Torah scholars (quite possibly it was R. Meir Shapiro, founder and dean of Yeshivath Ḥachmey Lublin). In one particular town there was a man noted for his immense wealth. Rumor had it that he was one of the richest in the country. So whenever the rabbi came to the town, accompanied by his devoted attendant, he always went to visit this Jewish Croesus — and always to no avail. Not only would this moneybags give nothing. He always berated the rabbi soundly into the bargain, for daring to trouble him.

One freezing winter night the rabbi and his attendant came to the town, in the course of their travels, and they stopped at an inn to rest and warm up a bit. Hardly ten minutes had gone by when the rabbi spoke up: "Come, Zelig, let us go. We will visit that very rich man."

11

"What," Zelig groaned, "him? We have been to see him at least a dozen times, and all you have ever gotten for your troubles is a series of ringing, stinging insults. On a bitter-cold night like this, after a long hard journey, would it not be better if we just rested here till the morning, getting a good night's sleep?"

The rabbi persisted, however, and away they went. They knocked at the door and entered, and there stood the rich man himself. As he recognized them, he began his usual charming tirade: "What? Are *you* back again?" Suddenly, however, he stopped and shrugged his shoulder. "Oh well, what is the use? If you insist on coming back all the time, I suppose I will have to give in. Here . . . here is your donation." And he gave the rabbi a most handsome amount, that made up for all the other dozen times.

Back at the inn, Zelig the attendant asked in excitement, "Just tell me, dear rabbi: What made you decide to go again to his house? I would have given up on him long ago."

"I will tell you," the rabbi replied. "What always stopped him from giving us any assistance for the yeshivah? It could only be his evil inclination, the element of Satan within him. Well, I simply learned from Satan. If he could be so persistent and energetic, that every time I came there he prevented the man from giving a penny (though we know that every Jew descended from Abraham is inherently kind and compassionate), and he made the man insult me instead — I decided that I must be just as energetic and persistent. If Satan never lets up, neither must I."

How do we do our mitzvoth, though? Consider a person going to the synagogue, to join a congregation in prayer. He goes slowly, his mind on something else (or perhaps on several "something elses"). On the way he may dawdle a bit. If this may make him late, the thought does not seem to disturb him. In the synagogue, his thoughts may continue their travels during the prayers. When the Torah is read, he may not always pay attention either, especially if a whispered conversation fascinates him.

Similarly, when the time comes to give charity, he may give some token amount listlessly, throw in a few pennies. But his heart won't really be in it.

What kind of angel do we create when we do a mitzvah like that? It will probably be a cripple, without proper hands and feet, unable to move vigorously, but only managing to shuffle along, aimless and woebegone.

Or it will be a cardiac case, with a diseased heart, suffering from cardiac insufficiency.

How well we would do to remember Abraham and Isaac at the altar. He was ready to give up his son's life, dearer to him than his own, if God but wished it. With this kind of dedication we can make our observance and faith a force in our own life and in the lives of those about us.

## ❧ THE LASTING EFFECT

WHETHER WE LIKE IT OR NOT, whatever we do or fail to do affects not us alone. And this is a lesson driven home to us by the immortal words of the Sages.

In the *Book of Ruth* we read of Naomi returning to her region of Bethlehem in the land of Israel, after ten years in Moab. With her came her daughter-in-law Ruth, a Moabite young woman, now widowed, who insisted on staying with her and becoming a member of the Israelite people. Since the two had to eat and Naomi was old, Ruth left her at home and went to the field of Boaz, a family relation of Naomi's; and there she gleaned the fallen, forgotten ears of wheat, while the wheat harvest was in full swing.

Boaz soon noticed her, found out who she was, and invited her to come to his field (and nowhere else) and gather wheat as long as the harvest lasted; and when she was thirsty, she could drink from the water prepared for the hired hands (Ruth 2:5–9). At lunch-time he invited her to come and eat, in the field; *so she sat beside the reapers, and he passed her some parched grain (ibid.* 14). On this the Midrash expounds:

אָמַר רַבִּי יִצְחָק : לְמַדְתְּךָ הַתּוֹרָה דֶּרֶךְ אֶרֶץ, שֶׁכְּשֶׁאָדָם עוֹשֶׂה מִצְוָה יְהֵא עוֹשֶׂה אוֹתָהּ בְּלֵב שָׂמֵחַ [שָׁלֵם]. שֶׁאִלּוּ הָיָה רְאוּבֵן יוֹדֵעַ שֶׁהַקָּדוֹשׁ־בָּרוּךְ־הוּא כּוֹתֵב עָלָיו, וַיִּשְׁמַע רְאוּבֵן וַיַּצִּלֵהוּ מִיָּדָם (בראשית לז כא), בְּכִתְפוֹ הָיָה טוֹעֲנוֹ וּמוֹלִיכוֹ אֵצֶל אָבִיו. אִלּוּ הָיָה

13

אַהֲרֹן יוֹדֵעַ שֶׁהַקָּדוֹשׁ־בָּרוּךְ־הוּא כּוֹתֵב עָלָיו, וְגַם הִנֵּה הוּא יֹצֵא לִקְרָאתֶךָ וְרָאֲךָ וְשָׂמַח
בְּלִבּוֹ (שמות ד יד), בְּתֻפִּים וּבִמְחוֹלוֹת הָיָה יוֹצֵא לִקְרָאתוֹ. אִלּוּ הָיָה יוֹדֵעַ שֶׁהַקָּדוֹשׁ־
בָּרוּךְ־הוּא כּוֹתֵב עָלָיו, וַיִּצְבָּט לָה קָלִי (רות ב יד), עֲגָלוֹת פְּטוּמוֹת הָיָה מֵבִיא וּמַאֲכִילָה.
(ויקרא רבה לד ח; ילקוט שמעוני, רות תר״ד)

Said R. Yitzḥak: The Torah teaches you a proper rule of behavior — that when a man does a mitzvah, a good deed, he should do it with a good [whole] heart. For had Reuben known that the Holy, Blessed One would write about him, *And Reuben heard it, and he saved him from their hands* (Genesis 37:21), he would have carried him on his shoulder and brought him to his father. Had Aaron known that the Holy, Blessed One would write of him, *Moreover, behold, he is coming to meet you, and when he sees you he will be glad in his heart* (Exodus 4:14), he would have gone out to welcome him with timbrels and dancing. Had Boaz known that the Holy, Blessed One would write of him, *and he passed her some parched grain* (Ruth 2:14), he would have brought fatted calves and given them to her to eat.[5]

So states the Midrash. Now, the Torah tells what Reuben did. Jacob sent his son Joseph to see how his ten other sons were doing; and as Joseph approached his brothers, who envied and hated him, they began hatching a plot to kill him. So Reuben intervened, *and he said, "Let us not take his life." And Reuben said to them, "Shed no blood; cast him into this pit, here in the wilderness, but do not raise a hand against him"* — in order that he might save him out of their hand and restore him to his father (Genesis 37:21–22). He saved Joseph's life; he stopped the brothers from killing the lad. But he never carried out his plan. Long before he could return to the pit to get Joseph home, the brothers sold the lad to foreign traders, and he wound up as a slave in Egypt.

Well, the Midrash notes, had Reuben known the Torah would record his good deed and humane wish, he would have thrown caution to the winds and defied his brothers. Then and there he would have put Joseph on his shoulders and carried him home to his father.

Again, Aaron did a praiseworthy thing. After years away in Midian, Moses returned to tell him that the two were to go together to get the Israelites out of Egypt. Only, Moses would always receive God's message, and Aaron would merely be the spokesman, although he was the older brother. Yet the Almighty predicted that far from being envious or resentful, Aaron would be delighted to see him — and so he was. Says the Midrash: Had Aaron known the Torah would tell this about him, he would

14

just about have "called out the band" and "pulled out all the stops." He would have given Moses a royal, scintillating welcome.

Finally we return to Ruth and Boaz. He was kind to her. He gave her a friendly welcome when she came as a stranger to his field; he invited her to come and gather fallen, forgotten ears of grain during the entire harvest; and when she was thirsty she could take a drink from the reapers' water supply. Then he invited her to lunch, there in the field, with himself and the hired hands. And he made one more gesture of hospitality and kindness: He handed her some parched grain, a few roasted ears of wheat — a small gift held out with his fingertips, as the Midrash notes.[5] Yet again the Midrash adds: Had Boaz known this would appear in Scripture, he would have brought her fatted calves to eat—the most sumptuous feast he could provide.

What sense are we to make of it? Does it mean that these people would have played to the gallery? Had Reuben known he was on stage (before the television and newsreel cameras of posterity) he would have hammed it up? Had Aaron known the Torah was giving him publicity, he would have exaggerated his natural affection and joy at seeing his brother again after years of separation? Had Boaz known he was getting a write-up in Scripture, he would have gone all out in his generosity? Are we (Heaven forbid) to think of these personages in the Torah as movie actors, ready to turn on splendid performances specifically under the bright lights of posterity?

The truth is that whether or not they were recorded in the Torah made no direct difference to them. They received no greater or lesser reward because their deeds were written down. And small, partial or limited though their actions might have been, they were still acts of goodness and generosity, worthy of being set down in Scripture. Had they realized, however, that their deeds would become part of the Torah, part of our basic text of education and inspiration for all the generations, they would gladly have done more, to set yet better examples for our moral guidance.

Actually, though, why *were* such small, partial acts preserved in the Torah, for us to read again and again? The answer is: to teach us that when a person does a mitzvah, a religious good deed, he can never know what the end result will be. Reuben did a simple thing: he talked his brothers out of killing Joseph. He never dreamed that as a result, Joseph would live to become viceroy of Egypt and would save peoples and nations in the Mediterranean world from starvation when famine struck for seven years. He never dreamed that some day this very Joseph would take care of the

15

entire family: Jacob and all his sons, with their wives and children. Had he known that, the Midrash implies, he would have carried Joseph home on his shoulders, then and there. Had he suspected the far-reaching consequences of his touch of kindness, he would have "given it all he had."

Aaron went out to meet Moses, and gave him a friendly welcome, a cheerful hello. It was genuine, from the heart. The Almighty foretold, *when he sees you, he will be glad in his heart* (Exodus 4:14). So Moses was encouraged to enter Egypt, and the two brothers joined forces to carry out the Divine plan to free the Israelites. How could Aaron suspect that from this happy reunion Moses would go on not merely to take the Hebrews out of Egyptian slavery, but also to become the leader of the people, mediating between them and God, until he made them God's people, as he brought the Torah to the world? Could Aaron have foreseen any of this, he would have come out with music to greet his brother.

The same holds true for Boaz and Ruth. It was a small gesture of kindness. She was hungry, and he handed her some roasted wheat. Yet there were consequences, as Scripture relates. The two married, with the result that Ruth had a descendant named David — king of Israel, founder of Israel's royal family line. All who sat on the throne in Jerusalem after him were his direct descendants. The ultimate king of Israel in the future, the righteous Messiah, will be his descendant too.

So, had Boaz had an inkling that thanks to his bit of kindness, things would work out to make Ruth the ancestress of David and Israel's line of royalty, he would have given her not a few ears of parched wheat but fatted calves.

What is the lesson for us? We too will always find opportunities for doing mitzvoth, good deeds of all kinds — to give a dollar for a yeshiva, give a poor woman a few coins, provide an orphan with a suit of clothes for Sabbaths and Jewish holidays. And you too may never know. The orphan may become a top student at the yeshivah. The suit, the new jacket and trousers that really match and look so handsome, may spark some touch of animation, ambition and enthusiasm — and he may grow into a great Torah scholar in Jewry. His generation may recognize him some day as the greatest man of piety and learning. Believe it or not, such things have been known to happen.

So when you do a mitzvah, do it with all your heart. You never can tell what the far-reaching consequences will be of this little thing you are doing now. Reuben, Aaron and Boaz did not know either what the results

16

of their small acts would be; but the Almighty knew, and He had their acts recorded in the Torah. And had they themselves known, says the Midrash, they would have done so much more.

Our small and simple good deeds can also have wonderful consequences, as they become woven into the tapestry of our community life. The Midrash we quoted, on Reuben, Aaron and Boaz, has a sequel: "In the past, a man would do a mitzvah and the prophets would record it. Now, when there are no prophets, who writes it down? — Elijah and the royal Messiah; and the Holy, Blessed One sets His seal to it."[5]

Every good thing we do, the Midrash implies, is important to Elijah and the Messiah, because it helps make the world a bit more ready for the day when the Messiah can appear, heralded by Elijah at last.

So learn to recognize a golden opportunity for a mitzvah when it comes along. And if you can do more, don't hold back. Then you won't have any regrets later.

## ❧ SETTING A PRICE

IN ACTUAL TERMS OF DOLLARS AND CENTS, THOUGH, just what does it mean to do a mitzvah or to give "with all your heart"? Does it mean giving everything away to the first hundred people who ask for a handout? Does it mean going bankrupt, because *that* is really "with all your heart"? Few of us could or would live like that, and it would do more harm than good. It is enough to follow the guideline of the Torah's law of *maasér*, the tithe. In ancient Israel a farmer had to give a tithe, a tenth of his produce, to the Levites. So observant Jews today generally set aside a tenth of their income for charity, thus following also the example of our Patriarch Jacob, who vowed to the Almighty, *of all that Thou wilt give me, I shall surely separate a tithe for Thee* (Genesis 28:22).

In some cases, however, a mitzvah demands its own price, whatever it may be, if we are to act "with all our heart"; and what that price is, we may discover in quite an unexpected way.

17

Let us dip into the Bible, our Written Torah, once again. In chapters 3 and 8 of *be-midbar*, the Book of Numbers, the Almighty bids Moses replace the firstborn with Levites. Ever since the Hebrews left Egypt, the firstborn — whatever son in any and every family who was the very first child — were destined to serve the Almighty by offering sacrifices, when a sanctuary would be built. In fact, says the Talmud (TB *Z'vaḥim* 112b), until the *mishkan* was built — the Tabernacle, the temporary and portable sanctuary in the wilderness — sacrifices might be offered up anywhere on *bamoth* ("high places"), and firstborn sons officiated in making the offerings. Once the *mishkan* was built, however, the tribe of Lévi had to take their place.

So we read: *Thus you shall separate the Levites from among the Israelites, and the Levites shall be Mine. And after that the Levites shall go in to do the service of the Tent of Meeting. . . . For they are wholly given to Me from among the Israelites; instead of all that were first from the womb, the firstborn of all the Israelites, I have taken them to Me. For all the firstborn among the Israelites are Mine . . . on the day I smote all the firstborn in the land of Egypt, I hallowed them for Me* (Numbers 8:14–17).

Because the Almighty slew all the firstborn sons of the Egyptians while none among the Hebrews were harmed, the Israelite firstborn became holy to the Almighty. Now, when the *mishkan* was up, however, the Levites had to take their place — because (as the Sages teach)[6] when the Hebrews made the Golden Calf, the firstborn sons had joined in worshipping it, but the tribe of Lévi had not.

So every firstborn Israelite had to be "redeemed" by a Levite: As a Levite took his place, the state of holiness was transferred from him to the Levite. There were, however, 273 more firstborn Israelites then Levites. How were they to exchange their state of holiness, to be able to lead ordinary lives? Said the Almighty to Moses: *And as for the redemption of the two hundred and seventy-three among the Israelite firstborn who are over and above the number of the Levites, you shall take five shekels, five shekels a head . . . and you shall give the money to Aaron and his sons as the redemption price of those who are in excess* (Numbers 3:46–48).

It was straightforward enough. Yet one thing is puzzling: why only five shekels? True, when a firstborn baby boy reaches the age of thirty days, he is always redeemed (at the ceremony of *pidyon ha-ben*) by giving five shekels to a kohen. But that is because he is only a baby. By the Torah's law, if someone vowed about another person, ערכּוֹ עלי "His valuation be

18

upon me," it means he would have to give to the Sanctuary treasury the *erech*, the "valuation" of that other person; and for a child under five the valuation was five shekels (Leviticus 27:6). For older persons, however, it had to be more (*ibid.* 3–5). They why was the redemption price here, for the 273 firstborn Israelites, specifically five shekels?

We find an unexpected answer in the commentary of Rashi: כָּךְ הָיְתָה מְכִירָתוֹ שֶׁל יוֹסֵף, עֶשְׂרִים כָּסֶף, שֶׁהָיָה בְּכוֹרָה שֶׁל רָחֵל "This was the price for the sale of Joseph — twenty pieces of silver (Genesis 37:28) — who was the firstborn son of Rachel."[7] A shekel was worth four pieces of silver; so those firstborn among the Israelites who needed to be redeemed actually had to give the equivalent of twenty pieces of silver: five shekels.

Yet the explanation needs an explanation. What connection is there really between the sale of Joseph by his brothers and the firstborn sons of the Hebrews? Did the Almighty decree this price simply as measure for measure, tit for tat?

Stop and consider, though. Who were those firstborn Israelites? They were the original servants of the Lord, intended from the start to serve as His ministers at the *mishkan*. They were to be His holy servants, offering up His sacrifices. When you come to redeem a servant of the Lord, says the Torah, do not sell him short. Let him not be worth less to you than what those Midianite or Ishmaelite traders who bought Joseph were willing to pay for a little servant boy. Pay for a servant of Mine, says the Almighty, at least what those heathen paid for a Hebrew boy — not less.

I do not know what the figures are today, but some time in the past it was calculated that on an average it cost between six and twelve hundred dollars to give one pupil one year of education in an American elementary school. Thus city, state and/or federal governments bore an expense of perhaps $9600 to put a boy through elementary school. To carry him through high school would require at least fifteen hundred dollars a year, which means an additional $6,000. Let the boy continue into a city college or univeristy, and it would mean a further cost of perhaps $15,000 till the boy had a bachelor's degree.

So when a good Jewish boy went through the public school system — elementary school, high school and college — the city, state and/or federal governments were willing to pay some $31,000 to make him (hopefully) a good, intelligent young man. Today the cost is certainly much higher. Then how much is it worth to us to develop a Jewish boy into a good, intelligent young Torah scholar?

19

In a case like this, the Almighty makes His point clear: Do not sell My servant short. Do not pay less to acquire him, to make him a healthy, creative part of My faithful people, than what others — outsiders — are ready to pay for him.

The next time you are asked to give generously for a yeshivah, to help support an effective, vital Torah school, bear in mind that here it is not enough to give a token amount. Pious wishes will not do. If we do not give enough for Torah education, with all our heart, to fulfill the sacred obligation our people have carried ever since Sinai, remember that the American culture is ready to give more (with no ill will, but only with the best intentions in the world) to draw our children away from the Torah, our only hope for spiritual survival.

Going further, I recall reading about a conference of missionaries held in Oakland, California. There was a comprehensive report of their activities and accomplishments, with all kinds of facts and figures; and after careful calculation they concluded that it cost them $50,000 to convert one Jew to their "true faith." This was the price they paid, if you will, to buy a Jewish soul.

Ever since I read this, I could not forget it. If ever the question should arise, "How much it it worth to us to save a Jewish soul?" I know that in Oakland, California the missionaries gave us an answer we dare not ignore.

Once I told Rabbi Aaron Kotler (of blessed memory) of this report from the missionaries' conference. "*Oy,*" he groaned: "a Jewish soul!" It gave this great Talmudic scholar physical pain to think of a Jew lured into a "salvation" that he knew to be perdition. At another time I had the opportunity to tell the same thing to the late David Ben-Gurion, Israel's famed first prime minister. "Fifty thousand dollars!" he repeated, marveling. He was impressed that people were willing to spend so much to gain the heart of a Jew.

The next time you hear how much a yeshivah needs to be able to take in another Jewish student, how will *you* react? Will you be impressed by the size of the cost? Will it seem overwhelming to you? Or will you follow the sainted Rav Aaron Kotler's way and think of the immeasurable value of a Jewish soul?

Remember the Almighty's rule: Do not sell My servant short! For a servant of Mine, do not give less than others would!

20

# ❦ THE VALUE VANISHES

WHY DO WE STRESS SO MUCH the importance of Torah in Jewish life? — because with Torah alone we find permanence. Only the Torah infuses the age-old, enduring values of our faith into our life, and lets us pass them on to the next generation. Anything else, however attractive, precious and wonderful it seems, eventually turns out to be ephemeral. The value vanishes, like smoke in the wind, leaving dross with a bitter aftertaste.

In symbolic terms, the Talmud (TB *Avodah Zarah* 17a) makes this clear by relating a story:

It was told of Eliezer b. Durdya that there was not one courtesan in the world with whom he had failed to become intimate. Once he heard that there was one particular woman of pleasure in a faraway region who took a purse full of *denarii* (coins) as her fee. He took a purse filled with *denarii* and went, crossing seven rivers on account of her. During the cultivation of their intimacy, she emitted flatulence. Then he heard a heavenly voice saying,[8] "Just as this [foul] wind will never return to its origin, so will Eliezer b. Durdya never be accepted in repentance."

He went and sat among the mountains and hills. Said he, "O mountains and hills, beseech mercy for me!" They replied, "Sooner than plead for you, let us plead for ourselves" — for Scripture says, *For the mountains shall depart, and the hills be removed* (Isaiah 54:10). Said he, "O heaven and earth, beseech mercy for me!" They replied, "Sooner than plead for you, let us plead for ourselves" — as Scripture says, *for the heavens shall vanish like smoke, and the earth will wear out like a garment* (ibid. 51:6). Said he, "O sun and moon, implore mercy for me!" They replied, "Sooner than plead for you, let us plead for ourselves" — as Scripture says, *Then the moon will be confounded, and the sun ashamed* (ibid. 24:23). Said he, "O stars and constellations, implore mercy for me!" They replied, "Sooner than plead for you, let us plead for ourselves" — as Scripture says, *And all the host of heaven shall moulder away* (ibid. 34:4).

Said he, "The matter depends on nothing but myself alone." He put his head between his knees and groaned in his bitter weeping, until his soul expired. A heavenly voice resounded, saying, "Rabbi Eliezer b. Durdya is eligible for life in the world-to-come."

Quite clearly this is a true story. The incident happened. Yet just as clearly, it is set down in the Talmud as an allegory, to teach us something by its symbolism (as the sainted R. Aaron Lewin, the late rabbi of Reisha or Rzeszow, Poland — who lost his life in the Holocaust — once explained).

In the world of Freud, where conjugal relations between man and woman were a matter for repression and severe denial from the conscious mind, he concluded that symbols in dreams generally alluded to just such relations. In other times and places, where no severe repression of this kind existed, the opposite was found: dreams of conjugal intimacy were symbols of achievement in life. Thus the Talmud teaches (TB *B'rachoth* 57a) that a dream of incest can foretell the gaining of understanding or wisdom; a dream of adultery can indicate the certainty of living on in the Hereafter. In our time at least one foremost psychoanalyst (Erik Erikson) has noted the precise prallels in human development between a person's way of functioning in everyday life and his way of intimacy with a life-partner. Whether in maturity or neurosis, one will parallel the other.[9]

So the pursuit of courtesans and women of pleasure can be taken as a symbol for the drive to achieve any goals that attract and allure, promising supposedly wonderful rewards. In the time of the Second Temple, for example, there was Hellenism; and enough of our Jewish youth pursued that with a vengeance. They were convinced that Hellenism would open to them the doors of a wider, better world. They could compete in sports against the athletes of neighboring countries, in the olympic games of the ancient world. Of course, it meant appearing in the nude (that is the way it was done), with the sign of circumcision surgically disguised. It meant making a gesture of worship to the Greek god that supposedly presided over the games. "But," said the eager, determined, impassioned Jewish youth, "so what?" ... And Hellenism would mean opening connections of business and trade with neighboring Greek-style cities, and participating in their "rich" cultural life. ... There was Greek culture, with sophisticated philosophy, that seemed so much more wonderful than the old, familiar Torah.

It needed the courage of a Mattithyahu, the aged father of the Maccabees, to rise up and kill a Jew being seduced by this harlotry (just as, long before that, a grandson of Aaron named Pinḥas rose up and killed a prince of the tribe of Shimon when he was being seduced by a more blatant and literal harlotry). Only that marked a full, determined stop to the movement away from observant Judaism which was gathering a frightening momentum. And it took a war by the Maccabees to regain the ancient Sanctuary and cleanse it from the defilement that it suffered, because so many Jews had eagerly espoused Hellenism.

The Hellenists among our people were enthusiastic in their time. They had drive and verve, vigor and vim. And the result was a bloody war, that cost our people untold death and suffering.

Who were the early Christians, that started *their* movement in Israel? They too were Jews. They found its teachings so beautiful, as in a dream. The Pharisees with their Talmudic law were too much into reality for their liking. But they never realized that you cannot live in a dream world; and if you insist on living there, you wake up in a nightmare.

They began a movement that seemed all loving-kindness and roses; and it evolved into a nightmare — with Jewish victims. When Roman emperors were converted to Christianity, Jews were taken to Rome and thrown into cages. Like the Hellenists before them, they were going to participate in sports — now in the arena of the gladiators.

Christianity flowered in Europe, and Jews were expelled wholesale from their lands of settlement, or were burned, or baptized — because originally other Jews espoused eagerly a new religion of love.

Emancipation came at last to the Jews of Europe. The walls of the ghetto began breaking down. And our youth saw new goals of harlotry to pursue. There was *haskalah*, intellectual freedom and equality, education in the literature and culture of an enlightened Europe. So a way was paved to assimilation, with Moses Mendelssohn leading the grand march.

In Germany the youth saw equality in their reach at last: equality in the culture and social life. They would be accepted into refined German society. So Germany became their new Jerusalem. From their prayer-books they threw out every mention of the original Jerusalem, every bit of prayer and supplication to return to the holy city. They had it made right where they were. They had their courtesan to pursue and win: a secure cultured life in Germany. It was a dream — till Hitler came and they awoke to find this a nightmare also.

Then there was Karl Marx, the son of a baptized Jewish father. He wrote an essay against the Jews with more poison in it than anything ever written by a Nazi theoretician like Goebbels. Yet that never bothered the

23

Jews who became inflamed with ardor for his socialist doctrine. He found a disciple in Lenin, and eventually, in 1917, there was a revolution in Russia. Who will ever know how much Jewish energy and enthusiasm, dedication and devotion went into that revolution? How many burning zealots like Trotsky came from our people, preaching the Marxist gospel, stirring up the masses in pre-revolutionary Russia, fomenting the upheaval that was going to bring utopia for all.[9a] They were in the forefront of the new Soviet government, destroying the age-old religion of their people as ruthlessly as they could. They formed the *yevsektsia*, the Jewish sections of the Soviet propaganda machine, grinding out the communist line with rare power and spirit — till 1930. By then, Stalin's purges had cleaned them out. Not a single Jew remained in the leadership of the Soviet communist party; and Russian Jews were singled out for the special attention of the full Soviet machinery of tyranny, cruelty and suppression.

Chaim Weizmann left his *shtetl* in Eastern Europe as a young man, to study chemistry at a Central European university (and in his *shtetl* he left behind all connections with observant Judaism). Then he moved to England, to pursue his academic career at the university in Manchester. And in the English people and their government he saw the key to his Zionist dream. The English were civilized, and they knew and loved the Bible. They would surely want to help the Jews, the people of the Bible, return to Palestine, the land of the Bible, in fulfillment of the Divine promise to the Patriarchs.

This too was a rosy dream; and it seemed to be coming true, as Britain issued its Balfour Declaration, and then became the ruler of the holy land under a mandate from the League of Nations.

From that dream too, Weizmann and his followers awoke with a bad headache. The British loved the Arabs too much and wanted their friendship too intensely to treat the Jews with any kind of fairness, let alone compassion.

So it was decided that the trouble lay in the government that England had. If only a labor government were in power, *it* would be friendly to the Jews in Palestine. A labor government took office, and it issued a White Paper, worse than anything which had gone before.... Thus it went, through the decades and eras of our history.

Eliezer b. Durdya, says the Talmud, went after every courtesan and woman of pleasure. There was not one he overlooked or neglected. He found delight with all of them. Our youth went after every attraction and appealing ideal that this world ever offered. We gave our strength, enthusiasm and passionate commitment. In the thirties, when mass rallies were held in Madison Square Garden (New York) in support of the poor, common Spanish people embroiled in a Fascist-fomented civil war, a disproportionately large number of young Jewish intellectuals filled the seats and responded with fervor. When volunteers from the Western world formed the Lincoln Brigade to fight in the Spanish Civil War, a good number of them were Jewish. In 1964 the time came for freedom marches and similar activities down south in the United States, to give the Negroes truly equal rights instead of lip service and Jim Crow laws; and in the forefront there were Jews again — until Michael Schwerner, a 24-year-old social worker from Brooklyn, and Andrew Goodman, a 20-year-old student from Queens (New York), were murdered in a small town in Mississippi on June 21. Whatever caught their hearts, our youth went to it with fervor, no matter what the cost.

The time came, says the Talmud, when Eliezer b. Durdya heard of one lady of the evening who was utterly superb, but frightfully expensive. Undeterred, he took money enough and crossed seven rivers to reach her. Just so was our youth never deterred. As long as the goal beckoned, promising some glorious achievement, no price was too high, no effort too much. We crossed seven rivers and seven oceans to reach our destinations — to build empires of industry in an America where that meant the acme of success; to gain entry into country clubs where *that* was the measure of achievement.

Eliezer b. Durdya came, saw, and wished to conquer. He began wooing the fabled lady of pleasure, when suddenly an offensive wind was in the air. With his goal in reach, he found it was all a foul, empty wind. All the worth and value of it vanished. Hellenism was vapid; the new religion of love was murderous in its cruelty. All the ideals and determined hopes left a vile odor behind them, in their utter disintegration. The heated, impassioned disciples of Marx and Engels and Lenin, sworn to achieve a worker's paradise in a socialist utopia, met sudden death in Stalin's purges or were sent to Siberian labor camps for "corrective re-education." Siberia had the ideal winds and temperature for cooling hot-heads and tempering impassioned thinking.

Generations of Jews wooed the goal of equality and security on German soil. They fervently espoused German ideals, German civilization, German culture. The last generation went to the concentration camps.

25

In the narrative of the Talmud, Eliezer b. Durdya reached a moment of truth. Just when he thought he "had it made," when he believed (in the words of a popular song) that "everything's going my way," he heard a strange heavenly voice telling him, "Just as the wind never returns to its origin, so will Eliezer b. Durdya never be accepted back in repentance." He was finished, *kaput*. He had made it to nowhere. In a flash he summed up his life. It added up to zero.

He had no one, nothing permanent left in his life, with which he could stay.... So he went to the hills and mountains. They were solid and dependable, like the Rock of Gibraltar. He asked them to pray for him, to help him find some anchor in life, some permanence.

My mind goes back to the early forties. The ghastly facts of the Nazi "final solution" reached us with the force of a sledge-hammer, and orthodox Jewry frantically organized its *Vaad Hatzalah*, its emergency rescue committee, to see who or what could be saved from the blazing inferno of Hitler's crematoriums and gas chambers. I was in the midst of the activities, and everywhere I could see Jews facing their own moment of truth, like Eliezer b. Durdya. As our people realized what was happening in Nazi-dominated Europe, they too felt (like Eliezer) their whole world turn to a shambles. All they believed in and hoped for in the world of man seemed to have crumbled.... And like Eliezer, they turned to the "mountains and hills" of the Western world, the great statesmen in whom they placed their trust, the supposed pillars of Western civilization.

At one point there were a thousand Jewish children somewhere in Europe destined for death in Germany's scientifically efficient timetable. The Jewish people turned to Anthony Eden, the polished urbane foreign secretary of England who had always opposed Neville Chamberlain and his jelly-like appeasement of Adolf Hitler. Eden had always believed in firmly opposing the Nazi threat. So the Jews, believing in him, pleaded with him: Take the thousand children into England and save them. Let them live!

The hills and mountains could not help Eliezer b. Durdya. "Pray for *you*, to gain some permanence in the world? We have to pray for our own future. The prophet foretold that some day we will be gone!" Earthquakes, upheavals in the earth's crust, can put a mountain under water before you can realize what has happened. Could Anthony Eden give a thousand children a foothold in life, to save them from extermination? He had to worry about his own political life, his precious career. What would the

British say? They would not be pleased at all if he overloaded their little island with a thousand foreign youngsters when they had their hands full with their own wartime problems. No, he could not save those children. He was sorry, but they would have to become statistics of the Holocaust.

Weizmann and his devoted followers believed in England as the savior of Zionism. The British, they said firmly, would make Palestine a homeland once again for the Jewish people. So England ruled Palestine, and our people built their new settlements there. And when we pleaded with the British to let Jews in from Hitler's inferno, they answered with White Papers. They flimflammed Weizmann and left him cooling his heels, while the victims of the Nazis perished. England, supposedly as dependable as its Rock of Gibraltar, was concerned with its own future in the Middle East, and so sacrificed Jewish interests for Arab good will. Those hills and mountains, you see, had their own worries. They could have precious little concern for us.

Information came through on the exact location of the crematoriums and gas chambers: Auschwitz, Buchenwald, and other names that acquired their grisly notoriety. So we ran to other hills and mountains. British Jews without number held Winston Churchill in high regard: a humane, compassionate statesman and leader, par excellence. And the Jews in America swore by Franklin D. Roosevelt. He was always so friendly and charming in his fireside chats. The Jews backed him passionately in every presidential election. So they went to Prime Minister Churchill in London and to President Roosevelt in Washington; and they explained and implored: The Nazis had a machine, a system of terrifying efficiency, and a timetable, to exterminate Jews by the millions at these specific places. Order a few air raids, to bomb those places out of existence. The Jews who were there at the time would thus be killed, but they were doomed anyway, by the Nazi timetable. And then the German beasts would no longer have the means to dispose of Jews by the millions.

Alas, the mountains and hills had their own problems. To save the world for democracy and ensure their place in history, Churchill and Roosevelt needed a great military victory. They had little time or concern for minor side-problems, like saving millions of innocent Jewish lives.

At one point 700 refugees from Holland managed to reach Cuba by ship. People pleaded with Franklin D. Roosevelt for permission to let them enter the United States. He could not be bothered. He was busy with matters of state. They had to return to Europe, to the Nazi death houses.[10]

27

Among the hills and the mountains Eliezer b. Durdya sat alone, abandoned, bereft. So strong and dependable they had seemed in all the years he had run his happy course. And now they could not help him. "O heaven and earth," he cried out, "beseech mercy for me!"

Surrounding the mountains and hills, above and below them, were heaven and earth. Perhaps they could help. Beyond the statesmen and countries that would not help us, there was the League of Nations. Perhaps *it* would come to our rescue. Perhaps it would speak out against Nazi Germany and stop its diabolic activities. Perhaps it would order England, which ruled Palestine by its mandate, to let Jews into their homeland without restraint. . . .

Neither could heaven and earth help Eliezer b. Durdya. The prophet foretold that they too would not last forever. They were only forms of mass and energy that would wear out and vanish one fine day . . . The League of Nations could not last either. It was moribund, needing only to wake up to realize that it was defunct.

In our time there is the United Nations; and occasionally we turn to it, not for mercy but at least for justice. And we find it going lopsided, overloaded with Arab influence.

Eliezer b. Durdya looked about him in his misery and despair. What was left for him to turn to? There was still the sun shining by day, the moon by night. So he begged them to pray for him — but again to no avail. They too had been promised by the prophet that one day they would go out of existence.

In ancient times the sun and moon had been worshipped as deities. In our time they are studied by scientists. The sun's composition is analyzed. Its gaseous emanations and radiations are minutely scrutinized. The moon has become our first station in space travel, and samples of moon rock have been brought back for analysis.

Once the sun and moon were worshipped as deities that ruled the world. Today science studies them, and knows better than to worship them. But instead, starting in the nineteenth century, mankind has taken to worshipping science. Its discoveries and developments have been so marvelous and magical, so incredible and amazing. So people developed the firm belief that science *must* lead mankind to a better life in a better world. We could certainly look to science (they comfortably assured everyone) for security and steady improvement.

28

Well, Germany was famous for its science. It had superb scientists. And they helped work out the most efficient ways of killing the six million victims of the Holocaust. They found methods to prevent the masses of dead bodies from starting an epidemic and ravaging Europe with disease. There were instant mass burials in huge graves that the victims dug before being shot to death. There were mass cremations. . . . They were very good scientists, even brilliant; only, they were not human. Some of them even used Jewish subjects for "experiments" in unimaginable cruelty.

Science gave the world new weapons and techniques, but no morality. It could pray for no one. It could help no one. . . . Even when it produced the most appalling weapon of all since human history began — the atomic bomb — scientists could only disclaim all moral responsibility and guilt. They could merely give mankind the products of their theories and experiments. It was for mankind and its leaders to decide where to go from there.[11]

Night came upon Eliezer b. Durdya, alone among the hills and the mountains. He looked up once more, and saw stars and constellations. "Pray mercy for me," he begged them; but this too was futile,

The world has many stars and luminaries that shine in their prominence. For instance, in the Vatican in Rome sits a gentleman in fancy robes whose word is law to millions of faithful followers. To this day it remains an unsettled question if the gentleman who held this post in Hitler's day ever moved in any significant way to help the Jews going by the millions like cattle to the slaughter. According to a stage-play by a non-Jewish dramatist ("The Deputy") he did a great deal of nothing. The Vatican itself differed, giving a fine casuistical answer to the question, to show that the Pope in Hitler's day did very much. Of course, it remains strange that wherever and whenever any other individual or group, people or country worked with energy and dedication to rescue Jews, we generally knew about it at the time or immediately after the war. Truth, like oil, has a way of rising to the water's surface and becoming visible.[11a]

At any rate, there is much to be learned from the instructive actions of a later Pope or two: for instance, when it became clear that in the nineteen years when Jordan held the Old City of Jerusalem, its Arab citizens tore down old historic synagogues and left Jewish holy places in utter ruins. They even used Jewish tombstones for building materials. The cry of outrage from the Vatican against such heinous acts of despoliation by the Arabs under Jordan was very significant — the cry of outrage that never came. From the Vatican we heard clear, undisturbed, diabolic silence. Only when Israel regained the Old City, in the wake of the Six-Day War, did the venerated gentleman in Rome display signs of anxiety and agitation: He felt *his* holy places were in jeopardy (and this has remained the charged emotion at the Vatican).

When Arab infiltrators entered Israel and slaughtered innocent people, including women and children, time and again the Vatican remained calm and still, in marvelous self-control. Then, in one particular retaliatory raid, Israel's defense forces landed in an Arab airfield, carefully removed every human being, and blew up thirteen planes. Not a soul was hurt. The Pope reacted, however. This shook him to the core. Yet when Nasser (Sadat's charming predecessor) solemnly promised to move the entire Jewish population of Israel slightly to the left — into the Mediterranean Ocean — the gentleman in the Vatican was again in admirable self-control. He remained still, quite undisturbed.

Some Jews may have always looked to American presidents and leading statesmen, from Dwight David Eisenhower down to our day, as shining stars in the firmament who would ensure Israel's peace and permanence. Whatever illusions we may have had, one by one, from one president to another, the illusions have faded away, like the stars at dawn.

Over and over, the symbolic story of Elezer b. Durdya has been repeated, by individuals and whole sections of our people. It is as if they caught the Torah's directive to serve "with all your heart and with all your soul and with all your might" (Deuteronomy 6:5), but they merely overlooked the first part: that this has to be the way to serve the Lord your God, and nobody and nothing else. They always thought they would make it to a great achievement some other way; they would find security or fame, strike roots, build something enduring and permanent. And always there came a moment of truth, when against their will they realized it was all a wind, a miasma of nothing, stench without substance.

Try as we might, the moment of truth cannot be avoided. There is a story told about R. Sh'néor Zalman of Lyady, the founder and first *rebbe* of the hassidic movement of Lubavitch (*habad*). When he began teaching his new concepts and ways in Divine worship (within the laws of the Torah), his innovations aroused such resentment and hostility among others that they were moved to bring accusations against him to the government of

the Russian czar: that he was a source of dissension and treasonous dis-
loyalty to Russia, etc. — until he was put under arrest and taken to the
prison in St Petersburg (called Leningrad today). As he sat in his cell, the
chief of police came in for some preliminary questioning; and he found
the aged rabbi sunk in his holy thoughts. For even in a prison cell his mind
kept working on the Torah. Suddenly a point came up in the police chief's
mind, which had been troubling him. Although a non-Jew, he loved to
read the Bible; and he found one thing in it difficult. "There is something I
would like to ask you," he told the sage. "Will you give me an answer?"

"Ask whatever you like," R. Sh'néor Zalman replied.

"Tell me: what does it mean when it says in the Bible, *Then the Lord
called to the man and said to him: Where are you* (Genesis 3:9)? How can we
imagine that the Almighty did not know where Adam was (because he and
Eve had just eaten the forbidden fruit and, hearing God approaching, they
had hidden)?"

Slowly the first *rebbe* of Lubavitch replied, "Do you believe that the
Bible was given for all time, and it applies always and everywhere, to every
generation and every person?"

"Oh, yes," replied the chief of police. "I believe that."

Said the hassidic sage, "This verse in the Bible means that the Almighty
always calls to everyone and asks, *Where are you?* Where are you at in the
world? Here a person is allotted a set number of days and years of life, so
that each and every day he can do some good for the Lord and for human
beings. Then ponder and consider: Where are you in your world? How
many years of your life have already passed by, and what have you accomplished in those years? For example, *you* have lived such-and-such a number
of years" (he gave the exact age of the police chief) "and what have you
accomplished in that time? Whom have you benefited?..."[12]

In the utter stillness of a man's reflection, the Divine question will suddenly
infiltrate, "Where are you?" We have to realize and decide on our position
and identity, and we have to answer for it. In our human condition, there
is no escape.

Take the case of Moses Hess in the mid-19th century, in some ways a
fascinating bit of a parallel or sequel to Eliezer b. Durdya. For years he
lived with a non-Jewish girl of sordid background, whom he had met in a
house of ill repute, until at last he married her (although she never converted
to Judaism). For most of his adult life, although from an orthodox back-

ground, he wanted nothing to do with Jews and Judaism. He was going to solve the problems of all mankind, with the help of the writings of Spinoza and Hegel. A contemporary (and would-be friend) of Karl Marx, he too spouted a brand of socialism; and as a result he shuttled between France and his native Germany, shadowed and hounded by secret police as a dangerous, unwanted radical.

For a while he worked with Marx on a socialist newspaper that they started, but they broke apart. To his fellow-Jews he was a radical; to his fellow-socialists he was a Jew; to his friends he was a burden and a bore; to his family he was a skeleton in the closet. So he lived a hand-to-mouth existence as a *luftmentsh*.

At last, in 1840, he was stirred to his roots by a dreadful blood libel in Damascus. He was forced to realize how brutally people in the world could treat the Jews, and how indifferent other people would remain. Like Herzl decades later at the trial of Dreyfus, he heard the quiet heavenly voice asking, "Where are you?" He had to face the fact that he was a Jew, and with his brethren he shared a special poignant vulnerability. With feverish intensity he began studying and pondering the history, character and destiny of the Jewish people.

In 1861 a new German emperor declared a political amnesty. After years as *persona non grata* there, Moses Hess could return at last to his native land; there he studied his fellow-Jews in Germany at first hand. And he was appalled. He found them turning to Reform Judaism with lightning speed, to achieve a total elimination or disguise of anything Jewish in their appearance and way of life.

Suddenly everything he had experienced and realized in the past two decades came to a boil. He sat down and wrote *Rome and Jerusalem*, anticipating everything Herzl and the Zionists were to declaim in later years. The enlightened radical socialist turned about and demanded of his people that they return to their spiritual origins *in their homeland*. And much in his book was directed specifically to his brethren in Germany. In the apt words of one current writer, "He prophesied disaster to those reformers who were seeking to transform the Mendelssohnian doctrine of enlightenment into an Israelite reflection of German secular culture. The man struck at the roots of their belief when, in a few sentences, he showed them that Judaism could not survive if served up as a pardonable accident of birth with slight abnormalities which could be successfully treated by a generous larding of Teutonic unction."[13]

32

After decades of a wasted life scattered to the winds of socialist theory, Hess found his moment of truth, and he warned his compatriots: "No reform of the Jewish religion, however extreme, is radical enough for the educated German Jew. But the endeavours are in vain. Even conversion itself does not relieve the Jew from the enormous pressure of German anti-semitism. The German hates the Jewish religion not less than the race; he objects less to the Jews' peculiar beliefs than to their peculiar noses."[14]

Alone among the hills and the mountains, Eliezer b. Durdya realized he had reached the end of the road. Courtesans, ladies of pleasure, the pursuit of fun and delight — all was futile. It all led to disintegration and nothing. And no mountains and hills, no heaven and earth, no sun and moon could save him or help him. It depended on him alone. Only he could help himself — by turning back to his origins and his Maker.

In his own way, as far as he could go, Hess attempted to do the same. He remained a *luftmentsh* before and afterward, blowing words in the wind. But this was his finest hour, when in stark self-realization he did his best to return to his spiritual origins, to the heritage of his people; and he called to his people to save themselves by doing the same.

From the moment of truth there is no other place to go. Eliezer b. Durdya put his head down between his knees and wept. He alone would have to help himself, to find his way back to his own identity.

In a sense this is what happened to the Jewry of the world, especially our people in America, when one group after another, one level after another realized the full scope and meaning of the Holocaust in Nazi Europe. Except for the fragments that managed to survive, European Jewry was wiped out. In the land of Israel the determination grew to establish an independent homeland, to provide a sure and final place of safety for our people. And in America and other lands of democracy, Jews who had hardly been aware of membership in this historic people awoke to a new sense of destiny and commitment. At the very least, they became members of the Jewish community, dedicated to the existence and survival of the emerging and growing State of Israel.

From the moment of truth there is no other place to go. Whether it makes us or breaks us, we *must* realize what a world of illusion and false hopes this is for the Jew. One after another, nations and leaders in the world turn into hostile, bitter enemies; and others remain neutral bystanders, chewing their gum (or cud) and watching with interest.

33

As Eliezer b. Durdya reached his tragic, inescapable conclusion (says the Talmud) his strength gave out. Head down between his knees, groaning in his wretchedness, he had no more heart or will to live. Death brought an end to his misery. . . . Then a heavenly voice resounded, "*Rabbi* Eliezer b. Durdya is eligible for life in the world-to-come."

When R. Judah haNassi learned of his (the Talmud continues) he wept and said, "One person may earn his eternal life [in the Hereafter] in a period of several years, while another may earn his eternal life in one short while." Then he added, "If it were not enough for *baaley t'shuvah* (those who achieve repentance) that they are accepted [by Heaven], they are also given the title *rabbi!*"

R. Judah haNassi spent years in patient, persevering study, to master the Oral Torah — till he could codify the six orders (sections) of the Mishnah as we know it today. It cost him years of concentration and self-discipline in relentless study till he received the title *rabbi*. Heaven bestowed the title on Eliezer b. Durdya because he reached a moment of dreadul, disintegrating realization, after a life of dissolute pursuit of pleasure — a realization of what his whole life amounted to — a realization so ghastly and crushing that he expired in grief.

The point of the Talmud might be that in the one moment of awful self-awareness, Eliezer b. Durdya learned as great and important a truth as any Torah scholar learns in years of study. As it were, he took a "crash course" in God's immutable truth, and what he learned (at the cost of his life) was equal in value to decades of Torah study. That moment of transfiguration entitled him to be called *rabbi*, as it entitled him to life in the Hereafter.

And perhaps this is why the story is recorded in the Talmud — so that we can know how important and precious is the lesson he learned — and make sure we never forget it: When we take stock of our place in the world, after all the pursuit of seductive chimerical goals, we can only turn to ourselves, to find our inner strength in our inner identity.

We were meant to be God's people, *a kingdom of* kohanim (*Divine ministering servants*) *and a holy nation* (Exodus 19:6). Establishing the State of Israel and becoming committed and dedicated to our people and our homeland are all steps in this direction. For we will be either God's people or nothing. . . .

In his immortal Proverbs, the wise king Solomon warned us: *And now, O sons, listen to me... Keep your way far from her* [a loose woman]... *lest you give your vigor to others... lest strangers take their fill from your strength* (Proverbs 5:7-10). And the Midrash teaches: This refers to the ten tribes, and the tribes of Judah and Benjamin; for all the Israelites are called "sons," as Scripture says, *You are sons to the Lord your God* (Deuteronomy 14:1). "Listen to me": he warned them to heed the Divine word.... Yet, continues the Midrash, the ten tribes became steeped in adultery. So, the Midrash adds, the Holy, Blessed One said to them, "About other sinful deeds I would have been patient with you. Now that you have taken up seduction, get up and go!" (*Be-midbar Rabbah* 9, 7).

The ten tribes went — out of Jewish history and into oblivion. And this is what we can expect, individuals or groups, if we invest our energy and commitment in the beckoning, alluring harlot attractions of this world.

From the moment of truth we can turn only to ourselves, our inner resources. And those resources are not physical but spiritual. Whatever we may do in self-defense, we cannot make a fist and punch out at the world. That only invites retaliation: a stronger fist punching back. Our strength evolves in our threefold way of *torah, avodah, g'milluth ḥassadim* — Torah study, worship in prayer, and acts of loving-kindness. Thus we can invoke Heaven's aid and move ahead on our predestined way.

To quote again from the Midrash:

כָּל נִסִּים שֶׁעָשָׂה הָאֱ־לֹהִים לְיִשְׂרָאֵל בְּמִצְרַיִם לֹא עָשָׂה אֶלָּא עַל שֶׁשָּׁמְרוּ עַצְמָן מִן הָעֶרְוָה.
(במדבר רבה ט יד)

All the miracles that God wrought for the Israelites in Egypt, He wrought only because they kept away from immorality (*Be-midbar Rabbah* 9, 14).

If we keep away from immorality and harlotry in its every symbolic sense, giving our heart only to the Torah and its laws, we have the power to invoke miracles, to go straight and clear on our Heaven-blessed way. Otherwise, like Eliezer b. Durdya, we will reach the end of a road leading nowhere....

35

## ❧ THE PRECIOUS SINGLE ANTIDOTE

Is it such an easy thing, though, to vanquish all the temptations of harlotry, in its thousand forms and varieties? Can we be proof against the lures and attractions about us? The milieu beckons and draws with a thousand wiles. It promises rewards of untold pleasures and satisfactions. Whatever can capture your heart, be it the prospect of fame, wealth, success, or delights of the senses, our affluent but costly society makes it seem available, within your grasp. And in our time we watch in dismay as the essence of harlotry, in its plain original sense, floods the marketplace anew.

In a world that has made commercial success *the* goal of goals, where the profit motive reigns supreme, justifying everything, and competition for the almighty dollar is fierce, pornography has been discovered as a most profitable commodity. It is vaunted and flaunted in the face of our youth, by every possible means of communication. We live on a spinning planet that would pay little heed to the warning of our immortal Sages: "Wherever you find immorality, calamity comes upon the world.... About everything the Holy One is patient and forbearing — except immorality."[15] Too many inhabitants of this planet seem determined to discover the truth of this teaching from personal experience....

As alternatives to licentious debasement and corruption, the environment offers new varieties of "religious" experience, from drugs that induce happy dreams and horrid hallucinations to Zen Buddhism, as well as (you should excuse the expression) *Jews for Jesus*. Somewhere in America's wild west, it is said, one can even find a self-styled "rabbi" ready to direct lost young Jewish souls into an American temple of *haré krishna*.

How poignantly it all brings to mind a parable in the Talmud:

אָמַר ר׳ חִיָּא בַּר אַבָּא אָמַר ר׳ יוֹחָנָן: מָשָׁל לְאָדָם שֶׁהָיָה לוֹ בֵּן אֶחָד, הִרְחִיצוֹ וְסָכוֹ וְהֶאֱכִילוֹ וְהִשְׁקָהוּ וְהִלְבִּישׁוֹ, וְתָלָה לוֹ כִּיס זָהָב בְּצַוָּארוֹ, וְהוֹשִׁיבוֹ עַל פֶּתַח בֵּית זוֹנוֹת. מַה יַּעֲשֶׂה אוֹתוֹ הַבֵּן שֶׁלֹּא יֶחֱטָא? (ברכות לב ע״א; ד״ס)

36

Said R. Ḥiyya b. Abba in the name of R. Yoḥanan: It can be likened to a man who had a single son. He had him bathed and ointment applied to his skin; he provided him with food and drink and clothing; then he hung a purse of gold about the lad's neck and set him down at the entrance of a brothel. What was the boy to do that he should not sin? (TB *B'rachoth* 32a).[16]

The mass immigration of our people from Central and Eastern Europe to the American shore occurred when the United States was on the verge of tremendous industrial and commercial expansion. From the grinding poverty of countries like Poland and Russia our people came determined to establish an economic base of security. They worked hard and moved toward their goals. In consonance with the style and aims of the American way of life, they were determined to provide well for their children, to give the youngsters every opportunity for happiness, advancement and achievement. The motto became, "We want our children to have everything we didn't have." In time this changed to the smug, satisfied litany of "We gave our children everything"; but often this was followed by a plaintive, despairing note: "What went wrong?"

There was money enough, but no values or guidelines, no channels or directions for idealism and commitment. What were they to believe in? Where the young generations did not turn to the blatant, bedazzling attractions of harlotry and hedonism, appreciating only the physical pleasures of a materialistic world, they sought and found ideals and causes far removed from the authentic Judaism that remained utterly foreign and unknown to them.

It sadly recalls another passage in the Talmud:

אֶלָּא מַהוּ שֶׁאָמַר מֹשֶׁה, וַיַּעֲשׂוּ לָהֶם אֱלֹהֵי זָהָב? ... אָמַר מֹשֶׁה לִפְנֵי הַקָּדוֹשׁ־בָּרוּךְ־הוּא: רִבּוֹנוֹ־שֶׁל־עוֹלָם, כֶּסֶף וְזָהָב שֶׁהִרְבֵּיתָ לָהֶם לְיִשְׂרָאֵל הוּא גָּרַם לָהֶם שֶׁיַּעֲשׂוּ אֱלֹהֵי זָהָב.

(יומא פו ע״ב)

Now, why did Moses say, *and they made themselves a god of gold?* ... Moses declared before the Holy One, "O Master of the world, the silver and gold which Thou didst give the Israelites in great abundance — that caused them to make the god of gold" (TB *Yoma* 86b).[16]

On behalf of his people, Moses was pleading with the Almighty to forgive them for the enormous sin of the Golden Calf. Surely it would have been enough for him to say, *I pray thee: this people has sinned a great sin*

(Exodus 32:31); why did he add, *and have made themselves a god of gold?*
The answer is that he wanted to make a point: The cause of it was the
abundance of gold they had. They had left Egypt laden with gold and silver
(Exodus 12:35–36). As the Midrash comments with a sardonic touch, had
they gone out carrying squash and pumpkins in their hands, would they
ever have made an idol?[17]

Whatever has beckoned their hearts, our youth has gone arunning, be
it to weird or base pleasures, or to seemingly noble and worthwhile ideals.
As one might put it, they have taken many trips.

There was a time when our people lived in separate quarters (called
ghettos) and spoke only Yiddish. Whatever went on outside their quarters
went on in Polish or Russian, Hungarian or Rumanian. It was, thank
Heaven, none of our business. In American and other lands of democracy
the common language is English, and our people learned it quickly
enough — if not the first generation, then the later ones. Even if one did
not read, there was the universal language of pictures (still and moving)
presented for mass consumption.

So our youth found and finds itself truly "at the entrance of a brothel,
with a purse of gold about the neck." How could they help sinning?
"עינא וליבא תרי סרסורי דחטאה The eye and the heart are the two solicitors
for sin," says the Talmud.[18] An environment of unbridled license sends its
messages through the eyes directly to the heart; and how is our youth to
find resistance and restraint without the sobering knowledge that Eliezer b.
Durdya finally gained at such great cost, that sin paves a sure road to disgust
and regret, guilt and despair? And if they avoid the lures of immorality and
sinful pleasure, how will they withstand the powerful call of alien and
illusory ideals? The pain was still fresh from the memory of all the young
Jews in Russia and America who worshipped and served the idol of communism, when we began lamenting anew over the number of Jews who
enrolled heart and soul in the cause of Negro equality and Negro rights,
only to find the dominant elements of the Black cause turning criminal in
their demands and methods, insisting that they were justified and not
hesitating to make Jews their first targets and victims.

What are we to do for our youth? How are we to prepare and equip
them to face the world and not be lured astray? "The eye and the heart,"
says the Talmud,[18] "are the two solicitors (or panders) of sin." As Rashi
remarks, the eye sees, the heart desires, and the body does the sinful acts.[19]
So the Talmud continues: *My son, give Me your heart, and let your eyes watch*

*My ways* (Proverbs 23:26). Said the Holy, Blessed One, "If you give Me your heart and your eyes, then I know you are Mine."

Here lies the answer: to give our young ones an alternative — to channel the eyes and the heart onto the Holy One; to teach them our faith: *Hear, O Israel, the Lord is our God, the Lord is one* (Deuteronomy 6:4). The world has one sole Creator, who is ever with us and about us, a personal God for each and every individual. Therefore *you shall love the Lord your God with all your heart and with all your soul and with all your might* (*ibid.* 5). Love, devotion, faith and commitment should center on Him. Aptly the Sages point out that here the Hebrew for "your heart" is *l'vav'cha*, not the usual *lib'cha*; there are two letters *béth* in the word — implying that we must love and serve Him with both inclinations of the heart, the good and the evil impulses.[20] All the forces and passions of the heart should be channeled and focused on His service.

How is this to be done? — *And these words, which I command you this day, shall be on your heart* (*ibid.* 6). The key to the matter is "these words": the Torah. Says the Midrash: Put these words on your heart; for as a result you will get to know the Holy, Blessed One, and you will cling to His ways. Great is Torah study, say the Sages, for it leads to reverent fear [of the Almighty]; reverent fear leads to caution; and caution leads to proper action.[21]

Torah teaches us to use care, discretion and restraint, out of a thorough-going awareness of the Divine Presence. It checks us from giving way to blind impulse and unbridled imagination. And the Sages assure us further: Whoever puts words of Torah on his heart will find annulled and negated for him thoughts of conflict, hunger, mad folly, immorality, evil impulse, etc.[22] The Talmud sums it up succinctly: בראתי יצר הרע, בראתי לו תורה תבלין I [says the Almighty] created the evil inclination; I created the Torah as the remedy for it.[23]

Every age and generation has its own battle of the *yétzer ha-ra*, the evil inclination, to face. Our time and our world may seem the worst of all in its terrible trials and temptations; but no Jews were ever free of the conflicts and stresses of temptation. The Torah, however, has always been the antidote and the remedy, the weapon and the armor to withstand and overcome it. Torah gives us a chance in the inevitable battle.

It is well worth noting these words of R. Naḥman of Bratzlav:[24] "Whoever breaks this desire for immorality can then break easily all cravings; and it is therefore a general remedy. Insofar as each and every person

39

removes himself from this desire, to this extent he comes closer to the revelation of the Torah; and this holds equally true in the opposite direction, Heaven forbid. Therefore, before a man can attain the [personal] revelation of the Torah, he must be put to the test in the crucible of that desire, which is the key trial and refining process. And when he withstands the test and breaks through the shell that precedes the fruit, he merits to attain the fruit, meaning the revelation of the Torah."

Every Jew faces his own inner strugle with the demons of desire and temptation, that lure either to ways of pleasure or to alien goals and ideals which mislead and corrupt. With a solid background in Torah, the struggle can be faced and the battle won. Insightfully called a remedy by the Sages, Torah acts like a vaccine for the spirit, giving it the ability to develop moral antibodies that will fight off the inevitable infection of wayward desires and ambitions. Then, as the central moral battle is fought and won, the Torah gains new meaning for a person. New layers of its sense and significance unfold for him. He gains increasing entry into its revelation, as the Torah becomes over more an integral part of his life.

Among secular Jews the disputes and discussions go on: What is the Jewish spirit? What is Jewish identity? What, or who, is a Jew? They look for answers, to stem the tide of the disappearance of the Jew into the miasma of assimilation and intermarriage.

Those who keep the Torah faithfully know that it alone is the answer. It is the precious single antidote to the moral poisons that fester and multiply in the environment — an environment whose moral pollution is far worse than its physical, ecological deterioration.

If only we gain the proper perspective, we will realize how blessed our people has been, that the Torah has never been completely forgotten. It has never been left in the holy ark of the synagogue or on the shelf of the library, as a precious heirloom or heritage from an ancient civilization, waiting for occasional readers or scholars to pore over its quaint letters and puzzle out its meaning. From one generation to another, we have had our great scholars, devoted teachers, and good students. There have always been people of energy and dedication, making sure that the tradition of sacred learning would not disappear from our midst.

Consider this striking passage in the Talmud:

כִּי הֲווּ מַנְצוּ ר׳ חֲנִינָא וּר׳ חִיָּא, אָמַר לֵיהּ ר׳ חֲנִינָא לְר׳ חִיָּא: בַּהֲדֵי דִידִי קָא מִנְצֵית? דְּאִי חַס־וְשָׁלוֹם מִשְׁתַּכְחָא תּוֹרָה מִיִּשְׂרָאֵל, מְהַדְרְנָא לָהּ מִפִּלְפּוּלִי. אָמַר לֵיהּ ר׳ חִיָּא

40

לר' חֲנִינָא: בַּהֲדֵי דִידִי קָא מִינְצֵית? אֲנָא עָבְדִי לְתוֹרָה דְּלָא מִשְׁתַּכְּחָא מִיִשְׂרָאֵל. מַאי
עָבֵידְנָא? אַזְלִינָא וְשָׁדִינָא כִּיתָּנָא וְגָדִילְנָא נִשְׁבֵּי, וְצַיְידְנָא טַבֵי, וּמַאֲכִילְנָא בִּישְׂרַיְיהוּ
לְיַתְמֵי, וַאֲרִיכְנָא מְגִילָתָא מִמַּשְׁכָא דְטַבְיָא, וְכָתֵבְנָא חֲמִשָּׁה חוּמְשֵׁי וְסָלֵיקְנָא לְמָתָא דְּלֵית
בָּהּ מִקְרֵי דַּרְדְּקֵי, וּמַקְרֵינָא חֲמִשָּׁה חוּמְשֵׁי לַחֲמִשָּׁה יָנוּקֵי, וּלְכָל חַד וְחַד אֲמִינָא, אַקְרֵי
לְחַבְרָךְ. וּמַתְנֵינָא שִׁיתָּא סִדְרֵי לְשִׁיתָּא יָנוּקֵי, וּלְכָל חַד וְחַד אֲמִינָא לֵיהּ, אַתְנֵי לְחַבְרָךְ.
וַאֲמַרְנָא לְהוּ, עַד דְּהָדַרְנָא וַאֲתֵינָא אַקְרוּ אַהֲדָדֵי וְאַתְנוּ אַהֲדָדֵי. וְעָבְדֵי לָהּ לְתוֹרָה דְּלָא
תִשְׁתַּכַּח מִיִשְׂרָאֵל. וְהַיְינוּ דְּאָמַר רַבִּי, כַּמָּה גְדוֹלִים מַעֲשֵׂי ר' חִיָּא. (בבלי, כתובות קג ע"ב; בבא
מציעא פה ע"ב וד"ס)

When R. Ḥanina and R. Ḥiyya fell into a dispute, R. Ḥanina spoke up to
R. Ḥiyya, "You would dispute with me? Why, were the Torah ever
forgotten in Jewry, Heaven forbid, I would restore it by my keen powers
of reasoning!" Said R. Ḥiyya to R. Ḥanina, "Would you dispute with me?
I took action so that the Torah should not be forgotten in Jewry. What did
I do? I went and planted flax and wove nets [from the flaxen cords] and
[with those] I trapped deer. I gave their flesh to orphans for food, and prepared parchment sheets from the hides of the deer. [On them] I wrote the
Five Books [of Moses], then went off to a town that had no school-teachers
for the children; and I taught the five Books to five children; and to each
one I said, 'Teach this to your fellow.' Then I taught the six orders (sections)
of the Mishnah to six children, and to each one I said, 'Teach this to your
fellow.' I told them, 'Until I come back, teach one another the Scripture
and the Mishnah.' So I arranged that the Torah should not be forgotten in
Jewry." Well, this is why Rabbi [Judah haNassi] stated, "How great are
the deeds of R. Ḥiyya!" (TB *K'thuboth* 103b, *Bava M'tzia* 85b).

These were two Sages in the time of the Mishnah. One had a brilliant mind,
a superb intellect developed and honed fine by years of Torah study. Were
he living today, if he wished he could certainly be a leading professor of
Talmud or Jewish Studies in a major university. When he found himself
disputed on some point of Talmudic law, forced to debate his view in the
*béth midrash* (the academy of sacred study), he retorted not as a boast but
as a matter of fact that were the entire Torah forgotten, he could restore it.
recreate it, bring it all back with his powers of reasoning. It would all be
there again: the Divine word as the center of a system of law and ethics
and morality.

Obviously his claim to fame was indisputable. Nobody challenged or
doubted him. Yet R. Ḥiyya, his opponent, had an effective answer. Perhaps

41

his intelligence did not burn so bright and fierce. He, however, made sure that the Torah would never be forgotten. He would make sure that R. Ḥanina never had a chance to show his spectacular ability in mental pyrotechnics.

What did he do? He started at the very beginning. He planted flax. When the crop grew, he made flaxen (or linen) thread, which he made into cord. From that he wove nets, which he used to trap deer. Deer are kosher animals; so he had them slain ritually, by kosher *sheḥittah*. Having no need of the meat, he gave the venison to orphan children. He wanted only the hides, to treat them until they became sheets of parchment — the only material on which a proper (kosher) Torah scroll may be written. Being evidently a trained scribe, he wrote out the entire Pentateuch on his parchment: the five Books of Moses, that every Torah scroll contains. In our scrolls, however, they are on one continuous roll of parchment, made from individual sheets stitched together. R. Ḥiyya left his Pentateuch in five parts, each Book in a separate scroll.

Then he took off for a town with no school-teachers, no little red schoolhouse, no proper education for the children. He took five youngsters, sat down with them, and taught each child one of the Five Books of Moses. When he finished, he told them in effect, "Each one teach one." Every child in the little group would become a teacher in turn, with each of the other four, for that part of the Written Torah which R. Ḥiyya had taught him. By the time they were finished, five children in the town would know the entire Pentateuch. They could start a school.

This was part one of R. Ḥiyya's "operation education," to take care of the Written Torah. But there was also the Oral Torah, the Mishnah, rooted in the authority of Scripture, and taught through the generations by teachers to pupils. For this R. Ḥiyya could write no text. In our time we have the Mishnah nicely printed with commentaries, and even with English translation. The time came eventually when R. Judah haNassi saw that it was in danger of being forgotten. It was becoming impossible to retain it all accurately by heart. So he decided that it had to be put into writing. That, however, happened some years later. At this time it was still literally *Oral* Torah, absolutely not to be put into writing.

So R. Ḥiyya took six bright children and taught each of them one of the orders or parts of the Mishnah; and then he told them too, "Each one teach one." Promising to be back, to reinforce their enthusiasm and perseverance, he left them as the nucleus of a budding Torah school.

42

In intellect R. Ḥanina was greater; R. Ḥiyya could not claim to match him. Yet R. Judah haNassi, the religious head of Israel, was moved to exclaim, "How great are the deeds of R. Ḥiyya!" It was *this* Sage he admired. Intellect steeped in Torah is valuable. A man like R. Ḥiyya is greater, though. His accomplishments rank higher, because he makes sure the Torah will be learned in the next generation too.

Potentially (as the commentary of Maharsha points out) R. Ḥanina was far superior. Should Jewry ever reach such a sorry, miserable state that the Torah was no longer known, he alone could recreate the sacred heritage of Divine law, with his powerful mind. In actuality, however, R. Ḥiyya's achievement was superior. He made sure that the Torah would *not* be forgotten; and thus R. Ḥanina never had the occasion to put his extraordinary ability to use.

The point of the little anecdote in the Talmud is clear. Yet, R. Aaron Kotler of blessed memory once noted, there is something quite puzzling here: Why did R. Ḥiyya have to plant his own flax, weave his own nets, and personally capture deer, and so forth? In fact, why did he have to write the Pentateuch out by himself? (And why did he have to tell about it?) Surely he could have achieved the same purpose by purchasing parchment and having a scribe write the Pentateuch? Or better still, he could have simply bought an already-written Torah scroll. What purpose did it serve that he did all this himself? Was it (perish the thought) exhibitionism? Did he want to do everything *davka* the hard way, so that he could say, "Look at me"?

Not at all, answered the sainted R. Aaron Kotler. R. Ḥiyya made a most important point: As Maharsha (R. Sh'muel Edels) notes in his commentary, from the very start his entire program of activity for the Torah was לשם שמים for the sake of Heaven. No other purpose or intention was mixed into it. Not even the parchment for the Torah was to come from an ordinary dealer or manufacturer. He wanted nothing that was made commercially, for sale at a profit. From the planting of the flax, all was for the single purpose of holy Torah study.

The Sage knew how important it was to teach this lesson — not in words, as one more pious rule among many, but by action, which speaks louder than words. He moved and acted with dedication and a singleness of purpose, and with no other aim in mind. Even when he was left with meat from the captured deer, he would not sell it. For people could then say that *this* was his main purpose, to turn a profit, and the rest was in-

43

cidental; or at least they could comment sarcastically that the pious dedicated rabbi "was not losing on the deal." So he gave the venison away to orphan children, in an act of charity.

This is the reason why R. Ḥiyya took such a difficult, painstaking course of action, and why the Talmud recorded it: to set an example for others to follow. Torah alone can safeguard authentic and meaningful Jewish life. But true Torah learning can be maintained and continued only by utter dedication and singleness of purpose, with no other thought in mind. This applies to the rabbis who serve as instructors and heads of our Torah schools; and it applies to every layman who understands the need to support a Torah school. There can be no thought of publicity or recognition, prestige or fame, as a major factor. The Torah can be perpetuated only out of a love for the Almighty who gave it to us; *and you shall love the Lord your God with all your heart.* Do not leave over in your heart what some psychologists call a fraud corner: a little private part where you harbor your own personal ambitions and wishes, that you hope to achieve by working for Torah education.

(And how appropriate it is that this point should have been made by R. Aaron Kotler of blessed memory. Past any doubt he was a worthy, outstanding successor to R. Ḥiyya in our time. Few ever equalled his fierce and constant concentration on the promotion of Torah study *lish'mah*, for its own pure and holy sake, to the exclusion of everything else.)

It must be stressed that this way that R. Ḥiyya showed, this example he set, was not a fancy display of bravura or moral gymnastics, to illustrate how religious he was. It was absolutely necessary.

What he asked of the children he taught was no small matter. Imagine sitting with five youngsters and teaching each one a whole Book of the Torah, then telling him to teach it to the others, and to learn from the others what he taught them. What of their precious playtime? Why should they sit for hours each day poring over Hebrew words in a parchment scroll while their friends were out romping and having a wild time? He was asking dedication of the children, and he could expect to get it only because he had the same dedication himself.

Children are innately honest. They can detect which teacher is in the classroom because *nebbach* (alas) this is his job, and he might as well get on with it, till the happy day when he can retire on his pension and never see those brats again. They can also detect which teacher is there because the

44

material he teaches is the most important thing in his life. And the children respond accordingly.

In every generation the children who respond, who catch fire (as it were) from the enthusiasm of devoted teachers, make the sacrifices worthwhile. Those children guarantee the continuity of an authentic Jewish people, in loyalty to the Torah. The purpose and the hope of a R. Ḥiyya is to inspire others to follow in his footsteps. And this is our hope and prayer for every Jewish child.

The famed R. Moses Sofer, the great leader of European Jewry in an earlier century, better known as the Ḥatham Sofer, once noted that there is a specific blessing we give a child at two particular occasions: When an infant boy is circumcised to enter him into the Covenant of Abraham, the people present exclaim, "כשם שנכנס לברית, כן יכנס לתורה ולחופה ולמעשים טובים" Just as he has entered the Covenant, so may he enter upon the study of Torah, marriage under the bridal canopy, and a life of good deeds." When a firstborn son reaches the age of thirty days, there is the ceremony of *pidyon ha-ben,* "the redemption of the son." The little boy's father gives a kohen the equivalent of five shekels to redeem the child from a state of holiness. There again, the kohen wishes the child, "יהי רצון, שכשם שנכנס לפדיון כן יכנס לתורה ולחופה ולמעשים טובים, אמן May it be Heaven's will that just as he has entered the state of redemption, so may he enter upon the study of Torah, marriage under the bridal canopy, and a life of good deeds; amen."

Now why, asked the Ḥatham Sofer, is this blessing given the child at these two specific occaions?

He replied: The Torah can be studied *lish'mah,* for its own sake, simply because it is our God-given guide to life; or it can be learned for some ulterior, personal reason. In the time of the Talmud this was known. Thus we read: It was taught: *to love the Lord your God* (Deuteronomy 30:20) — so that a man should not say, "I will study Scripture so that I will be called a wise man; I will study Mishnah so that I will be called rabbi (master); I will study Mishnah so that I can become an elder and sit in the academy." Rather, learn out of love [of God] and eventually honor will come (TB *N'darim* 62a).

In the time of the Talmud it was already possible to study Torah out of personal ambition, to gain status and prestige in the community. In our time this holds even more true. A young student may be far more interested in the admiration he enjoys or expects for his studies than in what he is

45

actually learning. He may pay far more attention to a title that might be added to his name than to the fine points of a Talmudic discussion in the *béth midrash*.

On the American scene of our time the possibilities of side interests and ulterior motives have grown. Today college credit is given for Talmudic study. Let a young fellow spend enough time in a yeshivah, and he hastens his progress toward a fine college degree. Again, you may sometimes meet a callow or shallow young man, and when you ask him what he does, how he spends his time, he may answer a bit smugly, "I'm a *ben torah*" — because he has good reason to believe that thus he has a status entitling him to a good *shidduch*, a marriage that will bring him a fine dowry and a life of ease.

Of course, even Torah study in such cases has value. R. Judah (we read in the Talmud) said in the name of Rav: Let a man ever occupy himself with Torah learning and mitzvoth, even if not for their own true sake; for from this level of insincerity, "not for its own sake," he will reach the level of *lish'mah*, "for its own sake."[25] We simply have to pray that such students will make the transition successfully, to realize and accept that the reward for Torah study lies in the learning itself, and in nothing else.

It is clear, however, that our sacred heritage can be studied for its own sake or for other reasons. The same holds true of marriage. A devout young Jew will go to the wedding canopy because the very first mitzvah in the Torah is the religious duty to "be fruitful and multiply" (Genesis 1:28), to have children and raise a family, in the pathway of the Torah. This is marriage *lish'mah*.

Human nature being what it is, however, there can be other motives.

The Mishnah recounts that on the fifteenth of Av and on Yom Kippur, the marriageable young girls of Jerusalem would go out and dance (by themselves), to give the eligible young men a chance to choose brides among them. Then we read in the Talmud: There were four families [clans] in Jerusalem. The pretty girls among them said, "Cast your eyes on beauty, since a woman is only for beauty." Those of aristocratic descent said, "Cast your eyes on those of good family, since a woman is only for [bearing] children." The rich ones among them said, "Cast your eyes on wealth." The average (plain) ones among them said, "Take your choice, for the sake of Heaven. . . ."[26]

From early times there could be various motives for marriage, not all of them praiseworthy.[27] In the 13th century R. Baḥya b. Asher wrote in his commentary on the Torah (Genesis 24:3): Let a man not wed a woman for her beauty, as Scripture plainly says, *Charm is deceitful, and beauty is vain* (Proverbs 31:30); nor for her wealth, because wealth can grow wings and fly / like an eagle into the sky; nor yet on account of the lordship (prominence) and power of her relatives and family, so that he can get their help and be able to attain a lordly position — because he will come to grief and be punished for each of these three motives.

With insightful wisdom a 14th-century scholar wrote in a fine work on Jewish ethics: If someone marries a woman whose relatives are strong and powerful, intending to gain position over people through them, should their might eventually leave them he will equally leave his wife. . . . If one marries a woman for the sake of wealth, he will ultimately reach a state of poverty. . . . If someone marries a woman on account of physical desire, he will ultimately be sated with her, turn from her in disgust, and divorce her. . . .[28]

Both literature and real life are full of bad marriages made for improper and illusory reasons. There was a wealthy American heir named Tommy Manville who kept marrying, divorcing and remarrying throughout his life. His motive was clearly beauty alone; his wives seemed to get younger as he grew older — until he became a laughing-stock in all America. . . . There are stories enough to be found in both fiction and reality, of a man marrying lonely older women and ending their lives, to enjoy their savings and their life insurance.

Sad to say, marriages are not always made "for the sake of Heaven." And neither are "good deeds" always done for the sake of Heaven.

Take a simple example of good deeds like charity. There are people who give money frankly to get publicity. They like to see their name in the papers. They glow at the sight of a plaque commemorating their gift. They thrive on the satisfaction of being the guest of honor at a banquet for a noble worthy cause. Well, there is nothing wrong with that. This too is a way of giving charity. The money generally goes toward a very good purpose. In our highly (and professionally) organized community life, people often give their contributions merely to avoid losing the standing and esteem that they enjoy among friends, acquaintances, colleagues and equals. This too is probably all to the good. Otherwise the money might be squandered foolishly.

Our Sages taught: If someone says, "I give this money to charity in order that my son may live," he is a complete tzaddik, an entirely righteous person (TB *P'saḥim* 8a). Even if his motive is to "buy" Heaven's help for a sick child, if he gives to the poor only because he wants in return his son's health, something more precious than money, it is all right. He has done a good deed. Yet obviously it is not charity *lish'mah*, for its own pure sake. Neither this man nor a person who suddenly gives a million dollars to a hospital or a school, so that a building will bear his name, is necessarily training himself in generosity and compassion. He is not working to become a *baal tz'dakah*, a "master of charity," a man who knows he must answer the needs and the pleas of unfortunate human beings.[29]

Think of an eight-day-old child, however, undergoing circumcision. He too is taking part in a mitzvah. He is entering the Covenant of Abraham. The pain of a minor bit of surgery is inflicted on him, only because the Almighty commaded, ובן שמנת ימים ימול לכם כל זכר *And he that is eight days old among you shall be circumcised — every male* (Genesis 17:12). About this mitzvah you can be sure: it is *lish'mah*. Neither the father nor the *sandek* nor the infant has any ulterior motive. None of them gains any personal advantage. It is purely for a mitzvah.

Similarly the mitzvah of *pidyon ha-ben*. The young father has paid the hospital and the attending physicians. The nursery is well furnished and equipped, complete with diaper service. He has his wife and little baby at home, and by thirty days after the little fellow's entry into the world, he has become used to this new, miraculous addition to his life. "My baby boy," he thinks with pride and wonder, and carries pictures in his wallet. Then, because it is the very first child his wife has ever borne, when the infant is all of thirty days old a kohen comes; the child is brought in; and the kohen asks the young father in Aramaic, "What would you rather do: give me your firstborn son . . . or do you wish to redeem him for five shekels . . . ?" All of a sudden the kohen, who might be a total stranger, tells the father that if he wants to keep the baby, he has to give him (the kohen) a lump sum of money. Why? Is it the kohen's baby somehow? Or is this some kind of hold-up?

Obviously this is a ritual that the Torah commands. There could be no other reason. For otherwise it would be a meaningless charade. So clearly it is a mitzvah done *lish'mah*, for its own pure sake, to obey the Almighty's order.

So, said the Ḥatham Sofer, the child is given the special blessing at these two occasions. At his circumcision and again at the *pidyon ha-ben*, he is blessed with the wish, the hope and the prayer that just as he has partici-

48

pated in these two mitzvoth *lish'mah*, two pure acts of religious observance uncontaminated by any unworthy side interests, so may he merit to study the Torah *lish'mah* when he grows older, then marry *lish'mah*; and finally, as a married man, the head of a family, and a member of the community, may be develop ways and patterns of doing good deeds *lish'mah*.

In short, may he find his way to live in accord with the Almighty's wishes, to really "love the Lord your God with all your heart and with all your soul and with all your might," and not to make this an afterthought, after he has set his sights on other, mundane life-goals.

## WHEN THE MOUNTAINS DANCED

THE TRADITIONAL, AUTHENTIC JEW goes through life with his Torah — nothing less, nothing more. *You shall not add to the word that I command you, neither shall you diminish from it* (Deuteronomy 4:4). We add on nothing, we take nothing away. We need all the mitzvoth, all the commandments and teachings; not one ever becomes outdated or superfluous for us; and nothing from the outside world is ever vitally necessary to go with it.

On the world scene the authentic traditional Jew has never really become an important, heroic figure. *Behold, it is a people that dwells alone, and it shall not be reckoned among the nations* (Numbers 23:9). No, among the nations we have never counted for much. Whenever the Jew received his neighbor's attention, he generally became an object of scorn and fun, a target of taunting and torment. We wore their badges of shame and suffered their outbursts of wrath or their studied cruelty.

Yet humbly, gently, quietly the spirit of the authentic Jew, learning his Torah, observing his mitzvoth, lives on. Whatever he does during the day to earn his living, he finds his real calling in the hours given regularly to sacred study. Then he comes into his own. With the Torah he breathes and thrives, grows and survives. With the Torah the Jewish spirit lives on past every wave of anti-semitism that rises and seeks to engulf us.

49

Where did the Jew learn this way of life? How did he learn to live so constantly, so faithfully with the Torah, indomitable in his modesty, unflinching in his humility? Who first taught the Jew to stick to our heritage through thick or thin, paying small heed to the clamors and distractions, the wiles and lures of the cultures in the world about him?

Perhaps he learned it at Sinai. After all, the Sages teach that every member of Jewry was there — not merely the Israelites alive and present at the time, but the life-spirit of every last Israelite, Hebrew and Jew ever destined to be born:[30] They (and we) were all there watching. And even before the Almighty revealed His presence on Mount Sinai to give the Torah (say the Sages) a little drama took place, that was really worth watching.

In the vision of the Psalmist, *When Israel went out of Egypt . . . the sea looked and fled . . . the mountains skipped like rams, the hills like lambs* (Psalms 114:1–4). And the Talmud explains: "the sea looked and fled" — when the Red Sea was divided; "the moutains skipped," etc. — at the time the Torah was given (TB *P'sahim* 118a).

So when the Almighty prepared to give the Ten Commandments, and the entire Torah that went with them, there was action. Things, as we might say, were jumping. *O God,* hymned the Psalmist, *when Thou didst go forth before Thy people, when Thou didst march across the wilderness . . . the earth trembled. . . . Why are you dancing, O high-peaked mountains . . . ?* (Psalms 68:8–9, 17).

Why indeed were the mountains dancing or skipping about in a fine frenzy? In the Midrash, R. Yosé of Galilee explains:

בְּשָׁעָה שֶׁבָּא הַקָּדוֹשׁ־בָּרוּךְ־הוּא לִתֵּן תּוֹרָה מִסִּינַי, הָיוּ הֶהָרִים רָצִים וּמְדַיְּנִים אֵלּוּ עִם אֵלּוּ: זֶה אוֹמֵר עָלַי הַתּוֹרָה תִּנָּתֵן, וְזֶה אוֹמֵר עָלַי הַתּוֹרָה תִּנָּתֵן. תָּבוֹר בָּא מִבֵּית אֵלִים, וְכַרְמֶל מֵאַסְפַּמְיָא... זֶה אוֹמֵר אֲנִי נִקְרֵאתִי, וְזֶה אוֹמֵר אֲנִי נִקְרֵאתִי. אָמַר הַקָּדוֹשׁ־בָּרוּךְ־הוּא: לָמָּה תְּרַצְּדוּן הָרִים גַּבְנֻנִּים (תהלים סח יז)? כֻּלְּכֶם הָרִים גְּבוֹהִים, אֶלָּא גַּבְנֻנִים — הֵיךְ מַה דְּאַתְּ אָמַר, אוֹ גִבֵּן אוֹ דַק (ויקרא כא כ). כֻּלְּכֶם נַעֲשָׂת עֲבוֹדָה־זָרָה עַל רָאשֵׁיכֶם. אֲבָל סִינַי, שֶׁלֹּא נַעֲשָׂת עֲבוֹדָה־זָרָה עָלָיו, הָהָר חָמַד אֱלֹהִים לְשִׁבְתּוֹ (תהלים שם): וַיֵּרֶד ה' עַל הַר סִינַי (שמות יט כ). (בראשית רבה צט א).

At the time the Holy, Blessed One came to give the Torah at Sinai, the mountains came running, quarreling with one another. This one said, "On *me* will the Torah be given," and that one said, "On *me* will the Torah be given." [Mount] Tabor came from Beth Elim, and [Mount] Carmel from Spain. . . . This one said, "I was called," and that one said, "*I* was called." Said the Holy Blessed One, "Why are you dancing about, you *harim gavnunim* (high-peaked mountains)? You are all high, tall mountains, yet nothing but *gavnunim* — cripples"; for so is it written, *or gibbén, hunchbacked, or a dwarf* (Leviticus 21:20). "Idol-worship took place on the tops of all of you. But Sinai, which never had any idol-worship take place on it — that is *the mountain that God has desired for His abode*" (Psalms 68:17). So *the Lord came down on Mount Sinai* (Exodus 19:20) (*B'réshith Rabbah* 99, 1).[31]

Evidently there was a furor of activity there in the wilderness, in the region of Sinai. In the words of the Midrash *Mechilta* (*baḥodesh* 5), the mountains were in stormy agitation, and hills were collapsing. Think of it: Revelation was coming. The Creator was about to give His imperishable message, His Divine law, to mankind. So the tallest mountains came rushing breathlessly, skipping and dancing with excitement. Reaching high into the sky, rising above the clouds, each was certain that *it* had to be the site for the Almighty's unique, unforgettable Revelation. What else could give Him a setting of such majesty and grandeur? They were the *harim gavnunim*. The word *gav* means a back; but it is also at the root of the word *gavoah*, "high, tall." So *gavnunim,* as Rashi and Radak explain, means "very high"; but as Meiri writes, it also denotes "high-backed," or, in the case of mountains, high-peaked.

This they were indeed. Their peaks rose far above earth. So there they were, clamoring for the Almighty to bring His *shechinah*, His Divine Presence, to rest on them. Each one shrieked or bellowed, "I was called" — this is *my* manifest destiny. I must be the setting for the Revelation!

Since its earliest beginnings, mankind has striven to rise from its primitive levels, to ascend from ignorance and brutality to refinement and culture. Realizing that he walked on two feet instead of four, and that this made a difference, man has tried ever more to stop being so crude and imbecilic, and develop a civilization worthy the name. Human beings strove to ascend; and for one people after another — one civilization, culture, and religion after another — the mountain, rising tall in natural splendor and majesty, became an important symbol. In human systems of thought and belief, mountains assumed significance.

For ancient Greece, there was Olympus, rising nearly 10,000 feet into the air, covered with snow at the top most of the year, massive in appearance. There, said the Greeks of old, on its summit of bare, naked rock, above rising precipices broken by ravines, dwelt the gods, in their idyllic home above the clouds. Its lofty top, said this ancient people, was the setting of the divine immortal beings who could affect and control their lives. And to those gods they gave their worship and devotion, as they developed their schools of philosophy, their mathematics and astronomy, and their unsurpassed art. Ancient Greece became famous for its civilization.

Then Rome conquered Greece, and inherited (or succumbed to) its culture and religion. The Greek gods became Roman gods. Only the names changed, to make them properly Roman. And Rome in turn pointed proudly to high mounds of earth. In the course of its development, it encompassed seven hills: (going clockwise) Capitoline, Quirinal, Viminal, Esqueline, Caelian, Aventine, Palatine. So it became known as the City of the Seven Hills.

Now, how did the second hill get its name? Roman legend told of Romulus as the city's first king. Abandoned as a child and raised by a she-wolf, he had grown to rule the city in majesty, and started it on its course to glorious empire. But one day, said Roman legend, he disappeared mysteriously in a thunderstorm. So the people decided he had been transformed into a god. They changed his name to Quirinus and took to worshipping him. And thus the second hill came to be called Quirinal.

Rome was proud. The legends of this City of Seven Hills told of seven kings (Romulus had been the first) who led it on to "world conquest": They overpowered the entire Mediterranean world and united it in one mighty empire, with one language and one religion. (Only Jewry, keeping its own language and its own religion, remained an exception — an exception that outlived the Roman empire.)

Then how can we Jews go on living with the belief that the Almighty — the one and only Creator of all existence — gave *us* (a small, puny, insignificant little people) His imperishable word, on a little bit of a mountain named Sinai that hardly anyone had ever heard of? The important, lasting message of culture and civilization, the great body of learning and values and knowledge for mankind to cherish and grow on, must surely have come to a far greater people, like the Greeks or Romans, on a far taller, more important mountain!

Yet a Jew with a fine Talmudic mind might find an answer: The Greeks and Romans of old had mainly a secular, worldly civilization, largely interested in man's material life on earth. The timeless word of God must be mainly concerned with lasting values and the spirit: with ethics and justice, piety, compassion and devoutness. So the Torah was given on Sinai.

Never fear: Here too we find "competition." After all, in the eyes of the world we are not unique in our belief in one God. The world speaks glibly of "the three great faiths of monotheism." Well, the central figure of one of these "great faiths," a Jew who hailed from Nazareth, is supposed to have delivered a famous "sermon on the mount." It is the longest speech of his in the purported writings of his disciples. So it became the highpoint of a "new religion" that was ready in turn to conquer the world. Why take any further notice of the Revelation at Sinai? It had happened so long ago, a minor incident in the dim recesses of a murky past. In the minds of the followers of the man from Nazareth, his mountain loomed bigger, his sermon rang better.

And lo and behold, *Rome* became the headquarters of this "new faith": There a "personal representative" of the Nazarene would always dwell, ruling in state over the far-flung flock of the faithful. Thus Rome gained a new name: It came to be called the Eternal City. As the seat of the faith, it was considered certain to last forever. Don Isaac Abarbanel, the great Jewish statesman who wrote a masterful commentary on Scripture, regarded the city with awe: In ancient times it had ruled a world as a military power. In his day it held an equal dominion over the spirits and souls of men.[32]

Wait, though: a third "great faith of monotheism" arose in the world— the Moslem faith. And this too, dear reader, came from a mountain. When its "great founder" was about forty, he took to going off by himself to Mount Ḥira (near Mecca) to meditate. Well, one day, in a cave of the mountain, a voice suddenly told him that he was God's (personal, indispensable) messenger. This started him off on *his* career, as "the true prophet"; and once again the Jews, the Torah, and Mount Sinai were supposed to pale into insignificance by comparison. As the Moslems proclaimed, the world now had a great new dazzling "religion of the faithful," which also had its origin at a mountain.

How perceptive was the wisdom of our Sages, how uncanny their vision. With a simple metaphor of mountains in a dance of frenzied excitement, they conveyed a timeless, transcendental truth.

When the Torah was to be given to human beings, said they, Mount Tabor came flying in. If there was to be a Divine revelation and proclamation from a mountain, it was ready for the job. Where did it come from? —

a place called *Béth Elim*, which could mean the house of gods, or "the home of the gods." As one contemporary scholar notes,[33] this could well be an allusion to Mount Olympus, which the ancient Greeks believed to be just that — the happy hunting (or romping) ground of the spirits they worshipped.

Another Midrash phrases Mount Tabor's "claim to fame," when it came a-running, in this way: "It is fitting for the *shechinah* to rest on *me*, because I am the tallest of all the mountains. On me the waters of the Flood never poured down!" (*Midrash T'hillim* 68, 9).

Greece with its pantheon of gods, its philosophy and science and art, believed itself superior to everything and everyone. Whatever disaster might strike the world, be it even the Flood in Noah's time, they had not the slightest doubt that Olympus with its mythical cast of characters could not be touched by it. Why, their gods and their culture were absolutely immortal!

Proud they were of their achievements in philosophy and art, mathematics and astronomy. They could build edifices of perfect, classic beauty. And they gave credit for it all to their gods. How certain they were that by the grace of the gods they had developed a civilization with a culture fit to bequeath to mankind, worthy of lasting forever. And how many in later centuries agreed, as they devoted themselves religiously to the classical heritage of ancient Greece.

With *its* pride, Rome was yet haughtier than Greece. Its achievements, thought the ancient Romans, were certainly greater. Just look at their far-flung dominion. They conquered and subjugated entire countries and peoples, and organized them into one tightly-knit empire.

Who can dispute their success? Their military prowess was brilliant, their organized strength was remarkable. None could withstand their onslaught as they overcame one peaceful nation after another, one peace-loving people after another.

How impressive their armies were in their stunning triumphs. After every success in war there was a splendid victory march in the city of Rome. Those victorious glorious soldiers carried their trophies in exultation — the most valued treasures of the defeated enemy. And behind came the wretched people taken captive, dragged along in chains, destined for the misery of slavery. With what zest and sparkle a Roman sculptor depicted in relief, on an arch of triumph, the victory march after Titus vanquished Israel and destroyed the Second Temple. In the sculptured marble you can see their haughty pride as they carried the *menorah* and other most holy objects, ransacked from our Sanctuary; and behind came the unfortunate Jews in chains, headed for wretched slavery.

Rome reveled in its glory and basked in its majestic power. It too considered its culture an imperishable treasure.

If mankind was to be given a lasting body of thought and culture, to educate the human spirit through the generations toward a civilized human life, Greece with its Olympus and Rome with its seven hills were ready to provide their culture, their way of life and thought.

In the imagery of the Sages, their mountains came dashing into the wilderness, ready to take the place of Sinai and give the world their kind of "Torah," their repository of learning and wisdom. And the thought is even echoed in Scripture: When the Torah was to be given, sang the Psalmist, *the mountains skipped like* élim (Psalms 114:4). Generally translated as rams (as the plural of *a-yil*, with a *yod* ommited), *élim* could also well mean gods (the plural of *él*).

Yes, those mountains of idolatry were there, dancing about, ready to thrust Sinai aside.... But how did the frenetic ballet ever end? The Talmud answers:

דָּרַשׁ בַּר קַפָּרָא: מַאי דִכְתִיב, לָמָּה תְּרַצְּדוּן הָרִים גַּבְנֻנִּים (תהלים סח יז)? יָצְאָה בַת קוֹל וְאָמְרָה לָהֶם: לָמָּה תִרְצוּ דִין עִם סִינַי? כֻּלְּכֶם בַּעֲלֵי מוּמִין אַתֶּם אֵצֶל סִינַי. כְּתִיב הָכָא גַּבְנֻנִּים, וּכְתִיב הָתָם (ויקרא כא כ) אוֹ גִבֵּן אוֹ דַק. (מגילה כט ע"א)

Bar Kappara taught: What is the meaning of the verse, *Why do you dance about* (t'ratzdun), *O high-peaked* (gavnunim) *mountains* (Psalms 68:17)? A heavenly voice emanated and said, "Why do you want a quarrel with Sinai? You are all cripples compared with Sinai" — for here גבנונים *gavnunim* is written, and elsewhere it is written, *or* גבן *gibbén, a hunchback, or a dwarf* (Leviticus 21:20) (TB *M'gillah* 29a).

Under the influence of old Aramaic, the Hebrew letters *tzaddi* (צ) and *kuf* (ק) sometimes interchanged in ancient usage. So *t'ratzdun* is understood as *t'rakdun*, from the root *rakkéd*, to dance. But, Bar Kappara indicates, it can also imply *tirtzu din*: "Why do you want a quarrel, a controversy?" This, says Bar Kappara, is what a heavenly voice called out: Why all the pushing and shoving and competing among the tall mountains? Compared to Sinai, the rest of you are cripples.

A person may be perfectly healthy and normal. Yet if he lacks one important organ or limb, he is a cripple. He is handicapped. In this respect he does not measure up to others.

Compared to Sinai, says Bar Kappara, Mount Olympus was a cripple. For what was Greek culture? The people of ancient Greece worshipped beauty and developed it remarkably in their art and architecture — but as an end in itself, for human pleasure, subject to no higher standard, serving no higher purpose. They venerated strength and developed skill in sports, training their youth to excel at their olympic games — but again, to no higher purpose. Their philosophy may have led people to feel urbane and civilized, polished and learned; but it brought no true morality to Greece. And their religion certainly led nowhere: Their gods obeyed no moral or higher law. Those "divine" beings might commit any foul deed or trickery they chose.

How truly R. Judah haLévi struck home when he wrote[34]

וְאַל תַּשִׁיאֵךְ חָכְמָה יְוָנִית
אֲשֶׁר אֵין לָהּ פְּרִי כִּי אִם פְּרָחִים

*And let not Greek wisdom lure you,*
*which bears no fruit, but only blossoms.*

In all that ancient Greece produced, in all the wealth of beauty and scintillating intellect, there was no fruit — nothing of substance to nourish a man's spirit so that he could survive and grow morally in the Almighty's world.

With all their culture, the Spartans saw nothing wrong in exposing their little babies (on a mountain!) to cold and neglect, so that only the hardy ones would survive. They wanted no weaklings, and it did not bother them if those died. It was at Sinai, through the Torah, that man began to learn that *all* human life is precious. The Torah made us know that man was created in the Divine image. If you bring death to anyone, big or small, you will answer to God for it.

Plato, perhaps the greatest of the Greek philosophers, preached that from the age of six, boys should be taught to ride horses (very necessary in battle in his day) and use the bow, the javelin and the slingshot.[35] From childhood, said that fine mind, they should be trained to use the dangerous battle weapons of his day. And by the age of seventeen, like young hunting dogs, they should "play in games of battle" and taste blood.

56

With all its fine philosophy, ancient Greece saw nothing wrong with needless wars of conquest, or with vile immoral practices when they were not at war, which could leave the people with no decent structured family life to speak of.

The Stoics said: Don't react to anything too strongly. Keep a poker face and a stiff upper lip. Bear it and grin. The Epicureans said: Enjoy yourself; it's later than you think. *Eat and drink, for tomorrow we die* (Isaiah 22:13). The architects built splendid structures with graceful ionic colums, and the sculptors carved human figures exquisitely. They offered a libation to their gods, immensely pleased with their "classical civilization" that produced blossoms — so utterly pretty when they bloomed. But blossoms are not food. They wither and rot. And so, as you might say, there was something rotten in olden Greece. It was empty and rotten within. Without a higher purpose at their core, without an absolute Divine law demanding moral integrity and compassion, they lacked one imporant limb; and their entire culture was crippled.

Certainly good health and physical strength are fine. It is important to have a healthy mind in a healthy body. *And you shall take great care about yourselves*, says the Torah (Deuteronomy 4:15). We are forbidden to do anything that will harm us physically, but have to live wisely and well to maintain good health. In our codes of law, from Rambam's *Mishneh Torah* to the *Kitzur Shulḥan Aruch*, you will find chapters on this very subject: rules and regulations for health, including exercise.[36] It is obviously necessary — but for a higher reason, not as an end in itself: *The dead will not praise the Lord* (Psalms 115:17). They are silent as the tomb where they abide. So *I shall not die, but live,* sings the Psalmist; for what purpose? — *and I will relate the deeds of the Lord (ibid.* 118:17).

We have a higher aim in life: to praise and worship the Creator in our prayer, to learn His Torah and obey His mitzvoth. Games and sport are fine, especially for the young, but only for this end. When Israel maintains professional athletes who play their scheduled games on the Sabbath; when it insists on sending teams to play in international olympic tournaments, even on Rosh haShanah, and eleven are murdered by Arab terrorists — we can only call the Jews involved by one name: *mithyavnim*, people who want to become ancient Greeks.

Good food is fine. The sections in our codes of law that were mentioned above deal with the subject of diet. But the Torah, as we know it, brooks no gourmets of the Epicurean school of philosophy who live only to savor and relish fancy dishes of exquisite delight. Meals have a somewhat different purpose for us. So the Talmud is quite clear: Whoever engages in Torah study is permitted to eat the meat of animals and poultry; and whoever does not engage in Torah study is forbidden" (TB *P'saḥim* 49b).[37] In His world of moral law, the Almighty gains nothing from either gourmets or gourmands (fressers in plain Yiddish).

Beauty is certainly a wonderful thing. It brings pleasure and delight into human life. But this too has its place for us, in a life with a higher ideal. *This is my God,* sang Moses with every Israelite after the miraculous rescue at the Red Sea, *and I will glorify him* (v'anvéhu; Exodus 15:2). This word *v'anvéhu,* however, is from the same root as *naveh,* "beautiful, handsome." So in the Midrash, R. Ishmael justly asks: Can a mortal being of flesh and blood possibly do anything to *beautify* his Maker? — to make Him more handsome, as it were? It must rather mean (he answers), "I will bring beauty to Him with the mitzvoth: Before Him I will have a beautiful *lulav,* a beautiful *sukkah,* handsome *tzitzith,* handsome *t'fillin*" (Midrash *Mechilta,* Exodus 15:2).

From time immemorial this has been the Jew's way of bringing beauty into his life. When the festival of Sukkoth comes shortly after Yom Kippur, he spends a tidy sum for a handsome, straight frond of a palm tree, called a *lulav.* He spends much more for a special variety of citrus fruit called an *ethrog,* the price depending on its lovely shape, color, etc. Why? — because on Sukkoth it is a mitzvah of the Torah to take these two, with some myrtle leaves and willow branches, say a benediction over them, and wave them.

By the same token, for this festival the authentic Jew constructs a *sukkah,* a booth covered with branches and boughs, where he will have his meals and perhaps sleep during Sukkoth. And he makes it as beautiful as he can, with gay decorations of fruit, etc.

To fulfill a commandment of the Torah he wears a *tallith katan,* a small four-cornered garment, with *tzitzith* (tassels) at the corners; and for morning prayer he puts on a *tallith,* a large garment with *tzitzith* at the corners. For these too he is ready to pay a good price, to have them handsome and well-made, the tassels prepared by devout people specifically for this mitzvah.

The same holds true for *t'fillin* (phylacteries), the leather boxes with straps attached, that contain portions of Scripture written on parchment. Countless Jews through the generations have paid far beyond their means to get the portions of Scripture written by a scribe of outstanding piety with a fine calligraphic hand. They have paid for leather of the finest quality, made into boxes that were perfectly square and colored absolutely black — because this is what the Torah's law, given Moses at Sinai, requires.

"Blessed art Thou, Lord our God, King of the universe, who crowns Israel with splendor." This is what the observant Jew says every morning, having in mind the *t'fillin* he has put on in preparation for prayer. *Bind upon yourself your splendor*, the Almighty told His prophet (Ezekiel 24:17); and by this, says the Talmud, He meant the *t'fillin* (TB *B'rachoth* 11a).

In the Songs of Songs (4:1) we read, *Behold, thou art beautiful, my love; behold, thou art beautiful.* As the Sages understood, it expresses the Almighty's thoughts about His people; and the Midrash interprets: "Behold, thou art beautiful" through the mitzvoth . . . with a *m'zuzah* . . . with *t'fillin* . . . a *sukkah* . . . the *lulav* and *ethrog* . . . (*Shir haShirim Rabbah* 4:1).

This has always been the way that the Jew filled his life, and his home, with beauty. Go into any Jewish museum anywhere in the world, and you will see what the precious objects are which our finest artists produced through the centuries: crowns and *rimmonim* for the Torah scroll; silver cups for *kiddush* and *havdalah*; menorahs for Ḥanukkah; velvet coverings for the Torah scroll, and for the *ḥalloth* (loaves) on the Sabbath table; spice boxes for *havdalah*. Into objects that had to be used for a mitzvah, in the worship of the Almighty, our people's artists poured their talents and their hearts. And these objects have enriched Jewish lives and adorned Jewish homes. Unlike the ancient Greeks, our people have known beauty *with holiness*; on this the Jewish spirit has thrived and survived.

As for astronomy, mathematics and philosophy, our great scholars were not ignorant in these fields either. The Talmudic scholar Sh'muél attested that the highways and byways of the heavens were as clear to him as the streets of his native city (TB *B'rachoth* 58b). Rambam mastered Greek and Arabic philosophy, and countered with a response rooted in Torah Judaism that remains unsurpassed. To this day the Jewish philosophers of the Middle Ages are studied with profit. For in their body of thought, nurtured by roots in the Torah, no rot of moral decay or depravity could set in.

Mount Olympus came out into the wilderness with its ancient Greek culture and classical civilization. It danced and postured, certain that it was taller and more handsome than Sinai. Said a heavenly voice: Why are you pushing and vying with Sinai? Compared with it, you are a cripple.

Sinai had the same healthy parts and limbs as Olympus — and one more, that Olympus lacked. Sinai presented the positive elements that Greek culture offered, but set them in place in the structure of the Torah, to be used in a Divinely ordained way of life.

Rome was even more proud than Greece. How great an empire it built and ruled! Its people were masters of organization and construction. We can still marvel today at their viaducts and aqueducts, their bridges and bathhouses.

Yet what sort of viable culture had *they* to give humanity, to be cherished and perpetuated? What spirit could be nourished, what character formed, by a culture of merciless strength without any conscience, arrant might without compassion?

Certainly the conquering soldiers could strike a dashing pose for the admiring audience, one foot poised on the neck of the enemy. They were sure they earned the awed respect of posterity. Yet how long could this posture be kept? After the applause and the accolades died away, the admiring audience petered out and all went home, there would be only the wind shrieking occasionally in their ears as it blew across the empty vistas of time. The rest was silence. . . .

And in the silence, perhaps they could catch an echo of the simple truth that Hillel taught. Once, says the Mishnah (*Avoth* ii 7), he saw a skull floating on the water's surface. Said he, "Because you drowned someone, you were drowned; and the end of your murderers will be that they will be drowned." Such is the harvest that even conquerors can hope to reap from the toll of human life that their conquests took. In their own contemporary history they could see the point underscored: Among their own supreme leaders, Caesar brought death to his fellow-Roman, Pompeii; Brutus assassinated Caesar; and Antony brought an end to Brutus's life.

Certainly no Roman had any need to doubt that his people were superior to the Jews. Just look at the political picture: Who ruled whom? So by the same token, their culture must have been very superior to the Torah, no? Yet the Talmud has a strange story to tell:

Onkelos the son of Kolonikus was a nephew of Titus, the very emperor who defeated Israel in the year 70 and destroyed the Second Temple. Yet one day this royal nephew decided to convert to the Jewish faith (TB *Gittin* 56b). In the midst of life at the royal court, with all its pomp and sparkle, he evidently felt an aching void that only the Torah could fill. So off he went to live among the Jews, and became one of them.

When the emperor learned of this, says the Talmud (TB *Avodah Zarah* 11a),[16] he sent a troop of Roman soldiers [to bring him back under guard]. He won them over, however, by [quoting] verses of Scripture, and he converted them to Judaism. So [the emperor] sent another troop after him, ordering them, "Say nothing at all!" [If they kept their mouths shut, Onkelos could never draw them into conversation, and thus would have no chance to persuade them to turn Jewish; they would simply arrest him and bring him back. It seemed a foolproof plan.] Well, as they took him and got going, he said to them, "Let me tell you just a plain, ordinary thing: [In a procession at night in Rome] the torchlighter carries the flame before the torchbearer. The torchbearer [carries the light] for the commander; the commander, for the governor; and the governor, for the imperial officer. But does the imperial officer ever carry a light before the people [who follow]?"

"Oh no," they answered him. [The plain people in Rome could follow — and stumble — in the dark, for all their fine, resplendent officers cared. After all, the Roman way of life was based on haughty pride.] Said he to them, "The Holy, Blessed One, however, held a light before the Israelites: for it is written, *And the Lord went before them by day with a pillar of cloud, to lead them on the way, and by night with a pillar of fire, to give them light* (Exodus 13:21)." They converted to the Jewish faith.

So he [the emperor] sent yet another troop after him, ordering them not to enter into any conversation whatsoever with him. As they took him and started going, he noticed the *m'zuzah* affixed by the door. He put his hand on it and asked them, "What is this?" [Piqued by curiosity, they forgot the emperor's strict orders, and] they replied, "Tell us." Said he, "It is the way of the world that a mortal king of flesh and blood sits within, and his servants guard him from without. As for the Holy, Blessed One, however, His servants are within, and He guards them from without — as Scripture says, *The Lord shall guard your going out and your coming in from now and forever* (Psalms 121:8)." They converted to Judasim.

He [the emperor] sent no more after him.

Did Rome with its seven hills want to compete with Sinai? Did it want its culture to become the timeless heritage for mankind instead of the Torah? "Compared with Sinai," said the heavenly voice, "you are all cripples."

61

Rome's culture was healthy and strong in its way, but it was crippled: It lacked one part of the body — a heart.

Military prowess can be necessary and most useful — to wipe out forces of absolute evil from the world, and to win a homeland promised by the Almighty. When the Hebrews needed a leader to command them in battle against the Canaanites across the Jordan, *Moses called Joshua and said to him in the sight of all Israel: Be strong and courageous* (Deuteronomy 31:7). Later on he told him again, in God's name, *Be strong and courageous, for you shall bring the Israelites into the land which I swore to them; and I will be with you* (ibid. 23).

Used to good purpose, physical strength is valuable. We pray to the Almighty for it; and every morning we say, "Blessed art Thou, Lord our God, King of the universe, who girds Israel about with strength." We need energy in our everyday life to do our work and deal with the host of problems that arise. But nowhere does the Torah hold up as an ideal the development of rippling muscles, "a gorgeous physique," or "the body beautiful." On the contrary: whatever a man gains in the world by using his strength, the Torah warns him not to say in his heart, "*My power and the might of my hand has made this wealth for me.*" *But you shall remember the Lord your God, for it is He who gives you power to get wealth* (Deuteronomy 8:17–18).

On the personal, individual level the Torah forbids pride and boasting about "the pile [of money] I made with my own two hands"; why? — because if a man recognizes no debt of gratitude to the Almighty for the help of His Divine providence, he will pay no attention to the Torah's orders to help others who have been less fortunate in life: *Now, if your brother grows poor and his means fail him, then you shall uphold him . . . that your brother may live, along with you* (Leviticus 25:35–36). In brief, the Torah wants us to have a heart. *If there is among you a needy man, one of your brethren . . . you shall not harden your heart nor shut your hand against your needy brother* (Deuteronomy 15:7). Given the Roman approach to life, however, that might was entitled to rule as hard and as far as it could, a man who "made it" in life would have a short and snappy answer: "I made my pile with my own two hands. Nobody helped me. Let that poor fellow go out and make *his* pile. If he can't, that's his tough luck!"

Rome with its seven hills lacked a heart; it was crippled. The purpose of Sinai was to give man a Torah that demanded compassion, a little kindness, in the name of God, the father of us all. It is for the strong to protect the weak, for the rich to help the poor.

62

As a nation we developed a crack army under Joshua, to conquer the Promised Land, which Canaan occupied. But the Torah forbade waging battles just for the sake of exultation in conquest and empire-building. We were given a specific land to take, and no more. And even when the Hebrew army went to wage battle, the Torah put down strict rules: *When you draw near to a city to fight against it, then call to it to make peace* (Deuteronomy 20: 10). If the city agreed to peace, there was a precise law on making the city tributary; and it was then forbidden to kill anyone.

As individuals or as a nation, authentic Jewry has always acknowledged the Almighty as the source of strength and might. *The voice of the Lord is powerful; the voice of the Lord is majestic.... The Lord will give strength to His people* (Psalms 29:4, 11) — for what purpose, though? — not to let us become a conquering world power; as Scripture continues, *the Lord will bless His people with peace.* This is the entire reason for our wish and prayer for strength: to be able to have tranquillity in a hostile, belligerent world.

One of the most pernicious pieces of propaganda ever produced against the Jewish people is the notorious *Protocols of the Elders of Zion.* Concocted over a century ago out the vapors of some sick, paranoid imagination, the pamphlet sees in Jewry an international conspiracy to gain control of the world. It was proven false over and over, yet it rears its ugly head time and again, in one language after another, in one country after another. And people believe it.

There is an old rule that every effective lie must have some kernel of truth behind it. And, believe it or not, this lie does too. At Sinai we received our assignment: the Torah — to be kept through centuries in Israel and centuries in exile. As we fulfill our destiny, scattered throughout the world, we move ever closer to the day when all will recognize and acknowledge the Almighty's absolute sovereignty. In that sense we move toward international, world-wide power — not the kind of power that Rome wielded, but the power to see Isaiah's prophecy fulfilled: *For out of Zion shall go forth Torah, and the word of the Lord from Jerusalem. And He shall shall judge between the nations, and shall decide for many peoples; and they shall beat their swords into plowshares, and their spears into pruning-hooks. Nation shall not lift up sword against nation, neither shall they learn war any more* (Isaiah 2:3–4).

When the time came to give the Torah, the Creator chose not the tall imposing mountains but modest, unnoticed Sinai. He had His own way of measuring and deciding. As the Midrash puts it: the Holy, Blessed One measured all the mountains and found none on which the Torah could be given but Mount Sinai (*Va-yikra Rabbah* 13, 2).[38]

The reason for His choice was simple: He wanted to give the Ten Commandments — all ten of them, with not any one left out. From Mount Olympus, the elysian home of the Greek pantheon, mankind would never hear the Divine decree, לֹא תִנְאָף *You shall not commit adultery*! Greek mythology is rife with stories of Greek gods who fancied pretty women, whereupon they appeared in human form, each one always looking exactly like the husband of the lady who had captured his fancy; and then of course he gratified his (animal) desire. The Greeks accepted these stories calmly, even with pride. In this way, said the myths, some of their great (divine) heroes were born.[39] So how could Greek culture be the vehicle to teach the world that Heaven hated and banned any kind of adultery or fornication?

Rome had seven hills. From which of them could the Almighty proclaim לֹא תִרְצָח *You shall not kill*! Rome's pride and glory was its army, that made it a world power by killing. The brazen, unflinching cruelty of the Romans was legendary. Reluctantly our father Isaac blessed his son Esau, *By your sword shall you live* (Genesis 27:40); and our Sages had no doubt that the Romans were the descendants of Esau.

A Jew from Nazareth supposedly preached a "sermon on the mount," and became the central figure in a new religion. Read certain books of historic fact which the Catholic Church placed on its "index" (its list of books forbidden for the "faithful" to read), and you may be stunned to find how many of the Ten Commandments the representatives of this faith managed to ignore in the course of some nineteen centuries. All too often, members of the clergy could not obey what they preached to the laity. Any careful, honest account of the Moslem faith will reveal the same story.

The tall mountains were puffed up with pride, full of their overweening superiority. Like static jamming the airwaves, the vibrations of their idolatry would block out some of the immutable Divine commandments that the Creator had to give mankind. In this important sense they were crippled — by pride. Only humble, unassuming Mount Sinai would let all ten come through. And only the Israelites, humbly receptive, eagerly responding, *We will do, and we will heed* (Exodus 24:7), were ready to receive them.

This is the way of the Almighty. He chose Sinai because He rejects haughtiness and welcomes lowliness and humility,[39] and He applies the same yardstick to cultures and religions.

64

As noted above, Don Isaac Abarbanel marveled at the role of Rome in world history: First it had been the hub of the empire of a vast military power. Then it became the center of the Catholic world, the "holy seat" of a new "empire of the faithful," wielding vast power again.

We told earlier about Onkelos the *gér* (the proselyte) who converted to Judaism one troop of Roman soldiers after another. Clearly the dry rot of their way of life was already being felt in ancient Rome, and many were more than ready for a true religion to heal them spiritually. They did not all turn *en masse* to Judaism, however. Instead, great numbers of Romans, and eventually a Roman emperor, embraced the "new religion" centered around a Jew from Nazareth, who supposedly had given a marvelous "sermon on the mount."

Of course his "sermon" sounded marvelous. Just about everything good in it came from our Written and Oral Torah.[40] Such a minor detail, though, never bothered the gentlemen of the new religion. They were sure their faith was different and better, and absolutely unique and wonderful. So of course it had to be rammed down our people's throats, to save their souls.

How well Don Isaac Abarbanel knew the cruel sheer power of this second Roman empire, the spiritual realm ruled from the Vatican. He felt its onslaught in his very bones.

By training he was a financial advisor to sovereign leaders; and in 1484 he was called to Castile, to serve King Ferdinand in this capacity. Ten years earlier, Ferdinand of Castile had married Isabella of Aragon, and thus enlarged his kingdom. Thanks in no small measure to the skill and resourcefulness of his new financial advisor and treasurer, Ferdinand was able eventually to wage a successful war against the Moors of Granada.

For over two centuries the Church in Spain had been working to force the Jews into its fold, on pain of death or expulsion. Unfortunately, the Jews played too important a role in the economic life of the country, and the governing heads had always hesitated to do anything very drastic. Now, however, the priest who served as confessor to Queen Isabella was a Dominican named Torquemada (who went down in history — and down is certainly the right word — as the originator of the Spanish Inquisition). With true Dominican zeal, like an importunate dog after a meaty bone, he kept insisting that the adamant, unyielding Jews must be expelled. And now that he had conquered Granada (thanks to the financial acumen of Don Isaac Abarbanel), King Ferdinand felt secure enough to consent. Besides, the war in Aragon had left him heavily in debt. Abandoned and confiscated Jewish property would be very useful. He listened to his wife and her "man of true religion," and ordered all unconverted Jews out of Spain.

On a fateful day in 1492, some 300,000 left Spain, with no clear destination. Don Isaac Abarbanel was among them. They were robbed and slain; they died of hunger and disease; and within a few years, only 10,000 of them were left.[41]

Rome, the Eternal City with seven hills, was very ready to replace Sinai as the source of a "Torah", a divine teaching for the world. It could claim the right to serve the Jews as well: After all, Spain, a country under its spiritual rule, had given the Jews safety for centuries. Yet Rome's essential stock-in-trade was a tall mountain's arrogance, that ruthlessly undid any kindness ever shown us.

The spires of the cathedrals always rose higher than our modest houses of worship. But we knew that as long as we had our "sea of Talmud" we need not look to the "holy see" for any Divine word. Compared to Sinai, their "mount" with its sermon, its gospels and testament, was a crippled thing.

Take, for example, the strict rule of celibacy that this Nazarene "faith" established for its clergy. It took an American (non-Jewish) scholar like Henry C. Lea, a man of independent means, to undertake a dispassionate study of the subject — how far the rule was observed, and what were its effects, in the observance and in the breach. And his books (which include a detailed study of the Inquisition, another interesting aspect of this "religion of love") have always ranked high on the Catholic Index, the list of works forbidden for the faithful to read. It remains a subject for clinical psychological study to evaluate the damaging, destructive effect of this rule on its practitioners and on their victims.

The founder of the Moslem faith went to the other extreme. For *his* faithful flock, polygamy has remained essential to this day. One wife could not possibly be enough for a devout follower of this "true prophet." In fact, so important was the matter for them that he could promise every loyal subject nothing better in the Hereafter than a harem of the most delightful and ravishing kind.

The faith of the Torah simply requires marriage for everyone, as early as feasible (we have no exempt clergy); and monogamy has been the rule. Pointedly the Talmud records the words of R. Ḥisda: "The advantage I have over my colleagues [in Torah learning] is because I married at sixteen;

and had I married at fourteen, I would have told Satan, *Here's an arrow in your eye!"* (TB *Kiddushin* 29b–30a).

Whatever mountains of culture and religion have arisen to dazzling heights to capture minds and hearts, through the centuries the pious Jew has paid them scant heed. Knowing that the Almighty ignored all the glorious mountains and chose Sinai, the Jew of faith has ever left aside all the cultures and beliefs currently in vogue about him, and has clung tenaciously — even at the cost of his life — to the Torah.

Unfortunately, this has been true only of the devout observant Jew. In one age after another, alas, too many of our flock have strayed, bedazzled indeed by the mountains of foreign cultures, faiths and ideals.

With what heartrending pain a prophet of ours cried out to his people, *Yet upon every high hill and under every green tree you reclined as a harlot* (Jeremiah 2:20). In his time, as a harlot gives herself to everyone, our people devoted themselves to every kind of idol-worship that they learned from heathen neighbors. And this, if you will, set a tragic precedent for our youth in many a later generation. Once we became exposed to a free world beyond the ghetto walls, every new ideal became an idol for our impressionable youth, and it claimed its victims. Our young folk took up new causes wholeheartedly, as they heard in them a siren song of hope for their people or for all mankind. They gave themselves with a naive idealism that was pathetic, never realizing that ultimately they would be left as bitterly abandoned and disillusioned as any harlot.

In the era of the Maccabees we had our *mithyavnim*, Jews who wanted to be a little Greek in their lifestyle, thinking that this way lay glory. In the decades of the 19th century, when the winds of socialist and communist theory began blowing across the face of Europe, Jewish voices rose in the forefront. Moses Hess wanted to outdo Karl Marx, to save mankind, as both preached their radical gospel. In the end, to the Jews he was a crank and an embarrassment; to the socialists he was a Jew, to be mocked and scorned. Like a harlot at the close of her career, he was left with a residue of bitterness and emptiness; and then his thoughts turned back to his Jewish people and their religious heritage.

In his youth, until he turned Fascist in the aftermath of the First World War, Benito Mussolini trumpeted aloud the glories of radical socialism. "Socialism is war," he bellowed, "and in war, woe to those who have humanitarian feelings."[42] He became a hero to be followed blindly by

Italy's radicals, including (for our sins) a good number of Jews. Then Hitler arose like a blazing comet straight out of hell, and the Fascist, posturing Mussolini became his ally. So many of his former worshipful followers ended their lives in Hitler's concentration camps.

As the 19th century moved to its end, the effect of Nikolai Lenin's communist preaching reached full strength. Countless thousands were intoxicated with his gospel, as certain as he was that a worker's paradise could be attained, and thus mankind could be saved. Need we add that Jews were among his most dedicated followers? Inspired beyond words by his "sermon on the mount," they worked with fanaticism to bring the "gospel" to the Russian masses. At last the revolution came, and Russia turned communist. Behold, there were Lenin's Jewish disciples in the forefront, organized as the *yevsektsia*, a special section with special authority. They worked with a rare dedication, that even Torquemada would have admired, to uproot every trace of religion from their fellow-Jews in the new Soviet paradise. They were doing just fine — till they were variously liquidated, assassinated and purged. Like any harlot, they too received a fine reward for their fine service.

A separate tragic chapter in our people's history, to read only if you have a strong stomach, concerns the anarchist movement in Czarist Russia. Jews joined in and sought to take the lead, wanting to solve their people's problems and troubles by merging them with the difficulties of all the oppressed workers and peasants. Jewish anarchists insisted on pushing to the forefront and carrying out the dangerous missions. They were caught and arrested, tortured and put to death. And the Jewish troubles and problems remained untouched and unsolved. The other Russians remained apart. All the devotion and sacrifice went down the drain of history.

In our time, in America, a bizarre thing called the hippie movement found Jews again prominently out front, with more misguided idealism that led nowhere. The Negroes began their impassioned battle for civil rights and integration, to correct wrongs that had been done them since the very birth of the American nation. And behold, Reform rabbis, without an idea in their heads of what their goals for Jewry should be, suddenly discovered a purpose in life. They flew down to Alabama and jumped into one swimming pool with local Negro residents. They felt great, joining the cause and showing solidarity.

To this day they probably remain too addlepated and bewildered to understand what happened next. Black militancy grew, becoming more

intense and nasty, and breaking out (like a sore) in the Black Panther movement, etc. And the immediate targets that the Negroes chose to attack,
verbally and physically, were their Jewish neighbors. Shops owned by Jews
in Negro neighborhoods were damaged, and so forth. Rabbis in name only,
perhaps even Jewish in name only, those Reform leaders had failed to know
a primary rule: Whenever a scapegoat is needed, the Jew is chosen.

*Upon every high hill and under every green tree you reclined as a harlot.* We
have only to read perceptively through our people's history in the last 150
years; we have only to learn what goals and ideals draw our youth today —
and we can realize how truly the prophet Jeremiah spoke. Every mountain
of foreign culture and foreign values beckons and lures, and our youth
follows bedazzled.

Looking outward at our people, past and present, it is easy enough to
see this. Yet alas, it has its truth in our midst as well, in the lives of loyal
Jews who do their duty toward God and toward man — and there it is not
so easy to see. Even when the Torah is kept, people may go and find their
mountains, other ideals to serve in devotion; and they may never even
realize it. . . . We have our business activities, our professions, our political
endeavors. And we take it for granted that there we have goals and ideals
to serve, standards to maintain, above all other considerations.

To set ourselves straight, there is a simple way: We only have to
remember why the Almighty chose Sinai above all other mountains when
He came to give the Torah: It was the lowest and most humble of all the
mountains.

The Baal Shem Tov emphasized how easy it is for a man to become
haughty, all puffed up with self-importance, and still imagine fondly that
he is really a learned man of distinction, a Godfearing tzaddik of fine
character, and most charming and pleasant. Such a man, said the Baal
Shem Tov, may even be sure that a noble person like himself should not
really associate with ordinary people; but he only does so in order that
people should not think him arrogant; and besides, it is a mitzvah to be
modest.

Such a man, says the Baal Shem Tov, is like a person in a horse-driven
coach, fast asleep, as the driver takes it up a high hill. When he wakes up,
the coach is on the top of the hill, where the road is straight. Should a
companion tell him that they are high up, he will not believe it; he sees no
evidence of it whatever. Only when they start going down the other side
does he realize with a shock how right his companion was.[43]

69

So the test is simple: Are the ideals and goals of our life on a basis of Sinai? Do they fill us with pride, or can we live with them in humility? And above all, as Sinai was the setting for the Torah to be given, so must we ask ourselves if our life has the Torah for its base. Are we willing to make everything in our life subservient to the Torah's ideals? Then morally and spiritually we can have a healthy, normal life. Otherwise we are serving the ideals of some tall, imposing mountain that has bewitched us past all rational thought. We have made some other goal (or goals) more important than our immortal faith. And we would do well to remember that in the Almighty's sight all the other mountains were crippled — by their arrogance. Any other ideals, set above the Torah, can only tax and cripple our lives, making us haughty, and ultimately having no healthy purpose or healthy results.

On Sinai alone the Torah was given, and nothing but the Torah. To stay clear of other, bedazzling mountains, we have to keep the Torah the central element in our lives. It is for us to learn, and to have our children learn. But even more important, it is essential to maintain our gifted students and great scholars — and the yeshivoth where they study. For the Talmud has fascinating names for the two basic types of great scholars. One type, the Talmud calls *Sinai*; the other type, it calls *okér harim*, "an uprooter of mountains" (TB *Horayoth* 14a).

One kind of Torah student works like a natural sponge. He absorbs a knowledge of the Torah, phenomenally retaining its thousand and one details. He deserves the name *Sinai*: for through him, as it were, the Torah is given anew to our people. In a hundred ways he makes the people about him aware of the Torah all over again. Through his daily life, his everyday actions, the laws of the Torah come alive. When a person does not understand something in the Torah, he can ask a *Sinai* and learn the answer from this "walking encyclopedia."

But there is also another outstanding type of scholar: *okér harim*, an uprooter of mountains. He has a mind with a fine cutting edge. He can think coolly, incisively and brilliantly. By simple, rigorous, relentless logic he can upset and overturn a whole mountain of false thought and illusion. In the realm of the Divine word he pursues his goal of truth, and mountains of bedazzling delusion and claptrap get short shrift with him. About the *amora* R. Shimon b. Lakish the Talmud attests that whenever someone saw him in the *béth midrash*, the House of Study, it seemed as if he was uprooting mountains and grinding them to dust against one another. And about the

70

*tanna* R. Meir the Talmud attests that he seemed to do the same with the very tallest mountains (TB *Sanhedrin* 24a).

Perhaps it is not by chance that this was the way of R. Meir. Very possibly he learned his method from his master teacher, R. Akiva. R. Shimon b. Elazar once told about him: I will illustrate it with a parable for you. To what is the matter like? — to a stonecutter who would do his cutting in the mountains. Once he took his axe in hand and went and sat down on a mountainside and kept hacking out thin splinters from it. So people came along and asked him, "What are you doing?" He replied, "I am going to uproot it and put in it the Jordan River." They retorted, "You cannot uproot the whole mountain." He kept cutting away, however, till he reached a large boulder. He got in under it [with his tools], dislodged it and pried it out, and sent it down into the Jordan, saying, "Your place is not here, but there!" (*Avoth d'R. Nathan* a 6).

Two types of Torah scholars have existed for us in every generation, as the study of our sacred heritage has continued uninterrupted. And with them the work of the Almighty in the wilderness lives on. With our "Sinais" the Torah He gave pulses and lives in our midst, as its thoughts and its truths echo and re-echo in our Houses of Study. And with our "uprooters of mountains" another important act of His lives on. When He came to give the Torah, He rejected the tall majestic mountains. He called them crippled in their arrogance, and disdained them. By their own Talmudic genius, our great Torah scholars have similarly "uprooted the mountains" of the world's "great" cultures and religions, grinding them into dust by showing how small is their value compared with the Torah. Learn to know and understand a phenomenal *talmid ḥacham*, a luminary of our time, and you will realize automatically how all the secular "mountains" of values and ideals in our modern world pale into insignificance.

The Almighty chose Sinai because it was the lowest and the lowliest of the mountains. It held itself humble. And this has remained a characteristic of our greatest Torah scholars and religious leaders. They have never felt it necessary to attain five university degrees and a full professorship, to fulfill their God-given task in the world.

It is told that a certain devout Jew who opposed the method and teachings of R. Menaḥem Mendl of Kotzk once sent word to this renowned hassidic leader, "I have attained such height in my learning that I now comprehend the seventh heaven." The *rebbe* of Kotzk sent back his reply, "I am so small that all the seven heavens bend down about me!"[44]

Our great scholars do not grow grand in their learning and piety, to tower above us in imposing hauteur. They bring the holiness of heaven down about them, even as Sinai found the Divine Presence abiding on it — and through them our lives become tinged with holiness.

One last point is worth noting about Sinai. As the Midrash tells it, Mount Carmel came dashing in from Spain, and Mount Tabor from Béth Elim (*Midrash T'hillim* 68, 9). Well, the Midrash then logically asks, "And where did Sinai come from?" (If the other mountains traveled in from elsewhere, it must have done the same.) Said R. Yosé: It was plucked out from Mount Moriah, like a loaf-sized piece from a batch of dough, from the site where our father Isaac had been bound on the altar. Said the Holy, Blessed One: Since their forefather Isaac was bound on the altar on it, it is suitable for his descendants to receive the Torah on it.

Sinai was the very place where Abraham had shown his readiness to sacrifice his only son, in obedience to the Divine command, and Isaac had shown his readiness to be sacrificed.

This has remained the essential quality amidst our people that has kept the Torah alive, a living force, ever taught and renewed for us by our great scholars as the vital source of our spiritual energy. Every outstadning *talmid ḥacham* in our history achieved his place in our annals through his own dedication and self-sacrifice. And you have only to read a little intimate history of our people in Eastern Europe, a bit of the details of their ordinary daily lives, to know how much self-sacrifice it took by everyone, common laborers and small shopkeepers, farmers and peddlers, to keep Torah study going at a high level in a hundred academies and a thousand schools.

This remains our sacred obligation too, in our time and age. Every Torah school is precious and important, and must be maintained whatever the cost and the sacrifice involved. Only our Torah schools give us a base and a hope for great Torah scholars, Sinai and *okér harim* types, in the next generation too. We dare not risk letting either type become extinct.

When the Almighty was ready at last to give the Torah at Sinai, said R. Abbahu in the name of R. Yoḥanan, no bird cheeped, no wing fluttered, no cow lowed, no angels flew or hymned, *Holy, holy, holy is the Lord of hosts* (Isaiah 6:3); the sea never stirred, and no humans spoke. The world was silent and still, as the voice proclaimed, *I am the Lord your God* (Exodus 20:2) (*Sh'moth Rabbah* 29, 9).

This is a voice that has never ceased calling, demanding of us to recognize His sovereign rule as the Creator, and to accept the Torah as His imperishable word. We can hardly expect the rest of the world to hear the call. People everywhere are far too busy with the delusionary, misleading "Torahs" of their own mountains — their own cultures, values and ideals that generate a cacophony of "sound and fury signifying nothing."

But if we fail to hear every day anew the Divine call from Sinai, there is another message that emanates from there daily, and Heaven help us if we ignore that. Said R. Joshua b. Lévi: Every single day a heavenly voice emanates from Mount Ḥorév [= Sinai], proclaiming, "Woe to the people for the Torah's humiliation!" (*Avoth* vi 2).

If we fail to turn a deaf ear to the raucous or beguiling noises of the world about us, so that we can hear the call from Sinai and respond to it, we will leave the Torah disgraced and humiliated. And without the Torah we will not survive as Jews.

Every generation in every age has made its sacrifices to keep Torah study alive. Sinai, says the Midrash, was a part of Mount Moriah — the part where Abraham had bound Isaac in complete readiness to sacrifice him if that should be the Almighty's will. And we have kept the legacy of Sinai alive ever since, with the same dedication and devotion and readiness for sacrifice. This has been a key part of the authentic Jewish way of life, that requires us to love the Lord our God with all our heart and with all our soul and with all our might.

And the day will yet come when we will see that all the dedication and sacrifice has not been in vain. The Midrash relates that one day Moses came to our people in Egypt and told them, "In this month you will be redeemed." Said they to him, "Our master Moses, how can we be redeemed? We have no good deeds to our credit." He replied. "Since He strongly desires your redemption, He will disregard your bad deeds. What will He regard instead? — the *tzaddikim* among you, and their activities." ... The Sages said ... they objected, "Our master Moses, how can we be redeemed, when all Egypt is befouled with our idol-worship?" He replied, "Since He strongly desires your redemption, He disregards your idol-worship and instead *He comes leaping over the mountains* (Song of Songs 2:8), and mountains signify nothing but idol-worship" (*Shir haShirim Rabbah* 2:8—1-2).

The prophet has promised us that the end of our present exile, in the era of the Messiah, will be like the liberation from Egypt in Moses' day. Very possibly, then too He may ignore what most of our people do, like lost misguided sheep in the woods of a non-Jewish world, He may pay attention only to our tzaddikim, loyally maintaining Torah study at any cost. Then, just as once before He ignored all other mountains and chose Sinai, He may consider only the "Sinai" in our lives — the loyalty to the Torah — and He will skip over all other mountains of false, idolatrous cultures and values, ideals and goals, that have so tragically misled so many of our people.

For us as a nation, history began at Sinai. In the Torah as our Sages understood it, there is a promise that we will achieve our goal, the fulfillment of our destiny, at Mount Moriah — the Temple Mount — the origin or matrix of Mount Sinai, in the vision of our Sages.

When Moses gave the twelve tribes of Israel his final blessings, before his death, we read that *to Zebulun he said, ". . . Peoples shall call a mountain; there they shall offer up sacrifices of righteousness . . ."* (Deuteronomy 33:19, literal translation).

What does it mean? One olden commentary[45] explains: [It refers to] all the nations, who will come seeking about for the *béth ha-mikdash*, the Sanctuary . . . and will offer up sacrifices there for the sake of Heaven [to worship the Almighty] — as written further in Scripture, [*And many peoples shall go and say*] "*Come, let us go up to the mountain of the Lord*" (Isaiah 2:3, Micah 4:2).

On the words of Moses the Midrash goes further: The nations of the world will leave their countries and come for the trade and commerce of land of Israel.[46] And they will say, "Since we have suffered the exertions and discomfort of all this journey, come, let us go up to Jerusalem and see what their life in the marketplace is like." So they will find all the Jews together, all eating one kind of food, all drinking one liquid, and all praying to one God. . . . Then they will say, "There is none like the God of Israel. It is worthwhile adhering to none but this nation"; and they will not budge from there till they convert to Judaism and offer up sacrifices to the omnipresent God . . . (*Midrash Tanna'im*, Deuteronomy 33:19).[47]

This is the vision of our inevitable future. Thanks to our sacrifice, devotion and perseverance, some day the Sanctuary will stand again in the holy city of Jerusalem, as in ancient times. When Passover, *Shavuoth* or *Sukkoth* will come along, all the Jews in the land will assemble in Jerusalem, on *aliyath regel*, to eat the meat of their offerings and celebrate the festival in sanctity. This is the sight that will move the people of the world beyond words: celebration in holiness, with families and communities joined in harmonious friendship; one common kosher food and drink for all to share; no lurid movies or television; no raucous notes of discord. . . . And the nations of the world will be moved to unite with us — to join the people of God.

Then עמים הר יקראו *nations shall call a mountain*: They will call Moriah, the Temple Mount, a "mountain" — a place on earth where the immortal truth of the Torah can be received, where the Creator can be worshipped. In this sense there will be no more thought of giving the name "mountain" (the source and focus of a proper faith or culture) to Olympus or Quirinal, Tabor or Carmel, or what-have-you.

May that day come soon, in our time.

##  YOU GRAB TOO

Wᴇ sᴀʏ ᴛʜᴇ ᴡᴏʀᴅs ғᴀɪᴛʜғᴜʟʟʏ every morning and evening: *And you shall love the Lord your God with all your heart and with all your soul and with all your might* (Deuteronomy 6:5). Yet is it so easy to serve Him "with all your heart"? It means concentrating and focusing our thoughts onto one concept and one purpose. What shall we do, though, when the world we live in has developed so many dazzling distractions? Once there were moving pictures, shown in movie houses or cinemas. So you could simply stay away from the movie houses, and the pictures would not possess your thoughts. Well, modern science found an answer to that: television. You simply put a box with a tube in your living room, turn a knob, and the moving picture (or the weekly installment of your beloved favorite adventure or comedy series) is right there.

We have a giant advertising industry that is devoted to seizing and holding your attention, to interest you in a thousand-and-one products, goods and services. By every possible means of communication you are cajoled and persuaded to buy this soap and that toothpaste, and to embark on this fabulous vacation. . . . How are we to learn, in this maelstrom of

75

Madison Avenue's creation, to concentrate our thoughts for a brief while at least, and pray properly and decently to our Maker?

It is told that at one morning prayer service (*shaḥarith*), after his congregation of *ḥassidim* finished *sh'moneh esreh* (the central part of the service, the long prayer recited silently, standing), the famed ḥassidic rabbi Reb Lévi Yitzḥak of Berdychev went over to some of the people and greeted them warmly with the words, *Sholom aleychem!* They were quite amazed. They were not guests or newcomers to the synagogue. They had not been away anywhere on a long trip. They came every morning to the prayer services. Why, they wondered, did they get such an effusive welcome, all of a sudden?

Reb Lévi Yitzḥak explained: "While you were whispering the words of the prayer, I could see by your faces that your minds were somewhere else altogether. You, for example, were thinking of the grain market in Odessa. *Your* thoughts were dwelling on the wool market in Lodz. Now that you have come back from such long journeys, it is only right for me to give you a friendly *Sholom aleychem*, to welcome you back!"[48]

If this happened to pious *ḥassidim* over 150 years ago, in Eastern Europe, how much more must it happen to us when we pray. Then what are we to do?

Long ago an English poet wrote, "My mind to me a kingdom is";[49] but a kingdom remains a valuable, well-regulated possession only when a sovereign king sits on the throne, strongly in control. So must we be master over our minds: like a king, firmly and imperiously ruling out the thoughts we don't want — especially when we stand in prayer before the Almighty, often called by the Sages the supreme King of kings. It is to Him that we have to make the kingdom of our mind completely subservient and loyal, by keeping our mental world disciplined.

Yet some of us may find this goal beyond us. A man's mind may prove too unruly for him to control, however hard he tries.

Well, it is told that a person once came to the Ḥafétz Ḥayyim (R. Israel Meir haKohen, the pious sage of Radun) with this very problem. Gently the Ḥafétz Ḥayyim answered him with a parable, an illustrative story:

A yeshiva student once married a fine young girl; and since he wished to continue devoting all his time to Torah study, she undertook to earn a living for both of them (a common practice in that place and time). She baked bagels and sold them at a little stand on the street.

One day the word spread that the army was to march through the town soon. Losing no time, the young woman baked twice her usual amount of bagels, and she gave the extra supply to her husband. "You stand with them at the other side of town," she told him. "With all those soldiers marching through, many are bound to be hungry and buy our bagels. In this way we can sell more and make more money."

When the soldiers came through the town, both of them were ready with their bagels. Luck, however, was not with the yeshiva student that day. When the army soldiers saw him standing, rather alone and forlorn, offering his wares for sale, they simply made a mad dash and snatched up the bagels helter-skelter. He hardly had a chance to realize what had happened before they were all gone — both the soldiers and the bagels.

Wearing a long look of sorrow, he came home and told his wife. She listened sympathetically and did her best to comfort him. After all, said she, there was very little he could have done about it. . . . After a while the young man asked his wife if there was anything to eat. With a sudden change of mood she turned on him and began berating him and shouting at him. He looked at her in perplexity. "I don't understand," he said. "When I told you what happened, you said not a word to criticize me. In fact, you were sympathetic. Now, when I ask for something to eat, instead of providing lunch as usual you raise your voice to me. Why?"

"When you told me that the soldiers seized all the bagels, I accepted it. There were a thousand of them, and you were only one. What could you do? But now, when you ask for food because you are hungry, you have only yourself to blame. They were grabbing and snatching? You could grab also. In the midst of all the frenzy, you could have grasped a couple of bagels and held on to them!"[50]

If we cannot control our thoughts, if all sorts of ideas and reflections march through your mind while you are standing in prayer, and they seize major parts of your attention — you grab too. Concentrate as much as you can. Make it a point to bring your mind back, over and over again. Focus on the meaning of a word here, a sentence there, a paragraph there.

The same applies to all the mitzvoth, all the religious good deeds that a good Jew should perform. The world about us, especially the business world, claims our attention to the point of distraction? You grab too. In the midst of a busy day, if the chance comes along to give a bit of charity, to help someone in need, don't pass it by. Value the opportunity and seize

77

it. If you can leave your office for a brief while in the afternoon to join a congregation for *minḥah* (the afternoon prayer-service), seize the opportunity. It is precious.

There is an old English saying, "Take care of the pence, for the pounds will take care of themselves."[51] If we take care of all the little chances we get to do small mitzvoth, little acts of kindness and religious devotion, it can all add up to an immense, impressive total of merit in our heavenly account book. This too is a way to "love the Lord your God with all your heart" — to grab every chance you get to perform a mitzvah, to do what you can when and where you can, and not sit back and wait for some special golden opportunity to do something dazzling and spectacular.

For this wise approach is found not only in an old English saying. Some 1500 years earlier the Sages of the Talmud taught: How do we know that penny by penny can all add up to a large sum? — Scripture says, *adding one to one to find the sum* (Ecclesiastes 7:27).[52] And human experience bears this out: Many a businessman has made a fortune out of a penny or two of profit on every item that he sold. We can make a "longer-lasting profit" — spiritually — from every penny we give to charity, from every word of prayer we say sincerely, from every mitzvah we do in happiness, because it is God's will.

# *Notes* TO PART ONE

1. R. Shimoh b. Tzemaḥ Duran (14th–15th century), *Magén Avoth*. Similarly Sh'moth Rabbah 32, 6: If a man does one *mitzvah* (religious good deed), the Holy, Blessed One gives him one angel; if he does two *mitzvoth*, the Holy, Blessed One gives him two angels.

2. The Midrash sees yet more in this action of Abraham: Said R. Shimon b. Yoḥai: The Holy, Blessed One told him, "As you live, I shall rank you on the level that had I bidden you to offer up your own life, you would have had no reluctance to obey — for the sake of My name." For here it is written, *since you have not withheld your son,* which already means Isaac explicitly; then what does "your only one" mean? — it denotes Abraham's life-spirit ... (Tanḥuma, *sh'laḥ* 14; Early Tanḥuma, 27; Be-midbar Rabbah 17, 2).

3. *Si-aḥ Sarfé Kodesh* (Lodz 1929), III 5.

4. *Kether Shem Tov*, ed. Slovuta, pp. 10a, 31a.

5. Va-yikra Rabbah 34, 8; Ruth Rabbah 5, 6; Midrash haGadol, Genesis 37:21; Yalkut Shimoni I §141; II, Ruth §604.

6. Tanḥuma, *b'haaloth'cha* 8; Early Tanḥuma, 13; Be-midbar Rabbah 1, 12; 15, 12.

7. Similarly P'sikta d'R. Kahana 2 (19b): Said the Holy, Blessed One: You sold Rachel's [firstborn] son for twenty pieces of silver, which are five *s'la'im* [shekels]. Therefore every one of you shall redeem his firstborn son for twenty pieces of silver. So too TJ Sh'kalim ii 4 (64d); Be-midbar Rabbah 4, 10; and Midrash Aggadah, Numbers 3:46.

8. This is the reading of *Haggadoth haTalmud* (Constantinople 1511), which is far more likely than the version in our Talmud editions, "Said she"; moreover, it is in accord with R. Ḥananel's reading (Talmud ed. Vilna, margin): During the cultivation of intimacy he heard it being said, etc.

9. Erik H. Erikson, *Childhood and Society*, etc. The thought is echoed in the very word "husband": We know its meaning as a noun; in earlier centuries it was also a verb: a man would "husband" his land by cultivating and tending it so that it yielded its crops.

9a. "Some political scientists put at roughly eighty percent the proportion of Jews in the ideological development of messianic socialism and communism" (George Steiner, *In Bluebeard's Castle*, London: Faber paperbacks, 1971, p. 41).

10. See in this regard: Gordon Thomas and Max Morgan-Witts, *Voyage of the Damned: the voyage of the St Louis*, London [1974] — the basis of a film with the same title.

11. In another sense too, science is every bit as impermanent, as destined to disappear, as the sun and moon in Isaiah's prophetic vision. How many people in the world, setting their belief firmly in scientific theories on the age of the earth, etc., abandoned the ways and norms of their ancestral religion as "outdated and disproved." Yet consider these words by a foremost scientific thinker and writer of our time: "To the alchemists there were two ... principles. One was mercury, which stood for everything ... dense and permanent. The other was sulphur, which stood for everything ... inflammable and impermanent. All material bodies, including the human body, were made from these two principles and could be remade from them. For

instance, the alchemists believed that all metals grow inside the earth from mercury and sulphur, the way the bones grow inside an embryo from the egg. And they really meant that analogy . . . That seems a terribly childish theory today, a hodge-podge of fables and false comparisons. But our chemistry will seem childish five hundred years from now. Every theory is based on some analogy, and sooner or later the theory fails because the analogy turns out to be false" (Jacob Bronowski, *The Ascent of Man,* pp. 138 40). In need only be added that, by the avowal of all honest scientists, science never produces final truths but only theories.

11a.  Since the writing of these lines, the Vatican has revealed the truth about its "great holy leader" in the days of Hitler: He had previously been a high-ranking clergyman in Berlin, and had developed a great affection for the Germans (one is tempted to think that *matza min eth mino*). When he sat on the throne of the papacy and the machinery for the extermination of the Jews went into operation, all this "great holy leader" requested was that nothing of this program should be carried out within sight of the Vatican. It was all right to round up Jews in Rome and ship them off in a cattle car to a proper destination of death, as long as this "holy man" could see nothing of this through a window. Then he could go on living with his "holy thoughts" undisturbed and his love for the Germans undiminished.

12.  Ḥayyim Meir Heilman, *Béth Rebbe*, Berdytchev 1902, I, pp. 57, 58.

13.  Barnet Litvinoff, *The Road to Jerusalem,* p. 32.

14.  Moses Hess, *Rome and Jerusalem* (trans. Meyer Waxman), p. 58.

15.  B'réshith Rabbah 26, 5; TJ Sotah i 5 (17a); Va-yikra Rabbah 23, 9; Tanḥuma, *b'réshith* 12.    16.  According to *Dikduké Sof'rim.*

17.  D'varim Rabbah ed. Lieberman, p. 7; Yalkut Machiri, Psalms, p. 156 top.

18.  TJ B'rachoth i 8 (3c); Tanḥuma, *sh'laḥ* 15; Early Tanḥuma, 31.

19.  Rashi to Numbers 15:39 (cf. Be-midbar Rabbah 10, 2).

20.  TB B'rachoth 54a.

21.  Sifre, Deuteronomy §33; *ibid.* §161, reading of the Vilna Gaon.

22.  Avoth d'R. Nathan, a 20.    23.  TB Kiddushin 30b; Sifre, Deuteronomy §45.

24.  R. Naḥman of Bratzlav, *Likkuté Etzoth*, s.v. *b'rith*, §40.

25.  TB Sanhedrin 105b, Horayoth 10b.

26.  Mishnah, Taanith in 8; TB 31a, version in R. Isaac Aboab, *Menorath haMaor*, ed. Mosad haRav Kook, p. 360; TB in *En Yaakov* and MS Munich, margin (*Dikduké Sof'rim* and Taanith ed. Malter).

27.  According to a fascinating passage in the Midrash, divergent and perverse reasons for marriage began with the seventh generation of mankind: *And Lamech took himself two wives* (Genesis 4:19) — R. Azaryah said in R. Judah's name: This is what the people of the generation of the Flood would do. Among them, a person would take two wives: one for bearing children, and one for conjugal relations. The one for bearing children would sit like a widow in his lifetime, whereas he would give the one for conjugal relations a sterlizing root-drink, so that she should not bear children; and she would sit before him decked out like a harlot (B'réshith Rabbah 23, 2). This strikingly recalls a practice in ancient Greece, whereby a man would take a wife to bear him children, and in the years that followed he would leave her at home to the drudgery of her endless tasks, while he would go for his entertainment and pleasure to his pretty, witty *hetaera*, who might best be described as the ancient Greek version of the *geisha* in Japan.

28.  R. Israel al-Nakawa, *Menorath haMaor*, IV pp. 44–45.

29.   In his commentary to the Mishnah, Avoth iii 18, Rambam writes: Good traits are attained not according to the magnitude of an act but by the increase and multiplication of acts. This means that fine traits are acquired only when a man repeats good deeds many times. In this way he can gain such a disposition — but not when a man does one particular great act of a good nature; for by that one action alone, an inclination for it will not be acquired. To give an example: When a man gives a deserving person a thousand gold pieces at one time, he will not gain the quality of generosity to the same extent that a person acquires it when he donates a thousand gold pieces in a thousand instances, giving each gold piece separately, out of generosity. For he has repeated the act of giving 1,000 times, and thus has acquired a strong disposition for it . . . (after ed. Kafiḥ).

30.   Tanḥuma, *yithro* 11; Sh'moth Rabbah 28, 6.

31.   The metaphoric teaching is also found, in various forms, in Mechilta, *baḥodesh* 5; Midrash T'hillim 68, 9; P'sikta Rabbathi vii; Be-midbar Rabbah 13, 3; Vehizhir I, p. 45-46; Yalkut Shimoni II §47; Targum Jonathan, Judges 5:5.

32.   See Don Isaac Abarbanel, *Ma'ainé haYeshuah* (commentary on Daniel): *mayan* 2, *tamar* 3 (ed. Jerusalem 1960, p. 290a) — that the ancient Roman empire and the realm of Christendom under the papacy in Rome may be regarded as one. In *mayan* 8, *tamar* 5 (*op. cit.*, p. 355b) he declares the sovereignty of Rome to have been very superior, beyond compare in wisdom and sagacity. Further on (p. 337a) he notes that the emperor Constantine converted to Christianity and handed over the scepter of royal rule to the pope of his time.

33.   Moshe Aryeh Mirkin, ed. B'réshith Rabbah, 99, 1. On the symbolic meaning of mountains in the ancient world, note Balaam's opening words when he began his oracular utterances for Balak king of Moab: *From Aram did Balak convey me, from the mountains of the east* (Numbers 23:7). Aram is not a mountainous country. Was this an arbitrary metaphor, or did he wish to imply that Balak meant him to use the full powers of idolatry which emanated, in heathen belief, from the tall majestic mountains where their gods supposedly dwelt? Moreover, according to the commentary of R. Jacob b. Asher (*baal ha-turim*, and his *pirush ha'aruch*) the phrase means not "from the mountains of the east" but "from the mountains of antiquity." Note also Numbers 23:28, that to get Balaam properly "inspired" Balak took him to the top of *Pe'or*. Targum Onkelos and (Ps) Jonathan translate it as a height, but Targum Yerushalmi (MS Neofiti 1) renders it as the top of the idol of Pe'or (a known heathen deity in the ancient world). See too Isaiah 65:7, Ezekiel 6:13, and Hosea 4:13, which speak of idolatrous worship and sacrifices on the mountains.

34.   R. Judah haLévi, דבריך במור in his *Diwan*, ed. Brody, II p. 166.

35.   Plato, *Laws* VIII, ed. Stephens p. 794; in his *Dialogues*, ed. Jowett, V p. 175.

36.   See e.g. Rambam, *Mishneh Torah, hilchoth deyoth* iv; *Kitzur Shulḥan Aruch* 32.

37.   Note also the passage in TB Bava Kamma 71b-72a, where in the morning R. Naḥman gave Rava a final, well-reasoned answer to a question in law, which differed from what he had told him previously; and R. Naḥman explained: "The reason why I did not tell you this last evening is that I had not yet eaten [my portion of] beef" (and thus he had been unable to put his mind fully to work).

38.   Thus the Midrash states: *A man's pride will bring him low* (Proverbs 29:23) — this applies to [the mountains] Tabor and Carmel, which came from the end of the world, proudly declaring that "we are tall, and on us will the Holy, Blessed One give the Torah"; *but the lowly in spirit will uphold honor (ibid.)* — this applies to Sinai, which abased itself, saying that "I am

low"; and as a result the Holy, Blessed One rested His honor and glory on it, and upon it the Torah was given (*Be-midbar Rabbah* 13, 3).

There is an interesting story told of R. Abraham the son of R. Dov Ber of Mezritch, the Baal Shem Tov's disciple. One day this young man (known for his great piety as R. Abraham *haMal'ach*, "the angel") came from his home town to visit his father-in-law, a renowned Torah scholar. In a body, the notable learned and respected members of the community entered his father-in-law's house to welcome him with honor. They found him, however, standing at a window and gazing in total absorption. The town lay at the foot of a mountain, and R. Abraham could not tear his eyes away from the tall, imposing sight.

The eminent worthy people waited impatiently for him to turn around and say some word of greeting and blessing. Yet there he stood staring intently, lost in thought. At last one distinguished young man, quite learned in the Torah himself, lost patience. The esteem of the people in the room, he felt, was being slighted. "Honored rabbi," he spoke up, "why can you not take your eyes off the mountain? Have you never seen a mountain before?"

"I am just looking and wondering," replied R. Abraham, "how a mound of earth could have become so filled with pride until it became a tall mountain!" (R. Israel b. Abraham Rapaport, *Divré David*, Chortkov 1904, p, 51; another version: R, Israel Shapira of Gradzisk, *Emunath Yisrael,* Warsaw 1917, p. 62a).

*One with haughty eyes and an arrogant heart — him I cannot bear* (Psalms 101:5). So, in the Sages' imagery, the Holy, Blessed One left all the mountains and hills aside and brought His *shechinah* to rest on Mount Sinai (TB Sotah 5a).

He even scorned Mount Carmel, which, as the Midrash tells, had its own strong claim to the honor. We read: Carmel came from Spain... and [it] said, "I was called. It is right that the *shechinah* should dwell on me, because I made myself into a spread, flat surface within [the Red Sea] and on me they crossed the sea" (*Midrash T'hillim* 68, 9).

Mount Carmel had a good argument. When the Egyptian were pursuing the Israelites to recapture them, it had filled the Red Sea and formed a flat hard surface, so that the Israelites could cross safely in the nick of time. It had saved the Hebrew people at a critical moment. Surely it deserved this honor as a reward?

Note, however, that in the imagery of the Sages, Mount Carmel came running from Spain. Spain indeed gave our people precious safety during a part of our history. Exiled from their homeland, our people eventually had to find some kind of existence in the countries of Europe during and after the years of the geonim. And for centuries our people found a haven in Spain. Torah learning flourished there, producing such luminaries as R. Abraham ibn Ezra and R. Judah haLévi, R. Joseph Albo and R. Ḥasdai Crescas. Spain allowed our people to find safety there. So in the Sages' metaphor, its mountain felt entitled to replace Sinai at the Revelation.

Yet there was a bitter aftermath in that land. R. Moses b. Maimon (Rambam, Maimonides) was born in Cordoba and even became bar mitzvah there. Then he had to flee with his family. Moslems ruled Cordoba with an iron hand, and Jews who would not convert to their faith were "infidels." What was this "faith" of theirs that they would ram down our people's throat? Their "holy scripture" is filled with a murky kind of religious poetry that seems most clear through a haze of hashish smoke. And their "great prophet" evidently spent most of his life marrying women and conducting wars. Still, there was never a glimmer of doubt in the minds of the "faithful" that their so-called religion was vastly superior to every other.

However, what our people in Spain suffered from the Moslems was as nothing compared to the treatment they were to receive from another of the world's "three great faiths of mono-theism," as related below in this chapter.

39.   Note that when the Torah reports something strikingly similar (Genesis 6:4 — which the commentaries, however, explain to mean not the sons of God or gods, but the sons of great men), the next verse reads, *And the Lord saw that the wickedness of man on the earth was immense.*

40.   See Gerald Friedlander, *The Jewish Sources of the Sermon on the Mount.*

41.   See e.g. Erwin I.J. Rosenthal, "Don Isaac Abravanel," in his *Studia Semitica*, I, Cambridge 1971; B. Netanyahu, *Don Isaac Abravanel, Philosopher and Statesman*, Philadelphia 1953; Ephraim Schmueli, *Don Yitzhak Abravanel v'Gérush S'farad*, Jerusalem 1963.

42.   Encyclopedia Brittanica [1947] volume 16, p, 29.

43.   R. Israel Baal Shem Tov, in *Kether Shém Tov*, ed. Slovuta, 17b.

44.   R. Yoétz Kim Kaddish, *Si-ah Sarfé Kodesh*, II (Lodz 1927), p, 26b.

45.   R. Meyuhas b. Eliyahu, *Pirush al séfer d'varim*, Jerusalem 1968.

46.   As the commentary *Lekah Tov* indicates, it was appropriate for Moses to put those words in his blessing of Zebulun, because the shores where travelers to the holy land would arrive were included in Zebulun's territory. It was the maritime tribe of Israel.

47.   Sifre, Deuteronomy §354, has a slightly different version.

48.   R. Israel Berger, *Esser Oroth* (*Séfer Z'chuth Yisraél*, III), Warsaw 1913, pp. 63-64 (quoting *Séfer Divré Hachamim*, §22); Newman and Spitz, *Hasidic Anthology*, pp. 344-45; Buber, *Or haGanuz*, p. 205. Cf. this notable hassidic dictum: "I heard from my master instructor [R. Israel Baal Shem Tov]: At the place where a person's thought reaches, there he is entirely" R. Jacob Joseph of Polonnoye, *Tol'doth Yaakov Yoséf, sh'lah* — Koretz 1780, p. 189c, top).

49.   First line of a poem by Edward Dyer (c. 1540-1607).

50.   For a different version see David Zaretsky, *Mishlé heHafétz Hayyim*, revised, expanded edition, p. 121.

51.   Cited in: Earl of Chesterfield, *Letters to his son*, November 6, 1747.

52.   TB Sotah 8b; TJ i 7 (17a); Tosefta, Sotah iii 1.

# 2

## A human dignity

וַיִּבְרָא אֱ־לֹהִים אֶת הָאָדָם בְּצַלְמוֹ, בְּצֶלֶם אֱ־לֹהִים בָּרָא אֹתוֹ,
זָכָר וּנְקֵבָה בָּרָא אֹתָם (בראשית א כז)

*So God created man in His own image, in the image of God*
*He created him; male and female He created them.*

(Genesis 1:27)

**T**HIS IS THE CLEAR VOICE OF THE TORAH across the ages
of chaos and confusion, as man gropes to find himself and understand
himself: Who is he? what is he? what should he be? Darwin built a theory of
evolution and convinced the world that the human beign is a descendant of
some variety of ape.[1] The Torah says otherwise: man is a new, unique
creature in the panorama of creation — unlike any ape or baboon. He is in
God's image.

But let's look a moment at the exact words in the Torah, as our
immortal Sages understood them.

The Midrash states unequivocally that wherever we find the ineffable
name of God spelled *yod, hé, vav,* and another *hé* (which we pronounce
*a-do-nai* and translate "the Lord"), it denotes His quality of mercy, in man's
encounter with Him. Wherever *e-lo-him* is written (which we translate as
God), it indicates His quality of absolute, strict law, in relation to nature and
man (*B'réshith Rabbah* 33, 3).

To the great sages who studied our Torah through the centuries,[2] it was
equally clear that each verb in Scripture's account of creation has its own
meaning: בְּרָא (*bara*) denotes the absolute creation of something out of
nothing — יֵשׁ מֵאַיִן; where nothing existed before, some new entity
appears. On the other hand, יָצַר (*yatzar*) means that out of materials that
already existed, He formed or wrought something new — יֵשׁ מִיֵּשׁ "something out of something" — akin to the manufacture of a product from raw
materials. Similarly, the verb עָשָׂה (*asah*) denotes a shaping or adaptation of
what already existed.

87

וַיִּיצֶר ה׳ אֱ־לֹהִים אֶת הָאָדָם עָפָר מִן הָאֲדָמָה, וַיִּפַּח בְּאַפָּיו נִשְׁמַת חַיִּים

*Then the Lord God formed man of the dust of the earth, and He breathed into his nostrils the spirit of life* (Genesis 2:7). The Creator is called by two names here. He is not only *e-lo-him* (God), achieving His will through the strict laws of nature. He is also *hashem*[3] (the Lord), the ineffable Ruler of mercy who can intervene in the laws of nature and bend them to His will.

First, says Torah, וַיִּיצֶר (from יצר): He shaped and fashioned man out of the same primeval earth that gave rise to all living creatures. וַיֹּאמֶר א־להים נעשה אדם *And God said: Let us make man* (Genesis 1:26) — from the same raw material as the vast array of animals. And thus far there is nothing in our written Torah to contradict a dazzling Darwinian theory that places man in a long chain of animal development (except that we see in it not blind nature but a purposeful, unerring Divine will. In it we discern, as one poet wrote,[4] "what I call God, and fools call nature").

But there is another part to the sentence (verse) in the Torah: *and He breathed into his nostrils the spirit of life.* In the luminous words of the Zohar, the mystic Book of Splendor, "the One who breathed [this spirit] thus infused of His own essence."[5] Something new was added to man: an element of the Divine spirit, an essence of the Deity Himself. And the verse in the Torah concludes, ויהי האדם לנפש חיה *then man became a living being* (Genesis 2:7). He became a distinct entity, leaving the animal realm behind. Thus ויברא א־להים את האדם God truly *created* man (*ibid.* 1:27). Functioning in and beyond the laws of nature, the Creator added a touch of Divinity, and man became an utterly new being that can never be explained by Darwinian theory.


## ANGEL OR ANIMAL

Psychologists who must "publish or perish" may delight in showing resemblances between human and animal nature. At least one book compares pictures of humans with photographs of animals, showing startling similarties in their expressions. To the student of Torah this is of scant significance.

Our Sages knew there is a duality in human nature: angel *and* animal. In the Midrash we read in the name of R. Eliezer: He created four elements from above in man — four qualities of heavenly beings; and four elements

88

from below — four characteristics of earthly creatures. The heavenly qualities: man stands upright like the ministering angels, speaks like the ministering angels, has understanding like the ministering angels, and has vision like the ministering angels . . . . The four earthly characteristics: he eats and drinks like the animals, begets children like the animals, excretes bodily waste like the animals, and dies like the animals (*B'réshith Rabbah* 8,11; 14,3).

Our physical self was made of the earth, like the animals; *the Lord God formed man of the dust of the earth* (Genesis 2:7). The human body may well be a reshaping, a refinement for human purposes, of the kind of body that serves for apes — with earthly passions and needs, and with earthly vulnerability to death.

But what of his spirit, the entity of life that pulses and thrives in the body? *He breathed into his body the spirit of life* (Genesis 2:7). This is a distillation of Divinity, an incarnation of angelic powers and possibilities. We can share ideas, visions, moods — in speech, books, and music. We can think and plan, invent and build. Which ape ever constructed a mighty bridge to cross a roaring river? Which gorilla ever built a hospital to care for the ill?

Yet many are delighted to wallow, like happy little piggies, in the Darwinian "truth" that man is an animal. There they find their level. They simply will not see any more. And "none is so blind as those that will not see."[6]

Well, man has the ability to choose his path. "On the way a man wants to go, there he is led."[7] Then he can live as an animal too, if he wishes. When Abraham took his son Isaac to bind him on the altar on Mount Moriah, because so the Almighty commanded him, we read: *On the third day Abraham lifted up his eyes and saw the place from afar. And Abraham said to his lads: Stay here with the donkey, and I and the boy will go yonder . . .* (Genesis 22:4-5). In the Hebrew pharse *im ha-ḥamor* ("with the donkey") the Midrash discerns an echo of *am ha-domeh la-ḥamor*, "a donkey-like people."[8] And the Sages said further: A slave is content in the state of irresponsibility.[9]

But it is not hard to teach a person (especially the young) the profound, blazing truth of the Torah — that man was created *a little lower than the angels* (Psalms 8:6). I was told of a little boy in a *yeshiva*, a Torah day school, who was weeping bitterly in the hallway. "Why are you crying?" a teacher passing by asked him. Pointing to another youngster, the little lad blurted out, "He called me a *ḥamor*, a donkey!" Gently, the teacher asked,

"*Nu*, is that a reason for crying?" The boy retorted, "I don't care about myself; but he insulted the image of God!"

Actually, when a man fails to live by the moral law of the Torah, when he will not recognize and live up to his Divine potential, he doesn't become an animal. He becomes lower than the animals. Long ago our Sages made the point:

R. Elazar said: The verse *Let the earth bring forth a living spirit*[10] (Genesis 1:24) refers to the spirit of Adam, the first man. . . . R. Shimon b. Lakish said: The verse *the spirit of God was hovering over the face of the waters* (Genesis 1:2) connotes the spirit of Adam, the first man. . . . If man is worthy, he is told: You were first in the entire order of Creation. If he is not worthy, he is told: The gnat came before you (*B'réshith Rabbah* 8,7).

Only man's body, say the Sages, was formed last, after all the other creatures (as we read in the Torah). His Divine-like spirit was created first. If he lives up to the Divine element in him, he is the first, the head — fit to rule the animal world. He is the supreme achievement in Creation. If he lives only as an animal, he belongs last in the order of Creation; he is the lowest. Even the tiny gnat outranks him.[11]

Time and again it was said that Darwin dethroned man from his place of honor in the Divine plan of creation. No Darwin can do that, but only a man's way of life, as he chooses it. He can pick his spiritual *mishpocheh*, to consider himself related to the ape, or formed in the image of God.

For a world that has taken so long to learn so little of our Torah, one thought remains: Man can fly higher than the eagle, and streak through water faster than the whale. But can he live like a man?

## DIGNITY AND RESPECT

THE WHOLE CIVILIZED WORLD has come to accept the Divine decree of the Torah, *you shall not kill* (Exodus 20:13). Mankind has learned the truth of these imperishable words: שׁוֹפֵךְ דַּם הָאָדָם בָּאָדָם דָּמוֹ יִשָּׁפֵךְ, כִּי

בְּצֶלֶם אֱ־לֹהִים עָשָׂה אֶת הָאָדָם *Whoever sheds a man's blood, by man shall his blood be shed; for in the image of God did He make man* (Genesis 9:6). Into the warp and weft of creation, the Almighty set a law of retaliation: Kill a man, and you incur a fate to be killed — by society deliberately, or through the workings of destiny.[12]

Hillel, the Talmudic Sage, once saw a skull floating on the water. Turning to it, he said, "Because you drowned [someone] you were drowned; and the end of the one who drowned you will be that he will be drowned" (Mishnah, *Avoth* ii 6).

But our sensitive Sages also knew of another kind of murder: insult, disgrace and shame. You can so ruin a man's esteem that he wishes he were dead. The Talmud calls it מַלְבִּין פְּנֵי חֲבֵרוֹ בָּרַבִּים "whitening another man's face publicly"— because, if you deeply insult someone, you can see the blood draining from his face, leaving him deathly pale. What real difference is there if you spill a man's blood or make it course unnaturally through his body, as he wishes he were dead? The Sages interpret Scripture's words so (in addition to the plain meaning): שׁוֹפֵךְ דַּם הָאָדָם בָּאָדָם "Whoever sheds a man's blood within the man" דָּמוֹ יִשָּׁפֵךְ "his blood shall be shed." A man can bleed to death from an internal hemorrhage, within his body, even though we see nothing wrong with him. This is how the Sages regard a deathly insult. And for this, says the Talmud, אֵין לוֹ חֵלֶק לְעוֹלָם הַבָּא a person loses his share of life after death, in the world-to-come (TB *Bava M'tzia* 59a).

The late but unlamented Senator Joseph McCarthy began teaching America something of this Talmudic truth. The country watched him on television, as fascinating as a snake, and realized what he was doing. It was definitively termed "character assassination." He dug up the most tenuous links between communism and people in positions of security, and implied that they were therefore a dire threat to America's safety.

He killed no one physically (although several did die as result of his unlovely work). Yet past any doubt, he was a murderer. He destroyed lives and careers.

Well, against this great negative commandment not to kill, either with a gun or with words, the Torah imposes a great positive commandment: כְּבוֹד הַבְּרִיּוֹת respect for humankind. Remember, say the Sages: יְהִי כְבוֹד חֲבֵרֶךָ חָבִיב עָלֶיךָ כְּשֶׁלָּךְ Let the esteem of your fellow-man be as dear to you as your own self-respect (Mishnah, *Avoth* ii 10).

With this rule, the Torah's teaching that man was created in God's image stops being an abstract principle in the philosophy of ethics. There is

91

something we must do about it: respect our fellow-humans. And the Torah furnishes moving examples of this respect, that touched the everyday life of our people in the ancient land of Israel.

When the *béth ha-mikdash*, the sacred Temple, stood in Jerusalem, a Jew had to bring a *ḥattath* (sin-offering) as an animal sacrifice for any sin he did *b'shogég*, unknowingly (Leviticus 4:27–35). Suppose the Temple existed today, and you lived in Israel. If one Saturday you forgot it was the holy day of rest, and by force of habit you smoked a cigar or drove your car — you would have to bring a female goat or sheep to the Sanctuary as a *ḥattath*.

It might seem strange, even unjust, that if you sinned through sheer forgetfulness, meaning no harm, the Torah should demand an animal offering. But as some of our great teachers explain it, the Torah has its reasons. First, if you were entirely good, utterly removed from evil, the sin could not have happened. If you committed it, no matter how, it was because the sin found an opening to get to you.[13]

The Zohar (III 23a) notes that about other, plain people who might sin without realizing it, Scripture starts with the word *im*, "If" the person sins; but about a ruler it says *asher*, "*When* a ruler sins" (Leviticus 4:22). For, says the Zohar, "his heart is proud within him, since the people must follow him, subjected to his rule." As the well-known proverb says, pride goes before a fall.[14]

The Talmud (*Shabbath* 12b) tells how R. Ishmael b. Elisha learned of the Sages' ruling that on Friday night a person shouldn't study Torah by an oil lamp: if he finds the light too poor, he may forget himself and move the wick to make it brighter — which is forbidden on the Sabbath. But R. Ishmael b. Elisha felt self-confident. "I will study Torah," he said, "and not move the wick." Said R. Nathan: The end was that as he sat studying by his oil lamp on Friday night, he forgot himself and did move it. Once the Sabbath ended, he took his account book and wrote in it, "I, Ishmael b. Elisha, did this-and-this. When the Sanctuary is rebuilt, I will bring a fat animal for a *ḥattath* (sin-offering)."

Again, even one accidental, unaware bad deed could start a habit. If a person had to do nothing in order to be forgiven, he could let it happen again, and again, and again — till it wouldn't be so unintentional any more. The Midrash makes this point.[15] Moreover, it could leave guilt feelings, even start a lifelong guilt-complex. So the Torah demands a *ḥattath*, a sin-offering. A possible bad habit is nipped in the bud, and the slate is wiped clean of guilt fellings.

92

Then assuming you lived in Israel and the Sanctuary existed, if you forgot yourself and smoked a good Havana on the Sabbath, you would have to bring your *hattath* to the Temple court. There the goat or sheep would be taken north of the altar, to be ritually slain by a *kohen*. There, *batzafon,* north of the altar, was the one right place for it.

But wait. Someone might then watch you bringing the animal, and seeing it ritually slain north of the altar, he could muse, "Aha! That must be a *hattath*. Yankel must have forgotten himself and smoked a cigar on the Sabbath. He just can't keep away from those Havanas!"

As his offering was sacrificed at the Sanctuary, a man had to be alone with his thoughts — to sense regret and remorse for the accidental wrong he'd done. The key part of bringing an offering was to rest both hands on the animal's head and confess the sin that made the offering necessary. Then, as he watched it put to death, its blood sprinkled on the altar, and parts of it burned on the altar, he was to realize — in a sudden moment of truth — that all this should have been done to him, since so great is the destructive power of sin.[16]

But if the exact place where your *hattath* is ritually slain is a "dead giveaway," telling any prying eyes that your offering is a *hattath,* for a sin, how do you concentrate on contrition and repentance, when you know you're exposed to possible shame or ridicule if anyone is watching? Man is above the animal realm in his ability to know guilt and seek forgiveness. But he is equally sensitive to scorn and disgrace. From this the Torah should surely protect him when he comes to the Sanctuary seeking Divine pardon.

Well, we read on and find another rule: *As the* hattath, *so the* asham (*guilt-offering*): *there is one law for them* (Leviticus 7:7). One law — so that an *asham* was also ritually slain north of the altar. Then if someone watched you bring an offering and saw it put to death there, he couldn't be sure; it might be an *asham,* which you would bring if you thought you might have sinned but weren't certain. Thus, if you were in a room with both kosher and non-kosher steak, and afterward you couldn't remember which kind you ate, you would have to bring an *asham*.

The situation would seem a little better, then. But is it? If a man swindled another out of money and swore falsely about it, when he decided to repent he too would bring an *asham* (Leviticus 5:21–22). Well, then: if your prying neighbor saw your offering ritually slain north of the altar, he could let his imagination really go: "Aha! Yankel must have forgotten

93

himself and smoked one of those Havanas of his on the Sabbath; or he couldn't keep away from the steak at that affair, and he isn't sure he ate the kosher kind; or else he swore falsely to God just to diddle someone out of his money. . . . Good old Yankel — hasn't changed a bit."

Never fear. If the Torah teaches that man was created in the Divine image, if it regards deep insult as a form of murder, and commands us to respect another as we would want ourselves respected — it protects a person from this kind of shame.

...כִּי דְּמַר רַבִּי לֵוִי בְּשֵׁם רַבִּי שִׁמְעוֹן בֶּן לָקִישׁ: בִּמְקוֹם אֲשֶׁר תִּשָׁחֵט הָעֹלָה תִּשָּׁחֵט הַחַטָּאת לִפְנֵי ה׳ (ויקרא ו יח) – שֶׁלֹא לְפַרְסֵם אֶת הַחַטָּאִים. (ירושלמי, יבמות פ״ח ה״ג)

. . . as R. Lévi taught in the name of R. Shimon b. Lakish: *at the place where the* olah *(burnt-offering) is slain, the* ḥattath *(sin-offering) shall be slain, before the Lord* (Leviticus 6:18) — so as not to publicize the sinners (TJ *Yevamoth* viii 3, 9c).[17]

You see, an *olah* was also ritually slain there, *on the side of the altar to the north, before the Lord* (Leviticus 1:11). And an *olah* was brought not for any sin or wrongdoing, but as a voluntary offering — a gift to God — especially if someone had sinful thoughts that left him feeling guilty. And as the Sages note, as a rule no one completely escapes sinful thoughts.[18] So there is no disgrace in bringing an *olah*. In fact, it's commendable. Your prying neighbor could watch you till the cows came home, as you brought your *ḥattath*. If he saw it slain ritually north of the altar, for all he knew, you might be bringing an *olah*.

Interestingly enough, Scripture mentions four times where the *ḥattath* should be but to death — and never once does it give the spot directly, but always, "at the place of the *olah*," etc.[19] — indicating how the sinner is protected. As Scripture notes, it is "before the Lord."[20] There you're safe from shame and disgrace, from "partial murder" by insult and character assassination.[21]

94

Today, in our time, we have no Sanctuary. In the age-old words of the *musaf* service on our festivals: "Because of our sins we were exiled and driven far from our homeland. We cannot go up to appear and bow down in worship before Thee, to fulfill our duty in Thy chosen House, in the great and holy Temple that was called by Thy name, on account of the hand that was let loose against Thy Sanctuary." However we sin, we can bring no offerings. Then what are we to do for our guilt?

אָמַר אַבְרָהָם: רִבּוֹנוֹ־שֶׁל־עוֹלָם...תִּינַח בִּזְמַן שֶׁבֵּית הַמִּקְדָּשׁ קַיָּם; בִּזְמַן שֶׁאֵין בֵּית
הַמִּקְדָּשׁ קַיָּם, מַה תְּהֵא עֲלֵיהֶם? אָמַר לוֹ: כְּבָר תִּקַּנְתִּי לָהֶם סֵדֶר קָרְבָּנוֹת; בִּזְמַן שֶׁקּוֹרְאִין
בָּהֶן לְפָנַי, מַעֲלֶה אֲנִי עֲלֵיהֶם כְּאִילוּ הִקְרִיבוּם לְפָנַי, וַאֲנִי מוֹחֵל לָהֶם עַל כָּל עֲוֹנוֹתֵיהֶם.

(תענית כז ב)

Said Abraham: Master of the world . . . all will be well while the Sanctuary stands; [the offerings will protect my children;] but when the Sanctuary is gone, what will become of them? He replied: I have already prepared for them the order of the offerings [in the Torah]; whenever they study these in My presence, I will deem it as if they had offered them up before Me, and I will forgive them all their sins (TB *Taanith* 27b).

Our father Abraham anticipated the problem. And he was given a simple answer: we need only study about the offerings in the Torah.

Yet this only begs another question: All is well and good for the Torah scholar. What should an ordinary Jew do, who doesn't know how to study the Torah, especially the fine print of the commentaries and the supercommentaries?

Consider this passage in the Midrash: The Jewish people pleaded, "Master of the worlds . . . we are poor; we haven't the means to bring offerings." Said He, "I want words . . . and I will forgive you all your sins" — meaning by "words" nothing else than words of Torah. . . . But they pleaded, "We do not know [the Torah]." He replied, "Weep and pray before Me, and I will accept that" (*Sh'moth Rabbah* 38, 4).

95

When the cruel, power-hungry Romans destroyed the Sanctuary over 1900 years ago, the Sages and scholars gathered at Yavneh, under the staunch leadership of Rabban Yoḥanan b. Zakkai, to establish the Torah as the very heart of Jewish life, the core of our way to serve the Creator and merit His protection. The offerings at the Sanctuary were no more. But scholars in every age, down to our day, have continued studying them, to know just how they were offered up. This, says the Talmud, is every bit as good.[22]

For the great masses of Jewry through the ages, who could not study the Torah, there was the benison of prayer, the balm of words whispered directly to a listening Creator who never removed His ultimate protection from His people. So we read in the Midrash: When a man would bring an *olah* (burnt-offering) [to the Temple] he had reward for an *olah*; if a *minḥah* (meal-offering), he had reward for a *minḥah;* and so for a *ḥattath* (sin-offering), *asham* (guilt-offering), or *sh'lamim* (peace-offering). But whoever is humble in his mind [before God], Scripture reckons it for him as if he brought all the sacrifices in the Torah; for it is stated, *The sacrifices of God are a contrite spirit* (Psalms 51:19).[23]

Well, it is fascinating to find that the same protection of a sinner from shame, scorn or ridicule, transferred over to the world of prayer, where the sinner must go for his forgiveness while the Sanctuary is gone.

אָמַר ר' יוֹחָנָן מִשּׁוּם ר' שִׁמְעוֹן בֶּן יוֹחַי: מִפְּנֵי מַה תִּקְּנוּ תְּפִלָּה בְּלַחַשׁ? שֶׁלֹּא לְבַיֵּשׁ אֶת
עוֹבְרֵי עֲבֵרָה; שֶׁהֲרֵי לֹא חִלֵּק הַכָּתוּב מָקוֹם בֵּין חַטָּאת לְעוֹלָה. (סוטה לב ב)

R. Yoḥanan said in the name of R. Shimon b. Yoḥai: For what reason was it instituted that prayer should be said silently? — so as not to shame those who have sinned; for you see, Scripture made no difference between the place for a *ḥattath* and the place for an *olah*  (TB Sotah 32b).

As Rashi notes, sinners now confess in the *amidah,* the long prayer of eighteen benedictions (*sh'moneh eséh*) that forms the central part of the three daily prayer services. Elsewhere the Talmud also notes that in this long prayer recited standing, at any and every appropriate place a person should also mention his personal needs — where he must have the help of Almighty. And if he feels so moved, he may even add at the end the full confession of sins that we say on Yom Kippur, the Day of Atonement.[24]

So the Sages clamped a "lid of silence" on the *sh'moneh eséh,* the central prayer of eighteen benedictions. What you say in it must remain strictly your business — and your Creator's.

96

# THE CONFESSION
## ON YOM KIPPUR

Let's NOW TAKE A LOOK at the lengthy confession that we always recite in the *amidah* (the silent prayer said standing) in every prayer service of Yom Kippur except the last (*ne'ilah*). It is the long list of lines beginning with the words על חטא (for the sin . . .").

In ancient times, when the Sanctuary existed, the central activity on Yom Kippur was the long service of sacrifices and offerings, carried out there by the *kohen gadol,* chief of all the *kohanim.* Today, we have the day-long prayer-services in the synagogue, the "little Sanctuary," a small center of holiness left us in place of the great House of God in Jerusalem.

Soon after the destruction of the Temple, the confession of sins was a fixed part of the Yom Kippur prayers, for the worshippers at the end of the *amidah,* and for the reader (*hazzan*) within the *amidah.* Parts of the confession we recite were instituted in the time of the *g'mara,* the later part of the Talmud (after the Mishnah). Its form developed further in the days of the *ge'onim* (from 500 CE on), and the full text was finally set in the Middle Ages.[25]

It is the age-old custom of the penitent Jew, as he says the lines of this confession, to beat his chest, about the area of his heart, each time he says the words על חטא to mark his contrition for each sin he avows.

Well, the story is told that once, in an earlier period of our checkered history, a smug, pompous Jew decided to visit the synagogue on a Yom Kippur for the first time in years, evidently in a mood of nostalgia. Dressed in his formal morning coat, he watched what the others did, and followed in his prayer-book, with an indulgent lordly air.

As the confession of sins began, he stood with the rest, and watched as everyone beat his chest, once for every sin. Coldly he looked at his prayer-book, noting the translation. Then he began reciting the lines. Instead of a good reasonable blow with a fist, however, he accompanied every על חטא with a flick of the thumb that made his fingernail strike a button of his morning coat. That made a nice interesting sound, which he considered entirely sufficient. After all, those sins in the prayer-book had no real, direct relationship to him. He definitely did not indulge in such things.

Suddenly he stopped short, his hand suspended in mid-air. *Could it be?* he wondered. *How did the author of the prayer-book know?* One sin amid the list had struck home. That indeed was a failing of his! "Ah, ah, ah," he exclaimed, nodding his head vigorously in acknowledgment. And he struck his chest a resounding blow.

This is only a humorous anecdote from our folk-treasury. But suppose it reflected actual practice. Suppose each worshipper selected out of the lines of על חטא only those sins that really applied to him, and he uttered only these before his Maker, beating his chest in anguished contrition. Or perhaps he would follow no text but use his own words. . . .

We would be right back with the original problem of Yankel and his *ḥattath* (sin-offering) at the Sanctuary. Then we feared that prying eyes might realize how he had sinned, and he would suffer shame. In the synagogue on Yom Kippur, prying ears could do as much. How easily a man could regale his friends afterward, "Boy, what I heard Yankel saying in the synagogue! I was right next to him during the confession. You'll never believe it . . . "

Well then, it's no accident or coincidence that the entire Yom Kippur confession is in the plural. In all the list, there is not one avowal of "a sin that *I* sinned"; each line begins "for the sin שחטאנו that *we* sinned." Listen to your neighbor as you will. You can hear only the sins of *k'lal yisraél,* the Jewish people in entirety. For them we beg forgiveness on the sacred Day of Atonement.

But then, you might ask, maybe something important is missing? Shouldn't there be the confession of personal sins as well — just as an individual brought a *ḥattath* to the Sanctuary for his own sin?

Let it be noted that our religious law permits, even encourages, confessing private sins among the collective ones on Yom Kippur[26] — but quietly, discreetly, for the same reason that our Sages decreed that the *amidah,* the long main daily prayer of eighteen benedictions, is to be said silently. Moreover, in reciting the "plural" sins, a person is free to bear in mind his own personal failings in the year gone by, wherever they coincide with what he is confessing on behalf of *k'lal yisraél.* He can simply "include himself in."

Yet another important theme is implied here, too. In our ancient history, before Nebuchadnezzar came and destroyed the first Temple, the prophet Jeremiah envisioned the exile of our people into centuries of woe — and he cried out, שה פזורה ישראל *Israel is a scattered, driven lamb* (Jeremiah 50:17). And the Midrash poignantly comments: Israel is well likened to a lamb: If a lamb is hurt on the head or in one of its limbs, all its limbs feel the pain [as its small, weak body is utterly shaken by the wound]. Even so is it with the Israelites (Jewry): *Let one man sin, and Thou wilt be angry with the entire community* (Numbers 16:22).[27]

We suffer collectively for the sins of individuals. The Midrash teaches: [Scripture states] *And if a soul shall sin* (Leviticus 5:1) . . . Why does it not say, "if souls shall sin"? — because all the Jewish people are called one soul . . . and if one of them has sinned, all are responsible for one another.[28]

Throughout the long hard Jewish exile, the rule has held: collective responsiblity, collective guilt. Form the Middle Ages onward, our history records cases enough where one Jew or a few were accused of a crime, and a community suffered. Jews might be expelled, their houses might be burned and pillaged, they could be massacred. . . .

A generation or two ago, as Jews read of some criminal act in the newspaper, their one anxious question about the offender was always, "Is he a Jew?" History taught them to ask, and to prepare themselves according to the answer. In our century, as communism flared in Russia, one philosopher there wrote, "A Jew often used to say to me: You don't have answer for Lenin being a Russian, while I shall have to answer for Trotzky being a Jew." Somewhere in his career, Albert Einstein (who understood "Jewish relativity" as well as physics) remarked, "If my theory of relativity is proven successful, Germany will claim me as a German and France will declare that I am a citizen of the world. Should my theory prove untrue, France will say that I am a German and Germany will declare that I am a Jew."[29]

This is a rule of life for us, before the world and before our Maker. We may well shudder when blatantly Jewish names flare up in headlines as leaders of hippies and yippies and destructive radical movements, acting out their psychedelic nightmares with never a care for the harvest that all Jewry may reap. We shudder equally when Jewish names "shine" among the "stars" of the world of organized crime.

Who has not heard this parable in the Midrash? R. Shimon b. Yoḥai taught: This can be likened to a group of people situated in a boat, where one took an auger and began boring a hole under his seat. "What are you doing?" the others asked. "What do you care?" he rejoined. "Am I not making it under my place?" "But you are flooding the entire boat for us!"[30]

A bearded tzaddik goes from Torah study to mitzvoth and back throughout the year. He rarely spends a free hour outside his *beth midrash,* his House of Study. In the prayer-book's long list of sins for the Yom Kippur confession, how many did *he* do? Yet this is why he says them with such fervor, beating his chest at every line, the tears streaming down his face. His people's sins are *his* sins, and on his confession his people's fate may depend.

You are all guarantors for one another, says the Midrash — responsible for one another: If there is even one tzaddik, one righteous man among you, you will endure in his merit; and not you alone, but the entire world as well: for Scripture states, *the righteous man is the foundation of the world* (Proverbs 10:25). But if one of you sins, the entire generation suffers. This, we find, was the case with Achan: was it not Achan b. Zeraḥ who violated the ban? yet there was Divine retribution against the entire Jewish community.[31]

So we stand in the synagogue on Yom Kippur, as members of God's own people. Accepting our common responsibility, we confess our sins in the plural — the sins of *k'lal yisraél.* And thus, as human beings created in the Divine image, our personal dignity is safeguarded.

## ARMY REJECTS AND DROPOUTS

THE FIERCE BATTLES that the Israelites waged to conquer the Promised Land were *milḥemeth mitzvah,* "war by religious command," ordained by the Torah. But after they were settled on the land, they would sometimes have to wage war also to gain more food or more land, in order to survive.[32] Such military ventures were called *milḥemeth r'shuth,* voluntary war, by choice — for which the king needed the authorization of the Sanhedrin, the Hebrew supreme court. Then he could summon men to his battle-standard.

But as the men marched off to the fighting, the Torah imposed an interesting set of laws. When they reached the border, ready to leave it behind and go on to the battlefield, they stopped; and a special *kohen* addressed them.

This *kohen* was called *mashuaḥ milḥamah,* "anointed for war." Chosen just for this purpose, to speak to the men before battle, he had been anointed with oil, just as a *kohen gadol* and a king were anointed to set them on their lifelong tasks.[33]

At the border, this *kohen* spoke: "Whoever hears this, let him go and hear it [again] in the war regulations of the *kohen* of battle, and let him return home"[34] — if these regulations so ordered. The *kohen* continued: *What man is there that has built a new house and has not dedicated it? Let him go and return to his house, lest he die in the battle and another man dedicate it. And what man is there that has planted a vineyard and has not enjoyed its fruit? Let him go and return to his house, lest he die in the battle and another man enjoy its fruit. And what man is there that has betrothed a wife and not taken her? Let him go and return to his house, lest he die in the battle and another man take her* (Deuteronomy 20:5–7).[35]

Before the Hebrews had time to ponder these words, perhaps the strangest regulations ever given before a war, they were marched to the battlefield, to form ranks. Waiting in silence, they heard again the *kohen* anointed for war, speaking from a high place: *Hear, O Israel. You draw near this day to the battle against your enemies; let not your heart grow faint; do not fear or tremble or be in dread of them; for the Lord your God is the One who goes with you, to fight for you against your enemies, to save you* (Deuteronomy 20:3–4).

The Talmud teaches that the *kohen* explained: They faced no mild, kindly opponent, but a cruel ruthless enemy that would show no mercy; this was no civil war against other Israelites. But they could rely on the Almighty's protection. He had helped and rescued His people miraculously in the past.[36] A *kohen* or *kohanim* repeated his words aloud, to make sure everyone heard them.[36] Then the anointed *kohen* spoke again, from his high place, to repeat the rules he had given at the border: *What man is there that has built a new house and not dedicated it,* etc. Again he proclaimed Scripture's law that these must return home and not take part in the fighting.

No sooner had he finished than an army officer or officers repeated his words in great voices, to make sure no one failed to hear.[36] Now came the

101

last regulation, spoken by the commanding officer: *What man is there that is fearful and faint-hearted? Let him go and return to his house, that the heart of his brethren shall not melt like his heart* (Deuteronomy 20:8). These words in turn were repeated by another officer or officers, for all to hear.[36]

Well, this last rule is easy to understand: fear is contagious. Let one man run because his nerve breaks, and ten others instinctively want to run, afraid with him of some unseen terror. Far better to lose one man before the battle than ten in the thick of it.

But why ever the Torah's three other exemptions? Imagine: if you built yourself a new home and didn't yet start living in it, you would leave the battlefield. In a new vineyard, the grapes of the first three years were forbidden. The fourth-year crop was to be eaten in Jerusalem; or you could sell it, and buy food in Jerusalem with the money. If you had a new vineyard and didn't yet enjoy the fourth-year crop, you would be sent home. Then, if you formed a marital bond with a girl by betrothal (*érusin,* which made her your wife legally) but did not go through the second ceremony, *kiddushin* (consecration), under the canopy, to begin married life together, you too would go home.

In heaven's name, why?

This is the touching, humane answer of Rabban Yoḥanan b. Zakkai:

רַבָּן יוֹחָנָן בֶּן זַכַּאי אוֹמֵר: בּוֹא וּרְאֵה כַּמָּה חָס הַמָּקוֹם עַל כְּבוֹד הַבְּרִיּוֹת, מִפְּנֵי הַיָּרֵא וְרַךְ הַלֵּבָב – כְּשֶׁיְּהֵא חוֹזֵר, יֹאמְרוּ: שֶׁמָּא בָּנָה בַיִת, שֶׁמָּא כֶּרֶם נָטַע, שֶׁמָּא אִשָּׁה אֵרֵשׂ. (מדרש תנאים, דברים כ ח)

Come and see how greatly the Almighty cares for the dignity of human beings. [This was all] for the sake of the fearful and faint-hearted person — that when he went back, people should say, "Maybe he built a house; maybe he planted a vineyard; maybe he betrothed a wife" (*Midrash Tanna'im,* Deuteronomy 20:8, 120; *Sifre* §192).

The Torah was willing to lose three extra men for every one who *had* to be sent home, so that he should suffer no insult or disgrace on his way back from the battlefield.

Note the words of R. Yosé of Galilee: "fearful and faint-hearted" (Deuteronomy 20:8) — this means a person who is fearful for the sins he committed; therefore the Torah associated all those [other exempted people] with him, that he might return along with them, in their wake (TB *Sotah* 44a). As the Midrash puts it: "fearful and faint-hearted" — he bears the private knowledge of a sin (*Sifre* §197).

102

This clarifies a point: The *kohen* anointed for war gave a ringing promise of Divine protection: *let not your heart grow faint; do not fear or tremble or be in dread of them; for the Lord your God is the One who goes with you to fight for you against your enemies, to save you* (Deuteronomy 20:3-4). After this, how could a man be "fearful and faint-hearted"? The answer is that sin lies on his conscience, and he cannot be certain of Divine protection.[37]

Imagine what would be if the Torah had given him no "protective cover." Think of a typical GI unit about to go into action, when the captain or chaplain calls out, "All right, fellows! Anyone who's sinned, go home. Dismissed!" Here and there, some would slink off, red in the face, desperately trying to meet no one's gaze directly. The jeers and catcalls would come thick and fast. "Hey," the shouts would fly from all sides, "look at those sinners! *Repent!*"

No, says the Torah: this must not be. A man who is unsure of Divine protection because he sinned, has a reverent fear of the Almighty and yearns for His pardon. Then he deserves to be kept safe from scorn and insult, just as much as a man who brought a *hattath* (sin-offering) to the Sanctuary. It is better to send home three extra soldiers with every one, and not let a human being, created in the Divine image, suffer shame.

Down through the centuries our sages were sensitive to the pain that shame causes. It is told that R. Israel Salanter (of blessed memory), the founder of the *mussar* movement in our world of sacred learning, once had to spend a Sabbath in a certain town. A prominent householder hastened to invite the distinguished scholar to his home, and R. Israel accepted.

After the Sabbath candles were lit, the two went to the synagogue for the prayer-service that would usher in the holy day of rest. Then they returned to the man's home, for *kiddush* and the evening meal. The householder noticed immediately, however, that the *halloth,* the two Sabbath loaves on the table, were not covered. It is an old accepted custom for the loaves to be covered with a fine cloth until after *kiddush* and the ritual washing of the hands for the meal; but in a flurry of last-minute preparations, the man's wife had forgotten this detail.

Piqued at the oversight, that might reflect badly on him in the eyes of his distinguished guest, the man of the house flew into a rage at his poor wife: "It is a shame and a disgrace!" he stormed. "How could you have forgotten a thing like that?" With an apology, the woman quickly placed her embroidered ḥallah-cloth over the loaves, as a deep flush covered her cheeks. R. Israel said not a word.

After the meal, however, he called his host aside. "Tell me, dear sir," he said: "What is the reason that the two loaves are covered until after the kiddush?"

"Oh, I know that," his host replied. "It is permissible to say the kiddush (the benediction for the holiness of the Sabbath) over a cup of wine or over the two loaves. Since we leave the loaves aside and take the wine, we do not want the loaves to see themselves slighted, whereupon as it were they would feel put to shame. So we cover them."[37a]

"Consider then," said R. Israel Salanter gently: "You were so very concerned for the assumed, hypothetical feelings of two pieces of baked dough; it disturbed you that they had been left uncovered. But you forgot to consider the feelings of your good wife, the pain she would definitely suffer at being insulted."


## THE COST OF AN OFFERING

LET US RETURN FOR A LITTLE WHILE to the subect of animal sacrifices brought to the Sanctuary of old in Jerusalem. For a sin committed unintentionally, unknowingly, a person brought a ḥattath, a sin-offering. But if you did something and then couldn't find out if it was a sin or not, you would bring an asham, a guilt-offering. Thus (as mentioned earlier) if there was both kosher and non-kosher steak in a room, and you ate some in all innocence, and then couldn't remember or find out what kind you had eaten, you would have to bring an asham taluy, a "hanging asham" — an offering for something left hanging in doubt.

In one case you know you sinned. In the other, you are unsure: maybe you did, maybe you didn't. Where would you expect the Torah to be more severe? Surely harshness would be more fitting where a sin was definitely done. In the other case, there is a fifty-percent likelihood that nothing wrong was done at all.

104

Yet the Torah rules otherwise: For an *asham taluy* a man brought a ram, a male sheep, in its second year of life; and it had to cost at least two shekels.[38] On this the Torah insists. If prices of sheep went down, and you could get the finest one, generally worth twenty, for one shekel, you would have to wait till prices rose and it cost you two shekels.[39]

For a *ḥattath,* though, there was no minimum price that had to be paid. Even if the animal cost a *danka,* a small Persian coin worth a sixth of a shekel — one twelfth the minimum price of an *asham* — the offering was acceptable.[40]

Did the Torah slip up here? Never fear: the Torah makes no mistakes. In his Bible commentary, R. Baḥya explains it very well:

The reason for this is that when a person's sin is known to him, he worries and suffers sorrow; and anguish over a sin is [itself] an altar for atonement and one of the ways of repentance, in the sense that Scripture writes, *For I confess my iniquity, I worry for my sin* (Psalms 38:19). But a man who sinned and did not know it [for certain] would not worry, would not feel pained with sorrow, and would not confess to it. It is therefore right for the Torah to be more severe with him ... his sacrifice is called a guilt-offering ... because he is guilty ... in that he did not worry and did not fret over it before the Lord who knows the hidden matters [in a man's heart].[41]

As Ramban (Naḥmanides) writes,[42] this man simply reckons, or takes it for granted, that no punishment is due him. He indulges in the wishful thought, "Oh, it dosen't matter. I'm sure it will be all right."

Man was created in the Divine image. When he feels sorrow and contrition, that has value; and less is demanded of him when he seeks forgiveness for sin.

## THE DEAD
## OR THE SYNAGOGUE?

IN THE CODE THAT GOVERNS OUR RELIGIOUS LIFE, the hard dry strict law, the dignity of a human being remains of greatest importance.

Suppose for a moment that you lived in a suburb in Israel. It is late afternoon. When darkness falls, it will be the night of Purim — the happy holiday that brings *groggers* (noise-makers) to the synagogue and joy to children's hearts. You set out early to the synagogue, looking forward to hearing the *m'gillah,* the Book of Esther, chanted at nightfall. On the way you meet the rabbi and the cantor, who will read the *m'gillah;* and since it's early, you all take a roundabout way, through wild bushes and trees. The scenery is idyllic in its pastoral beauty. And suddenly you stop short. There, before you, lies a dead person; and you don't know who in the world it is.

There, is not another soul in sight. If you shout, no one will hear you . . . "Come on," you might say, "let's go to the synagogue. After the *m'gillah* reading, we'll come back. This man is dead. What matter if he lies here another two hours? And then we can bring a *minyan* with us [a religious quorum of ten] and have a proper memorial prayer and *kaddish*. . . . Look, Rabbi: if we stay and bother with him, there won't be any *m'gillah* reading!"

Our religious law decrees that you stay. Forget the synagogue and the *m'gillah* for now. The body must be buried then and there.[43] This is a *méth mitzvah,* a dead person who imposes a religious obligation.

Another thought might occur to you: "Rabbi, let's carry him back to civilization at least — to the undertaker. Then he can get a proper, respectful burial."

Long ago R. Akiva had a similar idea. In his later years he reminisced,[44] "This is how I came to serve and attend upon the Sages [to learn from them]: Once I was walking on the way, and I found a slain man. I carried him a distance of four mils, till I brought him to a cemetery and buried him. When I reached R. Eliezer and R. Joshua, I told them about it; and they said: For every single step you took, it is reckoned to you as if you committed murder! I reasoned: If now, when I meant to do a good, virtuous deed, I brought guilt on myself, how much more guilt must I acquire when I have no such good intentions? From that moment, I never budged from attending upon the Sages [to learn from them]."

No: if you find a dead person like that, you do not move him. מת מצוה קוֹנֶה מקוֹמוֹ "A *méth mitzvah*," says the Talmud, "takes possession of his place" on earth. So "whoever finds a *méth mitzvah*, he must attend to him and bury him in his place" (TJ *Nazir* vii 5), no matter what other mitzvah you were on your way to do.[46]

Why is this law so firm and absolute? — because the esteem of a human being is involved. In death all dignity vanishes. Only the body remains, lifeless and helpless. As long as a man lives, say the Sages, his awe is cast over all living beings. Once dead, he casts no more awe. Once a man's end has come, all have dominion over him.[47] What honor is it to a human soul to leave his body above ground when it can no longer defend itself against the smallest creature? It desperately needs the gift of burial.[48]

Even after his death, Torah law remembers that a man was created in the image of God, and over and above any other religious obligation, we must grant him the last honor and the last kindness — Jewish burial.

## ❧ A DOG OR A LION

Now, INTERESTINGLY ENOUGH, as it happens, within the *m'gillah,* the Book of Esther mentioned above, there is one passage on which the Talmud and Midrash elaborate, that is very much concerned with the principle of *kavod ha-b'riyoth,* human dignity.

In the Book of Esther, we read how Haman gets King Ahasuerus's seal of approval on a proclamation to all 127 provinces of his empire, ordering the wholesale destruction of the Jews on a set day: the thirteenth of Adar. Mordecai informs his niece Esther, now the queen in the royal

palace, and persuades her to go plead with Ahasuerus to save her people —
although, if anyone goes to see the king without being called, that person
is put to death, unless the king holds out his scepter for the person to touch;
and she had not been called to his royal chamber in thirty days.

ויהי ביום השלישי ותלבש אסתר מלכות *And it was on the third day:
and Esther put on royalty* (Esther 5:1). But surely, the Talmud asks, it should
have said "royal clothing"? Said R. Elazar in the name of R. Ḥanina:
This teaches us that she clothed (enveloped) herself in the Divine Spirit (TB
*M'gillah* 15b).

She needed the protection of the Divine Spirit about her. She sorely
needed a heavenly presence and wisdom to guide her. Once in the king's
chamber, would she find a way to save her people? Or would she merely
be put to death for coming uninvited?

As she walked through the palace to the royal chamber, enwrapped in
the Divine Spirit, the Midrash tells that she whispered a prayer: psalm 22 of
*séfer t'hillim,* the Book of Psalms, that David in his prevision had composed
for her.[49]

Says the Midrash: There were seven chambers through which she had
to pass to reach king Ahasuerus. She went through three without mishap
(as none there knew she was going without a royal invitation). As she
entered the fourth, however, Ahasuerus caught sight of her. He gnashed his
teeth fiercely and said, "Woe for those who are lost and gone but not
forgotten! How I yearned and begged for Queen Vashti to come before me,
and she would not . . . and I sentenced her to death.[50] And this one enters
like a wanton, without permission!"

As the guards perceived the king's rage, they were ready to slay her.
But she remained midway in the fourth chamber. Those behind her could
not touch her: she had already passed them. Those ahead could not touch
her: she had not yet reached them. . . . And at that moment Esther prayed to
the Almighty, *Be not far from me, for trouble is near, for there is none to help.*[15]

With the Divine Presence about her, she felt protected, and walked on;
ותעמד בחצר בית המלך הפנימית *and she stood in the inner court of the king'
palace* (Esther 5:1). And there she prayed again, *Save my soul from the
sword . . . from the power of the dog* (Psalms 22:21). Said R. Lévi: Once she
reached the house of the idols, the *shechinah* (Divine Presence) withdrew
from her.[52]

The royal chamber was the king's private chapel, with his fine little
collection of idols that he worshipped. There she felt a deathly chill in her

108

spirit, and she knew the Divine Presence had abandoned her to her mortal peril. In alarm, she cried out again the opening words of her prayer, *My God, my God, why hast Thou forsaken me?* (Psalms 22:2).[52]

Suddenly a thought struck her: "Is it perhaps because I called him [Ahasuerus] a dog?" — as we read, *Save my soul from the sword ... from the power of the dog* (Psalms 22:21). חזרה וקראתו אריה She thereupon called him a lion instead — as we read, *Save me from the mouth of the lion* (Psalms 22:22).[52]

With that, the tide turned for her. Aided by Divine forces again, Esther found favor with Ahasuerus, and he held out the golden scepter.[53] Event followed event, till Haman and his sons (his valiant lieutenants) swung from the gallows, and the Jews in the empire could defeat their vicious enemies.

What turned the tide at the critical point? Esther changed her metaphor about Ahasuerus. Instead of the lowly derogatory dog, she chose the lion as an image for him. The lion is an animal too, but the king of the animals. The term "lion-hearted" is a noble epithet denoting courage. People willingly bear first names — Leo, Leon, Leonard, Lionel — meaning a lion. On the other hand, "dog" is never anything but an insult.

Esther may have had reason for calling him a dog. In fact, as the Sages evaluate his actions, their conclusions are most unflattering.[54] But they studied him long afterward, and gave conclusions, not insults. Esther was about to see a living, powerful king, and was praying to be able to make him spare her people. . . .

Frederick the Great, king of Prussia (1712-1786), once remarked, "They say kings are made in the image of God. I feel sorry for God if that is what he looks like."[55] The Jewish view goes beyond this surface humor. The Creator is מלך מלכי המלכים the ultimate sovereign over all rulers and potentates. If He saw fit to let human beings share or control some small part of His sovereignty on earth, we must respect His will; and when we see a Gentile king, no matter who, we say a blessing to the Almighty "who has bestowed of His glory on His creatures."[22]

As Rambam phrases it in his commentary on the *m'gillah*, when the *shechinah* left her, Esther grew confused and frightened, and she said, "Perhaps I committed a foolishness in what I just said, when I called him a dog — since the Holy, Blessed One imparted of His glory to creatures of flesh and blood. And for this the [Divine] radiance was taken from me."

109

In the Yeshiva of Slobodka in an earlier time, the pious R. Isaac Sher (of blessed memory) taught *mussar,* the ethics and morality of the Torah. He used to make the two points just presented here: (1) If a man finds a dead body, a *méth mitzvah,* on his way to hear the *m'gillah,* he must forget the *m'gillah* and inter the dead person. (2) At a most critical point, the Divine Presence left Esther because she called King Ahasuerus a dog; once she corrected herself and called him a lion, king of the animals, a noble epithet — all went well.

Said R. Isaac Sher: The first point is easy to understand from the second. What was Esther's sin in calling him a dog? — she failed to give him his due honor. If she would liken him to an animal in poetic imagery, by Divine will he was royal, and in her imagery he must remain royal. Else she stripped him of his God-given dignity.

Had Esther not corrected herself, said R. Isaac Sher, and given him his due esteem, she would have failed. Resented, unacknowledged by the king, she would have been slain for her trouble, for coming uninvited. Haman would have succeeded; the Jews in those 127 provinces would have been slaughtered; and today we would have no Purim to celebrate and no *m'gillah* to hear in the synagouge.

If we have a Purim holiday, it is only because Esther observed the supreme principle of כְּבוֹד הַבְּרִיּוֹת to give a human being the full honor due him. Hence, if going to hear the *m'gillah,* you find a *méth mitzvah,* a poor forlorn body with no one to attend to it, obviously you must stay and bury it. If we Jews, including Esther, didn't treat every human being with the full dignity he deserves, you wouldn't be going to hear the *m'gillah* in the first place. There would simply be no Purim.

# THE SMALL COIN
# OF HUMAN INTERCHANGE

IN PIRKE AVOTH (Ethics of the Fathers, iii 14) R. AKIVA TEACHES a truly striking thought: חביב אדם שנברא בצלם Beloved is man, in that he was created in the [Divine] image. By His grace the Almighty made man in His likeness, distinctly apart from any other creature. A noted American psychiatrist (Harry Stack Sullivan) once remarked that "we are all much more human than otherwise": the two most dissimilar people on earth will yet resemble each other far more closely than either resembles any animal.

Cast in the likeness of the Creator, the entire human race is an élite, a nobility. R. Akiva speaks of "man," not a Jew or a Chinese or a blond Nordic hero. It was simply *Adam,* the Hebrew word for man, the progenitor and prototype of all mankind, that the Almighty created in His image. And note the words of the Midrash on his formation: He began to gather the dust [raw material] of the first man from the four corners of the earth — red, black, white, and yellow-green.[57] The first man had no superiority of color. The Sages teach further: Adam was created alone, a single human being. Why?... that the righteous should not say, "We are the descendants of the righteous first ancestor," and the wicked should not say, "We are the descendants of the wicked one."[58]

So people the world over share in the nobility of the human race, whatever their color or the cast of their features. If the Torah calls Jewry the chosen people, it does not make us a privileged, lordly class at the expense of any others. *Thus says the Lord: the Israelites are My firstborn son* (Exodus 4:22). In every family the firstborn is "chosen": he receives privileges, being older; but he also carries responsiblities: more is expected of him than of the other children. And no normal family will allow the oldest son to lord it over the other children unjustly or to exploit them cruelly. Nor can he make it impossible or unnecessary for the other children to grow to his level of responsibility.

When the Temple was destroyed in Jerusalem, the Sages set their Torah academy and *sanhedrin* (supreme court) in Yavneh, as Israel's new

111

center of religious authority. They could have emphasized their own new importance, the honor due them. Instead, they developed a little personal testament, to say often:

מַרְגְּלָא בְּפוּמַיְיהוּ דְּרַבָּנָן דְּיַבְנֶה: אֲנִי בְּרִיָּה וַחֲבֵרִי בְּרִיָּה. אֲנִי מְלַאכְתִּי בָּעִיר וְהוּא מְלַאכְתּוֹ בַּשָּׂדֶה. אֲנִי מַשְׁכִּים לִמְלַאכְתִּי וְהוּא מַשְׁכִּים לִמְלַאכְתּוֹ. כְּשֵׁם שֶׁהוּא אֵינוֹ מִתְגַּדֵּר בִּמְלַאכְתִּי, כָּךְ אֲנִי אֵינִי מִתְגַּדֵּר בִּמְלַאכְתּוֹ. וְשֶׁמָּא תֹּאמַר אֲנִי מַרְבֶּה וְהוּא מַמְעִיט? שָׁנִינוּ: אֶחָד הַמַּרְבֶּה וְאֶחָד הַמַּמְעִיט, וּבִלְבַד שֶׁיְּכַוֵּן לִבּוֹ לַשָּׁמָיִם. (ברכות יז א)

"I am a human being, and my fellow-man is a human being. My work is in town, and his work is in the field. I rise early for my work, and he rises early for his work. Just as he would not presume to do my work, so would I not presume to do his. Yet perhaps you would say I do much and he does little?[59] We learned: One may do much and one may do little; it is all the same, as long as he directs his heart to Heaven" (TB *B'rachoth* 17a).

The Torah scholar compared himself with the farmer, and he saw both doing the Almighty's work, contributing to human welfare. And this holds true whatever the farmer's race or nation. Well, if everyone is in the Divine image, and all contribute, as a rule, to the general welfare, then everyone is entitled to be received courteously, with good manners.

Said Shammai: Welcome every man with a pleasant, cheerful countenance (*Avoth* i 15). Abbaye (a Talmudic sage) had a favorite saying: A person should always . . . promote peace with his brethren and his relatives, and with everyone, even the heathen in the street.[60] It was told of Rabban Yoḥanan b. Zakkai that whomever he met, even a heathen in the street, he had a ready greeting, a friendly *Shalom*. No one ever greeted him first.[60]

How important is this? Read *Avoth d'R. Nathan* (13) on Shammai's dictum: This teaches us that if a person gives someone all the fine presents in the world, but with his face turned to the ground in surly anger, the Torah deems it as if he gave him nothing; but if he receives him pleasantly, then even if he gives him nothing, it is as if he gave him all the presents in the world.[61]

Are there any people in the world who, for you, are not worth even a friendly "hello"? Before you would so dismiss any group, or even one person, with scorn, ask: Would the Torah agree? The most shiftless reprobate can father splendid children. Koraḥ rebelled insolently against Moses, and the earth opened under him to swallow him alive (Numbers 16). Yet his descendants, gifted with prophecy, sang psalms in the Temple.[62]

112

In our prayers of Rosh haShanah and Yom Kippur we say of an evil person who might deserve to die: וְעַד יוֹם מוֹתוֹ תְּחַכֶּה לּוֹ; אִם יָשׁוּב, מִיָּד תְּקַבְּלוֹ "Till the day of his death Thou dost wait for him; should he return in repentance, Thou wouldst accept him at once." As long as a man lives, Jew or non-Jew, he has the capacity to learn and improve, to change and leave evil behind him. Then everyone, good or bad, is entitled to a smile of welcome, a word of friendship, when you meet him. In that way we "seek peace and pursue it" (Psalms 34:15).

It takes a thousand little acts of cheer and good will, smiles and friendly greetings, to help a person feel welcome in the world — needed, valued, appreciated. And this is something we all need from one another. Wisely the Talmud teaches: If a person knows his neighbor is used to greeting him [every time they meet] let him greet him first. If a person is used to greeting his neighbor [whenever they meet] and one day he does not, he transgresses Scripture's precept, *seek peace and pursue it* (Psalms 34:15). And if the other man greets him first and he does not return the greeting, he is called a robber.[62]

Is someone always gives you a pleasant *Hello* and a cheerful word, don't answer with some perfunctory sounds or a grunt. Give as well as you get. The other needs your friendly smile too. If it is your habit to greet a neighbor every morning, don't break the habit one day because you feel miserable. Make an effort and give a smile. And if the other takes the first step and gives you a cheerful *Hello,* return it. Otherwise you rob him of something precious: a bit of feeling all right. You leave him crestfallen, wondering what he did wrong. (Bear in mind, too, what the pious *Ḥafetz Hayyim* of blessed memory once remarked: Isn't it peculiar that we greet someone with a question, "How are you?" [or, in the short form of out time, "Hi"] and we don't even wait for an answer?)

In these simple ways, say the Sages, you "seek peace and pursue it". It is up to us ordinary citizens of the world to promote friendship and good will like that. On the level of the politicians in the world's capitals, the cause of peace is largely hopeleess.

Simple courtesy and good cheer — just that — can form the solid foundation of a blessed way of life with a good harvest. Take Hillel, the wise, humble Sage. He was considered as great in his time, in making the Torah established and known, as Ezra had been when the Israelites returned from Babylonia to their land.[63] Now, it was Hillel's colleague Shammai who taught in *pirké avoth,* "Receive every man with a pleasant, cheerful countenance" (Ethics of the Fathers, i 15). Yet if someone seemed to tread on the Torah or the Jewish faith in any way, his own good cheer vanished. Where the Torah was concerned, he would brook nothing that smacked of foolishness or insolence. Still, our Sages taught: Let a man ever be gentle, humble like Hillel, and not critical and impatient like Shammai. And they relate some relevant stories:[64]

What was the humility of Hillel like? Two men once made a wager between them, saying: Whoever [of the two] will go and get Hillel angry, will receive 400 *zuz* [from the other].[65] Said one, "I will make him angry."

It was late Friday, before the Sabbath, and Hillel was washing his head [in preparation for the holy day. The man] went, came over to his door, and knocked. "Is Hillel here? Is Hillel here?" he cried; "where is Hillel?" [He did not call for Hillel the elder or Hillel the patriarch — just Hillel.] The Sage put on a robe and went out to him; "My son, what do you want?"

"I have a question that I must ask."

"Ask my son; ask."

"Why are the heads of the Babylonians round?"[66]

"My son," said the Sage, "you have asked a great question. It is because they have no bright, intelligent midwives" [to give the infants proper care].[67]

The man went away, waited a while, then returned to knock at his door. "Is Hillel here? Is Hillel here? Where is Hillel?" The Sage put on a robe and went out to him: "My son, what do you want?"

"I have a question that I must ask."

"Ask, my son; ask."

"Why are the eyes of the Tarmodians [in Palmyra] mere slits, and bleary?"

"My son," said the Sage, "you have asked a great question. It is because they live among the sands of the desert. The winds come and blow the sand into their eyes."

The man went away and waited a while. Then he returned and knocked on the door. "Is Hillel here? Is Hillel here? Where is Hillel?" The Sage put on a robe and went out to him. "My son, what do you want?"

"There is a question I must ask you."

"Ask, my son; ask."

"Why are the feet of the Africans wide?"

"My son, you have asked a great question. It is because they live in the marshes, and every day they tread [barefoot] in the water."

114

Said the man, "I have many questions to ask you, but I am afraid you may mind and be vexed." At that the Sage put on proper clothing and sat before him. "All the questions you have to ask," said he, "ask!"

Then the other said, "Are you the Hillel whom they call the *nassi* (the patriarch, religious head of Israel)?"

"Yes," said the Sage.

"If you are Hillel, may there not be many like you in Israel!"

"My son, why?"

"Because I have lost 400 *zuz* on account of you!"[68] [He must certainly have expected this above all to enrage Hillel, as the Sage realized the exact reason for those questions.] "Be careful of your temper," said Hillel. "Calm yourself. Hillel is well worth it that you should lose 400 *zuz* and another 400 *zuz,* and Hillel should not be vexed and angry."[69]

The Talmud and Midrash[64] then tell of a non-Jew who came to Hillel asking to be converted, but on condition that he should teach him only the Written Torah (Scripture), since he did not believe in the Oral Torah (embodied now mainly in the Mishnah and Talmud). Hillel accepted him.[70]

The first day, Hillel taught him [the first letters of the Hebrew alphabet] *alef, béth, gimmel, daleth.* The next day he reversed them for him [reading them, *daleth, gimmel, béth, alef*].[71] The man protested, "But yesterday you did not teach me thus!" He replied, "Must you then not rely on me? Then rely on me also about the Oral Torah."[72]

Do *we* ever realize how utterly each generation depends on the one before it for its concepts and meanings? Since human language began, it goes from one generation to the next by oral transmission. Hillel made the man realize that the same holds true for our Oral Torah — which necessarily began when Moses explained the words of sacred Scripture.

The Sages tell further[64] about a certain heathen who wanted to be converted to Judaism on condition that the whole Torah should be taught him in the time that he could stand on one foot. Hillel accepted him.[73]

Said Hillel [In fulfillment of the condition] "What is hateful to you, do not do to your fellow-man. This is the whole Torah. The rest is commentary on it; go and learn it."

(On this, Rashi quotes Proverbs 27:10, *Your friend and your father's friend, do not forsake.* This "friend" denotes the Almighty, says Rashi. Just as you would hate it if a good friend didn't respect your wishes, so is the

Holy One offended if we fail to observe His mitzvoth. So "the whole Torah" is, first and foremost, a solemn commitment to observe its precepts *mé'aha-vah,* for the sake of a bond of friendship with the Creator, who rewards and protects His flock.)

Then the Sages recount:[64] It once happened that a certain heathen was passing behind a *béth midrash,* a House of Study, when he heard the teacher's voice reciting,[74] *And these are the garments which they shall make: a breast-plate and an éphod and a tunic,* etc. (Exodus 28:4). He went to the teacher and asked, "Explain these things to me"; and the teacher explained. "But for whom are these?" the heathen wondered; he told him, "For the *kohen gadol.*" So the heathen mused, "I will go and convert on condition that they make me *kohen gadol.*"[75]

He came before Shammai and said, "Convert me, on condition that you appoint me *kohen gadol.*" That Sage drove him off with the builder's measure that was in his hand. He then came before Hillel and said, "Convert me, on condition that I become *kohen gadol.*" He converted him; then the Sage said, "Is anyone ever appointed to serve before a king unless he knows all the arts and ways of royalty? Go learn the arts of royalty."[76]

So he went and studied all the Torah's laws on the *kohanim.* When he reached the words, *and the stranger that comes close shall be put to death* (Numbers 1:51), he asked him, "To whom would this verse apply?" Replied the Sage, "Even to David, king of Israel." The man drew the conclusion for himself: "If the Israelites, who are called sons of the omnipresent God,[77] — and out of the love He bore them, He called them *Israel My firstborn son*[78] — if for them it is written, *the stranger who comes close shall be put to death,* how much more must this apply to a mere convert who comes along with his walking-stick and knapsack!" Then and there his mind was soothed and set at rest.

He went to see Shammai and admitted, "Am I then eligible to be a *kohen* at all? It is written in the Torah, *the stranger who comes close shall be put to death.*" Then he went to see Hillel and said, "Humble, gentle Hillel, may blessings rest on your head, that you brought me under the wings of the *shechinah* [the Divine Presence, by converting me]."

In time the three met in one place. Said he, "The exacting impatience of Shammai sought to drive us from the world; the gentle humility of Hillel brought us under the wings of the *shechinah.*" It is told that two sons were born to that convert. He named one Hillel, and the other Gamliel; and they were called Hillel's converts.[79]

116

Hillel was patient and modest. He reckoned that if the Creator put a person on earth, his life must have value. If someone tried to vex him just to win a wager, he was content to teach him patiently the importance of patience at all costs, even at the cost of the 400 *zuz* that the man had wagered. The man might live on a little better, a little wiser, as a result.

When others came with demands and conditions that Shammai might find insolent, Hillel always assumed that the person before him had a reason. Without anger, he looked for a way to channel the strong demand, so the person could move toward the Jewish faith.

One man wanted Judaism by the Written Torah alone. Perhaps he wasn't ready to trust in the sheer accuracy and reliability of an oral tradition that began for us with Moses in the wilderness. Many today "accept" only our Written Torah, paying it glorious lip-service, but with scant attention to its clear, precise laws, that form the backbone of the Oral Torah. As for doubting the Oral Torah, for years you could have heard anything from scoffing skepticism to sneering denial about it, from so-called leaders ("religious" and otherwise) who knew only how to mislead and distort.

(Such leaders might have read with profit the preface of Herbert Danby, a non-Jewish clergyman, to his translation of the Mishnah. Both there and in his introduction he shows a rare appreciation of the importance and value of the Mishnah as the cornerstone of the Oral Torah in its recorded form. And he states: "Throughout, both in translation and notes, traditional Jewish interpretation has been followed. Considering the centuries of intensive study devoted to the Mishnah and its associated literature by Jewish commentators from the time of the Talmuds to the present day, to neglect or ignore their results is as presumptuous as it is precarious."[80] How refreshing to find, in this unexpected quarter, a view so in accord with that of observant Jewry, which Hillel subtly conveyed in his own way.)

Hillel began with the Hebrew alphabet, and showed the convert how crucial oral tradition and transmission are right there. And he left it to the convert to draw his own conclusions about the Oral Torah. Bible students of our time have been amazed to find, by evidence, how accurate the *massorah*'s text of Scripture has remained over long centuries of time — originally the result of oral transmission.

The one who wanted to learn the entire Torah while standing on one foot might have been afraid the Torah was too much, too complex to master. After all, scholars have devoted a lifetime to it, then said they merely scratched the surface, or took a drop from the sea of the Talmud.

117

So this man wanted to grasp the essence of the Torah in a nutshell, as it were. Then he could go on to learn the myriad details, a few at a time. With a nutshell-knowledge of the essence in hand, he would never feel he was floundering in the sea of the Talmud.

As for the one who wanted to be *kohen gadol*, there is still a child in every adult. So he saw a vision of glory that he thought in his grasp. Hillel let the resulting eagerness and enthusiasm of the man carry him along, to study and grow in religious maturity. The benefits remained when the child's vision had to be given up.

How did Hillel develop his blessed approach? — by the principle of כְּבוֹד הַבְּרִיּוֹת : by respecting every human being as an image of the Deity, with a Divine value and purpose on earth.

## ꙮ DUST, ASH & A WORM

ACTUALLY, LONG BEFORE HILLEL'S TIME, there were several esteemed, renowned members of our people noted for their humility and modesty. In the Talmud, R. Eliezer b. R. Yosé of Galilee teaches: *Not because you were greater than any people did the Lord set His love upon you and choose you* (Deuteronomy 7:7). Said the Holy, Blessed One to the Israelites: I set My love upon you because even when I bestow greatness on you, you humble yourselves before Me. I raised Abraham to greatness, and he said, *I am but dust and ashes* (Genesis 18:27); Moses and Aaron — and they said, *but what are we?* (Exodus 16:7,8); David — and he said, *But I am a worm and no man* (Psalms 22:7).[81]

Abraham was the first in the world to renounce idolatry and worship the one true Creator. His descendants would form a people to keep this faith of truth. And he was renowned: *Hear us, my lord,* the Hittites told him: *you are a prince of God among us* (Genesis 23:6). Yet as he began to plead with the Almighty for Sodom and Gomorrah, he said, "I am but dust and ashes."

118

Moses was the leader of the new Hebrew nation. Through him this people left Egypt, free. At the close of the Pentateuch, the Almighty bears witness that never, before of after, was there a prophet like Moses. Yet when the Hebrews turned quarrelsome, all he and Aaron said was, "what are we — [nought] — that you quarrel with us?"

David was a king of Israel, founder of the royal dynasty that would never be replaced. Yet in prayer he said, "I am a worm, and no man."

Well, now, were these three equal in humility? No, says R. Yoḥanan in the Talmud.[81] Abraham called himself dust and ashes. In dust of the earth, things can grow. Where the earth is bare today, a tree may grow tomorrow. The dust of the earth has a future. Ashes are the result of burning wood. Where ash lies today, a tree perhaps grew yesterday. Ashes have a past. David, on the other hand, called himself a worm. More than a past or a furure, it has a present. It exists; it aerates the earth, helping plant life. It is food for birds, bait for fishermen.

Moses, however, called Aaron and himself *mah, "what"* — a zero, nothing — a question mark without an answer. So Scripture rightly states, והאיש משה עניו מאד מכל האדם *the man Moses was very humble, more than any man* . . . (Numbers 12:3). The Hebrew for "man" is *adam,* made up of the letters *alef, daleth, mem.* Then we could take it as an acrostic denoting Abraham, David, Moses: Among these three, he was the most humble.

Well, we ordinary mortals need only the benign humility of an Abraham, if we are to be worthy of being not just his descendants but also his disciples. In *pirké avoth* (Ethics of the Fathers, v 19) we read: Whoever possesses these three traits is among the disciples of Abraham our father . . . a good (generous) eye, a lowly spirit, and a modest, humble soul. To this, *Avoth d'R. Nathan* (b 45) adds: How do we know about a modest, humble soul? — because it is stated, "I am but dust and ashes."

Certainly, to learn and practice humility constantly, is to invest wisely. You get valuable dividends from it: First, you avoid a major disease. As one wise man said, conceit is the most incurable disease of the human soul.[82] Then it prepares you and paves the way for you to practice *g'miluth ḥassadim,* acts of charity and kindness. Consider this striking passage in *Avoth d'R. Nathan* (a 7):

Teach your household gentle hu mility. For when a man is modest and his family is modest, then if a poor man comes and stands at the householder's door and asks them, "Is your father here?" they answer, "Yes; come in."

Before he yet enters, the table is readied for him; he comes in, eats and drinks, and [in the grace after meals] he blesses the name of Heaven. Thus he [the master of the house] will have great spiritual pleasure. But when a man is not gently humble and the members of his household are harsh and vexatious, then if a poor man comes and stands at his door and asks, "Is your father in?" they answer No, rail at him in anger, and drive him away in disgrace.

If you remain modest and don't inflate yourself like an automobile tire in order to be a "big wheel" and "go places," it's easy to receive every person with courtesy and respect, and to give each his due, within your means: to your neighbor, a cheerful greeting, a warm word of welcome; for the poor, a share of your charity. So you set a path for your children to follow. In time you establish בית נאמן בישראל a "faithful house" in Jewry.

Most things in life you cannot take with you into eternity. But this is an achievement of merit that you can "send on ahead" — to enjoy the reward (like dividends) in the Afterlife.

Moreover, modesty and humility make it easy to recognize the Torah's truth and hold to it. R. Ḥanina b. Idi said: Why are the words of Torah likened to water?... to tell you that just as water always leaves a high place and goes to a lower level, so do the Torah's words endure only in one whose mind is humble (TB *Taanith* 7a).

Hillel and Shammai each developed an academy, where generations of students continued studying the Torah that they had taught. Between the two academies, *béth Hillel* and *béth Shammai,* there were differences in questions of religious law: In many instances, where one school said *Yes,* the other said *No;* what one permitted, the other forbade. For three years, says the Talmud, the two schools were in conflict, each contending that its views should be followed. Finally a heavenly echo was heard: The rulings of both were "words of the living God"; but in general, *béth Hillel* should be followed. The Talmud then asks: If both taught "words of the living God," why did *béth Hillel* merit that its rulings should become law? — because they [Hillel's disciples] were gentle and humble (TB *Eruvin* 13b).

What began with Hillel as a "game of patience," a way of being kindly and humble with all, ended with an ability in his disciples to establish norms of religious law for all Jewry.

In this he left a lesson for us all. In *pirké avoth* (Ethics of the Fathers, iv 12) R. Meir teaches: "be humble in spirit before every man." If you see a younger person, remember: when he reaches your age, he may be greater than you.[83] An older person deserves your respect for the age and experience he has attained.[84] The rich are to be respected for their ability to attain wealth.[85] And in the presence of a poor person, bear in mind: If he had your money, perhaps he might have done much more with it.

So is it possible to "be humble in spirit before every man" and live with a becoming modesty, leaving one's horn at home, unblown. It is a policy well worth trying.

## A FAVOR FROM THE POOR

As *Avoth d'R. Nathan* INDICATED ABOVE, it's no more than a natural step to take, in gentle humility, from treating every human being with courteous respect to giving the poor a fair measure of charity. But for this, you must accept the Torah's teachings simply, whole-heartedly. For about the Torah's precept to help the poor[86] it is easy to be "clever" and ask sharply: If I have amassed a modest sum by my hard honest toil, why should I share any of it with the poor? Did I make them poor? Did I prevent them from striving and succeeding like me?

You could even quote Scripture: *For the poor man will never cease out of the land* (Deuteronomy 15:11). The needy and indigent will always be with us, no matter what. There will always be recessions, depressions, unemployment. Some are fated to be poor. Then am I responsible for economic conditions, economic troubles, and human fate? By what right does Scripture continue, *therefore I command you, saying: you shall surely open your hand to your brother, to your poor and needy one . . . (ibid.)*?

Long ago, Tineius Rufus, the Roman governor of Judea, scornfully asked R. Akiva,[86] "If your God loves the poor, why does He not support them?" R. Akiva gave the Roman a simple answer: "It is so that we may be saved through them from the punishment of Gehinnom (purgatory)." We need the merit of our charity to save us from suffering and grant us life in the Hereafter.

121

But Tineius Rufus would not buy that at all. "On the contrary," said he, "that will condemn you to Gehinnom. Let me give you a parable: to what is this like? — to a mortal king of flesh and blood who became angry with his servant and put him in prison, ordering that no food or drink be given him. Yet one man went and provided him with food and drink. When the king heard of it, would he not be angry with the man? And you [Jews] are called servants, as it says, *For to Me the Israelites are servants; they are My servants* (Leviticus 25:55)."

R. Akiva answered with his own parable: "To what is this like? — to a mortal king of flesh and blood who grew angered with his son and put him in prison, ordering that no food or drink be given him. Yet one man came and gave him food and drink. When the king heard of it, would he not send the man a present? And we [Jews] are called sons, as it says, *You are sons to the Lord your God* (Deuteronomy 11:1)."[86]

So every indigent person brings us a precious opportunity to earn life in the Hereafter, rather than purgatory. R. Dostai b. R. Yannai reinforces the point vividly: If a man brings a present to a [mortal] king, it is uncertain if it will be accepted or not. If we assume it is accepted, it is uncertain if he will be admitted into the king's presence or not. Not so is the Holy, Blessed One: If a person gives but a penny to a poor man, he will merit to receive the *shechinah,* the Divine Presence [in the Hereafter]. . . . R. Yoḥanan added: What does it mean that *he who is gracious to the poor lends to the Lord* (Proverbs 19:17)? Were it not plainly written in Scripture, we would not dare say it: As it were, *the borrower is a servant to the lender* (Proverbs 22:7).[86]

You see, why are we so sure of such a great reward for giving charity? We read in the wise words of king Solomon, in the Book of Proverbs, that whatever you give the poor in kindness is like a loan to the Almighty; and in the same Book of Proverbs we are told that a borrower's debt makes him like a slave to the lender, till he pays back his loan. To this extent the Almighty bound Himself to repay us for our kindness to the needy. No wonder the Midrash pungently states in the name of R. Joshua: יותר ממה שבעל הבית עושה עם העני, העני עושה עם בעל הבית More than the master of the house does for the poor man, the poor man does for the householder.[87] And an early writer on ethics adds: Whoever deals charitably with an indigent man, let him not imagine he is doing the needy person a favor; in truth, it is rather the needy man who is doing him a favor.[88]

A little folk-story bears this out: It is told that a poor man once came to Anshel Rothschild in Frankfort, the pious founder of the great banking family in Europe, and he asked for the loan of a thousand *kronen*. "You see," he explained, "now I go about begging, and receive charity. What I get, I spend; and I'm as penniless as before. If I could have some capital, I could buy goods and sell, and make a bit of profit. Then I wouldn't need to beg any more."

Anshel Rothschild saw the man was young, intelligent and energetic. Despite his dirty, ragged appearance, such a plan might work. But Rothschild was a cautious banker. "I might lend you the money," he said slowly; "but you would need an endorser, someone to guarantee payment if you should fail and be unable to repay it yourself."

The poor man shrugged. Who in the world would co-sign or guarantee a loan for the likes of him? With a little grin he replied, "Only the *ribbono shel olam,* the Master of the world, would endorse something like this." The answer took Anshel Rothschild quite unawares. Pious as he was, what objection could he make? "Done," said he; "here is a thousand *kronen* for three months." And in the next three months Rothschild realized over and over that his good deed was taking effect. His banking affairs flourished as never before.

Three months later, to the day, the poor man appeared — no longer poor. His plan was working quite well. And he came to repay the loan. But Anshel Rothschild only shook his head. "Never you mind," he said. "Your endorser already repaid me."

Yet it's puzzling. Does this mean that the Almighty gives some people a life of misery in poverty, making them unable to survive without help, just so that if you aid them, if you move them to a better position on the chessboard of life, you will be aided and moved to a better position in the Hereafter?

A great *maggid,* a preacher of an earlier age, gave a masterful parable to explain it: A man of means made a banquet in his home, to which he invited twenty people. As befit his status, the settings were entirely of silver. At each place lay a silver plate, silver spoons, a silver knife and fork, etc. The guests arrived, and one by one they took their seats. Finally the last man came. But as he took his pace, he beckoned to his host. "Mendl," said he, "what is this? At my place there is no setting — no plate, no spoons, nothing. Did you forget about me?"

Mendl the host went to the head of the table. "Friends," he said, "I prepared a setting for each and every guest. Yet one setting is missing —

123

obviously because one of you took two. Whoever it was, please put the extra setting back!"

The *maggid* drew his moral: The Creator did not overlook the poor or play any games with them. When He brings people to life on earth, He supplies enough on earth, crops and oil, diamonds and gold, copper and iron, to provide for all. כִּי לֹא יֶחְדַּל אֶבְיוֹן מִקֶּרֶב הָאָרֶץ For the poor should not be overlooked, forsaken, to fail, out of the midst of the earth (Deuteronomy 15:11).[89] The riches out of the midst of the earth are enough to provide for him too. The Almighty prepared for him as well — enough food, potentially, to provide for all at the banquet of life. If some face malnutrition or starvation, it is because others have taken more than their rightful share. Whether they know it or not, the Almighty watches and waits for all this to be straightened out, like Mendl the host at his banquet table.

In his Divinely inspired wisdom, King Solomon wrote:

לְבַד רְאֵה זֶה מָצָאתִי, אֲשֶׁר עָשָׂה הָאֱ-לֹהִים אֶת הָאָדָם יָשָׁר, וְהֵמָּה בִקְשׁוּ חִשְּׁבֹנוֹת רַבִּים

*Behold, this only have I found: that God made man decent, upright, but they have sought out many devices* (Ecclesiastes 7:29). Originally, God made man, Adam, as the progenitor of the human race: no separate nations, peoples or groups, but one family on earth, from one father. All was to be *yashar*: decent, honest. In one family, what the father provides should be shared equally and reasonably, with no quarrels and no outcasts. If some are more fortunate in life than others, they should not build walls between the Haves and the Have-nots, between the acceptable and the unacceptable.

Yet the verse continues: "but they" — by the time there was no longer one man but a large plural "they" — people went looking for *hish'vonoth*, schemes and devices, to gather wealth. This Hebrew word, though, written in Scripture without vowel marks (*n'kudoth*), could also suggest *heshbonoth*, calculations.

Many a businessman runs through the month at a furious pace, then calls in his accountant to discover what (if any) his profits were. Often, though, the accountant may make more than one calculation. If figures are needed to show competitors, or employees demanding salary increases, the real profits must be wholly or partly hidden in the balance sheet. If a large bank loan is needed, or a report must be issued to stockholders, the accountant must make a different calculation — to show the firm bursting at the seams with dynamic vitality and potential.

Thus, as we might understand King Solomon's words, they "seek many calculations." And if they are reluctant to give a fair share to the poor, with the proper accountant's report they can cry poverty as piteously as any penniless man.

Well, the poor man has his accountant also:

אָמַר ר׳ אַבִּין: הֶעָנִי הַזֶּה עוֹמֵד עַל פִּתְחֶךָ, וְהַקָּבְּ״ה עוֹמֵד עַל יְמִינוֹ; דִּכְתִיב: כִּי יַעֲמֹד
לִימִין אֶבְיוֹן (תהלים קט לא). אִם נָתַתָּ לוֹ, דַּע שֶׁמִּי שֶׁעוֹמֵד עַל יְמִינוֹ עָתִיד לְשַׁלֵּם שְׂכָרֶךָ. וְאִם
אֵין אַתָּה נוֹתֵן לוֹ, דַּע שֶׁמִּי שֶׁעוֹמֵד עַל יְמִינוֹ עָתִיד לִפָּרַע מִמְּךָ. (ויקרא רבה לד ט, מהד׳
מרגוליות)

Said R. Abin: This poor man stands at your door, and the Holy, Blessed One stands at his right — as it is stated, *He stands at the right hand of the needy* (Psalms 109:31). If you give him [alms] know that the One who stands at his right is destined to pay you your reward. But if you do not give him, know that the One who stands at his right is destined to exact payment from you (*Va-yikra Rabbah* 34, 9).

Human accountants may make "many calculations" for different purposes. As the poor man's accountant, the Almighty makes only one simple calculation: He records what you give or do not give. If you give the poor their fair share, you're distributing what is properly theirs. Then you can go on earning and enjoying what is properly yours. If not, eventually He has to settle accounts with you — by His calculation or accountant's report, not yours. And don't count on taking along your checkbook into the Hereafter and making out a sizable check there to charity. In heaven your check is worthless. There they accept only "receipts" — of the charity you give on earth.

Well, about this matter of helping the poor, the Sages give us another thought to ponder. We read in Scripture: *You shall surely give him* [your poor fellow-man] *and your heart shall not be grieved when you give to him;* כִּי בִגְלַל
הַדָּבָר הַזֶּה *for on account of this matter, the Lord your God will bless you in all your work* (Deuteronomy 15:10). To the Sages in the academy of R. Ishmael, the word *big'lal* (on account of) suggested the verb *galal,* to roll; and the standard object that rolls is a wheel. So the School of R. Ishmael taught: It is a wheel that revolves in the world.[90]

All mankind was meant to live on one level, as one family, sharing equally in the earth's bounty. But when some found ways to wealth, it suited them better to be superior, above the less fortunate, as an aristocracy

125

of wealth. As it were, the members of human society took their places on a wheel of life, and the wealthy pushed on the wheel to make it take them ever higher.

Of course, those nearest the top always want the wheel to stop turning. But there are always some below who are amassing *their* pile and pushing and straining to rise in the world. The rotation doesn't stop.

"Fortune turns round like a mill-wheel," wrote Cervantes in the 16th century, "and he who was yesterday at the top lies today at the bottom."[91] Who doesn't know the term, "wheel of fortune"? The kernel of the idea originated in the School of R. Ishmael.

Sometimes, though, a man may feel absolutely safe from its turning. He may have too many gilt-edged bonds to ever see the specter of poverty haunting his life. Then let him ponder this little passage in the Talmud: R. Ḥiyya told his wife, "Whenever a poor man comes, go greet him directly with bread, so that others may welcome your children directly with bread." Said she, "Are you cursing them" [that they should be beggars]? In reply, he quoted the School of R. Ishmael: "It is a wheel that revolves in the world."[90]

R. Elazar haKappar spells out exactly what is implied here: Let a man ever beseech mercy about this fate [of poverty] — for if he does not come to it, his son will; and if his son does not, his grandson will.[90]

So we read in the Written Torah: *For the poor shall not cease out of the land. Therefore I command you, saying: you shall surely open your hand to your brother, to your poor and needy* (Deuteronomy 15:11). And the Midrash interprets: It is good advice I am giving you, for your good. . . . Beware of withholding compassion; for in whatever way you withhold compassion, so will it be withheld from you (*Midrash Tanna'im*).

We quoted above what the Midrash teaches in the name of R. Joshua: More than the master of the house does for the poor man, the poor man does for the householder.[87] With every bit of charity you give, you're paying for some very important insurance.

# UNDERSTANDING THE POOR

W HEN IT IMPOSES ON US the mitzvah, the privilege, and the blessed duty of giving charity, the Torah is not merely concerned with giving the wealthy an insurance policy for a good life in the Hereafter, and a way to cushion their own children against poverty. It is also very concerned for the poor. The Torah knows well that poverty, as one English poet described it, is the "mother of miseries."[92]

In Scripture the wise Solomon says truly, *the ruin of the poor is their poverty* (Proverbs 10:15); and the thought is poignantly echoed by Ben Sira (38:19): "The life of the poor is a curse of the heart." With compassionate insight the Talmud notes that once a man is reduced to needing the help of others, his face changes color.[93] Nor do R. Ammi and R. Asi exaggerate when they add: It is as if he were punished with both fire and water.[93]

None is so vulnerable as the needy to shame and humiliation. None needs the concern of the Torah more to protect his esteem as a creation in the Divine image.

So our codes of religious law, from the *Mishneh Torah* of Rambam (Maimonides) to the *Shulḥan Aruch* of R. Joseph Caro, contain whole sections on charity and the care of the poor.[94] Everything is worked out in detail, from rules of collection to rules of distribution. And Rambam notes, almost casually, "Never have we seen or heard of a community in Jewry that did not have a community charity chest." Which other people could have a statement like that in a code of law? (But then, which other people has the Torah?)

Moreover, which other people has a system of law that lists, as Ramban does, eight different ways or levels of giving charity, one more noble than another?[95] For a Jew, Rambam writes, it is not enough to give a coin when a mendicant stretches out his hand. If you have learned to give grudgingly, learn to give with a smile. You will be happier also. If you've learned to give when asked, train yourself to help before you're asked. If you now

127

give your alms face to face, learn to give indirectly. It's less shaming for those who are helped. Find ways of helping so that your money reaches the needy without their ever seeing you, and without your knowing who gets it. Finally, there is the fine art of giving charity so that the one who benefits never knows it is charity.

The main thing is to have insight, to understand something of the poor man's plight. Scripture states, אשרי משכיל אל דל *Happy is he who acts wisely with the poor* (Psalms 41:2). Said R. Yonah: It is not written, "Happy is the man who gives to the poor," but *maskil,* who considers the penniless man and acts wisely. Consider him well, to find how to help him (*Va-yikra Rabbah* 34, 1).[96] In the verb *maskil* (acts wisely) lies the noun *séchel,* "brains, intelligence." This is what you need to help someone who is down and out without shaming him.

Well, R. Yonah acted according to his own teaching. We read further in the Midrash: This what R. Yonah did: When he saw a member of a fine, distinguished family who had come down in the world and lost his wealth, and was ashamed to take charity, he would go to him and say, "I have heard about you that you have come into an inheritance in a country overseas. Here is this precious object to help tide you over.[97] Once you come into your inheritance, you can return it or pay me for it." And as he handed it over to him, he would say,[98] "I have given it to you as a gift."[99]

This is how one Sage mastered the fine art of helping the needy without hurting their spirit. Thank Heaven, the art did not die with him. In every age the Torah's wisdom has guided scholars and sages to treat the poor with tact.

In Eastern Europe R. Israel Salanter (of blessed memory) brought the study of *mussar* into the *yeshivoth* (Torah academies) of Lithuania, so that the ethics and morality of the Torah should be learned well, along with its laws.[100]

It is told that one year, shortly before Passover, a man came with a question: "Rabbi, at the Passover *seder,* would I be allowed to use milk instead of wine?"

The first two nights of Passover in the lands of exile (only the first night in Israel) the Jewish family has a *seder* at home — an evening of festive ceremony to celebrate our people's liberation from Egypt under Moses. At four points in the *seder,* everyone drinks a cup of wine. Yet this man wanted to use milk instead of wine, for the Four Cups.

"What is the matter?" asked R. Israel. "Are you ill? Has the doctor forbidden you wine?"

"Oh no," said the man. "I am quite healthy, thank Heaven."

R. Israel turned to his good wife, who was sitting ther, listening. "Please go and give this man twenty-five rubles for wine for Passover."

"Rabbi!" exclaimed the man. "I came to ask a question of law, not to ask for charity, Heaven forbid."

R. Israel looked at him gently. "Who said anything about charity? This money is a loan — until, with the Almighty's help, things go well with you again."

Satisfied, the man took the money and left. But then the sage's good wife turned on him: "Now what, in Heaven's name, made you give the man twenty-five rubles? You know wine for Passover costs only two or three rubles."

R. Israel Salanter gave a grumble. "You heard his question: Might he use milk for the Four Cups at the *seder*. If he were making a proper *seder* like every Jew, with chicken or meat for the festive meal, could he even ask such a question? Since meat and milk are forbidden at one meal, he would not even put them on the same table. Then what did I learn from the question? — that he has not even enough for meat on Passover. So I gave him enough for everything."

Closer to our time lived R. Israel Meir haKohen (of blessed memory), the most pious sage of his generation, better known as the *Ḥafetz Ḥayyim* (from the name of a work he wrote). In the town of Radun, Lithuania, he devoted himself to teaching Torah in his yeshiva.

Once the Russian authorities that ruled over Radun found someone in his yeshiva whom they suspected of spying activities. (In every age Russian authorities have been ready to see spies in every nook and cranny.) They arrested the suspect, of course; and for good measure, since the *Ḥafetz Ḥayyim* was the head of the Torah school, they took him as well, for questioning before the magistrate.

The attorney who came to defend the suspect was the famed Gruzenberg, who had defended Mendel Beilis in the notorious blood-libel case in Kishinev. A good friend of the *Ḥafetz Ḥayyim,* Gruzenberg was startled to see this devout scholar there — a man so steeped in Torah study that he couldn't possibly have the remotest relevant information about any spying. The attorney went up to the magistrate, to have him send the sage home.

"Your honor," said he, "do you know who this man is? He is the *Ḥafetz Ḥayyim*."

"What does *that* mean?" asked the magistrate, unimpressed.

"He is a great sage, a world-famous Torah scholar."

"So what?" asked the magistrate, half suspecting a "Jewish plot" here.

"Do you know what they tell about him?" continued Gruzenberg. "One night, as he and his wife were sleeping, a burglar broke into their home. He was quiet, but not quiet enough; and the sage's wife heard him She woke her husband and told him she was going to try and stop the thief. 'Oh no,' said the *Ḥafetz Ḥayyim*, 'you must not do that.' His wife was puzzled: 'Why not?' He answered, 'How big a town is Radun? We probably know everyone in it. Well, the thief must be local, from around here. Who would come from another town to steal our few possessions? Then if you go to him, you will recognize him, and he will be mortally embarrassed; and this the Torah forbids: We may not insult or embarrass a human being, ever!'"

But the Russian magistrate understood vodka better than fine points of ethics and morality. "Tell me," he asked coldly, "do you believe this story?"

"You can believe it or not," snapped Gruzenberg, "but one thing I can say for certain: They do not tell such stories about you and me!"

If the man was stealing some of his meager possessions, the *Ḥafetz Ḥayyim* wasn't troubled. The things could be replaced. And the thief was probably poor, stealing to keep body and soul together. His self-respect, though, was of tremendous importance to the pious sage. If his wife embarrassed or humiliated the thief by confronting him, his self-respect would be shattered; and that could not be replaced. And the burglar too was created in the Divine image.

130

# THE CHARITY
## THAT STOOD STILL

ONE AMERICAN COMEDIAN, I recall, was given to saying laconically, "I have been rich, and I have been poor; and believe me, rich is better." Well, the Torah also knows the bitter other side of this: Poor is worse. For this reason it stresses the importance of a mitigating charity, to alleviate the unjust woe in the world about us. And as the towering intellect of Rambam (Maimonides) makes it clear in his code of law, to take a coin from your pocket and give it indifferently is far from enough. There is a need to grow and develop in the art of charity, to treat the poor as human beings.

One *maggid,* a preacher from the Old World, used to quote the verse הוֹן וָעֹשֶׁר בְּבֵיתוֹ וְצִדְקָתוֹ עֹמֶדֶת לָעַד *Wealth and riches are in his house, and his* tz'dakah *(righteousness) stands forever* (Psalms 112:3). This, said the *maggid,* is a puzzling piece of Scripture. Whom is the Writ describing? . . . Only in America, said he, did he find the answer:

Zalman was among the masses that came from Eastern Eurpae to New York's Lower East Side. To earn a living, he acquired a pushcart and spent his days by it among the hundreds of other pushcarts on Orchard Street, to cry and peddle his wares.

As the months went by, Zalman could thank Heaven: he was not doing badly. He could hold his head up among his neighbors. Saturday mornings, he went to the little synagogue around the corner; and when an appeal was made sometimes for an important charitable cause, Zalman made it a habit to pledge a dollar — a handsome amount in those years on the Lower East Side. His fellow-worshippers invariably commented with admiration on his generosity.

But Zalman's earnings were generous too. He saved his money, and soon opened a store (shop), leaving his pushcart forever. In a while he moved to a better apartment, in a better neighborhood. Saturday mornings, he now went to a large synagogue that boasted a cantor. His family spent more on clothing. And in the summer, thank Heaven, his wife and children could leave the sweltering city for a place in the country.

131

One thing, though, remained the same. When an appeal for charity was made in the synagogue of a Saturday morning — for the same kind of vital cause as in the little synagogue near Orchard Street — Zalman still pledged a dollar — the same dollar. It had always seemed to him a fine, substantial response to any appeal in the synagogue. He remembered the appreciative comments every time he had made his pledge in the little synagogue on the Lower East Side. So he saw no reason to change his ittle habit. . . .

Times changed. He sold the store and became an importer of choice wares, selling "wholesale only, to the trade." Prospering in the land of opportunity, Zalman moved to a palatial home in an exclusive neighborhood. He acquired a car with a chauffeur, a butler and a maid, and two television sets. Of course, by now "the dollar wasn't a dollar any more": its value had gone down tremendously since his early days on Orchard Street. But in some things Zalman was a creature of habit, set in his ways. . . . So when an appeal was made of a Saturday morning in the magnificent ultra-modern synagogue that Zalman now attended — an appeal for one of the same good, vital causes as in the little synagogue near Orchard Street — Zalman pledged the same amount as ever: one dollar. It still seemed to him a nice, solid pledge.

The *maggid* returned to his verse: הוֹן וָעֹשֶׁר בְּבֵיתוֹ *Wealth and riches are in his house;* Zalman had a home with everything his heart could desire and money could buy; וְצִדְקָתוֹ עֹמֶדֶת לָעַד *and his* tz'dakah *stands forever* (Psalms 112:3). The word *tz'dakah* is usually translated as righteousness, but for generations of our forefathers it has meant charity — and Zalman's charity indeed stood forever. It stood absolutely still for ever and always. He always gave the one dollar.

In charity, Zalman lost the capacity to grow. As a psychologist might say, he was fixated at the level of one dollar — perhaps because he took the phrase "the almighty dollar" too seriously. The Jew who would be worthy the name must grow in his charity. As Rambam teaches,[95] there are different ways and levels of giving. It is better to help the poor cheerfully rather than grudgingly, anonymously rather than pompously.

Let us remember Scripture's words, אַשְׁרֵי מַשְׂכִּיל אֶל דָּל: Happy is the one who uses *séchel,* intelligence, for the unfortunate in our midst. With compassion and understanding, if you "give till it hurts," you can make sure it hurts only you and not the one who needs the help. But with proper growth in your charity, you can change that motto to "give till it feels good."

One easy way to reach this stage of growth was suggested by R. Elḥanan Wasserman (of blessed memory), the saintly dean of the Yeshiva of Baranovich, Lithuania, in an earlier time. It was his serious suggestion that every Jew should take off, regularly, ten percent of his earnings and put that into a special bank account, for *tz'dakah*. Scripture bids us עַשֵּׂר תְּעַשֵּׂר *Tithe shall you tithe all the yield of your seed* (Deuteronomy 14:22). In olden Israel, when the Sanctuary stood, every farmer was required to take off *maasér,* a tithe, a tenth part of all his crops, that had to be given to the poor during certain years. If we cannot fulfill the mitzvah itself today, we can at least keep its humane spirit, its compassionate intention, by following R. Elḥanan Wasserman's suggestion (as pious Jews have done on their own in every age).[101] In fact, since the verb in the Scriptural verse is doubled, some would always set aside not one tithe for the poor, but two — not ten percent, but twenty. (The United States government allows yet more to be deducted for charity from taxable income.) Well, if R. Elḥanan's idea is good, this idea is twice as good.

The great value of this plan is that when the time comes to give, there is no need to give of your own and deprive yourself of anything. You hand over to the poor a part of what is already theirs, that was only given you for safekeeping.

## ❧ GRATITUDE

IT COULD BE SAID that the Torah impresses on us, past any doubting, that we may not take people for granted. Human beings are in the image of *hashem,* the Creator Himself; so they must be treated with courtesy and respect. The poor are in His image too; then they must not be forgotten.

But what if someone does you a significant favor, and you have reason to be grateful? Then you also acquire an obligation to show your gratitude when the time comes, and not be an ingrate. (The Torah does not accept

133

the famous American retort, "Yes, I know all that you did for me; but what have you done for me lately?")

Here too כְּבוֹד הַבְּרִיוֹת the principle of respect for human beings, is involved. If I ignore someone who has done me a favor, choosing to forget his kindness, I fail to pay him the respect and honor he has earned. And so I insult an image of God. Thus we read in the Midrash:

מִפְּנֵי מָה עָנַשׁ הַכָּת׳ בְּיוֹתֵר לְכַפּוֹיֵי טוֹבָה? מִפְּנֵי שֶׁהוּא כְּעִנְיָן כְּפִירָה בַּהַקָּבָּ״ה. אַף הַכּוֹפֵר
בַּהַקָּבָּ״ה כּוֹפֵר טוֹב הוּא. הָאָדָם הַזֶּה הוּא כּוֹפֵר טוֹבָתוֹ שֶׁל חֲבֵרוֹ – לְמָחָר הוּא כוֹפֶה
טוֹבָתוֹ שֶׁל קוֹנוֹ. וְכֵן הוּא אוֹמֵר בְּפַרְעֹה, "אֲשֶׁר לֹא יָדַע אֶת יוֹסֵף" ‏(שמות א ח)‏ וַהֲלֹא עַד
הַיּוֹם הַזֶּה מִצְרַיִם יוֹדְעִין חַסְדּוֹ שֶׁל יוֹסֵף? אֶלָּא שֶׁהָיָה יוֹדֵעַ וְלֹא הִשְׁגִּיחַ עָלָיו; וְלִבְסוֹף
כָּפָה טוֹבָתוֹ שֶׁל הַקָּבָּ״ה, שֶׁאָמַר: לֹא יָדַעְתִּי אֶת ה׳. ‏(שמות ה ב; משנת ר׳ אליעזר 137)‏

Why did Scripture prescribe punishment especially for those who are ungrateful? — because it is akin to denying the Holy, Blessed One. A man who denies the Holy One is also denying a favor.[102] This man shows no gratitude now for his neighbor's kindness; tomorrow he will be ungrateful for his Maker's kindness. Thus we read that Pharaoh *did not know Joseph* (Exodus 1:8); yet does not Egypt know to this day of Joseph's kindness [that saved it from famine]? The truth is that he knew of him, but he gave him no thought, and was simply ungrateful for his kindness. And in the end he was ungrateful to the Holy One, declaring, *I do not know the Lord* (Exodus 5:2) (*Mishnath R. Eliezer*, 137).

Said R. Abin: This can be likened to a man who threw stones at the statue of a high commander. Exclaimed the king, "Off with his head! Now it is the commander's [image he attacks]; tomorrow he will set to work on mine" (*Midrash Tanḥuma, sh'moth* 5).[103]

So the point of the Midrash is clear: If anyone becomes an ingrate, he cannot draw the line between people and the Creator. He will become a blind, self-destructive heretic.

Moses himself showed how important gratitude is. In the wilderness, at the burning bush that was not consumed, the Almighty first spoke to him, to bid him go to Pharaoh in Egypt and liberate the suffering Hebrews. Yet after this direct command from the Almighty, he did not go at once. Instead, *Moses went and returned to Jether* [Yithro] *his father-in-law and said to him,* "*Let me go, I pray, and return to my brethren in Egypt . . .*" (Exodus 4:18).

134

Isn't it incredible? The Almighty tells him to go rescue his people from their cruel servitude. Yet first he stands on ceremony!

But the Midrash explains: When the Holy, Blessed One told Moses, *And now go, and I will send you to Pharaoh* (Exodus 3:10), Moses replied, "Master of the world, I cannot; for Yithro welcomed me and opened his home to me; I am like a son to him. . . . Yithro received me and treated me with honor. Can I then go without his permission?"[104]

He had come to Midian a refugee, fleeing a death sentence in Egypt. With Yithro he found shelter, a home; and he married Yithro's daughter. So before he could return to Egypt on the Almighty's mission, he had to have Yithro's permission. It was more than courtesy. It was an obligation of gratitude. To ignore it would be tantamount to scorning the Almighty Himself.

R. Isaac Sher (of blessed memory), the noted spiritual guide of the Yeshiva of Slobodka, used to continue in the same vein: If the Almighty wanted the Hebrews out of Egypt, free, surely he could have arranged it in the twinkling of an eye? Supreme Master of the universe that He is, able to supersede the laws of nature at will, certainly nothing about such a task was beyond Him. Then why send Moses to Pharaoh to plead with him? Why send one plague at a time, to see after each one if Pharaoh had grown agreeable? What purpose did it serve for Moses to return to this obdurate ruler over and over?

Here too, said R. Isaac Sher, the principle of הכרת טובה was at work: the obligation to acknowledge a favor and show gratitude.

The Hebrews came to Egypt originally at a critical point. Famine raged in Canaan then, and there was food only in Egypt. Though gathered and stored and managed by Joseph, that food belonged to the Pharaoh who then ruled. Only by his royal permission could the Hebrews come to stay in Egypt. And he had graciously consented. So Jacob and his sons could settle with their families in Goshen and be safe from starvation.

The Hebrews owed a debt of gratitude to the country that gave them refuge and hospitality. Although the Egyptians subjected them to cruel, bitter servitude, and by Divine justice they had to be taken out and set free, that debt of honor had to be paid. So they could not simply up and leave. It had to remain the present Pharaoh's royal privilege to decide their fate. They had to honor him by staying, subject to his rule, till he permitted them to go.[105]

This all-important principle clears up another strange point in the Torah. We read: *No Ammonite or Moabite shall enter the assembly of the Lord; even to the tenth generation, none of them shall enter the assembly of the Lord — for ever; because they did not meet you with bread and with water when you came forth out of Egypt; and because they hired Balaam against you . . . to curse you* (Deuteronomy 23:4-5).

No member of the nations of Ammon and Moab could ever become a Jew — not even if he underwent conversion a thousand times; not even if ten generations converted and they kept every mitzvah in the Torah perfectly.

Yet, considering the Torah's reasons, doesn't this seem a bit harsh? What, after all, were the great crimes of Ammon and Moab? (1) When the Israelites came, in their journey through the wilderness, to the territory of these two nations, they didn't come out in cheefrul welcome with bread and water. (2) They hired Balaam the sorcerer to curse the Hebrews.

Well, about the bread and water, we find no hint Scripture that the Israelites suffered because they didn't get any. The manna fell every day for them; and the Sages tell that for Miriam's sake, a well (called Miriam's Well) traveled along with them in the wilderness, underground, giving them water as they needed it.[106] Then at the most, Ammon and Moab failed to show courtesy. They were not polite.

As for Balaam's curses, read what Scripture itself says right afterward: *Nevertheless, the Lord your God would not hearken to Balaam; and the Lord your God turned the curse into a blessing* (Deuteronomy 23:6). Ammon and Moab were hostile, but Balaam's curses had no ill effects. As an old proverb goes, "Sticks and stones may break my bones, but words will never hurt me."[107] Then why this extreme law in retaliation, that never allows someone from Ammon or Moab to become a Jew?

Well, the Midrash notes that Lot benefited greatly from his uncle Abraham several times (in the years when his name was still Abram): When the Patriarch left Ur of the Chaldees for Canaan, he took Lot with him. As a result, Lot prospered and became wealthy. Then Lot settled in Sodom, and when Sodom became involved in war, the enemy took him captive, with all his possessions. Abraham counter-attacked, defeated the enemy, and set him free. Finally, when Sodom was to be destroyed for its evil, Lot and his two daughters were rescued for Abraham's sake.[108]

Let it now be noted that the nations of Ammon and Moab were descended from Lot and his two daughters.[109]

The Midrash continues: In return for these [favors, Lot's] descendants were duty-bound to pay us back with favors. Yet not only did they not recompense us with kindnesses, but they actually repaid us with acts of evil ... (*Mishnath R. Eliezer*, 136).

Indeed, the things that Ammon and Moab did were not so bad in themselves. What the Almighty could not forgive was their sheer ingratitude to the descendants of Abraham. An ingrate, who forgets and denies favors done him, sins against the Divine image of man. Then the Almighty wanted no part of such ingrates among His people.[110]

Few of us realize what place this principle of הכרת טובה, of acknowledging every favor and kindness, holds at the very foundation of our faith. In the Midrash we read: The Holy, Blessed One declared to the Israelites [as He began the Ten Commandaments], *I am the Lord your God*; but why did He add, *who brought you forth out of Egypt* (Exodus 20:2)? He said to them, in effect, "Beware, take care that you do not turn ungrateful, for ingrates cannot accept the kingship of Heaven" (*Mishnath R. Eliezer,* 137–38).

Had He begun the Ten Commandments as "the Lord your God who created heaven and earth," there could be ways of throwing off the Divine obligation of the Torah. A person might retort that if He is the Creator, all mankind owes Him allegiance equally; why "pick" on the Jews?

Instead, the Ten Commandments begin with a ringing, imperishable reminder that He rescued our ancestors from a servitude that could have left them a slave people forever. He did this with miracles and wonders, so that no Hebrew there could possibly doubt His existence or His participation. This became a tradition of faith among our people, handed down from one generation to the next, from the exodus itself to this day.

For this reason, says the Creator, you have an obligation to obey Me and observe the Torah — in gratitude, in הכרת טובה.

In the kaleidoscopic history of mankind, the Jewish people has endured through every kind of vicissitude — and only a special Divine providence can explain it. It can only mean that our Creator remains our protector. He continues "taking us out of Egypt" through the ages. If we are perceptive enough to see this, we can live in our faith, with our Torah, in gratitude for His abiding kindness.

137

# ❧ PAYING THE TOLL

Let me bring this essay on human dignity to a close by relating a minor little incident out of a summer day, when the sainted R. Aaron Kotler (of blessed memory) had to travel by car to the mountains of New York State. One of his students accompanied him. As the car sped along a state highway, it approached a toll gate. The driver could pass by either of two booths. At each the cost was the same: a quarter of a dollar. But at one there was an attendant, ready to give change, while the other was an automatic affair: If you had a quarter, a coin in the exact amount, you could throw it into a net and ride through.

R. Aaron's student had a quarter, and the driver headed for the automatic booth, to get through quickly. But in an instant the great Talmudic scholar understood the situation, and directed the driver to the other booth.

And he explained: The automatic booth is devoid of heart or mind. Cold, impersonal, the machine lets you through according to a strict law: If you throw a quarter into the net, you pass. If you have no quarter, you do not. It's of no concern to the machine.

Did he exaggerate the importance of the matter — this genius who transplanted pure advanced Talmudic study from Kletzk, Lithuania to Lakewood, New Jersey? Was he overdramatic? Did he go to extremes?

Remember: we live in an age of increasing automation. Robot-mechanisms run our elevators and calculate our bills. To your telephone company, electric company, and bank, you're not really a human being. You're a series of holes punched in a card.

The flashing lights of digital computers make ever more decisions affecting our lives. And to the computers it makes no difference whether we're human beings or blocks of concrete. They calculate and solve problems. But no automated device can be programmed to show compassion or understanding. And ultimately there are banks of computers in the great military centers of the world, capable of destroying whole sections of mankind at the touch of a button — without compassion or understanding.

R. Aaron Kotler's thought was simple: Wherever a machine replaces a human being, it implies that there a man, created in the image of the Creator, is not needed; we can do without him; and so in one area after another of man's relations with his fellow-man.

R. Aaron's action was a small reminder that *in the image of God did He make man* (Genesis 9:6). How wise are we to set machines in power and control over us? Will automation help us live more as human beings? It may be worthwhile working to safeguard human dignity. The dignity you save may be your own.

# *Notes* TO PART TWO

1.  Charles Robert Darwin, a neurasthenic who could not manage a regular occupation, and did not have to, took a long trip on a slow boat and amassed a mountain of facts. Alone in his room, slowly, painstakingly, he fit the mountain of facts beautifully into his theory of evolution — that through the "survival of the fittest" in the "jungle" of nature, all forms of life evolved and developed from the simple to the ever more complex. Thus he gave man a new image of himself: as the last in the evolutionary chain of development, with the right to act as an animal in the jungle, so as to be one of the "fittest who survive."

Today, Darwin's theory is accepted with reservations, if at all. Later theory is inclined to believe that one species came from another not by evolution but by mutation, a sudden jump or change in genetic continuity (or by both). In the laboratory, however, scientists can produce only small, minor mutations in insects, etc. When the Almighty brought the ten plagues on ancient Egypt, Pharaoh's wizards could imitate the first two; the third they called "a finger of God" (Exodus 8:15), and they gave up trying to imitate any more. In startling parallel, modern science produces minor mutations in the laboratory, but can neither imitate (reproduce) nor explain the great mutations which, by their postulate, produced the vast array of living creatures on earth. Why such mutations at such points in time?

Beyond time, the Almighty waits for mankind to learn the truth of the immortal words of the Torah: the creation is a pure expression of the Divine will.

(For recent thinking on the theory of evolution, which has led at least one eminent scientist to a new awareness of the Deity in human development, see Alistair Hardy, *The Biology of God*.)

2.  B'réshith Rabbah 1,9; and see R. Shimon Kasher, פשוטו של מקרא I, 5–6.

3.  Literally, "the name," the Hebrew word generally used for His supremely holy name (see two paragraphs above) that may not be pronounced as written.

4.  Robert Browning, *The Ring and the Book*, X.

5.  Quoted in R. Sh'néor Zalman of Lyady, *Tanya*, chapter 2.

6.  Matthew Henry, *Commentaries*, Jeremiah XX. There is also the famous Indian tale of the blind men and the elephant. In one version (John G. Saxe, *Clever Stories of Many Nations*, Boston 1865, pp. 61 ff.) there were six blind men. One fell against the elephant's hide. He described the animal as very like a wall. The second reached a tusk, near its mouth. So for him the creature resembled a spear. The third blind man, at the front, caught hold of the elephant's trunk. Lo, he said afterward, the animal resembled a snake. The fourth got to one of the creature's knees — thick, sturdy, straight. He described the elephant as very like a tree. The fifth blind man, tall, chanced upon an ear, waving to chase away the flies. He marveled how this animal resembled a fan. The sixth, bringing up the rear, got his hands on the tail. For him, then, the creature was very much like a rope.

So too, some see how man resembles the animals in his bodily functions; in his emotions; in his reactions to stimuli. They can describe him as a thinking animal, a feeling animal, a

140

working animal, a creative animal. But they have not the vision to see, in his full *gestalt,* in his unplumbed potential, the image of Divinity.

7.   TB Makkoth 10b, etc.

8.   Pirké d'R. Eliezer 31; i.e. *im* (עם) *ha-ḥamor* is interpreted as though it read *am* (עם) *ha-ḥamor.* It is interesting to note the full passage in the Midrash: As Abraham the Patriarch came in sight of the hills, he saw the glory of the *shechinah,* the Divine Presence. Atop one hill he saw a pillar of fire blazing from earth to heaven. Said he to Isaac, "My son, do you see anything on one of these hills?" *Yes,* his son replied. "What do you see?" asked the Patriarch. "I see a pillar of fire reaching from earth up to the heavens." Thus Abraham knew [that this hill was the place meant by God for the sacrifice, and he knew] the boy was acceptable for the sacrfice.

Then he asked [his servant lads] Ishmael and Eliezer, "Do you see anything on one of those hills?" *No,* they replied. Said he to them, "Then *stay here with the donkey* (Genesis 22:5), you people akin to the donkey. Just as the donkey here sees nothing [on that hill] so do you see nothing" (bracketed additions from Midrash haGadol, Genesis 22:4).

Those who are ready to perceive the Divine element in man can see the fire on the hill or the mountain — the challenge of the Almighty's demands, to be met and surmounted, even at the cost of pain, hardship, sacrifice. Those who want only creature comforts and pleasures, to wallow on earth like happy animals, will never see the Divine element in man, and will never grow in moral stature.

9.   TB Gittin 13a.

10.   Literal translation; generally rendered, "the living creature."

11.   Note also this Talmudic passage: Said R. Yoḥanan: Had the Torah not been given, we should have to learn about modesty from the cat, about robbery from the ant, immorality from the dove, etc. (TB Eruvin 110b). Here too, we have the point that those for whom the Torah has not been given yet, who live blind and deaf to its Divine message, are lower than the animals: They have much to learn from the creatures of the world.

And indeed, which cats ever trafficked in immorality and indecency for profit? Ants live by strict laws, committing no robbery. They need no police. The male dove is always faithful to its mate. Nor does any animal use a pill to enjoy a "new morality." They are likewise free of problems with alcohol and drugs.

Animals may kill creatures of other species for survival — for food or self-defense. None will murder their own kind on account of "racial superiority" or "to save their souls" or for the sake of "the survival of the fittest."

12.   Note Cain's words to the Almighty when he had killed his brother and in his encounter with the Almighty he had to acknowledge his guilt: . . . *from Thy face I shall be hidden, and I will be a fugitive and a wanderer on the earth; and whoever finds me will slay me* (Genesis 4:14).

13.   In this the Torah gives us a basic teaching that Freud later "discovered": He wrote an entire book (*The Psychopathology of Everyday Life*) to show that for every mistake or slip a person makes, "by accident," there is a reason in his unconscious.

14.   Based on Proverbs 16:18, *Pride goes before destruction, and a haughty spirit before a fall.*

15.   Midrash Tadshé 18 (in *Béth haMidrash* III 183; A. Epstein, מקדמוניות היהודים xxxv): Why did the Torah decree upon every man who sins unwittingly, to bring an offering for himself — and the man cannot go clean of guilt till he brings an offering for his inadvertent sin? It is only that a person should not [come to] do this sin before the Almighty deliberately, intentionally.

141

16. So Ramban (Naḥmanides), commentary, Leviticus 1:1. It is borne out by a subtle point in the Midrash: Scripture writes of a bullock as an *olah* (burnt-offering), and of a sheep or goat as an *olah*. In both cases we read that the entrails and legs should be washed with water, then burned on the altar (Leviticus 1:9, 13). But there is a small difference: about the sheep or goat it says that the *kohen* "shall offer it all (*v'hikriv*) and burn it on the altar"; about the bullock it simply says that he "shall burn it all on the altar"; the word *v'hikriv* ("and he shall offer it") is not there.

Well, *v'hikriv* is from the root *karav*, to come close; so it can denote bringing close or near. Says the Midrash: If a man can afford a young bull, a fine head of cattle, he is evidently wealthy. He might easily think, "Let me go and do all sorts of vile, ugly things not fit for decent people. Then I can bring a splendid bullock with plenty of meat on it, and have it offered on the altar. The Holy One will surely be gracious to me and forgive me."

No, says the Midrash: *v'hikriv* is missing about a bullock. If you bring the finest animal with such an attitude, the offering will not bring you closer or nearer to your Maker. Rather, devote yourself to good deeds and Torah study. Then bring even a thin mangy sheep for an *olah*, and God will be with you in mercy, to accept your repentance. There will be *v'hikriv*: you will be brought closer to your Maker (Tanna d'vé Eliyahu [6] 7 — ed. Friedmann 36; Va-yikra Rabbah 2 end; Yalkut Shimoni I § 444).

That a *ḥattath* (sin-offering) might be ritually slain only north of the altar is derived from Scripture in TB Z'vaḥim 58a–b and Sifra, *va-yikra, dibbura d'ḥova, parashah* 6, 10.

17. *Korban ha'Edah* comments on this passage in the Jerusalem Talmud: For this reason [the Torah] did not set a separate place for its ritual slaying, so that onlookers should not see that it is a *ḥattath*, whereupon he would be shamed. For with an *olah* [too] the one who brings it stands by it, and also places his hands on it shortly before it is ritually slain.

Similarly *Moshav Z'kénim*, a commentary, etc. on the Pentateuch, mostly by the scholars of *tosafoth*: "he shall slay it at the place where one slays the *olah*" (Leviticus 4:24) — R. Elazar of Worms explained: it is in order not to shame him publicly; for if they would ritually slay it in another place, all would know he had sinned (*Moshav Z'kénim*, London 1959, p. 248).

18. TB Shabbath 64a: If we have gone free of the power of sin, we have not gone free of the grip of improper thoughts. See also TB Bava Bathra 164b, that sinful thought is one of three transgressions from which no one escapes for even a day.

19. Leviticus 4:24, 29, 33, 6:18.   20. Leviticus 1:11, 4:24, 6:18.

21. Note also this passage in the Midrash: Why did He decree upon the *kohanim* [who ministered in the Tabernacle and Temple] not to eat an ordinary person's *ḥattath* outside the Sanctuary, but only within the court of the Tabernacle [and the Temple]? — so that no other man may learn from them that this person sinned, thus making him ashamed (Midrash Tadshé 18, in *Béth haMidrash* III, 182, and A. Epstein, מקדמוניות היהודים xxxv).

In the Mishnah (Z'vaḥim v 3) we read, "*Ḥattath* (sin) offerings . . . of an individual . . . are eaten within the hangings by the male *kohanim*." The hangings, great lengths of cloth, formed the boundaries of the *mishkan,* the Tabernacle in the wilderness. Within the hangings was the court, an area for the *kohanim* alone. In the Sancturay, the court was within the stone walls that bounded the Temple. Only there the male *kohanim* were allowed to eat the flesh of a *ḥattath* (Leviticus 6:19, 22).

Well, a good sheep or goat provides plenty of fine meat. All would probably gather round as it was roasted, and have a feast. They would relax, and tongues enjoying the feast might start to wag.... "That Yankel deserves the Almighty's forgiveness. He certainly gave us a splendid *ḥattath*. It's really good!" And so forth. Then everyone in earshot would know you had sinned. The Torah could not silence *kohanim* at their meal; so it restricted them to their own quarters in the Sanctuary, where no ordinary Israelite was permitted.

22. This teaching is also found in TB M'naḥoth 110a, Va-yikra Rabba 7, 3 (ed. Margulies), Midrash T'hillim 134, 1 (which states of "the Torah scholars who devote their study to the laws of the Temple service: I [God] reckon it for them as if the Sanctuary were [thereby] rebuilt in their days").

23. Tanna d'vé Eliyahu 18 (ed. Friedmann, 104). Similarly P'skita d'R. Kahana 25 (ed. Buber, 158a; ed. Mandelbaum, 353): How do we know that if a person turns in repentance, it is reckoned as if he went up to Jerusalem, built the Sanctuary, built the altar, and offered up on it all the sacrifices? From this verse: *The sacrifices of God are a broken spirit; a broken and contrite spirit, O God, Thou wilt not despise* (Psalms 51:19); and what is written afterward? *Do good in Thy favor to Zion, build Thou the walls of Jerusalem. Then wilt Thou delight in the sacrifices of righteousness,* etc. (*ibid.* 20-21).

24. So TB Avodah Zarah 8a. Note also this most interesting passage in *Moshav Z'kénim* (p. 258; see note 17): "*In the place where the olah is slain, the ḥattath shall be slain* (Leviticus 6:18) — this is the reason why the ritual slaying of the *ḥattath* was in the same place as the *olah*: because the Torah was particular to protect sinners, so that the people should not perceive anything and make the sin known — for you see, the *ḥattath* comes to bring atonement for the sin. In the same vein, we find in the Mishnah tractate Avoth (v 5): [the people at the Sanctuary] would stand pressed close together, yet would bow down in worship with ample room. Rashi explained 'with ample room' to mean that everyone was four ells away from his neighbor. And R. Hai explained that for this reason there were four ells between everyone and his neighbor, so that no one should hear the confession of his neighbor, whereupon he would be despised by him; for the Torah was particularly concerned to protect the sinner."

25. See Daniel Goldschmidt, מחזור לימים נוראים II, introduction, 10-11.

26. See e.g. R. Abraham Danzig, חיי אדם, § 143.

27. Va-yikra Rabbah 4, 6; also Yalkut Shimoni, Jeremiah § 334 and Job § 920; Mechilta d'R. Shimon b. Yoḥai, Exodus 19:6.

28. *Kundres aḥaron l'midrash y'lam'denu,* in *Béth haMidrash* VI 84. It might also be noted that in the 20th century it became fashionable to preach that society is responsible for its offenders. Our people learned this when they left the wilderness to conquer Canaan under Joshua's leadership (and the lesson stayed with us). They conquered Jericho easily. Yet at Ai, which they should also have taken swiftly, they suffered defeat (Joshua 7:4-5). The Almighty told Joshua why: *The Israelites have sinned* (*ibid.* 11). Casting lots to find the sinners, Joshua found only one guilty man: Achan had taken forbidden war booty from Jericho (*ibid.* 6:18, 7:18-21). Well, the Talmud and Midrash make it clear that this was not Achan's first offense; he had done similar things in Moses' day (TB Sanhedrin 43b-44a; TJ vi 3, 23b; B'réshith Rabbah 85 end; Be-midbar Rabbah 23, 6; Tanḥuma, *mass'é* 5). Then at some time, neighbors must have spotted something wrong about him; yet he was never reported to Moses or Joshua. The neighbors evidently "minded their own business," deciding they "didn't really know anything for sure." So the Israelite army was defeated at Ai, all being held guilty for his crime. Whoever has it in his power to prevent wrongdoing and doesn't, is punished for the selfsame crime (TB Shabbath 54b, Avodah Zarah 18a).

29. Nicholas Berdyaev, *Christianity and Anti-Semitism,* 32; Albert Einstein, *Address at Sorbonne, Paris.*

30. Va-yikra Rabbah 4, 6; also Zohar III 122a; cf. Tanna d'vé Eliyahu (11) 12 — ed. Friedmann, 56.

31. Tanḥuma, *nitzavim* 2; Early Tanḥuma, 5. About Achan see note 28.

32. Thus TB B'rachoth 3b tells of Hebrew elders coming at dawn for an audience with King David. "Our lord the king," they would say, "your people Israel need the means to live." He replied, "Go and earn a living from one another." They rejoined, "A handful of food does not satisfy a lion [or: a lion cannot be satisfied by licking its own paw — *Shittah M'kubetzeth*] nor can a pit be refilled [only] with the earth taken from it." [So Rashi; alternatively: a well will not be filled by rainwater, or by the water from its opening or its source; sluices must bring water to it from the sourrounding earth. See *tosafoth, tosafoth haRosh,* and *Otzar haGe'onim* I 3.] Then he said, "Go and prepare yourselves to attack in troops."

33. TB Sotah 42a.

34. Tosefta, Sotah vii 10; TB 42a–b.

35. Rambam MT *hilchoth m'lachim* vii 2 (see *Kessef Mishneh, Leḥem Mishneh*); Me'iri to Sotah 42a, pp. 98–99.

36. TB Sotah 43a.

37. The behavior of our father Jacob bears out this point. When he journeyed to his uncle Laban, at his parents' bidding, he received the Almighty's firm promise: *Now behold, I am with you, and will guard you wherever you go, and will return you to this land; for I will not leave you till I have done that about which I have spoken to you* (Genesis 28:15). With an iron-clad promise like that, from the highest power on earth, he could surely face anything without fear. Well, he had hardly returned from Laban to the land of Canaan when he learned that his brother Esau, his sworn enemy, was coming with 400 men. *Then Jacob was greatly afraid, and he was distressed. . . . And Jacob said: O God of my father Abraham . . . deliver me, I pray Thee, from the hand of my brother, from the hand of Esau, for I fear him* (Genesis 32:7,9,11). So the Talmud and Midrash ask: A man whom the Holy, Blessed One assured was yet frightened and fearful? And the answer is given: But Jacob said, "Woe is me. Perhaps the iniquity [I committed] will cause it" — cause him the loss of the Almighty's protection. In all his years with Laban, his crafty double-dealing uncle, he might have committed some small forgotten sins (Mechilta, *amalék* 2; MdRSbY Exodus 17:14; Aggadath Esther 4, 14; Esther Rabbah 6, 11; Tanḥuma, *b'shallaḥ* 28; TB B'rachoth 4a, Sanhedrin 98b).

About sinners who must leave a Hebrew army before battle, the Tosefta (Sotah vii 14) quotes the verse, *Why should I fear in days of evil? — the iniquity of my heels will surround me* (Psalms 49:6). To the Sages this strange phrase, "the iniquity of my heels," means sins that a person tramples with his heels, as it were, because they seem so trifling to him. As a result, he develops an Achilles heel, a vulnerability that Divine protection cannot cover. And the Midrash adds a trenchant proverb of its time: The scorpion topples the camel by stinging it in the heel, and it says, "As you live, I will reach till your head" (Yalkut Shimoni II § 764).

37a. So Tur Oraḥ Ḥayyim, §271 — because ordinarily, when both bread and wine are to be taken, the bread is to be eaten first, since in Deuteronomy 8:8 Scripture lists wheat, the basic source of bread, before vines, the source of wine.

38. If someone used a sacred object from the Temple for an ordinary purpose, Scripture writes, *he shall bring his* asham *to the* Lord, *a ram . . . worth silver shekels in your evaluation . . .*

(Leviticus 5:15). As R. Abraham ibn Ezra notes, "shekels" (plural) means at least two; hence *asham me'ilah*, a guilt-offering for a breach of holiness, must cost at least two shekels. By one of the thirteen rules for interpreting Scripture (*g'zérah shavah*) the rule is applied to three other kinds of guilt-offerings, including *asham taluy* (TB K'rithoth 22b; Z'vaḥim 90b, Rashi s.v. ובאין בכסף שקלים).

39. TB K'rithoth 27a.

40. Mishnah, Sh'kalim ii 4; TB Z'vaḥim 48a, K'rithoth 22b.

41. R. Baḥya, commentary on the Pentateuch, Leviticus 5:17 (ed. Chavel, II 416–17).

42. Ramban, commentary on the Pentateuch, Leviticus 5:15; see also R. Yonah (Ramban's disciple), cited in Ramban ed. Chavel, II 25, notes.

43. See TB Yevamoth 89b (Eruvin 17b, Nazir 43b).

44. TJ Nazir vii 1; minor tractate S'maḥoth 4.

45. Mishnah, Sotah ix 3; TB Eruvin 17a.

46. TB B'rachoth 19b, etc. Even if a rabbi is on his way to teach Torah to a hall packed with students, should he find a *méth mitzvah*, he must stay and bury the body — although Torah study is as important as all the mitzvoth together, since a Jew cannot observe them properly without learning the Torah. A kohen may attend no funeral except for certain close relatives. The *kohen gadol* in Temple times was banned even from the funeral of such relatives. Similarly, if a man vowed to be a *nazir* for thirty days, he was then also forbidden to attend the burial of the closest relative. He had to remain the thirty days in ritual purity, like the *kohen gadol*, undefiled by the dead. Yet let a man who was both *kohen gadol* and a *nazir* find a *méth mitzvah*, and he too would be duty-bound to bury him, losing his ritual purity (Mishnah, Nazir vii 1; TB 47b).

47. TB Shabbath 151b, N'darim 41a.

48. It is clear from Scripture that burial is the ideal fitting way to deal with the dead: When Sarah died, Abraham rose from his mourning to negotiate persistently with the Hittites till he acquired burial ground (Genesis 23:2–20). When Abraham died, his sons buried him in the same sepulcher (Genesis 25:8–9). So the Writ mentions other interments, time and again (Genesis 25:9, 35:19,29, 49:31; Numbers 11:34, 20:1; Deuteronomy 34:6; etc.) in keeping with the Almighty's words to Adam: *For dust you are, and to dust you shall return* (Genesis 3:19). On the other hand, not to find burial after death is clearly a curse and punishment in Scripture (e.g. II Kings 9:10, Jeremiah 8:2, 14:16, 16:4,6, 25:33). Furthermore, anyone who must attend to a departed person's burial is freed from all other mitzvoth (Mishnah, B'rachoth iii 1); and it is a sin to delay an interment overnight without good reason (TB Mo'éd Katan 22a).

Note this too: If a man blasphemed God or worshipped idols, he was to be stoned to death, and his body hung from a tree, as a warning to others not to follow in his ways (Deuteronomy 21:22; TB Sanhedrin 45b). Yet the Torah ordained that his body was not be left overnight. The very day it was hung, it was to be taken down and buried (*ibid.* 21:23).

Said R. Meir: A parable — to what can this be likened? — to two twin brothers in a certain city [who resembled each other closely]. One was chosen king, and one turned to banditry. [When he was captured] the king ordered him hung. But whoever saw him said, "Why, the king is hung!" So the king gave orders, and he was taken down (TB Sanhedrin 45b; bracketed additions after Rashi to Deuteronomy 21:23).

It was a token hanging: close to sunset he was sentenced and stoned to death; then the body was hung; one man tied it to a tree, and one man took it down (TB Sanhedrin 45b; Sifre, Deut. §221, etc.). For even in death, evil as he had been, this man was a creature in the

Divine image. To leave it hang longer would be, as it were, to mistreat or insult the Almighty in effigy; *for a curse of God is hung there* (Deuteronomy 21:23); then it had to be taken down at once.

49.   Midrash T'hillim 22, 7 end; the psalm is generally interpreted as her prayer throughout § 22.

50.   Esther 1:10–21.

51.   Psalms 22:12. Midrash T'hillim 22, 24; Yalkut Shimoni, Psalms § 687; Aggadath Esther 26a.

52.   TB M'gillah 15b.

53.   According to the Midrash, the churlish king was still riled at her uninvited presence, and he kept his face averted. An angel then slapped his face and said, "You wicked man! Your noble wife is standing outside, and you sit thus within?" (Midrash T'hillim 22, 27; Aggadath Esther 52). In the Talmud we read: Three angels then came in on her behalf. One held her head high; another cast a thread of grace over her face; the third stretched out the scepter of Ahasuerus till it reached Esther standing in the doorway (TB M'gillah 15b).

54.   Thus we read in the Talmud and Midrash: *This was Ahasuerus* (Esther 1:1) — this was he in his wickedness, from beginning to end. Ahasuerus had a putrid, vapid mind. He was a stupid king. He killed his wife because of his friend [Vashti, on Memuchan's advice; Esther 1:16–21] and his friend because of his wife [Haman, at Esther's plea; Esther 7:5–10] (respectively: TB M'gillah 11a; Esther Rabbah 4, 1; M'gillah 12a; Esther Rabbah, proem, and 1, 1). The Midrash notes further: about one woman [Vashti] he took advice, but about an entire people [the Jews] he took no advice (Midrash Panim Aḥérim, 56). He blindly let Haman issue a royal decree to destroy them.

55.   Quoted in Evan Esar, *The Treasury of Humorous Quotations*, p. 81 §3.

56.   TB B'rachoth 58a.

57.   Pirké d'R. Eliezer 11; Yalkut Shimoni I §13.

58.   Tosefta, Sanhedrin viii; TB 38a.

59.   My work is important and his is not?

60.   TB B'rachoth 17a.

61.   This thought has found its way into the literature of the world: 17th century: "The manner of giving is worth more than the gift" (Pierre Corneille, *Le Menteur*, act 1 sc. 1); 18th century: "For the will and not the gift makes the giver" (Lessing, *Nathan der Weise*, act 1 sc. 5); 19th century: "The gift without the giver is bare" (James Russell Lowel, *The Vision of Sir Launfal*, II 8); "Rings and jewels are not gifts, but apologies for gifts. The only gift is a portion of thyself" (Ralph Waldo Emerson, *Essays, second series: Gifts*); "It is not the shilling I give you that counts, but the warmth that it carries with it from may hand" (Miguel de Unamuno, *Essays and Soliloquies*, 136).

62.   TB B'rachoth 6a, with marginal reading in Ms Munich (*Dikduké Sof'rim*, note).

63.   TB Sukkah 20a.

64.   TB Shabbath 30b–31a; Avoth d'R. Nathan a 15 (both sources, and variant readings in *Dikduké Sof'rim*, have been used).

65.   Obviously Hillel's patience was famous.

66.   Avoth d'R. Nathan has "long." The question was deliberately chosen, as Hillel was from Babylonia; and his manner of calling Hillel was obviously offensive and insulting.

67.   Avoth d'R. Nathan reads: When a child is born, it is reared in the care of male and

female slaves; hence their heads are long [see note 66]; but here we have intelligent midwives: when a child is born, they raise it in cradles and rub its head; therefore their heads are round.

68.  About four months' earnings of an average worker then (Talmud, ed. Steinzaltz)·

69.  Avoth d'R. Nathan b 29 has a different version: Once a man came to anger Hillel the elder. He waited till the Sage was sleeping, then knocked and called out, "Is Hillel here?" "What do you want?" asked the Sage. "I have a question to ask." Hillel arose and opened the door, put on a robe and sat. "What is your question?" he asked. "I have forgotten," replied the other. "Calm yourself," said the Sage [literally, "Be careful of your temperament"]. "Why," asked the man, "is a cow's tail long and a donkey's tails short?" "You have asked a great question said Hillel. "It is because the donkey carries a saddle [or pannier] on its back; hence its tail [need] reach only halfway up its haunch [to swish the flies away]. A cow's hide is exposed; hence its tail is long, so that it can reach all of its hide with it. Do you have any other question?" "No," said the other, and he stood up and went away, while the Sage went up to sleep. When he was sleeping, the man began knocking [again]. "Is Hillel here?" he called. "What is it?" asked the Sage. "A question," he replied. The Sage arose, opened the door, put on a robe and sat. "Ask your question," said he. "I have forgotten it." "Then calm yourself." Said the man, "Why are the heads of Babylonians long, while in this land people's heads are round?" "You have asked a great question," answered Hillel. "It is because there are no cradles in their localities; all his days [an infant] is raised in his mother's lap. But in this land, once a child is born, she [his mother] takes him and puts him in a cradle; so their heads become round. Have you any other questions?" "No," said the other [and so on, as above, till the next question]: "Why are the bottoms of Africans' feet wider than those of other people?" "My son, you have asked a great question," the Sage replied. "It is because their dwelling-place is among marshes, and they walk day and night in water. Their feet spread from water, and therefore they are wider than those of all others. Have you another question?" [etc. as above, till the man asked] "Why are the eyes of the Tarmodians narrower than those of all other people?" He replied, "You have asked a great question. It is because they are close to the desert, and the wind blows the sand into their faces, and their eyes fill with water." Said the Sage, "Have you any other question?" "No"; and so the Sage went to sleep. At that the other began shouting, "Woe is me because of you, Hillel! Woe is me because of you!" "What is the matter?" asked the Sage. "Your humility made me lose 400 dinars." Hillel replied, "Better for you to lose 400 dinars and again 400 dinars, than that Hillel should be called impatient, hot-tempered even a brief while before the Almighty.

70.  The original reads: A certain heathen once came before Shammai. "How many Torahs have you?" he asked. "Two," that Sage replied: "one written, and one oral." Said the other, "About the Written Torah I believe you; about the Oral Torah I do not. Convert me to Judaism on condition that you teach me [only] the Written Torah." Shammai berated him roundly and sent him off with an angry rebuke. When the man came before Hillel, he converted him.

71.  So R. Israel al-Nakawa, *Menorath haMa'or*, IV, 268.

72.  Avoth d'R. Nathan a 15 has instead: "My son," said Hillel, "sit"; and he wrote down the Hebrew letters for him. "What is this?" he asked. "An *alef*," the other replied. "This is not an *alef*," said Hillel, "but a *béth*. What is this?" "A *béth*," the man replied. "This is not a *béth*," Hillel retorted, "but a *gimmel*." [Apparently the man protested] and Hillel asked, "But how do you know this is an *alef* and this is a *béth*? It is only because our fathers so transmitted them to us. Just as you accepted this on faith, so must you accept [the Oral Torah] on faith."

147

73.   The original reads: A certain heathen once came before Shammai and said, "Convert me to Judaism on condition that you teach me the entire Torah while I stand on one foot." That Sage simply drove him off with the builder's measure that was in his hand. The man them came before Hillel — and he converted him.

74.   Another version: when he heard a child's voice (Midrash haGadol, Exodus 28:4; *Exempla of the Rabbis,* p. 23).

75.   After the verse, Midrash haGadol reads: Said he, "For whom is all this honor?" They told him, "For the *kohen gadol,* who stands and ministers at the altar." Said he, "I will go and convert on condition that they make me *kohen gadol,* and I will thus serve at the altar." (So too *Exempla,* but it starts: Said he to him — i.e. to the school-child; see note 74.)

76.   Since he wished to serve as *kohen gadol* before the sovereign King of the universe, let him learn the relevant laws of the Torah. (His request of Hillel is found in Midrash haGadol and *Exempla*; the sentence that follows is in MhG.) In MhG, when Shammai drives him off, he berates him, "You foul leather vessel! Are there not enough [people to be *kohen gadol*] among the Jews that we should need foreigners?" *Exempla* reads: Said he to him, "Are there then no *kohanim g'dolim* among the Israelites except this Gentile who has come with his knapsack?"

77.   Deuteronomy 14:1.

78.   Exodus 14:22; the verse is relevant because originally the firstborn were hallowed to serve in the *mishkan* (Tabernacle) and the Sanctuary; only later were the *kohanim* and Levites chosen instead (Numbers 3:12–13, 41,45, 8:14–19). However, MhG and *Exempla* (see note 74) have instead: and of them the *shechinah* said, *you shall be to me a kingdom of* kohanim *and a holy nation* (Exodus 19:6).

79.   *Exempla* and three MSS of Midrash haGadol (ed. Margulies) add: and their father [the original convert] was Onkelos the Proselyte, who translated the Torah [the Pentateuch, into Aramaic].

80.   Herbert Danby, *The Mishnah,* Oxford 1933, vi.

81.   TB Ḥullin 89a.

82.   Henry Ward Beecher, *From a Plymouth Pulpit.*

83.   There is the American anecdote of a father who was berating his young boy for his indolence by comparing him (unfavorably) with Abraham Lincoln: "Why, when Lincoln was your age, he chopped wood every day for his mother, did all the chores around the log cabin house, then walked three miles so that he could borrow a book to read, to educate himself." The boy replied laconically, "Yes, Pa. And when he was your age, he was president."

84.   For this reason the Torah commands, *You shall rise up before a hoary head, and honor the face of an old man* (Leviticus 19:32).

85.   Thus R. Judah haNassi used to honor the rich (TB Eruvin 86a). Furthermore, the rich are in a position to do good deeds that are beyond the means of the poor.

86.   TB Bava Bathra 10a.

87.   Va-yikra Rabbah 34, 8 end; Ruth Rabbah 8, 9.

88.   R. Israel al-Nakawa, *Menorath haMa'or,* I, 33.

89.   The verse is generally rendered, "For the poor shall never cease out of the land"; but it can equally bear this translation. Note also this sagacious comment on Exodus 22:24, *If you lend money to any of My people, of the poor with you*: For this reason does an obligation lie on you to lend to him, because the money of the poor is to be found in your possession ... for the law is that if a man deeds his possessions in writing to one of his sons, he has made him no

more than a guardian or trustee, for the purpose that he should divide the possessions among the other sons [since we so understand his intentions] (*Ma'aseh Roke-aḥ*, in A.Z. Friedman, תורה של מעינה II 101). Thus, "of the poor with you" (literal translation) is taken to denote the money that properly belongs to the poor, which the Almighty assigned to your care. If it is your task to manage it for him, you must at least let him have some of it as a loan when he asks.

90. TB Shabbath 151b.

91. Miguel de Cervantes, *Don Quixote*, part I chapter 20.

92. Robert Southey, *The Vision of the Maid of Orleans*, book iii.

93. TB B'rachoth 6b.

94. Rambam, *Mishnah Torah, hilchoth matnoth ani-yim* vii–x; *Tur* and *Shulḥan Aruch Yoreh Dé'ah*, §§ 247–259; etc.

95. Rambam *ibid.* ix 3.

96. Also TJ Pé'ah viii 9, Sh'kalim v 6; R. Israel al-Nakawa, *Menorath haMa'or*, I, 31.

97. I.e. either to sell it or borrow against it.

98. Evidently not too audibly.

99. Va-yikra Rabbah 34,1 and sources in note 96. Interestingly enough, a story about an inheritance overseas has been used by "con men" (confidence tricksters) in our time. A handsome young man would find a simple trusting soul and spin a glib yarn about a grand inheritance (complete with castle) waiting for him in Spain. He just needed a modest sum to travel to Spain and authenticate his claim. Then he would certainly reimburse this simple trusting soul lavishly for advancing him this modest sum. Once he had the money, he would vanish; and alas, so would the castle in Spain. Thus, if you will, R. Yonah used a confidence trickster's game long ago, but in reverse—to help someone in need. גם את זה לעומת זה עשה הא־להים *God also made the one opposite the other* (Ecclesiastes 7:14). For everything evil in the world, the Almighty made something equal and opposite that can be used for good.

100. The story that follows appears in print about R. Yoshe Ber, the noted rabbi of Brisk (Brest-Litovsk), Lithuania, founder of the illustrious Soloveitchik dynasty of Torah scholars. However, I heard it originally about R. Israel Salanter, and so I relate it.

101. Thus, for example, Safed in the 16th century had a remarkable Jewish community, devoted to piety and Torah study, led by masters of religious law (including R. Joseph Caro, author of the Shulḥan Aruch) and original teachers of *kabbalah* (e.g. the Ari). In a list of "good and holy customs" current in Safed among the men of piety, drawn up by R. Abraham Galanti, number 27 reads: There are precious, remarkable individuals who keep the mitzvah, "Tithe shall you tithe"... i.e. two tithes, which means a fifth of every profit or fee that comes into their hand; and they leave it in a chest to be ready at hand for any mitzvah that comes along, to give generously the deposit left with them for safekeeping... and even someone who is poor, we know he is accustomed to do this (Schechter, *Studies in Judasim*, II 296–97).

102. I.e. the favor or gift of life, sustenance, good fortune, etc.

103. Also Midrash haGadol, Exodus 1:8.

104. Tanḥuma, *sh'moth* 16; Sh'moth Rabbah 4, 2.

105. A similar thought, essentially, can be found in the Midrash. When the Israelites in the wilderness reached the land of the Amorites, we read: *Then Israel sent messengers to Siḥon king of the Amorites, saying: "Let me pass through your land... we will go by the king's highway, until we have passed through your territory." But Siḥon would not allow Israel to pass through his territory; and he gathered all his men together... and fought against Israel. And Israel slew him... and took*

*possession of his land* (Numbers 21:21–24). Yalkut Shimoni I §764 cites *Midrash Y'lam'dénu*: Said Moses to Him [the Almighty], "Let us send messengers." He answered him, "I said, *I have given into your hand Sihon the Amorite, king of Heshbon, and his land; begin to possess it, and contend with him in battle* (Deuteronomy 2:24), and you would send messengers of peace?" Said Moses... "I learned from Thee... When Thou didst wish to take the Israelites out of Egypt, Thou didst say, *Come now, and I will send you to Pharaoh* (Exodus 3:10)."

Similarly Midrash Tanḥuma, *d'varim*, addendum 10 (p. 6): [The Almighty bade Moses "*Behold, I have begun to give Sihon and his land over to you; [begin to take control, to take possession of his land]*" (Deuteronomy 2:31). What is written above? — *and contend with him in battle* (ibid. 24). Yet they did not do so, but rather, "*I sent messengers... to Sihon the king of Heshbon, with words of peace*" (ibid. 26). Said the Holy, Blessed One: I said, "contend with him in battle," and you would propose peace? *There is no peace, says the Lord, for the wicked* (Isaiah 48:22).... Said Moses to Him, "I learned from Thee... Thou couldst have sent one flash of lightning to burn up the Egyptians, and Thou didst not do so, but didst rather send me to Pharaoh" — as it is stated, "*Let My people go*" (Exodus 5:1).

The last part is cited by Rashi to Deuteronomy 2:26.

106. So Séder Olam 5; Early Tanḥuma, *ḥukath* 47; TB Taanith 9a; Be-midbar Rabbah 1, 2; Yalkut Shimoni I §733. In fact, Va-yikra Rabbah 34, 8 states explicitly: Did the Israelites then need them [Ammon and Moab]? All the forty years that the Israelites were in the wilderness, did the manna not fall and the well not come up?

107. Robin Hyman, *The Quotation Dictionary*, 226. Similarly G. L. Apperson, *English Proverbs and Proverbial Phrases*, 601; *The Oxford Dictionary of Quotations* (ed. Smith and Hesseltine), 403.

108. Mishnath R. Eliezer, 136; as proof-texts, the Midrash quotes respectively Genesis 12:5, 13:5, 14:14–16, 19:29.

109. Genesis 19:36, 38.

110. Note also these passages in the Midrash: Adam, the first man, was driven from the Garden of Eden for no other reason but ingratitude: for it is stated, *And the man said: The woman whom Thou didst give to be with me, she gave me [fruit] of the tree* (Genesis 3:12; Mishnath R. Eliezer, 135; cf. Midrash haGadol, Numbers 21:5, 383, and sources given there). Facing guilt for having eaten the forbidden fruit, Adam blamed Eve for giving it to him, and he blamed the Almighty for having given her to him. He forgot how he had found no partner in life before her creation, and how he had welcomed her as his true helpmate. This was ingratitude.

The Midrash continues: So too our forefathers in the wilderness: For ingratitude alone the Holy, Blessed One became enraged with them — as it is stated, *the people spoke against God and against Moses... "and our soul has come to loathe this too light, miserable food"* (Numbers 21:5). Said the Holy, Blessed One to them: Kings choose only light food to eat, and you complain and say, "our soul has come to loathe it"? At once *the Lord sent fiery serpents among the people* (ibid. 6; Mishnath R. Eliezer, 135–36). In Be-midbar Rabbah 7, 4 we read: Our Sages said: They had no need to move their bowels like ordinary humans. Why? — because God said: Just as the angels have no need for that, so let it be necessary no longer for them.... But they began to speak mockingly of it. Said one to the other... By your life! Did you ever see anyone put wheat into a millstone and it should not be ground and come out? So do we eat the manna and it does not emerge. His friend replied: I fear that finally, one day, my stomach will swell up and burst open, since we do not evacuate it.

The Midrash above (Mishnath R. Eliezer, 136) continues: Now why, out of all possible punishments, did He send only serpents? — The Holy, blessed One had told it [the serpent], *dust shall you eat all the days of your life* (Genesis 3:14), and it did not complain about its food; and these were grumbling aloud about theirs. Then let this creature come and exact punishment from them. (Similarly Tanḥuma, *ḥukath* 19; Early Tanḥuma, 45; Be–midbar Rabbah 19, 22.)

# 3

## At home in America

*What is the home that you would build for Me, and what place is there for My repose?* (Isaiah 66:1)

 

THE SACRED TORAH RELATES STORIES AND ANECDOTES, and (*l'havdil*) so do books by the thousands that appear every day. What is the difference between them? An ordinary novel is read once (a few times at the most) and put away. Today's best-seller is tomorrow's forgotten book (and then people wonder what everyone saw in it). But the Torah we read through every year, without fail. On *Simḥath Torah* we finish the last chapter, with the death of Moses; and immediately we start again from the beginning, with the majestic account of creation. Why? — because there is always more to learn from those words, that came from the almighty Himself.

Take the story of Jacob and Esau in their youth. They were twins born to Isaac and Rebekah (Esau was a few minutes older), but how different they were as they grew. Esau took to the field to hunt (and as the Sages note,[1] he hunted down people too; it was all sport to him); while Jacob took to the tents of Shem and Ever to study Torah, Divine wisdom.[2]

One day, says the Torah, Esau came home from his hunting tired out, dead to the world; and he found Jacob cooking lentil soup. He didn't know exactly what it was, but tired and famished as he was, it must have smelled to him like the finest food in the world. Sprawled perhaps on a hassock, he told Jacob, הלעיטני נא מן האדם האדם הזה *Give me, pray, some of that red red stuff to gulp down* (Genesis 25:30). As the Midrash puts it, he opened his mouth wide as a camel and said, "Just keep pouring it down my gullet!" (*B'réshith Rabbah* 63, 12).

155

But now comes something astounding: Instead of feeding him, Jacob begins bargaining with him: "*Sell me as of this day your birthright*" (Genesis 25:31). Well, Esau decided he didn't care about his rights as the firstborn anyway, and he sold them to Jacob. And only after Esau swore to it also, then *Jacob gave Esau bread and lentil soup. And he ate and drank, and rose up and went his way; and so Esau despised the birthright* (ibid. 34)

Is this how Jacob should have acted? The Torah tells that he was *a simple sincere man who dwelt in tents* (ibid. 27). And the Midrash explains that he is called *ish tam,* a simple sincere man, because he was honest and straightforward all his life, innocent of any robbery or sin, or any ugly deed.[3] Then how could he take advantage of Esau like that? Imagine a man in the desert, long parched with thirst, who meets someone with a pitcher full of cool delicious water. In every way he pleads for some. "Wait," says the other. "That's a mighty fine watch you have there, ticking away. First you give it to me, and then you drink all the water you want." Of course the man will hand it over even if it is a precious heirloom. Better to lose it than die of thirst. And having drunk his fill he may even mutter, "Oh well, it wasn't a very good watch anyway. I didn't really care for it."

Doesn't this seem to have happened here? Yet how could Jacob exploit his poor brother in his plight? (In fact, this is asked in the Zohar, I 139a, of R. Shimon b. Yoḥai: How could Jacob refuse to give Esau the lentil soup till he sold him his rights as a firstborn? And indeed Esau [later] told Jacob, *he has supplanted me me these two times* — Genesis 27:36.)

In his fine commentary R. Meir Leibush Malbim gives the answer: That isn't at all what happened. Imagine, rather, a man standing by the raging ocean with a purse in his hand, filled with precious jewels — and he wants to hurl it into the sea. To him it's just a heavy burden. He is convinced the jewels are so much worthless junk. Another man happens to be there, and he says, "Look: why don't you give me that purse, in exchange for a good hearty meal?" The first man is actually famished, and he accepts eagerly, convinced that he has made an excellent trade with a blithering fool!

For what exactly was this birthright? Malbim quotes Don Isaac Abarbanel: The firstborn son was always to devote himself to spiritual matters, while the other sons pursued worldly occupations. The Midrash notes that till the *mishkan* (the Tabernacle) was constructed, firstborn sons did the work of the *kohen,* offering up sacrifices for others to the Almighty.

True, Jacob sat in the tents of Shem and Ever studying Torah; but he kept an eye on Esau; and he thought, "Is this wicked person to stand and offer up sacrifices?" So he decided to bend every effort to get the birthright (*B'réshith Rabbah* 63, 13).

Esau was only too happy to sell it. He was a hunter. What he caught in the field had value: it could be eaten and enjoyed. But a religious ritual? "*Here I am going to die* (Genesis 25:32) anyway," he asserted. As the Midrash puts it, he said, "I should offer up sacrifices and be burdened with the service of God — and then I'll die like all other human beings, who don't make offerings? Then what do I need all that bothersome toil for?" (*Midrash Aggadah*). So the Zohar (I 139a) explains: Yet before this incident Esau hated the birthright, and he begged Jacob to take it from him, even without payment.

Hence, the Midrash notes, he now told him, "This birthright that you think is valuable — give me a bowl of these lentils, and I'll give it to you" (*P'sikta Rabbathi* xii — 48a). And so it is written (the Zohar concludes) *he ate and drank, and rose and went; and Esau despised the birthright* (Genesis 25:34).

In the traditional *ḥéder* where generations of children were reared, the *rebbe* would drive the point home by noting how Scripture underlines Esau's behavior with his lentil soup: *he ate and drank,* never first washing his hands in the time-honored ritual and saying *ha-motzi,* the benediction over bread; *and he rose and went,* never saying *birkath ha-mazon,* the Grace after meals to thank the Almighty. Then what else could we expect but that as he left, *Esau despised the birthright?*

The Midrash rounds out the picture nicely: He started gathering crowds about Jacob, saying, "Do you know what I did to this fellow? I ate his lentils and drank his wine, and I diddled him, selling him my birthright for it!" [We can imagine him ending off with a hearty laugh.] Said Jacob to him, "Eat and enjoy yourself" (*Midrash haGadol,* Genesis 25:34). He remained unruffled, knowing that "he laughs best who laughs last."

Now, what meaning does this have for us? The Talmud teaches that מעשי אבות סימן לבנים the deeds of the fathers are a sign, an augury for the children (TB *Sotah* 34a). Whatever the Patriarchs did points the way for us, their children, to follow.

Esau was a hunter, a man of action and solid achievement. He brought home, if not the bacon, at least the venison. Jacob learned Torah, Divine wisdom in his tents. So he knew to pick up easily something of immense value that Esau scorned.

אַתְּ מוֹצֵא שְׁלֹשָׁה שֵׁמוֹת נִקְרְאוּ לוֹ לְאָדָם: אֶחָד מַה שֶּׁקּוֹרְאִים לוֹ אָבִיו וְאִמּוֹ, אֶחָד מַה שֶׁקּוֹרְאִים לוֹ בְּנֵי־אָדָם, וְאֶחָד מַה שֶּׁקּוֹנֶה הוּא לְעַצְמוֹ. ‎(תנחומא, ויקהל א)

You find (the Sages teach) that a person is called by three names: one is the name his father and mother call him; one is what people call him; and one is the name he earns for himself (*Tanḥuma, va-yakhel* 1).

When Esau said הַלְעִיטֵנִי נָא מִן הָאָדֹם הָאָדֹם הַזֶּה (Genesis 25:30) the scholars of *tosafoth* explain that he meant, "Give me, please, some of that red stuff to gulp down — [me] this red fellow."[4] Esau was born ruddy, all reddish in tinge (*ibid.* 25), but till then no one called him *Edom*, the Hebrew word for Red. It isn't proper to give someone a nickname that he might find derogatory; there could be a shade of insult in that. But Esau went and pinned the label on himself, saying heedlessly, in effect, "Pour that red stuff into this red guy." Well, if he gave himself the name, *therefore his name was called Edom* (*ibid.* 30): everyone called him "Red."

Jacob bought the birthright, however — and it became an augury and precedent for his descendants: *Thus said the Lord: Israel is my firstborn son* (Exodus 4:22) — meaning our people enslaved in Egypt;[5] and it holds true for all time. From its "birth," God (our spiritual "parent") called our people Israel, and among mankind we are His firstborn, His "oldest son," with all the privileges and responsibilities that this involves.

Ravaged by the canker of anti-semitic hate, there were always people who gave us names of *their* making. Thanks to Shakespeare, many of us were called Shylock (having been forced by the world of these people into Shylock's trade); and "Jew" became an ugly verb in the dictionary.

Yet there remains the name we can earn for ourselves — not as the Jacob whom Esau later saw with eyes of venom, but as the Jacob whom the Sages describe: the honest man of Divine learning who strove to pick up spiritual treasures that were there for the asking.

The most precious jewels of spiritual value are ours, if we only want them — through the Torah and the *mitzvoth*. The ḥassidic luminary R. Menaḥem Mendl of Vitebsk said, "Rejoice that you have an opportunity to sing to God. . . . Rejoice that you're able to pray, to learn Torah, to do His will."[6] Pray with sincerity, keep the Sabbath as the Torah ordains, give charity, support Torah study, do a mitzvah when you can — and you earn your proper name, that Heaven meant for you. Then no names that people of hate may call us (projecting their aberrations onto us) can touch us.

Consider a classic example: When the Israelites finally left Egypt, after over two centuries of servitude, the Egyptians showered presents on them as "loans": gold and silver objects, clothing, etc. (Exodus 12:35–36). The Israelites left loaded with wealth. One man, though, left loaded with a different "luggage": *Moses took the bones of Joseph with him, for Joseph had imposed a solemn oath upon the Israelites, saying, "God will surely remember you; and you shall carry up my bones from here with you"* (Exodus 13:19).

All the Israelites had sworn to Joseph that when the liberation from Egypt came, their descendants would take his remains for reburial in the land of Israel. But only Moses went and obeyed the oath. Says the Midrash:

לְהוֹדִיעַ חָכְמָתוֹ וַחֲסִידוּתוֹ שֶׁל מֹשֶׁה, שֶׁכָּל יִשְׂרָאֵל עוֹסְקִין בַּבִּזָּה וּמֹשֶׁה עוֹסֵק בְּמִצְוַת

עַצְמוֹת יוֹסֵף. עָלָיו הַכָּתוּב אוֹמֵר (משלי י ח): חֲכַם לֵב יִקַּח מִצְוֹת. (מכילתא, ויהי, פתיחתא)

This shows Moses' wisdom and kindly piety. For all the Israelites were busy with the spoils [the "loot" from the Egyptians] and Moses busied himself with the mitzvah, the religious duty of Joseph's remains. To him applies Scripture's verse, *The wise of heart will take mitzvoth* (Proverbs 10, 8; *Mechilta, va-y'hi,* proem).

The sainted genius of Torah, R. Aaron Kotler (of blessed memory) once asked about this: "Isn't it puzzling though, why the Sages call him wise for this? Pious, devout, yes; but wise?" If you and I were there, at the great exodus from Egypt, wouldn't we rather think it intelligent to gather a heap of good things from the obliging neighbors, leaving the matter of Joseph's remains to someone else? Then how was Moses wise?

Well, said R. Aaron, the Midrash itself proves its point. Less than a week after leaving Egypt, laden with their "loot," the Israelites came to the Red Sea, and stopped: dead end. They looked behind, and saw the Egyptians in full pursuit after them. They seemed to have a simple choice: they could either let the Egyptians capture them and go back into perpetual servitude, or take a flying jump into the sea and drown. But then *Moses stretched out his hand over the sea . . . and the waters were divided; and the Israelites went into the midst of the sea on dry ground* (Exodus 14:21-22). In the vision of the Psalmist, *The sea looked and fled* (Psalms 114:6), leaving a dry path for the Israelites (and when the Egyptians went after them, the waters returned and drowned them).

159

"The sea looked and fled." But what exactly did it behold, the Sages ask, that made it run like that? One answer is that it saw Joseph's coffin (*Midrash T'hillim* 114, 9).[7] With all the wealth they had gathered, the Israelites made no impression on the Red Sea. All that wealth with which they were laden could only help them sink faster if they entered the water. It took the remains of Joseph the *tzaddik* to make the water divide. With Potiphar's wife he had never yielded to temptation. Sold into slavery by his brothers, he later supported them through years of famine. When Moses came with his coffin because his dying wish had been to be reburied in the land of Israel, the Red Sea had to make way.

Then who was really smart and clever when they left Egypt: the Israelites who took wealth (not to migrate penniless) or Moses with Joseph's coffin? Hence the verse is applied to him: "The wise of heart will take *mitzvoth*." The bones of Joseph "insured" the safety of all the wealth. *That* was wisdom.

An American folksong has a refrain that sings of "one more river, and that's the river to cross." Life brings us at times to "one more river to cross," one crisis or difficulty after another that must either defeat us or be overcome. The question is: What equipment will we take along to get us over the rivers and oceans of life — till the final river, beyond which lies the Afterlife? "The wise of heart will take *mitzvoth*."

The equipment we amass and take along determines not only how we fare at the rivers, the barriers and hurdles in life. It also determines the character of the home we make and live in, while we travel on in time through the journey of life. It determines the atmosphere in which our family lives and our children grow.

We can amass the finest equipment to furnish a splendid home with every luxury and convenience. With no ideals of Torah and *mitzvoth* that the parents uphold, on which the children can grow, the children may turn to crime and drugs and a freakish search for meaning in the realms of hallucination — as experience has tragically shown.

The Torah and *mitzvoth* are there for the asking. We need only follow the examples of Jacob and Moses. And remember: If the father doesn't take along the bone-structure of the past, the *atzmoth* of the *tzaddik*, our sacred heritage, into his life and the life of his children — who knows where all the gold and silver he gathers will ultimately land? In one or two generations at most, some "Egyptians" will inherit it.

# A PLAGUE IN THE HOUSE

THE ISRAELITES CROSSED THE RED SEA IN SAFETY, and afterward spent forty years in the wilderness. The old generation died off, and a new generation grew up, with the courage to conquer the promised land of Canaan. What sort of homes would they have in that land once it was theirs?

In the Torah that Moses taught them, they learned a strange passage:

כִּי תָבֹאוּ אֶל אֶרֶץ כְּנַעַן אֲשֶׁר אֲנִי נֹתֵן לָכֶם לַאֲחֻזָּה, וְנָתַתִּי נֶגַע צָרַעַת בְּבֵית אֶרֶץ אֲחֻזַּתְכֶם.
(ויקרא יד לד)

When you come into the land of Canaan, that I am giving you for possession, I shall put a tzaraath disease into a house of the land of your possession (Leviticus 14:34). The Torah then teaches how the owner of the house is to report it to a kohen, how the kohen is to examine the infection in the walls of the house and reach his decision, and how he should deal with it.

Yet that first sentence certainly has a peculiar phrase: וְנָתַתִּי נֶגַע צָרַעַת "I shall put a tzaraath disease into a house" — apparently deliberately; it won't just be pure bad luck. And indeed, says R. Judah, "They were given news that the infections [of the home] would befall them."[8] This only leaves one question: Why? Moreover, R. Ḥiyya asked. "Was this then good news for them, that such infections would be inflicted on them?" (Va-yikra Rabbah 17, 6). Even if it was fated to happen, why tell them about it so far in advance?

The Midrash gives the answer: R. Shimon b. Yoḥai taught: Once the people of Canaan heard that the Israelites were coming to attack them, they arose and hid their possessions in the walls. . . . Said the Holy One, "I didn't promise their fathers that 'I will bring your sons into a desolate land' but rather into a land filled with every good" — as it is written, and houses full of all good things (Deuteronomy 6:11). What did the Holy One do? — He would inflict a tzaraath disease on a person's house, so that he would demolish it and find the hidden treasure (Va-yikra Rabbah 17, 6, ed. Margulies).

161

So Rashi explains:[9]

בְּשׂוֹרָה הִיא לָהֶם שֶׁהַנְּגָעִים בָּאִים עֲלֵיהֶם: לְפִי שֶׁהִטְמִינוּ אֱמוֹרִיִּים מַטְמוֹנִיּוֹת שֶׁל זָהָב בְּקִירוֹת בָּתֵּיהֶם כָּל אַרְבָּעִים שָׁנָה שֶׁהָיוּ יִשְׂרָאֵל בַּמִּדְבָּר, וְעַל יְדֵי הַנֶּגַע נוֹתֵץ הַבַּיִת וּמוֹצְאָן.

They were given news that the diseases would come upon them, because the Amorites hid treasures of gold in the walls of their houses all the forty years that the Israelites were in the wilderness; but on account of the *tzaraath* infection a person would demolish his house and find them.

You see, like the Arabs today, the Amorites didn't expect our people to last on the land. A few wars of attrition or annihilation, perhaps, and the land would be theirs again, intact. Well, there's an old Yiddish saying:[10] דער מענטש טראַכט און גאָט לאַכט Or: man proposes, and God disposes.[11]

In *K'li Yakar*, the commentary by the inspired preacher R. Ephraim Sh'lomo of Lenczyca (Luntschitz) we find another explanation:

וְיֵשׁ אוֹמְרִים שֶׁטַּעַם נִגְעֵי הַבָּתִּים לְפִי שֶׁהָאֱמוֹרִיִּים בָּנוּ בָּתִּים לְשֵׁם עֲבוֹדָה זָרָה; עַל־כֵּן הַקָּדוֹשׁ־בָּרוּךְ־הוּא מֵבִיא נְגָעִים עַל הַבָּתִּים, כְּדֵי לְנַתֵּץ אוֹתָם.

Some say the reason for the *tzaraath* infections of the houses is that the Amorites built the houses for the sake of idol-worship. Hence the Holy One would inflict such diseases on the houses, so that they would be demolished.[12]

Dedicating their homes to idolatry, the Amorites could very likely have put idols in the walls, to enjoy their (supposed) "benign influence and protection." When the Hebrews moved in they would see only blank walls and suspect nothing. So in time those walls would develop a sickly tinge, until the owner of such a home would have to go to a *kohen* and complain, כְּנֶגַע נִרְאָה לִי בַּבַּיִת *Something like a* tzaraath *disease seems to me to be in the house* (Leviticus 14:35). The walls would be torn down and the idols destroyed. Then the house could be rebuilt in purity and holiness, to fulfill in some small measure the Divine order, *So let them build Me a sanctuary, that I may dwell in their midst* (Exodus 25:8).

Each year we read through the Written Torah (the Five Books of Moses) in the synagogue, a portion every Sabbath morning, in the trustworthy belief that it always has something more to teach us. The Torah is our basic commentary on our human life. It can guide and illuminate our way,

162

if we listen and study in reverent receptivity. So this text too, on *tzaraath* infections in homes, has a cogent bearing on American Jewish life in our time:

The immigrants who crossed half a world to get from Eastern Europe to the American shore found life gruelling. They starved and hungered, and worked long inhuman hours so that their families could have a piece of bread. For cooking and heating the home (in New York's Lower East Side) there was a coal stove, where you could also burn wood, from boxes found in the street. For light at night you put a quarter (of a dollar, 25 cents) into the meter, and you could light the gas jets for a week.

To make sure they would have that quarter, people worked eighteen hours a day in the sweatshops. As a rule they weren't paid by the hour but for "piece-work": so much for every article or thing done. Our ancestors enslaved in Egypt used to work with a desperate urgency and frenzied will to finish a daily quota of bricks, building store-cities for Pharaoh. In startling parallel, the generation of immigrants to the United States labored in grim concentration to make their daily and weekly quotas of "piece-work," to earn their quotas of money. They focused on a single goal: זהב gold; and there was room for nothing else in their lives.

When Moses came to his enslaved people in Egypt and told them that God the Creator of heaven and earth saw and knew their suffering and promised solemnly to liberate them; when Moses called on them to lift their heads up from their row of bricks and see a wider horizon of freedom, where they could grow spiritually in Divine faith and worship — *they did not listen to Moses on account of shortness of temper and cruel bondage* (Exodus 6:9).

In the same way no one could talk to those immigrants of our sacred heritage: to have at least a *m'zuzah* on the doorpost, and a few *s'forim*, volumes of Torah learning, in the home, to look into of a Friday evening. In so many cases there could even be no talk of keeping the Sabbath. There was one goal: זהב gold — money to be earned. Nothing else mattered. That was the great theme that permeated the home, saturating the very walls.

For the children, they were grateful that public schools provided a good secular education. But about a Torah education of some sort, they couldn't think. There was no time; "time was money." A *lo yutzlach,* a person who could succeed at nothing else, would open a one-room "religious school" for the afternoon hours. At one point, one such "educator" on

New York's Lower East Side charged two cents per pupil per lesson, where-upon a competitor sprang up who charged one cent. And no one seemed able to lift his head from his "piece-work" and really care. Missionaries did a "good business" luring Jewish children off the streets (where they were told to go and play, so as not to bother the hard-working parents) by giving them sweets, carols and "inspiring" stories — and still no one was able to care. They were dedicated completely to זהב their material goal. They had to earn enough (and how much was enough?).

The years went by. A second generation grew up alongside the first. The weekly quarter (25 cents) for gas was always there now; and when gas ranges replaced the coal stoves, and electric lights burned at night instead of gas jets, there was money for that too. Gone also was the hovering fear of being put out on the street with the family's meager possession, for lack of the monthly rent. Yet the single-minded drive for זהב gold, material wealth, continued.

The late genial comedian Eddie Cantor used to tell of two laborers in a factory who stopped work at the lunch-hour, sat down, and took out their sandwiches. One of them sighed: "Peanut-butter sandwiches, that's all I get every day — just peanut-butter sandwiches — day in and day out. I tell you, I'm sick of them." The other man was surprised. "Why don't you just tell your wife to make you something else?" he asked. "What do you mean, my wife?" the man retorted. "I always prepare my own lunch."

The American Jew "prepared his own lunch," determined the goals and values of his life, day after day. Yet it remained always the same. It seemed that the people worked with their machines for so long that they became machines themselves, as it were — capable only of running to make money.

So the homes of American Jewry were built on money. That formed the walls and the wallpaper, the floors and the carpeting. Money set the pace of the home and drove its pulse. It was the goal and the achievement. And then, one day, many a householder would have to go to his rabbi. Just as an Israelite of old would have to go to a *kohen* and say כנגע נראה לי בבית "There seems to me to be something like a *tzaraath* infection in my house" (Leviticus 14:35), so would such a man have to report the infection that appeared, ugly and frightening, in his home life: "My daughter is going out with a non-Jew. My son is dating a Gentile girl. My children are beginning to violate the Sabbath. They're starting to scorn our Jewish faith, everything we hold sacred!"

The nature of infectious disease is to spread. At first the sickening tinges and hues of this plague troubled only Orthodox Jewry, bound in loyalty to our age-old faith of Torah and *mitzvoth*. And then the cry came as well from the ranks of Conservative and Reform Jews: כנגע נראה לי בבית American Jewry is ill! We're plagued by assimilation, ravaged by intermarriage. Jewish life, Jewish values, the Jewish home — all is disintegrating!

How did the *K'li Yakar* explain the infection? In the words of an earlier commentary, the reason was that when the Canaanites began building a house they would say, "Let it be in the name of this-and-this idol"; so an atmosphere of uncleanness took possession of the house from the ground up.[13]

The Israelites who captured Canaan took over the homes they found, lock stock and barrel, unaware of the spiritual pollution that made it vital to destroy those structures and build anew, clean and strong. The Jews who came to America accepted American-style homes, permeated by the pervasive goal of money-making. And so the homes grew empty of *yiddishkeit,* the lifeways and values we have cherished since time immemorial — and the vacuum was filled by the culture of the street.

There was a precious freedom in America — freedom from the ghetto life of Eastern Europe with its persecutions and pogroms and grinding poverty. But it became a freedom to go to horse races, and shout and scream with extra frenzy, louder than others, for the "right" horse to win. Jewish children found the freedom to attend "important" baseball games and watch with greater excitement than others. Minds that would have absorbed pages of the immortal Talmud in other circumstances, became filled with "batting averages" and other vital statistics of star baseball players. They became walking encyclopedias of the sport. And a heaven-blessed identity, carried and cherished through the centuries since Sinai, disintegrated.

Even if Jewish youth formed impassioned ideals, they were concerned with socialism and civil rights and equality for others. *They made me keeper of the vineyards, but my own vineyard I did not keep* (Song of Songs 1:6). For their own lives as Jews, entrusted with a Divine heritage and destiny, they had no ideals, no passionate loyalties or commitments. What did it mean, anyway, to be a Jew? They hadn't the vaguest idea.

And at last the parents came, stricken, pathetic, to cry כנגע נראה לי בבית "There is something terribly wrong in my house. It has to be cured!" There were "men of distinction" who held symposiums and wrote impressive articles on what Jewish identity is or should be, and how to give the

165

youth positive attitudes toward their Jewishness. It was all "full of sound and fury, signifying nothing."[14] *He that troubles his house inherits the wind* (Proverbs 11:29). They were only troubling the diseased house of American Jewry, solving nothing; and they could only inherit the wind of their own pompous pontifications.

How do you heal the נגע בבית the sickening infection in the home? You break down the walls, says the Torah, and build new ones: with a *m'zuzah* at the door, to attest to out faith and God's protection; with a picture of a great pious sage on the wall, such as the *Hafetz Hayyim,* for example, to shed an aura of holiness; with candlesticks and a *kiddush* cup on display, to use in honoring the Sabbath.

Insecure in their uncertainty, the immigrants took to American homes fearing they *had* to sacrifice everything for enough money, for a solid economic base. Rashi (Leviticus 14:34) indicates otherwise. The Israelites were intended to break down the Canaanite and Amorite walls, and they would find the gold that was there. In the teeming, burgeoning American Jewish community there were strong individuals who stood firm against the money-centered goals and values of the environment. Those goals and values were perhaps mighty as a wall in their milieu. In their homes they smashed those "ideals" and raised their families on Torah and *mitzvoth* instead. And they found their "gold"; they discovered their way to a livelihood and a firm economic base. But above all, they found the spiritual treasure of a life rich in meaning and lasting worth.

From such pioneers who went against the mainstream came the Rabbi Jacob Joseph School on the Lower East Side of New York, the first Torah day school for the young. Other *yeshivoth* followed, to provide authentic, lasting Jewish education from the elementary to the university level — and Jewish life worthy the name was established on the American shore.

# THE CLAN THAT WAS DIFFERENT

EARLY IN THE CHAPTER WE noted that Jacob became determined to buy from Esau the rights of the firstborn son, because then it was the firstborn's duty and privilege to minister before the Almighty, offering up sacrifices at at a consecrated altar. Amongs the Hebrew in the wilderness, however, this sacred duty was given over to the *kohanim,* the lineal descendants of Aaron (in the male line). And so, when the Sanctuary stood in Jerusalem of old, in its holiness and splendor, only they might minister there.

Yet it couldn't be left to them to come when they chose. For then at one time there might be no *kohanim* there, and a week later they might be falling over one another in the congestion. התקינו נביאים הראשונים עשרים וארבע משמרות So the early prophets established twenty-four *mishmaroth,* "watches" (Mishnah, *Taanith* iv 2) — twenty-four divisions of the *kohanim,* by family groups or clans.

This was the rule that Solomon established anew when the *mishkan* (the Tabernacle) was replaced by the first Sanctuary (II Chronicles 8:14). And when our people returned with Ezra from the exile in Babylonia and built the second Temple, the Sages recount: Four *mishmaroth* [groups or watches of *kohanim*] came up from the [Babylonian] exile (Ezra 2:36–39)... Then the prophets among them arose and divided them into twenty-four (TB *Taanith* 27a-b), since their number, like the population, grew. And Scripture bears this out (I Chronicles 24:1–18).

This, then, was the arrangement at the Sanctuary: the twenty-four clans served each a week at a time (in a set order) twice a year, the "changing of the guard" always taking place on the Sabbath. At the three annual pilgrimage festivals, though, when the entire male population had to come, bringing offerings, every *mishmar* was needed, to handle the immense volume of work.[15]

On any ordinary Sabbath, then, one *mishmar* (family group, clan) of the *kohanim* arrived and one left. We therefore read in the Mishnah (at the end of tractate *Sukkah*): הנכנס נוטל שש והיוצא נוטל שש ... "The

167

*mishmar* entering would take six, and the one leaving would take six." In the previous chapter we mentioned that every Friday twelve loaves were baked at the Sanctuary, and on the Sabbath they were brought into the holy chamber and placed on the gold-covered table. They were the *leḥem ha-panim*, the "showbread" that the Torah ordained (Exodus 25:30, Leviticus 24:5–9). The loaves remained in the holy chamber till the next Sabbath, when they had to be taken out to make room for the new batch. But (as noted in the last chapter) the old loaves were then always as fresh as when they had been brought. So the Mishnah tells us that they were divided between the old *mishmar* and the new one: six to each.

הַנִּכְנָסִין חוֹלְקִין בַּצָּפוֹן, וְהַיּוֹצְאִין בַּדָּרוֹם

"Those entering (the Mishnah continues) divided them [among themselves] at the north, and those leaving, at the south." Once a clan received its six loaves, it divided them into pieces and shared them out among the members, as each was entitled to a piece of the hallowed, blessed bread. But the new clan, that just came, did this at the northern part of the Temple forecourt, while the old clan, about to leave, did so at the southern end.

What was the reason for that? One Sage in the Jerusalem Talmud (*Sukkah* v 8) explains that it was to honor the incoming *mishmar*. As the commentary *Korban haEdah* notes, the northern part was where קדשי קדשים the most holy sacrifices had to be ritually slain; hence it was a distinguished area at the Sanctuary. But another Sage differs: Is was only (he says) because whoever entered went to the right, circled around, and went out from the left side (TJ *ibid.*). The entrance to the Temple Mount was east of the altar (as *Korban haEdah* notes); so turning to the right, a person would head north. The Tosefta explains that they went north because that was close to their place of work (*Sukkah* iv 25) — where the most holy offerings were ritually slain. But at any rate, as the Babylonian Talmud remarks, this system made it clear to all that this *mishmar* was coming, and that one was going (TB *Sukkah* 56b).[16]

But, says the Mishnah, there was an exception to the rule: בלגה לעולם חולקת בדרום "Bilgah always divided it up in the southern part." Even on a Saturday when it arrived, the clan of Bilgah, listed in Scripture as one of the twenty-four (I Chronicles 24:14), shared out its six loaves of showbread among the members at the southern end — so that, as the Tosefta notes (*Sukkah* iv 28), this *mishmar* always seemed to be leaving, never arriving.

168

And, says the Mishnah, there were peculiar things about that clan: וטבעתה קבועה "its ring was fastened down." Set in the pavement north of the altar, where the *kohanim* ritually slew the animal offerings, there were twenty-four rings (evidently pieces of curved metal or wood, described in the Jerusalem Talmud as "wide below and narrow above") — one for each *mishmar*. To keep an animal from moving and being injured instead of ritually slain, the ring would be turned to enclose the creature's neck and hold it securely in place (Tosefta, *Sukkah* iv 26).

The ring for the *mishmar* of Bilgah, however, was fastened down. It couldn't move. When that clan had to serve at the Sanctuary for a week, the men had to ask another *mishmar* if they might please use its ring.[17]

וחלונה סתומה "And," the Mishnah concludes, "its niche was blocked up." Every *mishmar* had a cubbyhole, a niche or container, where the members kept the garments that a *kohen* had to wear when he served at the Sanctuary (so Rambam's Mishnah commentary); and there they kept their knives[18] — which always had to be razor-sharp and free of the slightest nick or flaw in the cutting edge. So every other *mishmar* kept its special clothes and instruments locked up when it wasn't there. Not so the clan of Bilgah, however. Their niche or cubbyhole was blocked up, unusable. They had to carry everything with them.

Why this severe discrimination against one *mishmar* out of the twenty-four? Did those *kohanim* have bad manners or a bad odor, or something? — The Talmud gives the answer:

תָּנוּ רַבָּנָן: מַעֲשֶׂה בְּמִרְיָם בַּת בִּלְגָּה שֶׁנִּשְׁתַּמְּדָה וְהָלְכָה וְנִשֵּׂאת לְסַרְדְּיוֹט אֶחָד מִמַּלְכֵי יְוָנִים. וּכְשֶׁנִּכְנְסוּ יְוָנִים לַהֵיכָל הָלְכָה וְטָפְחָה בְּסַנְדָּלָהּ עַל גַּבֵּי הַמִּזְבֵּחַ וְאָמְרָה "לוּקוֹס לוּקוֹס: אַתָּה מְכַלֶּה מָמוֹנָן שֶׁל יִשְׂרָאֵל, וְאֵי אַתָּה עוֹמֵד לָהֶן בִּשְׁעַת דָּחֳקָן!״ וּכְשֶׁשָּׁמְעוּ חֲכָמִים בַּדָּבָר, שָׁלְחוּ וְקָבְעוּ אֶת טַבַּעְתָּהּ וְסָתְמוּ אֶת חַלּוֹנָהּ. (בבלי סוכה נו ב, ד״ס)

Our Sages taught: It happened that Miriam the daughter of Bilgah[19] became an apostate from the Jewish faith, and she went and married a military officer of the royal Greek rulers. When the Greeks entered the Sanctuary, she went and beat the altar with her sandal, exclaiming, "You wolf, wolf! You consume the property of the Jews, but you do not stand by them when they are sore-pressed!" When the Sages learned of the matter, they sent and shut down its [the clan's] ring and blocked up its niche (TB *Sukkah* 56b).

A girl named Miriam cast off all traces of her people's religion and converted to the Greek faith, with its culture and its pantheon of gods.

169

Her heart was taken by an army officer of the Syrian-Greek empire, and she married him. Then came the year 168 BCE. Antiochus Epiphanes was foisting his Greek religion ever more harshly on the Jews in Israel; and at last his army tramped headlong into the *béth ha-mikdash,* the Sanctuary itself, to set up a Greek idol there. Prominent among those soldiers marched Miriam's high-ranking husband, undoubtedly resplendent in his uniform. And with him came Miriam, into the Sanctuary, where her own people would never allow her past the women's forecourt (*ezrath nashim*), all excited and triumphant now to be on the side of the victors and not among the victims.

*Slap, slap, slap,* went her sandals on the pavement. And then she was slapping the altar with a sandal — the altar where animal sacrifices beyond number had been offered up reverently to the Almighty in response to His will, that the Torah taught. It was a deeply shaming form of punishment to slap someone with a sandal. The Greeks used it on children who needed disciplining. As it were, Miriam was thus telling the altar, "You bad bad boy!"[21] But her words had a much sharper sting: "*Lukos, lukos!*" she cried — the Greek word for wolf. And she hurled her accusation: the altar could only burn up and ruin good Jewish money, and it could not give the people the protection which in her belief a Greek god could give, when the people were in dire trouble.

The year was 168 BCE. From a spark of rebellion in the village of Modiin, the Maccabees organized and fought back. In time the Greek Syrians were driven out; the idol was removed from the Sanctuary; it was completely cleansed and dedicated anew. From then on we had a new holiday, Ḥanukkah, to celebrate every year. And the twenty-four *mishmaroth* of *kohanim* came again to the Sanctuary, each to serve a week, twice a year.[22]

But there was a difference now. Once the Sages learned about Miriam's "performance" at the altar, they made it impossible for the clan of Bilgah to use its ring or its niche any more; and the clan was ordered to share out its loaves of showbread at the southern end of the forecourt when it arrived, not at the northern end.

At this point we could expect any Jewish liberal reading this to rise up in outrage against the "establishment" of the Sages: How could they punish a whole group with such humiliation for what one individual happened to do?

170

Well, the Talmud itself asks the question: "On account of her, because she sinned, we penalized the entire *mishmar*?" — Said Abbaye: Indeed yes. As the saying goes,[23] the prattle of a child in the street is either from its father or from its mother (TB *Sukkah* 56b).[20]

When Bilgah's daughter Miriam set off on her path in life, scorning the Jewish faith and marrying out of it; when she showed her ingrained attitude at the altar in the Sanctuary — it wasn't the reasoned philosophy and measured conclusion of mature thought. It was a strong emotion-laden view that could only have taken root in childhood. Where could a little girl learn to feel so scornful and think so critically about her people's sacred faith and the altar of our Almighty God, where her own father ministered? The seeds could only have been planted and watered by a parent at home. And when she grew up, these attitudes and thoughts "flowered" and bore their bitter fruit.

Still the logical Talmud isn't satisfied: Very well, we grant that her parents were at fault. "But then, because of her father and mother, we penalize the whole *mishmar*?" — Said Abbaye: אוי לרשע ואוי לשכנו Woe to the wicked man and woe to his neighbor! (TB *ibid.*).

The parents didn't live in a vacuum. A *mishmar* was a clan. Linked by kinship, the families quite certainly lived in one area. They were bound to share attitudes, ideas, views of life. . . .

You see, Miriam's father couldn't really have been irreligious. Had he violated the Sabbath or eaten ham, the other members of the *mishmar* would surely have reported him. There is a firm rule in the Talmud: כל כהן שאינו מודה בעבודה אין לו חלק בכהונה Any *kohen* who did not accept and acknowledge the Temple service [as a sacred essential Divine worship] could have no share in the duties and privileges of a *kohen* (TB Ḥullin 132b). Had Bilgah turned bad outright and his *mishmar* connived to conceal it, all would have been "drummed out of the service." That clan could not have continued serving at the Sanctuary.

Miriam's father Bilgah was surely a good, upstanding member of the clan. Only, something must have crept into his behavior, his thinking and point of view. Perhaps he had dinner once at a gathering where a Greek Syrian officer attended. And then at home he praised the man: such elegance, such suave polish, so cultured a gentleman. And as a result, maybe he came to admire Greek philosophy and wisdom, poetry and art.

He would not have been the only one thinking and feeling like that. It was the period before the revolt of the Ḥashmonaim (led by Judah the

171

Maccabee). Many in Israel became *mithyavnim* then, in love with everything Greek. Eventually a Greek-style stadium was built in Jerusalem, opposite the Sanctuary, for Greek-style sports.[24]

It's not hard to have your head turned by an invitation to join the mighty, the successful of another people. How often has an American Jew felt deeply gratified and dazzled to be invited to golf with a famous general or with corporation executives at an exclusive country club. In all likelihood Miriam's father had his head turned similarly — if not 180 degrees, at least 30 degrees.

Letting our imagination run on, we can see him regaling his family with details of the fine Greek-Syrian officer he met, and how fascinating Greek culture was. And his little daughter Miriam drank it all in, in rapt wide-eyed attention.

What was the next step? — quite likely letting dear little Miriam get an education in that wonderful Greek culture: Let her learn that beautiful language, whose cadences made such lyric poetry. Let her learn Greek song, Greek dance, and the famed philosophy that ultimately left us the legacy of Socrates, Plato and Aristotle.

No, Bilgah didn't violate any laws of the Torah. When his *mishmar* went on duty at the Sanctuary, he was always there to serve properly for the week. Only, the further fields of Greek Syria looked greener. So by comparison the native fields looked sere: yellowing a bit, perhaps, and sickly with age. When the time came to go again for a week at the Temple, there might have been a *krechtz* (midway between a sigh and a groan): "Here I go again: same old routine: just offerings and sacrifices all day, one after another. You know? that altar is almost like a wolf. It just keeps devouring animals, with never a stop!"

At that point Miriam's mother might have chimed in, "It is true. Just think: A man vows to be a *nazir*. He doesn't drink wine or cut his hair for thirty days. Then he has to bring an offering. If someone does the slightest sin unintentionally, he has to bring an offering. There is no end to it. It is a shame the way that altar just robs the poor Israelites of all that good, precious livestock. As if many of them were not poor enough already!"

"And you know?" Bilgah might well have rejoined (like a Greek antiphonal chorus), "I don't see where that altar gives anything in return. I don't see where it protected us particualry in the past, when we were threatened or attacked. We just serve it blindly!"

172

Oh yes: he went to the Sanctuary and served when he had to, but not happily. The Psalmist hymns, עבדו את ה' בשמחה *Serve the Lord with joy* (Psalms 100:2). But this message never reached Bilgah. His heart was taken with Greek culture. . . . So his daughter's heart went that way too. She evidently learned her Greek lessons well. And eventually she married a Greek-Syrian martial officer — just the kind her father might have admired when she was a little girl. And she learned the Greek language so well that when she marched up to the altar at last and slapped it with her sandal, she burst out not in her native Hebrew but in her polished, cultured Greek, that she adopted for its elegance. "*Lukos, lukos!*" she cried — the Greek word for wolf.

Centuries afterward in Babylonia, as the later Sages of the Talmud considered the incident, Abbaye perceived immediately that Miriam's action was simply the result of her parent's influence. (Similarly, present-day psychologists have found that when children commit crimes, they are generally acting out the suppressed hostilities and frustrations of the parents.) At the very least, Miriam's father had a splendid lack of enthusiasm for his service at the Sanctuary. Had he loved his Divine duty and found deep meaning and satisfaction in it, his daughter could never have turned out as she did.

But, said Abbaye, Bilgah didn't live alone. He lived with the rest of his *mishmar;* and he was evidently an "influential" (to borrow a term from Madison Avenue) who cast his influence on his fellow-*kohanim*. Had the others been *tzaddikim,* truly pious, he would have given up his Greek-loving views, and Miriam would have lived a different life. One way or another, the whole *mishmar* developed something of his attitude.

How do we know? There is another passage in the Talmud, from the time of the Mishnah, that gives an alternative reason for the strong penalty mposed on the clan of Bilgah:

וְיֵשׁ אוֹמְרִים מִשְׁמַרְתָּהּ שֶׁהָיְתָה לָבוֹא, וְנִכְנַס יְשֶׁבְאָב אָחִיו וְשִׁמֵּשׁ תַּחְתָּיו.

iSome say the *mishmar* once tarried and failed to come on time, and its fellow-*mishmar* Yeshevav came in and served in its place (TB *Sukkah* 56b).[20]

Every Sabbath the *mishmar* that was leaving offered up the daily *olah* (burnt-offering) of the morning, and the incoming *mishmar* offered up the daily *olah* of the late afternoon. Well, one Sabbath when the clan of Bilgah was to arrive, the time came for the afternoon *olah,* and there was no sign of the new *mishmar*. So the outgoing *mishmar,* Yeshevav (which always

173

served the week before Bilgah) stayed on to bring the afternoon *olah*, and then remained all week,[25] in place of the late clan of Bilgah.

In psychoanalytic theory, lateness indicates resistance. People come late because some part of them would rather not come at all. Our Sages understood this quite well. They "got the message" that the *mishmar* of Bilgah thus sent. For ordinarily, says the Talmud, כהנים זריזין הן the *kohanim* were alert and efficient (TB *Shabbath* 20a). They had to be, to do everything properly when they served at the Sanctuary. Then here, as Rashi puts it, "it was obvious that they did not cherish this Divine service."

One scholar astutely notes[21] that both incidents (the clan's lateness and Miriam's act at the altar) must have happened in the same period in our people's history. Hence the Sages couldn't recall later which of the two was the specific cause that brought the penalty down on the *mishmar*. But whichever was the main cause, both surely helped the Sages reach their decision. For in effect, what did the penalty mean? From then on, when the *mishmar* of Bilgah arrived they went at once to the southern end, so that they should seem to be leaving instead of just arriving.[26] As one commentary notes,[27] it was a way of showing that even when they came they were only fit to leave. As it were, they were always given a tacit message on arrival: "We wish you could go home. Who really needs you here?" And the thought was reinforced when they found their ring (to use in ritual slaying) fastened down, and their niche (for storing clothes and knives) blocked up.[28] They were thus reminded that had it lain in the Sages' power to remove one of the twenty-four *mishmaroth* completely, they would indeed have been "retired" from their duties.

Surely there lies some small lesson in this for the American Jewish parent in his home. How important it is to measure our every word in the presence of sensitive, impressionable children. As the common saying went in Abbaye's time, "the prattle of children in the street comes either from the father or from the mother." We little realize how easily and drastically we can shape lasting ideas in our children's minds.

But better than watching our words, it is far healthier to develop sound, decent attitudes toward our age-old faith. When an appeal is made in the synagogue for a yeshiva, a Torah day school, don't yield to a momentary impulse to say afterward at home, "Those appeals just keep eating up our money. That school is always short of funds for something. Why, they're just like ravenous wolves." Bear in mind that if a day school is short of funds, it's because it is doing its job honestly, properly, with integrity. When a *m'shulaḥ* comes — a distinguished scholarly visitor — to ask for a contribution for an academy of advanced Talmudic study, don't say, "There's just no end to them. They simply keep coming. And every Saturday there's another appeal at the synagogue."

It is easy enough to echo the outcry of Bilgah's daughter Miriam at the altar: "*Lukos, lukos* — wolf, wolf! How long will you go on devouring the property of the Jews?" The altar might have seemed to be doing just that, requiring an endless stream of animal offerings. Yet in every age, from Moses to the Sages of the time of the second Temple, our great prophets and leaders knew that the Divine ritual at the altar gave far more than it took — bringing Divine forgiveness, protection and blessing.

Bilgah's daughter Miriam exclaimed also that the altar didn't stand by the Jewish people when they were sore-pressed and beset by troubles. This is a theme that many have repeated in bitter words of their own, through the great calamities and nightmares our people have known. We might be tempted to complain similarly, "What do we get for all our charity, for all we do and give for our faith?" Yet our faith has sustained our people through every age and every vicissitude. And it goes on maintaining our existence. Whether we can see it or not, Heaven rewards every good deed and act of faith.

So before we hastily say anything like the outcry of Bilgah's daughter, let us stop and think about the charity asked of us. First, be thankful that you have the opportunity and the means to give. Remember that in Heaven's accounts they don't honor bank balances but only receipts — for generous donations. Secondly, if you give in good cheer, you inculcate valuable attitudes in your children. They will learn to follow in your blessed ways. And thirdly, when we support Torah study, we maintain what our people needs most vitally and crucially for its spiritual survival.

## WHEN THE LIGHTS
## ARE EXTINGUISHED

As FRIDAY EVENING COMES and dusk is changed to nightfall, we welcome the holy Sabbath with prayer. After *l'chah dodi* and *mizmor shir l'yom ha-shabbath* (*A psalm, a song for the Sabbath day* — Psalms 92), etc. before we begin the main part of the service with ברכו (Bless the Lord, who is blessed), in the Ashkenaz rite there is an entire chapter of the Mishnah (*Shabbath* ii) that we say, so as to prepare for the main prayer with a bit of Torah learning. Beginning with the words במה מדליקין ובמה אין מדליקין (With what may we light, and with what may we not light, the Sabbath lamp) the chapter goes on to deal with the various laws about the light (for example, candles or an oil lamp) that is kindled before Friday evening to honor the holy Sabbath. One interesting paragraph reads:

הַמְכַבֶּה אֶת הַנֵּר מִפְּנֵי שֶׁהוּא מִתְיָרֵא מִפְּנֵי גוֹיִם, מִפְּנֵי לִסְטִים, מִפְּנֵי רוּחַ רָעָה, אוֹ בִּשְׁבִיל הַחוֹלֶה שֶׁיִּישָׁן – פָּטוּר. כְּחָס עַל הַנֵּר, כְּחָס עַל הַשֶּׁמֶן, כְּחָס עַל הַפְּתִילָה – חַיָּב. (משנה שבת ב ה)

If someone puts out the [Sabbath] lamp because he is afraid of Gentiles, robbers, or an evil (nervous) seizure, or for the sake of a sick person, so that he will sleep — he is free of any guilt. But if [he does it] so as to spare (save) the lamp, the oil or the wick, he is guilty [of violating the Sabbath] (Mishnah, *Shabbath* ii 5).

Today the observant Jewish homemaker generally lights candles in honor of the Sabbath; but at the time of the Mishnah oil lamps with wicks were used, and they shed a bright light.

Well, suppose, says the Mishnah, that on Friday night a man puts out his Sabbath lamp for fear of Gentiles; and Rashi explains: for example, the Persians had a religious holiday when they would allow light to burn after dark only in their idolatrous temple. Or, says the Mishnah, the man fears robbers: Violent outlaws might see the light from afar and be drawn to attack. Or else perhaps someone in the house suffers from a nervous disorder and light disturbs him. Rambam notes in his commentary that the

Mishnah means an illness called melancholia, in which a person loses control and becomes agitated when he sees a bright light or finds himself in company. He needs darkness and isolation to find a healing calm and tranquility.

Again, says the Mishnah, a man may put out the Sabbath lamp to let a sick person, critically ill, find restful healing sleep; for without sleep his life may be in danger; and the patient cannot be moved elsewhere, nor can the light be blocked.

In all these cases, says the Mishnah, there is no guilt for violating the Sabbath. (And Rambam notes that right from the start, initially, the Sabbath lamp may be extinguished in such cases, because danger to life is involved, and this is the sole reason for putting it out.) But should the main purpose be to save the lamp (because, as Rashi says, he sees it is getting spoiled; or, as Me'iri explains, with the oil almost gone he fears the lamp may crack) or he wants to save the oil or the wick — that is a violation of the Sabbath.

Isn't it strange, though, that we say this every Friday evening at prayer? After all, today we generally don't light oil lamps for the Sabbath; and the exact problems in this text aren't likely to occur nowadays. . . . Yet consider the times we have lived through and known, and you will see how meaningful the passage is.

The original text was actually המכבה את הנר מפני שהוא מתירא מפני גוים "If someone puts out the lamp because he is afraid of Gentiles." Under the impact of Gentiles looking over our shoulder and the censors they appointed, it was changed long ago to read מפני עכו״ם "because he is afraid of worshippers of stars and heavenly constellations." They wanted to make sure the Mishnah wouldn't mean them. But the change changed nothing for our people. It still meant a fear of people with other religions — and they gave us reason enough to fear them.

A certain religion took control of 15th century Spain, and the Inquisition burned Jews at the stake, to "save their souls," because it was a "religion of love." Others were hung by their thumbs and left to die in agony, at the express orders of bishops whose hearts were filled with the "love" that informed their theology.

So the Sabbath lights were put out. Thousands who couldn't make the supreme sacrifice at the stake became Marranos. Officially they converted to the faith of the "loving" bishops; and no Sabbath lights ever appeared again at their windows. They didn't dare show the slightest adherence to the Jewish faith. Only in secret cellar rooms, safe from prying eyes, they still observed the Sabbath and kept the *mitzvoth*. Yet time did its work of erosion. As the generations continued, the neighbors' "loving" faith was accepted more and more, and the secret practices of authentic Judaism slipped away from memory. In countless families the Sabbath candles went out for good.

(Of course, in our time there has been much talk of ecumenism and dialogue and bridges of understanding. The descendants of those whose hands applied mortal torture and death by fire now stretch out their hands to welcome us — in the framework of the same neighborly "religion of love." They even offer us forgiveness for the great murder we are supposed to have committed, on the founder of their faith — a murder that remains an unfounded, unproven aberrant claim of theirs. Only a few honest individuals among them recognize the documented, indisputable murders in their annals, that added grisly chapters to our martyrology, which really wait for atonement and forgiveness.)

In one country after another in the Middle Ages (and afterward), credulous neighbors, filled with superstition and half-baked ideas and rumors, hurled blood accusations at us — that our people slew Gentile children and used the blood in baking matzoth for Passover. On the strength of those wild accusations too, Sabbath lights went out. Countless Jews were tortured and put to death. Homes, entire districts, were destroyed in pogroms that ensued. And whole communities were sometimes expelled from a city, a province or a country.

There was good reason to beware of "robbers" also: not to show any lights in the window that might attract their attention. In the Middle Ages and afterward, if Jews gave their neighbors any reason to think they found some glow of peace and comfort in their homes, they were the target of envy and greed. So many trades and skills were barred to our people, while heavy taxes of every kind were imposed, to extract every last bit of possible income for the treasuries of the noblemen on whose land our people lived.

When that wasn't enough, a nobleman would simply kidnap a venerable scholar, the religious head of a Jewish community, and keep him imprisoned till his community paid the required ransom for him. When the scheme worked and then the nobleman ran short of money again, he would simply kidnap the venerable sage again. Thus it was that R. Meir of Rothenburg finally forbade his loyal followers to pay any more ransom for him, and he died in a medieval German dungeon.[29] And his disciple, R. Asher

b. Yeḥiél (the Rosh), fearing the same "preferential treatment" when he became head of the Jewish community, fled to Spain.

No, it was best to put out the Sabbath lamp and live in the dark, "for fear of Gentiles, for fear of robbers." Our people learned to live unobtrusively. In fact, about the time of Passover they wouldn't dare show their faces at all, even on the ghetto streets. A religious holiday generally came then for their neighbors, and priests and bishops filled with "love" would inflame their parishioners with passionate vicious hate against the Jews.[30] So we learned to live discreetly, to attract as little attention as possible. Yet that didn't spare the Jewish communities in France and Germany the "special attention" of the Crusaders, who attained glory for their devout cause by slaughtering and massacring helpless men, women and children merely by the way, as they passed by on their journey to their holy wars.

If you ever have the privilege to see a whole community or neighborhood with candles in the windows of a Friday evening, the sight is beautiful. I saw this in a Jewish neighborhood in Havana, Cuba, back in 1927. You can find it in Jerusalem now, in the section called *Mé'ah She'arim.* You walk through the old narrow streets, and candles (or little oil lamps) cast their gentle glow through the windows; and the effect is magical. It is as though you have wandered into a bit of *gan éden,* paradise, left by mistake in a forgotten part of the earth. You get a momentary prevision of the kingdom of Heaven on earth, in exquisite tranquility.

All is quiet and peaceful. You can feel the angels hovering in the air, who accompany every Jew on Friday evening from the synagogue to his home (TB *Shabbath* 119b).

Yet we read in the Mishnah, "If someone puts out the lamp because he is afraid of Gentiles, robbers, or רוּח רעה an evil wind of derangement..." The Nazis came to power in Germany in the thirties, and the lights went out for our people — for all three reasons. They were Gentiles, of a special kind. Aryans, they called themserlves, flying bravely in the face of scientific fact — and therefore superior; while the Jews (they said) were too inferior to live. So if Jews didn't put out their own Sabbath lights and flee the country, "heroic" storm-troopers were ready to smash their windows and put out the lights for them. And certainly the Nazis earned membership in any union of robbers, bandits and outlaws, as they seized Jewish property freely, under convenient "laws" of their own

179

making. As for רוח רעה "an evil spirit" of nervous disorder, how else would you describe their "spirit of the future"?

They moved across the pages of our history, and for six million of our brethren the lights were indeed extinguished, as the world moved on in silence.

Yet often enough it was more than Sabbath lamps that went out. כי נר מצוה ותורה אור *For a* mitzvah *is a lamp, and the Torah is light* (Proverbs 6:23). At times our physical existence wasn't threatened directly; we could live safe and sound. Only, it was forbidden to study Torah and observe its sacred precepts. When ancient Rome ruled in cruelty over Israel, such restrictions wers imposed. So we read in the Midrash of defiant Jews going bravely to their punishment:

מַה לְּךָ יוֹצֵא לֵיהָרֵג [לְסָקֵל]? עַל שֶׁמַּלְתִּי אֶת בְּנִי. מַה לְּךָ יוֹצֵא לְשָׂרֵף? עַל שֶׁקָּרָאתִי בַּתּוֹרָה [שֶׁשָּׁמַרְתִּי אֶת הַשַּׁבָּת]. מַה לְּךָ יוֹצֵא לִצָּלֵב [לֵיהָרֵג]? עַל שֶׁאָכַלְתִּי הַמַּצָּה. מַה לְּךָ לוֹקֶה מֵאָה פַּרְגּוֹל? [עַל שֶׁעָשִׂיתִי סֻכָּה] עַל שֶׁנָּטַלְתִּי לוּלָב [עַל שֶׁהִנַּחְתִּי תְּפִלִּין... עַל שֶׁעָשִׂיתִי רְצוֹן אָבִי שֶׁבַּשָּׁמַיִם]. (מכילתא, בחודש ו) [ויקרא רבה לב א]

"Why are you going forth to be executed?" one was asked. "Because I circumcised my son," was the reply. "Why are you being taken to be burnt at the stake?" another was asked. "Because I studied the Torah," he replied [or, "Because I observed the Sabbath"]. "Why are you going forth to be crucified?" a third was asked. "Because I ate *matzah* [on Passover]" said he. "Why are you being taken to be scourged with 100 lashes of the whip?" they asked others. And the replies came: "Because I built a *sukkah*, or took up a *lulav* [and *ethrog*, at the festival of *Sukkoth*]; because I put on *t'fillin* . . . because I did the will of my Father in heaven" (*Mechilta, bahodesh* 6) [*Vayikra Rabbah* 32, 1].

In the Europe of the Middle Ages they were more subtle. They took our sacred volumes of Talmud and Torah learning, gathered them in the public square, and set fire to everything.[31] So there were times when it was extremely difficult, if not impossible, to study Torah. Yet our people persevered. Through the centuries Torah study continued, and even thrived. In the years of the Nazis and the Second World War, entire *yeshivoth,* academies of Torah learning, were moved across oceans and countries; and for a while Torah study flourished in Shanghai.

But it remained for Stalin to prove that history can repeat itself. Just as in ancient Israel under Roman rule, the Jews in the Soviet Union found their age-old faith utterly restricted. Every Jewish school of any kind was shut down. Synagogues by the dozens were closed (many being converted to "clubs" where good Soviet citizens could drink vodka and give free rein to their alcohol-inspired imagination about the "nefarious activities" of Jews in the synagogues). With synagogues closed, rabbis were left "unemployed"; and many of them were sent to Siberia. (There is always plenty of work in Siberia, in the slave-labor camps, from which most people never return.)

Circumicision in the Soviet Union was declared a "primitive barbaric rite"; and a *mohel* was likely to go to Siberia if he was caught entering a child into the Covenant of Abraham. Our age-old religion in general was declared "counter-revolutionary." If it became known that someone kept the Sabbath or taught his children Torah, the secret police (KGB) would take a "special interest" in him. If he wasn't despatched to Siberia (for no particular reason) they found ways of dealing with him (for instance, calling him frequently for questioning, always unexpectedly and always in the early hours of the morning) — ways that were guaranteed to shorten his life.

Once more the light of authentic Judaism went out מפני גוים, מפני רעה מפני רוח רעה, מפני לסטים, for fear of Gentiles, robbers, and an "evil wind" — the foul spirit of communist ideology that declared all religion to be "the opium of the masses." It brought our people in the USSR to so pathetic a level of ignorance that few even knew the sentence of שמע ישׂראל (*Hear, O Israel: the Lord is our God, the Lord is one*) — the fundamental affirmation of Jewish faith.

And so, says the Mishnah, there are times in our history when the Sabbath light is put out in Jewish homes — when the illumination of the Torah and its sacred commandments is darkened. And we are פטור free of any guilt or blame. For Torah study, Sabbath observance, *kashruth*, even prayer, have all become impossible. There is nothing we can do then but survive till our way of faith can flourish again.

It is then בשביל החולה שיׁשן "for the sake of a sick person, that he should sleep." At such a time the Jewish spirit is in a sick situation, and it must be left to slumber. And as we read in Scripture, אני ישׁנה ולבי ער, *I am asleep, but my heart is awake* (Song of Songs 5:2) — waiting for a chance to return to our heritage.

But, says the Mishnah, sometimes a person puts out the Sabbath lamp simply to economize: כחס על הנר, כחס על השׁמן, כחס על הפתילה Why let the

181

lamp burn needlessly and get spoiled? Why waste oil or the wick? Then, says the Mishnah, he is guilty of violating the Sabbath.

At times a person decides observant Judaism is too "expensive": He can make more money operating his factory on the Sabbath also. Why have kosher meat, if it costs more? And why send his son to a good Torah day school, when it will cost him 500 dollars a year? Moreover, think of all he can save if he makes no response to any appeals in his community for the institutions that keep the Torah alive, and the institutions of humane charity and compassion. Perhaps he is good at accounting, and he can show you figures, black on white.

*Nu,* if we read the words of our Sages, we need not be impressed. Note that the Mishnah says כחס על הנר, כחס על השמן, כחס על הפתילה which means literally, "It is as though he saves on the lamp, the oil or the wick." It does not say חס על הנר וכו׳ "If he saves on the lamp," etc. It only seems to him that he gains something. He can go along for months, even years, feeling quite proud of his "economies", and suddenly an illness in the family or an audit by a government tax agency can take from him all he ever "saved" and more. . . . Heaven has its own way of balancing budgets and settling accounts.

Note the certainty in this Talmudic passage: R. Taḥlifa . . . taught: The entire income of a man[32] is allotted to him [by Heaven] from one *Rosh haShanah* (beginning of the year) to the next, except for his expenditures for the Sabbath and the festivals (*yom tov*), and for the Torah education of his children: If he spends less [for these purposes] he is given less; if he spends more, he is given more (TB *Bétzah* 16a).[33]

At *Rosh haShanah,* when a new year begins by our traditional reckoning, Heaven determines its allotment for each and every one: how much he will earn till the next *Rosh haShanah*. If we're extravagant, we have to bear the hardship when we run short. But for expenses to celebrate the Sabbath and festivals properly, as the Torah prescribes, and for educating our children in the Torah, the budget remains open: If we spend more, we get more.

So we have the abiding word of our Sages that if we spare no expense to make our home truly Jewish in faith, honoring the Sabbath as a holy day of rest, by the Torah's law — if we make the home a setting of spirituality that the Almighty can share with us — we won't lose by it. And this applies to a Torah education for the children as well, so that they can appreciate the home of holiness we make for them, and contribute to it.

Now, a proper amount for charity is included in Heaven's yearly allocation: There is a certain basic total that we are expected to give during the course of the year. The Almighty Himself tells us in Scripture, *do not harden your heart and do not shut your hand against your needy brother* (Deuteronomy 15:7). *You shall surely give to him, and let your heart not be grieved when you give to him; for on account of this the Lord your God will bless you in all your activities* (ibid. 10).[34]

Consider, furthermore, this most instructive story in the Midrash: R. Shimon b. Yoḥai went to sleep on a night of *Rosh haShanah,* and he saw in his dream that his sister's sons would be fined 600 *denarii* by the imperial government [of Rome, which ruled Israel]. He thereupon compelled them to become *parnasim,* managers of the communal charity [to provide for the poor]. "But whose money shall we spend" [to sustain the poor]?[35] they asked him. "Spend your own," he told them, "and write everything down [keep an exact account]. At the end of the year we will make a reckoning, and I will compensate you [for all you have spent]."

At the end of the year, slanderous false information was given [to the Roman government] that they were dealing [illegally] in bulky silk.[36] An aged official of the imperial government came then, and he told them, "Either you make a robe of royal purple (velvet) for the king, or you will be fined 600 *denarii*." Then he took them and put them in prison.

When R. Shimon b. Yoḥai learned of this, he went to see them. "How much did you spend?" he asked them — meaning on charity in the course of the year. "Here is the written account before you," they replied; "take it and read." He scanned the written record, and found that they had given out 600 *denarii* less six [that is, 594 *denarii*]. So he told them, "Give me six *denarii,* and I will get you out." In reply they scoffed, "Just come and look: That old official is demanding 600 *denarii* from us, and you say, 'Give me six and I will get you out'?" Said he to them, "Give me the six *denarii,* and let it be no worry of yours."

They took six *denarii* and gave them to him, and he [in turn] put them in the old official's hand as a bribe. At that the old man lowered his head and went away [leaving the priosners free to go]. When he was gone, they asked R. Shim'on b. Yoḥai, "Did you know perhaps [in advance] that we were going to be fined?" He replied, "As you live, since the night of *Rosh haShanah* I knew you were to be fined 600 *denarii.*"

"But," they protested, "had you told us, we would have given the six *denarii* also to charity" [and thus they would have been spared this whole trouble]. Said he, "Had I told you, you would not have believed me, and I would have had to pay for you" [the full 600 *denarii* as a fine, out of his own pocket].

It is written (the Midrash concludes) *Are you not to share out your bread to the hungry?* (Isaiah 58:7). If you merit [you give your charity] for the hunger of Jacob [Jewry's poor]; if not [you give it] for the fullness of Esau [the rich heathen] (*Va-yikra Rabbah* 34, 12–13).[37]

From the incident in the Midrash let us move ahead many centuries in time, to the home of a Jew in Berdychev, in Russia under the czars. The story is told that while the famed ḥassidic leader R. Lévi Yitzḥak was there visiting, a burly cossack came bursting in, and in a booming voice he shouted, *Yevrei, davai kushets* — "Hebrew, give food to eat!" Afraid that the powerful soldier might start smashing furniture, the Jew hastened to bring the best dishes he had, while R. Lévi Yitzḥak sat off in a corner, watching.

When the cossack had eaten his fill and left, R. Lévi Yitzḥak began musing aloud, with something of a Talmudic chant: "This whole thing is very odd. Four questions may be asked: (1) Why did the cossack have to come to you for food? He gets plenty to eat in his barracks. The czar feeds his soldiers well. (2) Why did he walk many miles to come to you, and to no one else? (3) Why did he address you as *Yevrei,* "Hebrew," a refined title? Why did he not say *Zhid,* the usual derogatory name they use for a Jew? (4) Why was he in such a rage?"

For a moment the noted ḥassidic rabbi thought in silence. Then he continued, "There can be only one answer: A poor Jew must have come here begging for food, and you turned him away. The prophet said firmly, וַהֲלוֹא פָרוֹס לָרָעֵב לַחְמֶךָ *Are you not to share out your bread to the hungry?* (Isaiah 58:7). If you refuse, there is an alternative: וַעֲנִיִּים מְרוּדִים תָּבִיא בָיִת *you will bring unruly, rebellious poor people to your home* (*ibid.*). If you don't give Jacob, you will have to give Esau. . . . This is why the cossack (a Russian, a descendant of Esau) came to your home and nowhere else — to collect what you owed the poor. This is why he did not eat his own good food in his barracks: he had to collect from you. And of course he was angry — that you troubled him to walk all the way here. Hence he said, *Yevrei davai kushets* — a Hebrew you should give food to eat — so that you won't have to bother with a cossack!"

It is human nature to try to save and economize. But we have to know when and where. Above all, let us not do it at the expense of the Torah and the faith it had given us. A young couple planning a home may think it wise to move to a non-religious neighborhood, where they can live as if the Torah doesn't mean them at all when it expresses the Almighty's will. Or they may believe naively that our authentic way of faith can be observed just as well there.

Remember what Abbaye said about Bilgah and his daughter Miriam: אוֹי לרשע ואוֹי לשכנו "Woe to the wicked and woe to his neighbor." Families in one vicinity exert an abiding influence on one another. If you see Sabbath candles glowing in the windows all about you, it is easy to light them in your home too. If there are good Torah day schools in the neighborhood, to which other children go, it will be easy to have your children go also. It can be a tragic mistake with lasting consequences to move to a neighborhood where it is hard to light the Sabbath candles, to kindle the glow of Torah and observant Judaism in the home (because it means sticking out like a sore thumb) — and then it is so easy for that flame to go out. A home in a soundly Jewish neighborhood, weekly Sabbath candles, a commitment to the Torah's way of life — these form a strong insurance policy against the tragedy of intermarriage and assimilation that now ravages American Jewry. Invest in it.

## INHERITANCE AND BETROTHAL

WHEN WE READ THE TORAH THROUGH EVERY YEAR AND STUDY IT, not only the chapters give us new insight and inspiration, and not only the sentences. At times the meaning in a word opens up a new point of view.

In the very last portion (*sidrah*) of the Five Books of Moses, we read תּוֹרה צוּה לנוּ משה מוֹרשה קהלּת יעקב *Moses commanded us the Torah, an inheritance of the community of Jacob* (Deuteronomy 33:4). The word מוֹרשה *morashah* is linked with the verb *yarash,* to inherit; so it means, properly, an

185

inheritance. Since our ancestors received the Torah at Sinai, each generation inherits it from the one before, to uphold it and transmit it to the next generation in turn. Thus the Torah has been rightly called our heritage.

Yet the Sages give it another meaning: אל תקרי מורשה אלא מאורשה Do not read it *morashah,* an inheritance, but *me'orasah,* betrothed. This teaches that the Torah is betrothed to Jewry (*Sifre,* Deuteronomy §345).

Our Sages are not given to playing word games by free association, just for the fun of it. Obviously they found the plain meaning here inadequate by itself, or possibly misleading. They wanted to drive home the point that the Torah is not merely something we inherit from our fathers and forefathers.

For how do people treat an inheritance? A man may be left a million dollars — and off he goes to Las Vegas to indulge at last his passion for gambling, a little "night life," and "a good time" generally. *Why not?* he thinks? What does he have to lose? — only money he received as a gift. He didn't have to work for it. Why not have "fun"? When gambling in Las Vegas palls, there are horses running in Florida — great excitement at the races. He has money to spend; and in the words of the popular saying, easy come, easy go.

The Torah is not an inheritance in this sense. If a person is born into the most pious, upstanding family of Talmudic scholars, there is no guarantee that he will necessarily be pious, moral and learned in turn. It will require effort and hard work of his own. He may be born with the most gifted mind and natural aptitude for Talmud study; under the influence of his home and family he may shine brilliantly as an עלוי, a young Talmudic genius. Yet he may grow up morally corrupt and squander his heritage, frittering away his talents and knowledge (as experience has sometimes tragically shown).

In fact, the Talmud asks: Why is it unusual for the sons of Torah scholars to turn out to be Torah scholars also? Said R. Yoséf: So that they should not say the Torah is an inheritance for them [and therefore, Rashi explains, they will feel no need to study it — since, as R. Nissim notes, they expect to "inherit" it]. . . . Ravina said: It is because they do not say a blessing over the Torah first (TB *N'darim* 81a). The sons of Torah scholars would feel no need to say a blessing first, to thank God for the Torah and be grateful for it. They would take it for granted.

*No,* say the Sages: the Torah is not merely מורשה an inheritance, to take for granted and squander. The *alef* is often a silent letter, appearing

186

unvoiced, unnoticed in a word. Assume an *alef* in this word; read it as מְאוֹרָשָׂה betrothed. It has this meaning too.

When a couple becomes engaged, the young man acquires responsiblity, not an inheritance to squander. He must buy a ring to make the engagement official. A home has to be acquired and furnished. And it means more than an initial investment. There will be weekly and monthly expenses, a wife and children to support, bills to pay. Of course, the rewards gained from a good marriage, a happy home life, as a fine family is raised, are beyond price. But it means a sober acceptance of life with responsibility.

This is what the Torah means to us: a lifelong commitment to maintain it in honor and dignity — to study it ourselves and obey it, and support the scholars who devote their lives to it. We are obligated to see to it that the Torah remains a vital living force.

And more: An inheritance, we noted, can be gloriously frittered away, till it all goes down the drain. But there is another way of treating an inheritance: A fine painting or art collection can be kept in a suitable setting at home, or donated to a museum. The paintings are preserved and cared for, and people come and admire. They may be impressed, even moved deeply. But as a rule their life then continues as before, in no way changed for the better.

Reform Judaism revels in thinking of Jewry as "the people of the Book." But a precious book received and treated as an inheritance, as an heirloom, can mean no more to us than a Rembrandt in a museum. There are rich men in the world with fine libraries in their homes. The shelves are lined with complete sets of Shakespeare, Scott, Tennyson, Dickens, and so forth, all bound in the finest tooled leather. Fine heirlooms indeed — but those books have never made anyone particularly moral, kindly or devout.

In the New York Public Library at Fifth Avenue and 42nd Street, you can even find a Bible treated with reverence. In the Rare Book Room is a Latin Bible printed by Gutenberg in the 15th century, one of the few perfect copies in the world. It is kept in a glass case. Every morning an attendant opens the case and turns the page; that is the best way to keep the volume in good condition. But the words in that book of Scripture speak to no one.

Manuscripts of parts of our *tanach,* our Hebrew Bible, were found in the Qumran caves in the land of Israel, and judged to be about 2,000 years old. At the Israel Museum in Jerusalem a special building was constructed to house those leaves and fragments, a building with a roof like an over-turned saucer. A host of scholars and experts have studied and written about those fragments and leaves, creating a small mountain of literature. So far,

187

though, the discoveries at Qumran have brought new faith to no one. Even a pair of *t'fillin* was found there; but it hasn't particularly moved anyone to put on *t'fillin* every morning and pray.[38]

At the Metropolitan Museum of Art we can stand in awe before priceless relics from ancient Egypt and Greece. All are the heirlooms of mankind, telling of ancient cultures with their beliefs and thoughts, dreams and hopes. Yet how far can they influence us? In the school that turns out Conservative "rabbis" there is a beautiful *aron kodesh* (holy ark) in the room used as a synagogue, where the students pray on the Sabbath. Several hundred years old, it was brought there from a faraway land. Yet it has not deterred the students from going out to congregations and making a travesty of the synagogue and the Sabbath, by the norms of historic *k'lal yisraél* — by having mixed seating and encouraging the use of the car to come to services.

Again, heirlooms are precious objects, meant to last for generations, to be kept and treasured. The only trouble is that one man's impressiveness may be another's boredom. One man's heirloom may be another's worthless thing that wastes needed space. One day I may bring home my departed grandfather's tall old clock and place it lovingly against the wall in the living room. It is 100 years old, and holds nostalgic memories for me. I think it looks handsome there. Then my wife may walk in and ask, "Now why did you bring that piece of junk into the house?" And soon the "grandfather clock" will leave the living room, to hold its memories for me in the attic.

Mordecai M. Kaplan was a child prodigy. At eighteen he received *s'michah* (rabbinic ordination) in Eastern Russia. Then he came to America and read John Dewey; and he was never the same since. In his book *Judaism as a Civilization* he tried to convince me, the reader, that the reason why I wear *tzitzith* (ritual tassels or fringes at the corners of a *tallith katan,* a four-cornered grament) is that my father wore them, and his father before him. It was meant to be a learned book (by then Kaplan was a Doctor and a Professor), "reconstructing'" Judaism with a show of profundity. It fell just a little short of the truth.

You see, my father ate with a wooden spoon. Further back in the family line a forebear took his food perhaps from a circular (concave) depression hollowed out in a wooden table, chinaware being yet unknown. Thank Heaven, I use cutlery and china at my meals, and I can still observe authentic Judaism as the *shulḥan aruch* (code of Jewish religious law) details it.

188

However, were I to stop wearing a *tallith katan* with *tzitzith* at the corners, something vital would cerainly be lacking. The Torah specifically orders us to wear it so that *you shall see it and recall all the commandments of the Lord and observe them, and not go straying after your heart and eyes* (Numbers 15:39). It is a soldier's uniform, if you will, to keep me mindful of my duties and my restrictions as a member of the Almighty's spiritual army. Civilizations may come and civilizations may go, using knives, forks and spoons as they will (or not), and the pious Jew will yet wear his *tallith katan.*

Our Torah is indeed *morashah,* an inheritance, received from our fathers and forefathers. The word never loses it plain meaning.[39] There is an added pride and significance in wearing the *tallith katan* with the knowledge that all the preceding generations wore it too. We are a link in a chain of historic observance that began at Sinai.[40] But were it only a "quaint custom" bequeathed to us, we would merely have kept a few such garments, carefully preserved, in our "museum of Judaism."

The Yiddishists bequeathed their youth an inheritance: a wealth of Yiddish literature describing so lovingly their childhood world in Eastern Europe. It was all there: the Sabbath candles that mother lit with tears in her eyes and a prayer for her family on her lips; the *latkes* sizzling at Ḥanukkah, the *graggers* sounding on Purim, the stolen *afikoman* and Elijah's cup at the Passover *seder,* the green leaves gathered for Shavu'oth — the whole panorama of faith and observance, by such master writers as Peretz and Sholom Aleichem.

The result was a great big zero. The children fled the Yiddish schools and left the literature behind, to moulder. A handful of students take university courses in Yiddish, as a dead (or expiring) language. Yet in our Torah academies and religious communities, Yiddish continues as a living language among those who never read Peretz or Sholom Aleichem, because it is the vehicle of Torah study and an observant way of life.

How wisely our Sages said אל תקרי מורשה אלא מאורשה "Do not read it *morashah,* inheritance, but *me'orasah,* betrothed." When a young man falls in love with a girl and becomes engaged to her, wanting to marry her, it is not because she is an heirloom. He needs her. Without her something most important is missing from his life. And he certainly will not preserve her under glass. With Heaven's help they will build a life together and raise a family. Certainly they take along norms and values from the past, but they give those norms and values new life and vitality into a new generation, with their own belief and commitment.

189

We do not observe the Torah mechanically as a mouldering relic, dusting it dutifully every day. In *Sh'ma yisraél* we say, "And these words which I command you *today* shall be on your heart" (Deuteronomy 6:6); as one commentary aptly interprets: Let them be in your eyes as though new every day, as though you just received them today from Sinai.[41] It is God's gift to us — ever fresh, vital and new.

Every time a young man meets his betrothed, he feels happiness. He is ready to devote himself to making her happy. In the spiritual dimension this is how the devout Jew relates to the Torah. As we say in our evening prayer, the Torah and the *mitzvoth* are "our life and the length of our days." In a good marriage the two never take each other for granted, but remain always, in a sense, in their engagement. And so the Midrash asks: How do we know the Torah is betrothed to Jewry? — because it says in Scripture, *I will betroth you to me forever . . . I will betroth you to me in faithfulness* (Hosea 2:21–22; *Midrash Tanna'im* 33:4). We are bound to it in everlasting betrothal, to remain faithful to it forever, *with all your heart and with all your soul and with all your might* (Deuteronomy 6:5).

One point remains: For want of a better word, we translate *me'orasah* as betrothed (engaged); but in ancient Israel, when a girl became *me'orasah* ("betrothed") to a man, legally she became bound to him like a wife. To separate, they would need a full divorce. For a year, however, the girl would remain in her parents' home, preparing her trousseau, household furnishings, etc. Then there was *kiddushin,* the ceremony of marriage, and the couple embarked on their married life together. (Today both ceremonies — *érusin,* "betrothal," and *nissu'in,* "marriage" — are performed together under the wedding canopy.)

Consequently, if נערה מאורשה a betrothed maiden is seduced or violated, the crime is punishable by death. Since she has the status of a married woman, it amounts to adultery. If she is attacked where people are within earshot, the Torah makes it clear that she has a duty to cry out, and all who hear her must come to her rescue (Deuteronomy 22:23–28). Well, this duty must certainly apply to her betrothed bridegroom.

Only too obviously, for our sins, the Torah is desecrated throughout the ranks of the Jewish people.

בְּכָל יוֹם וָיוֹם בַּת קוֹל יוֹצֵאת מֵהַר חוֹרֵב וּמַכְרֶזֶת וְאוֹמֶרֶת: אוֹי לָהֶם לַבְּרִיּוֹת מֵעֶלְבּוֹנָהּ שֶׁל תּוֹרָה.

"Every single day a heavenly voice emanates from Mount Ḥorév (Sinai), proclaiming: Woe to the people for the Torah's humiliation!" (*Avoth* vi 2). To such a large dismaying extent it is simply ignored. Where it is honored, the tribute is so often only lip service.

Needless to say, this maltreatment of our sacred heritage stems mainly from sheer ignorance, not from any evil intent. Nor is it within our means to correct the entire spiritual misfortune. But if we see the Torah violated by our children, by good neighbors, by fellow-worshippers in the synagogue, and we have the power to amend the situation, we must speak up and act.

America has developed a convenient policy of "mind your own business." As a result we have become dreadfully callous when misfortune strikes someone in our midst — even when we see an innocent victim violently attacked.

If the Torah is מאורשה betrothed to us, let us learn from the law of נערה מאורשה a betrothed maiden: על דבר אשר לא צעקה *because she did not cry out* (Deuteronomy 22:24). Where an outcry can be raised, where protest and alarm can be sounded, and we remain still, we share in the guilt of the desecration. The Talmud has a firm rule: שתיקה כהודאה דמיא Silence is tantamount to consent (TB *Y'vamoth* 87b). If we just look on and nod benignly, we grow inured to the constant desecration of the Torah; and then, deny it though we will, it goes on with our tacit consent.

At the beginning of the Book of Psalms (*T'hillim*) we read: "Happy is the man who does not walk in the counsel of the wicked . . . but his delight is in the Torah of *the Lord*, and in *his* Torah he meditates day and night" (Psalms 1:1–2). Rava notes the interesting fact that "at first it is linked with the name of the Holy, Blessed One, and then with his name" (TB *Avodah Zarah* 19a) — it is called "his": the Torah of the one who studies it. And so R. Judan said: if you toil in it, it will be called by your name (*Midrash T'hillim* 1, 16).

If you toil and strive in the Torah and for the Torah, to know it, live by it, and put in honest effort to uphold it loyally, then it becomes your Torah — a lasting possession gained in life that will never prove worthless.

191

Lᴇᴛ ᴜs ʀᴇᴛᴜʀɴ ꜰᴏʀ ᴀ ᴍᴏᴍᴇɴᴛ ɪɴ ʜɪsᴛᴏʀʏ to our ancestors in the wilderness, as they traveled steadily on their journey from Egypt to the promised land. In the third month since their journey began, it was their finest hour when they stood at Sinai to receive the Torah, and 600,000 strong, the entire people responded in unison, "All that the Lord said, we will do and we will heed!" (Exodus 24:7). In the poetic image of the Sages, angels came and set royal crowns on their heads (TB *Shabbath* 88a). Never before and perhaps never again would our people be so close to God. And Moses made a covenant with the people then, a solemn agreement that their acceptance of the Torah should be for all time, for all future generations.

Then we read in the Torah: *And they saw the God of Israel; and under His feet there was as a form of a sapphire brick,*[42] *like the very heaven for clearness. And to the nobles of the children of Israel He did not put His hand; and they beheld God, and ate and drank* (Exodus 24:10–11).

In general, being "heavenly," these sentences are obviously abstruse and very difficult. As an Englishman said long ago,[43] "Heaven were not heaven if we knew what it were." The Targum (Aramaic translation) makes it clear that they saw not the Almighty Himself (no human being can do that and survive, as we read in Exodus 33:20), but rather "the Divine glory" (or, in the words of Targum Yerushalmi, the glory of the *shechinah,* His immanence). As for the phrase "under His feet," the early commentary of R. M'yuḥas explains that it denotes not His throne of glory (as *Lekaḥ Tov* writes) but an ottoman or footstool beneath the *shechinah;* for the throne of glory itself is all-consuming fire.

But why does the Torah mention "a brick of sapphire"? What is *that* supposed to mean?

Targum Jonathan throws some light on the subject:[44]

וּתְחוֹת אַפִּיפוֹרִין דְּרִיגְלוֹי דְּמִיצַע תְּחוֹת כּוּרְסֵיהּ הֵי כְעוֹבַד אֶבֶן סַפִּירִינוֹן, מִידְכַר שְׁעַבּוּדָא דְּשַׁעֲבִּידוּ מִצְרָאֵי יַת בְּנֵי־יִשְׂרָאֵל בְּטִינָא וּבְלִיבְנִין; וַהֲווֹן נְשַׁיָּא בְּטִשָׁן יַת טִינָא עִם גּוּבְרֵיהוֹן. הֲוַת תַּמָּן רִיבָּא מְפַנְּקְתָּא מְעַבַּרְתָּא וְאַפִּילַת יַת עוּבְּרָא וְאִתְבַּטַּשׁ עִם טִינָא.

נָחָת גַּבְרִיאֵל וְעָבַד מִינֵּיהּ לְבֵינְתָּא וְאַסְקֵיהּ לִשְׁמֵי מְרוֹמָא וְאַתְקְנֵיהּ גְּלוּגְדַּק תְּחוֹת אֲפִיפוֹרִין דְּמָרֵי עָלְמָא.

. . . and under His footstool, set beneath His throne, there was a form of a sapphire stone, a reminder of the slavery to which the Egyptians subjected the Israelites, with clay and bricks. The women would trample and tread on the mortar [in Egypt] together with their husbands. One delicate pregnant young woman was there and she dropped her unborn child, whereupon it became trodden into the clay. So Gabriel came down and made a brick out of it, which he brought to the heavenly heights; and he set it as a footstool under the throne of the Master of the world.[45]

Enslaved in Egypt, our ancestors were given hard, back-breaking work to do: to make a specific number of bricks each day out of straw and clay, for Pharaoh's ambitious building program. At first they were given the straw; then they had to go out and find it themselves, and still make the same number of bricks every day. It was inhumanly cruel, but the taskmasters with the whips left them no chioce. So the women and children joined in.[46] There was no other way. All had to trample and tread the clay, using their bare feet to knead it with the straw, till it was fit to mold into bricks.

But as the Midrash tells,[46] the only place they could find straw was out in the wilderness, and it was so hard and thorny that it made their feet bleed. So they worked in a welter of blood, the daily shouts and whiplashes of their taskmasters adding to the unbearable tension and pain.

In this setting, says Targum Jonathan, a young woman — just a girl, really — reared in gentleness and ease, came to help her husband, although she was pregnant — according to the Midrash,[46] in a very advanced state of pregnancy. And she lost the baby; she had a miscarriage.

There was a time when we did not believe such stories. They were too horrible to be true, we said — too grotesque or gruesome. Such things just couldn't happen! . . . Today we are sadder and wiser. In our own twentieth century the Nazis subjected our people, old and young, to far greater atrocities. They really happened, in a period of modern history. And so the cruel, bitter enslavement by the Egyptians really happened, in a period of ancient history.

Today artists create paintings and abstract sculpture to commemorate the nightmare events of out time that have appalled the human mind. Thus when German airplanes bombed the innocent town of Guernica in the

193

Spanish Civil War, Picasso painted a mural that became world-famous, which hangs today in New York's Museum of Modern Art, kept in trust for the common people of Spain, till the day they will be free of authoritarian rule. When our people labored and toiled so long ago, in a welter of their own blood, on the construction sites of ancient Egypt, there were no artists to commemorate their travail. So an angel came down and took that unborn child, lying squashed and trampled into the clay — an unborn child that would never be born alive — and he made a memorial of it before the Creator and Father of humanity, who rules with compassion and justice.

In the maelstrom of frantic brickmaking, who could notice the poor girl's miscarriage? Amid all the tension and shouting by the taskmasters, who could listen to her pathetic lament? The angel made a brick out of that stillborn child — and God saw, and knew, and remembered. We read in the Midrash:[47] That very night, the Holy Blessed One appeared and struck down all the firstborn sons in Egypt.

Consider now the Jewish home in America through the decades. In a sense, when the Jews of Eastern Europe arrived *en masse* in the New World, they became busy kneading clay and making bricks. Coming from a background of grinding proverty, needing to survive and establish themselves on the new soil, they took to "making bricks," building an economic base. It was a question of dollars and cents, and time was money. They labored in the sweatshops and did "piecework," because the rent had to be paid, and they wanted to put something by besides. There was no time to think of the children: What kind of education would they get? What values would they learn to live by?

You can build solid structures with bricks: factories, industrial plants. The immigrants became busy making their daily number of bricks, and the wives and children pitched in to help. Then the children grew and became builders with those bricks, establishing empires of manufacture, commerce and trade. And what of their spirit? their Jewish soul? That, unfortunately, was stillborn. The soul and heart that should have learned our Jewish heritage with pride, that should have grown to keep the Torah with joy, was buried in with the bricks. We hardened into a mold to build our businesses, our money-making systems, with hardly a thought for the holy Sabbath or a word of honest prayer.

In ancient Egypt the angel Gabriel took the stillborn child out of the mud, the loam and the clay, to bring it to the very heights of heaven, to

194

the Almighty's throne of glory. In America too there were angels: human beings who gave time, money and effort to build our Torah day schools. In New York's Lower East Side, the Rabbi Jacob Joseph School came into existence, and other *yeshivoth* followed. There a new link could be forged in our timeless chain of tradition. A new generation could take up Torah study as of old. In the words of the prophet, *they shall seek Torah at his mouth, for he is an angel of the Lord of hosts* (Malachi 2:7). And the Talmud adds: If the teacher resembles an angel of the Almighty Lord, let them seek to learn Torah from his lips (TB *Moéd Katan* 17a). When teachers inspire children to learn the Torah and obey it, they are like angels indeed. Like Gabriel in ancient Egypt, the teachers of Torah in America have taken the spirit of the young out of the materialistic milieu, out of the morass of bricks and mortar and clay, to lift it to the very throne of glory.

How many prophets of doom foretold that *yiddishkeit* must be stillborn in America, that it could not be transplanted alive from the Old World. And how many adults seemed to bear them out. Go back to the decades of mass immigration and pick a Jewish family at random — and you will likely find that the young men who grew up in it became successful in their endeavors; but of *yiddishkeit* they know little. They can hardly read a word of a Hebrew prayer. Jewish history is a total blank for them; and as for a religious holiday, they haven't a notion of what it is about. With their "bricks" they did (and do) "just great." They can erect magnificent synagogues and Jewish centers. But they don't know how (or to Whom) to pray.

Wherever a Jewish child receives no living, healthy Torah education, there the road is paved to intermarriage. And wherever (Heaven forfend) an intermarriage occurs, there a Jewish family line becomes bricked up, dammed up. There the living Jewish spirit becomes stillborn forever.

Hope for us lies only with the angels of the Torah day school, with all who participate and contribute to lift a Jewish soul to the very heights of heaven, to the glory of our Divine heritage.

In those mystic sentences of the Torah we read: *and they beheld God, and ate and drank* (Exodus 24:11). As the Midrash explains, they feasted their eyes on the *shechinah,* the Divine Presence (*Va-yikra Rabbah* 20, 10); and Rashi in the Talmud (TB *B'rachoth* 17a) adds: that is like food and drink. With one generation following another in our Torah schools, we too can feast our eyes with *nachas,* true satisfaction in the knowledge that spiritually (where it counts) our people has a future.[48]

# RADISH AND HONEY

IN OUR EXPANSIVE MOMENTS OF PRIDE, when we risk dislocating an arm by patting ourselves on the back for all the Torah day schools we have in the United States, we assert sometimes that they are continuing the golden chain of tradition; they are the direct continuation of the fine schools that flourished in the Eastern Eurpoe of a bygone era. Actually, since the Torah requires us to be truthful, it must be admitted that on the elementary and high school level they are not the same. Unlike the *yeshivoth* of the past in the vanished communities of the Old World, our Torah day schools also give a full secular education through the elementary and high school years (which, incidentally, can compare favorably with the instruction given in any public school).

Some have argued that this added secular education is a good thing; others, that it detracts from a truly and fully Jewish education — especially where, in an attempt to be 200% American, a school gives too much attention to the secular studies.

One popular preacher (a *maggid*) once presented his view on the question by giving free rein to his imagination, producing a parable in his flight of fancy: A black radish (said he) once decided to get married, and he took a great liking to a fine mass of honey in a beehive. The honey, he decided, would be his bride. (Remember, please, the old Yiddish saying, *Oyf a maisseh fregt men nisht keyn kashes;*[49] about a story you don't ask questions. You just listen.) Well, off he went to the bee that had produced this honey, and he said, "I would like to marry your daughter".

The bee buzzed in fury. "What, you? Look at you, so filthy and dirty with all that earth on you. I won't have you in my family! And my daughter is so sweet and lovely. . . . Get out!"

Away went the radish without a word (he may have paled at the scathing rejection, but under his black, dirt-covered skin, no one could tell). He washed and scrubbed and cleaned — and back he came. "Please, sir," he asked the bee, "may I marry your daughter now?"

196

"Heavens, no. Not with that skin on you. Did you ever see the color of my honey? So golden clear ... Do me a favor: Go away."

Again without a word the radish left. He scraped and rubbed a long time, till all his dark covering was gone. He was now a clean, gleaming white. And this time, when he came to the hive, the "papa" bee was impressed. He accepted the radish for a son-in-law. In short, there was to be a wedding.

Well, how could such a marriage really be made? There is a traditional Jewish delicacy called *eingemachts* (a kind of jam) that was usually made for Passover: The radish is cut into little pieces and boiled with the honey. What better way could there be to make a "marriage" between a radish and a lovely mound of honey? So this was the wedding ceremony: they made *eingemachts*.

But then the question arose: What kind of *b'rachah* should be said over this tasty combination — what benediction to thank the Almighty for it before eating it? The *b'rachah* over a radish is *bo-rey p'ri ha'adamah* (Blessed art Thou ... Creator of the fruit of the earth). The *b'rachah* over honey is *shehakol nih-yeh bid'varo* (Blessed art Thou ... by whose word everything comes into being). Which of the two should be said over the combination?

Off they went to ask an authorized and authoritative rabbi. His answer was: *bo-rey p'ri ha-adamah* — because the main ingredient is the radish; the honey is a secondary ingredient, to give taste and flavor. Of course, the "papa" bee didn't like that. He tried to argue. It was no use, though. The rabbi was firm.

The bee began to weep: "I never wanted this big lump of a vegetable in my family in the first place. The moment he came to me, all black and dirty, I knew I wanted no part of him. And now look: he is the main, important ingredient, and my beautiful honey is just secondary — a minor ingredient. *Oy vey!*"

The *maggid* drew his moral: Originally the Sages of the Talmud wanted no part of *limmudey ḥol*, secular studies. The Almighty said in Scripture, *Let this book of the Torah not draw away from your mouth, but you shall meditate in it day and night* (Joshua 1:8). So when R. Joshua was asked if a man might teach his son Greek, he said *Certainly* — but at a time that was neither day nor night, because in this sentence we are commanded to stop learning Torah neither by day nor by night.[50] The Greek language was beautiful; the Sages said it would be an ornament for a girl to know it (TJ *Sotah* ix 15). Yet they

197

wanted no part of it. Greek philosophy was certainly the finest product of the human intellect in the secular world, sheer wisdom of its kind. Yet when R. Ishmael's nephew asked him if he might study Greek philosophy, having already learned the entire Torah, R. Ishmael gave him the same answer: Find a time for it that is neither day nor night (TB *Menaḥoth* 99b); then you are free from the obligation to keep studying the Torah and deepening your understanding of it.

As we might paraphrase it today, there is only one small room in your house where you cannot learn Torah. There you may read *limmudey ḥol.*

How right the Sages were, we learned afterward, in the centuries of exile. We lived among non-Jews; and somehow, whatever learning and culture they developed, it led them to plague and harass and murder us. They developed their own versions of monotheistic religion, and it meant that they had to torture us and put us to death "to save our souls." They developed art and literature and music and science, nowhere better than in Germany; and within living memory they burned children in the crematoriums. They used their brilliant advances in science and technology to exterminate millions of our people efficiently, so that they should not become a burden, needing food, or cause an outbreak of pestilence (this in addition to the "scientific" experiments in human torture).

The towers of non-Jewish learning and culture were the universities. There the most erudite minds with the most advanced knowledge were to be found. And there, in one European university after another, the Jewish students who gained admittance came face to face with virulent anti-semitism.

In America, though, *dina d'malchutha dina*: it is the law of the land that in our elementary and high schools there must be secular education. We accept it. And thank Heaven, our youngsters do consistenly well. In statewide competitive examinations their grades are remarkably high.

Let us not forget, though, what the so-called culture of so-called civilization did to us for 2,000 years: We were pogromed, exiled, and burned at the stake. We were gassed, cremated, and buried alive. Yet we clung to our Torah tenaciously. In this age of enlightenment, in our land of the free, some of the "muck on the radish" was removed, so that secular education appears white and clean — an American opportunity to grow and achieve. So we accepted it into the curriculum of our *yeshivoth.*

But in this "marriage of the radish and the honey" we must never allow the radish to become the *ikkar,* the main ingredient. It is for the sacred studies in our Written and Oral Torah that we can say a *b'rachah,* to bless and thank God wholeheartedly — for spiritual illumination and moral values to give richness and meaning to our lives. Secular studies may be essential to a good career. But their inherent content and substance is nothing to thank God for.

This in essence marks the criterion between the good Torah day school and the non-orthodox imitations that have sprung up: What do they consider the *ikkar,* the main, important ingredient in the program of studies, and what the *tafél,* the secondary, subordinate element? A small switch of a piece of railroad track can send a train in a completely wrong direction.

This is important for parents to remember too. They establish the values and the emotional climate in our Jewish homes. If they take the attitude that "of course that Torah stuff is all very nice, but it's the secular studies that count; that's how you can really get somewhere" — the children may pick up the attitude and make it their own. And then the children may indeed "really get somewhere" when they grow up — but not where the parents ever wanted them to go.

## THE MITZVAH
## WE COULD DO WITHOUT

IN THE SAME VEIN, NOW, there is a fascinating story that I once heard from the renowned Talmudic scholar R. Elḥanan Wasserman (of blessed memory).

About 1780 the great ḥassidic leader R. Lévi Yitzḥak settled in Berdychev, and under his mighty influence the town became a stronghold of ḥassidic life. But for a few decades the movement called *haskalah* ("enlightenment") had been around. The leaders of the movement clamored that it was time for the Jews to leave the ghetto intellectually (they couldn't leave it physically). All should learn our entire Hebrew Scripture, especially the *n'vi'im,* the Books of the Prophets, since it was beautiful literature. And the Jews should also learn the language and literature of the nations of Europe. Then, said the leaders of *haskalah,* the Jewish people would gain recognition, esteem and equality.

Had they meant sincerely only to spread the knowledge of *tanach,* our sacred Hebrew Scripture, and to improve the lot of their fellow Jews, the *haskalah* movement might have been a good thing in its way. But soon enough their real intention showed through: to tear down the whole fabric of Jewish religious life, wrenching it away from its roots in the Talmud and the *shulḥan aruch.* Like Ben-Gurion in our time, they wanted to derive *halachah,* authoritative norms for Jewish life, from their understanding of the Hebrew Bible, principally the Books of the Prophets.

(In our time generations of children have been raised on the *tanach* in the national schools of Israel. They learned their fill of the lofty humanity and noble ideals of social justice in the writings of the prophets. But about the Talmud and the *shulḥan aruch* they were given ignorance and scorn. The result is generations without any genuine Jewish values, with no basic commitment to the age-old sacred ideals of our people, and often even without the Zionist ideals they were supposedly taught.)

At any rate, the story tells that a clever young *maskil* (member of the *haskalah* movement) came one day to R. Lévi Yitzḥak in Berdychev, with maybe just a little gleam of malice in his eye. "Dear rabbi," said he, "I can prove that a person has to learn *haskalah,* everything they say we have to learn. It is written plainly in the Talmud!"

"Indeed? Where?"

"In the tractate *Kiddushin* 29a: It is stated there האב חייב בבנו ללמדו אומנות a father has an obligation to teach his son a trade, a profession. Under the program of *haskalah* a person will learn Greek, Latin, French, German. He can go and find employment in a high school or a college instead of living here in grinding poverty, starving half the time. Then you see, *haskalah* is *umanuth,* a profession; it is a *mitzvah* for a father to let his son gain the knowledge."

R. Lévi Yitzḥak looked at the young man thoughtfully and stroked his beard. "I don't know," he said. "It may be that you are right. I shall have to look into it." For a moment he sat musing. "You know," he said, "this is not the only *mitzvah* that a father has to perform for his son — to have him learn a trade or profession. For instance, in the very same paragraph of the Tosefta (in the tractate *Kiddushin*) there is also *milah,* circumcision. A father

200

has a duty to have his son circumcised. Well now, would you say that this is a greater *mitzvah* than *milah,* to have his son learn a profession?"

"Oh no, no," said the young man hastily, "certainly not. By *milah* a child becomes a Jew. He enters the covenant of Abraham."

"Very well," said R. Lévi Yitzḥak. "We find in the Talmud that if a father had two or three sons and they were circumcised, and each one in turn took sick and died on account of the circumcision, if he has another son, that one should not be circumcised in infancy.[51] We have to assume that there is some hereditary weakness in the man's children that makes circumcision a danger to their life when they are infants. As Rambam [Maimonides] writes, the father has to wait till the boy is quite grown and strong before having him circumcised.[52]

"Here," R. Lévi Yitzḥak of Berdychev continued, "a whole generation has died spiritually because of this *mitzvah* of learning *haskalah.* No, my son: This *haskalah* may be a *mitzvah* indeed; but we may not subject any more of our precious children to it."

According to the Torah, two witnesses prove a case (Deuteronomy 17:6, 19:15). Let us recall Moses Mendelssohn, who showed how superbly *haskalah* could be used as a profession. He combined his Hebrew background with his secular learning to gain esteem in Germany as a scholar; and his son converted out of the faith. Martin Buber delved into the Bible and ḥassidic teachings, and produced a philosophy of existentialism that had not the slightest trace of authentic Judaism in it. A Jew made of his people's sacred heritage a non-Jewish philosophy, and he became a world-renowned philosopher — an extremely successful instance of *haskalah* as a profession. In his old age he went to Germany, the land where the murder of six million of his brethren was conceived and put into effect — to receive a high award from a university.

If these are the products of *haskalah,* we can (and must) do without it. Secular education in our schools we must have, but let us never lose the blessed perspective of our great sages and scholars.

201

THE TERM "WISE GUY" is purely American. So many might think that the wise guy (or "smart-aleck") is a purely American type, born and bred on American soil, the very finest examples of the type coming from Brooklyn. Actually it isn't so at all. We can find him in the flesh in a story many centuries old, in *Séder Eliyahu Zuta* (beginning of chapter 4):[53]

פַּעַם אַחַת הָיִיתִי עוֹבֵר [מְהַלֵּךְ] מִמָּקוֹם לְמָקוֹם וּמְצָאַנִי אָדָם אֶחָד וְהָיָה מֵלִיץ [מִתְלוֹצֵץ] וּמַלְעִיג בִּדְבָרַי וּבָא כְּנֶגְדִּי. וְאָמַרְתִּי לוֹ, בְּנִי, מַה תָּשִׁיב לְאָבִיךְ שֶׁבַּשָּׁמַיִם לְיוֹם הַמִּשְׁפָּט [לְיוֹצֶרְךָ לְיוֹם הַדִּין]? אָמַר לִי, רַבִּי, יֵשׁ לִי דְּבָרִים שֶׁאֲנִי מֵשִׁיב לְאָבִי שֶׁבַּשָּׁמַיִם לְיוֹם הַמִּשְׁפָּט: אוֹמֵר אֲנִי לוֹ, בִּינָה וְדֵעָה לֹא נָתְנוּ לִי מִן הַשָּׁמַיִם [שֶׁאֶקְרָא וְאֶשְׁנֶה]. אָמַרְתִּי לוֹ, בְּנִי, מַה מְּלַאכְתְּךָ? אָמַר לִי, צַיָּד אֲנִי. אָמַרְתִּי לוֹ, בְּנִי, מִי אָמַר לְךָ [לִמֵּדְךָ] שֶׁתָּבִיא [שֶׁתִּטֹּל] פִּשְׁתָּן וְתַאַגְדֶנּוּ [וְתַאַרְגֶנּוּ] מְצוּדוֹת וְתַשְׁלִיכֵם לַיָּם וְתַעֲלֶה דָּגִים מִן הַיָּם? אָמַר לִי, רַבִּי, בָּזֶה בִּינָה וְדֵעָה נָתְנוּ בִּי מִן הַשָּׁמַיִם. אָמַרְתִּי לוֹ, בְּנִי, וּמַה לְהַשְׁלִיךְ מְצוּדוֹת וּלְהַעֲלוֹת [מַה לִטֹּל פִּשְׁתָּן וְלֶאֱרֹג מְצוּדוֹת לְהַשְׁלִיכֵהוּ לַיָּם לְהַעֲלוֹת בָּהּ] דָּגִים מִן הַיָּם נָתְנוּ בְּךָ [לְךָ] בִּינָה וְדֵעָה [דַּעַת וּבִינָה] מִן הַשָּׁמַיִם, לְדִבְרֵי תוֹרָה, שֶׁכָּתוּב בָּהֶם "כִּי קָרוֹב אֵלֶיךָ הַדָּבָר מְאֹד~ [דברים ל יד], לֹא נָתְנוּ בְּךָ [לְךָ] בִּינָה וְדֵעָה [מִן הַשָּׁמַיִם]? מִיָּד הָיָה מִתְאַנֵּחַ וְהָיָה מֵרִים קוֹלוֹ וְהָיָה בּוֹכֶה, וְאָמַרְתִּי [עַד שֶׁאָמַרְתִּי] לוֹ, בְּנִי, אַל יֵרַע לְךָ, אֶלָּא שְׁאָר בְּנֵי אָדָם [שֶׁכָּל בָּאֵי עוֹלָם] מְשִׁיבִין בְּאוֹתוֹ עִנְיָן [תְּשׁוּבָה זוֹ], מַעֲשֵׂה יְדֵיהֶן מוֹכִיחִין עֲלֵיהֶן [אֲבָל מַעֲשֵׂיהֶן יְהוּ מְעִידִין בָּהֶן]. עָלָיו וְעַל כַּיּוֹצֵא בּוֹ וְעַל הַדּוֹמִין לוֹ וְעַל הָעוֹשִׂין כְּמַעֲשָׂיו, מַהוּ אוֹמֵר: וּבֹשׁוּ עֹבְדֵי פִשְׁתִּים שְׂרִיקוֹת וְאֹרְגִים חוֹרָי (ישעי׳ יט ט). (סדר אליהו זוטא רפ״ד; ילקוט שמעוני א תתק״ס סוף פ׳ נצבים — נוסחאותיו באריכיים)

Once I [the prophet Elijah] was going from one region to another, when I came across a man sneering and jeering in his talk as he came toward me. "My son," I asked him, "what answer will you give your Father in heaven on the day of judgment?"

"Rabbi," he answered me, "I have an answer to give my Father in heaven on judgment day: I will tell Him I was not given any understanding or intelligence so that I could study Scripture or Talmud."

202

I asked him then, "My son, what work do you do?"

"I am a fisherman," said he.

"Well, my son, who taught you how to take flax and weave it into nets, and then throw them into the ocean to gather fish from the sea?"

"Oh rabbi," he replied, "for that I was given understanding and intelligence from heaven."

Said I, "My son, if to take flax, weave nets and throw them into the sea to catch fish, Heaven gave you the sense and the mind — for the words of the Torah, of which it is written, *the matter is very close to you* (Deuteronomy 30:14), understanding and intelligence were *not* given you from heaven?"

There and then he took to groaning; he raised his voice and began weeping — until I told him, "Do not grieve, my son. All human beings have the same answer to give; only, their activity, their occupation bears witness against them."

About him, everyone like him and similar to him, and everyone who acts like him, what does Scripture say? — *Then the fishermen shall lament, and all who cast hook in the Nile will mourn, and those who spread nets upon the water will come to grief. And the workers in combed flax will be disgraced, and so the weavers of cotton* (Isaiah 29:8–9).

We can almost picture this "wise guy" of ancient times, an olden version of a hippie perhaps, with a great big jeering grin smeared over his face as he met Elijah the prophet on the road. All he saw was a pious Jew with a long white beard (in all likelihood), a member of "the orthodox establishment." It was a chance to make fun of the old man, "have himself a ball." Later he could tell his friends about it, and they would laugh uproariously in appreciation, embroidering and embellishing the incident with their own witty contributions.

So Elijah prodded the young fellow gently, saying in effect, "You won't live forever, you know. Some day you will go back to the world of the spirit, to face your Maker. You will be asked if you learned any Torah, our Jewish faith, our Jewish heritage. You will be asked if you did anything for your fellow-Jews, for *k'lal yisraél,* for our religion. And then what answer will you give to explain this lovely personality of yours, this picturesque way of behavior?"

If chewing gum had existed in those times, the young man would surely have had a big wad in his mouth, and at this point he would have chewed with a big show of enjoyment. We can almost hear him answering, "Don't you worry about that at all, Grandpa. You see, when the brains were given out up there in heaven, I wasn't around. I didn't get my rightful share. Who has the brains for that there Hebrew Bible and Mishnah and Talmud? That learned stuff is for the *iluyim,* the bright yeshiva boys in the Torah establishment. No siree, that stuff is not for me. No brains, that's why."

As the jeering grin on his face improved, Elijah asked him, still ever so gently, what he did for a living. He was a fisherman, he said. And if he was around today, he might have added, "That's my thing, fishing. That's where it's at for me, out there in the open with the sea and the sky, the sunshine and the moonlight. It's great, man."

But now came another question from Elijah (and we can see that he would be superb at cross-examination in the courtroom): "Who taught you how to be a fisherman? Who taught you to comb flax and make threads and then weave nets from it? And how do you know where and when to throw your nets into the ocean so that they will come out laden with fish?"

"Oh, that just comes natural. It's a gift. I just kind of picked it up, you know? Heaven surely gave me the brains for that."

Now Elijah drove home his point: To go far afield and gather flax, comb it and work it into thread and weave nets — for this he had sense. To go out in a boat come rain or shine, risking his life against the elements in order to bring in his catch — for this he had brains and ability, no matter how far the tides and the wind might take him. But כִּי קָרוֹב אֵלֶיךָ הַדָּבָר מְאֹד *this matter* of Torah *is very close to you,* בְּפִיךָ וּבִלְבָבְךָ לַעֲשׂוֹתוֹ *to observe it with your mouth and with your heart* (Deuteronomy 30:14). It is right there, near you, accessible. You can approach it easily. Learn to say the words of the Torah with your mouth, till they become familiar. Take them to heart, to observe the mitzvoth faithfully. Thus you implant faith in your life.

Elijah's point struck home. There was once a motion picture in which the hero mused with regret, "I coulda been somebody."[54] This was the kind of realization which now dawned on the wise-acre hippie of long age. Instead of just building a boat and a fisherman's shack, he could have built a life within the Torah, with self-respect and meaning. He had squandered something precious, which could never be recovered.... It struck him with such force that he broke into tears and wept aloud.

So Elijah comforted him: "Do not give way to despair. You are in good company." Everyone gives the same answer, wherever you go: on Wall Street, in New York's garment center, in the fur trade, everywhere. "I only know how to run my business. Who has a head for studying? That Torah is for the rabbis and the yeshiva students."

Yet their business acumen, their skill at making money, is ample proof of intelligence. If a person takes his bankbooks to heaven with him, he won't be able to make any withdrawals, because "you can't take it with you"; but they certainly "may be used in evidence against you."

So Elijah concludes by quoting the prophet Isaiah: The fishermen, the workers in combed flax and cotton, all the skilled craftsmen who do well in their trades, will be sorry indeed when they have to account for their lives. Those who fish only for money in the American marketplace, those who knit and weave systems for increasing their profits — always too busy for a daily hour of Torah study or the needs of the community — will have cause for grief and regret.

For the symbol of a net is truly apt. With Torah study too you weave a net, strand by strand. After all, this is also how the *yétzer hara,* the evil inclination, works. As the Talmud expresses it (TB *Sukkah* 52a), "At first the *yétzer hara* is like a spider's thread" with which it spins its web — a gossamer thing, a little sinful act, insignificant, something so easy not to do that the person hardly pays attention to it. But every time the sinful act is repeated, it is another gossamer thread, and the strands twine together. "At the end," the Talmud continues, "it is like wagon ropes." The person is tied and hooked to the *yétzer hara,* with a "need" or habit that he cannot break.

Yet in the same way a Torah life can be built. In the words of the Midrash, a fool throws up his hands in despair. "Who can learn the Torah?" he asks. "The tractates of *n'zikin*[55] are thirty chapters; the tractates of *kélim* are thirty chapters!"[56] But what does a wise person say? "Today I will learn two laws, tomorrow two laws ... until I learn the entire Torah" (*Va-yikra Rabbah* 19, 2).

The words of the Torah are also strands, that you can weave into your daily activities and your home life. With the Torah you can do mitzvoth, blessed religious good deeds, to bring a new level of goodness into your life. With the Torah, Saturday can become the holy Sabbath, making your home a haven of relaxation and spiritual pleasure.

Persevere, keep at it, and the strands will twine together into thick strong bonds. Keep learning and doing, and you weave a net to bring you a plentiful catch from the ocean of Torah wisdom — a harvest from the sea of age-old Jewish learning, to enrich your life.

# ❧ THE WRESTLER

Long ago, says the Torah, when the world was still young, there were two brothers, and one hated the other implacably. Esau was supposed to get his father's blessing, and Jacob managed to get it instead; and for that Esau was determined to kill his brother. So Jacob fled to his uncle Laban in Aram-naharaim, where he eventually married Laban's two daughters and raised a family. At last he returned to Canaan, prosperous, laden with flocks and herds — only to find that Esau was as determined as ever to do away with him. The man was coming with an army of 400 to take his bloody revenge.

Our father Jacob prayed for Divine help, and sent a huge present to his brother, hoping to pacify him. Then, as night came, he slept. *And he arose that night and took his two wives, his two handmaids, and his eleven children, and crossed the ford of the Yabbok. He took them and sent them across the stream, and sent over what he owned. So Jacob was left alone; and a man wrestled with him until the break of day* (Genesis 32:23–25). Alone for all the world, as though there were no one else on earth, the two struggled and writhed. As the Torah tells, when this strange, unknown man saw he could not win, he injured Jacob in the hollow of the thigh. Then as dawn came, he blessed Jacob and was gone (*ibid.* 26–29).

Now, why does the Torah tell us this? It cannot be just to regale us with "another fine, thrilling incident in an action-packed adventure story." Every incident, every sentence and word in the Torah has a vital significance for every generation. Moreover, just who was this man who came to wrestle with Jacob?

As the Sages unravel the mystery, he was no ordinary mortal but an angel. Later Jacob called the site P'niél, *because I have seen* elo-him *face to face* (Genesis 32:30). This Hebrew name usually denotes the Almighty, but not always. Sometimes it denotes judges.[57] Here, as the Targum and the Midrash[58] make clear, it means an angel.

Yet what sort of angel was this, to come and attack Jacob viciously in the still of the night, when he was all alone? (And the Midrash adds that he meant to kill the Patriarch.)[59] The answer is that he was no sweet benign messenger from heaven. As the Sages teach, he was the guardian angel of Esau.[60] Every major nation in the world (say the Sages) has a patron or guardian angel in heaven that protects it and looks after its interests.[61] Esau's sons and grandsons were already the nucleus of the future nation of Edom. So he had a guardian angel — who came now in the darkness before dawn, insisting on a wrestling match to the death.

Scripture calls him a man, though, because so he appeared. Then what sort of person did he look like? The Sages have some very interesting answers. In the Talmud we read:

ר' שְׁמוּאֵל בַּר נַחְמָנִי אָמַר, כְּעַכּוּ״ם נִדְמָה לוֹ ... ר' שְׁמוּאֵל מִשְׁמֵיהּ דְּרַבָּה בַּר עוּלָּא אָמַר, כְּתַלְמִיד חָכָם נִדְמָה לוֹ. (בבלי, חולין צא ע״א ד״ס)

R. Sh'muél b. Naḥmani said: He appeared to him as an idol-worshipper, a heathen priest. R. Sh'muél said in the name of Rabbah b. Ulla: He appeared to him as a learned scholar (TB *Ḥullin* 91a).[62]

In the Midrash[63] we find this:

ר' הוּנָא אָמַר, בִּדְמוּת רוֹעֶה נִדְמָה לוֹ, לְזֶה צֹאן וּלְזֶה צֹאן, לְזֶה גְּמַלִּים וְלָזֶה גְּמַלִּים. אָמַר לוֹ, הַעֲבֵר שֶׁלָּךְ וַאֲנִי מַעֲבִיר שֶׁלִּי. הֶעֱבִיר יַעֲקֹב שֶׁלּוֹ, חָזַר וְרָאָה שֶׁמָּא שָׁכַח דָּבָר [נ״א כֵּיוָן שֶׁהֶעֱבִיר יַעֲקֹב אָבִינוּ אֶת שֶׁלּוֹ, אָמַר נַחֲזֹר וְנַחֲמֵי דִילְמָא אַנְשִׁינָן כְּלוּם]. מִיָּד [מִן דְּחָזַר] וַיֵּאָבֵק אִישׁ עִמּוֹ.....רַבָּנָן אָמְרִי, לְאַרְכִילִיסְטִיס נִדְמָה לוֹ. (בראשית רבא עז ב; ילקוט שמעוני א קלב; שה״ש רבה ג י)

R. Huna said: He appeared as a shepherd. This one [Jacob] had sheep, and he also had sheep; this one had camels, and he also had camels. Said he to Jacob, "Take yours across and then I will take mine over." So Jacob took his stock across [the Yabbok]. Then he went back to see if he had forgotten anything. [Another version: Once he took his stock across, the other said, "Let us go back and see if perhaps we have forgotten something."] Immediately [once he returned] *a man wrestled with him.* . . . The Sages said: He appeared to him as a bandit chief. . . .

The guardian angel of Esau, his guiding spirit, came with all the hatred of Esau himself, intent on killing our father Jacob. The Almighty's plan was that Jacob should raise twelve sons as loyal and devoted to God as he was, so that they would found the twelve tribes of our people. Esau's demon angel cared nothing about that, filled with Esau's hate as he was.

What human form did he take? One answer is: he came as a heathen priest. Long ago the Sages taught: מעשי אבות סימן לבנים the events in the lives of the Patriarchs remain a sign, an augury for their descendants (TB *Sotah* 34a). There was not just one Esau at one point in our early history. He was a "pioneer," setting a satanic pattern with his demon angel that others have followed through the centuries. When the Seleucid kings of Greek Syria ruled Israel, they tried to force our people into their kind of idol-worship, so that Israel could be "homogenized" into their empire. So they too appeared as "heathen priests."

Whoever knows the history of our people in Spain and Portugal is familiar with the role of priests there too, especially a man named Torquemada. They too wrestled with us and injured us — giving us the splendid choice of leaving the two countries (for some unknown destination; as one might say, "Get lost"), burning to death at the stake (to have our souls saved), or converting to their faith.

A hundred years ago there was hardly a Jew who hadn't heard of Edward Mortara. His story was a sensation. In 1853 or '54, when he was about two, he became seriously ill. A servant girl in the home (in Bologna, Italy), thinking he would die, baptized him secretly, to "save his soul before it was too late." The boy recovered, however, and the servant girl kept her secret — till 1858, when to relieve her conscience she revealed in the confessional what she had done. The news went post-haste to "headquarters," and on the night of June 23, 1858, when the boy was six, he was forcibly taken from his home by the papal police.

Although it was by no means the first case of its kind, it raised an outcry all over the world. High officials of other governments, including Napoleon Ill, protested and brought influence to bear. Moses Montefiore went to Rome. Nothing was of any use. The boy's soul remained "saved": He was raised for the priesthood, and he became a devout preacher in six languages.

(When we hear stories like this, we have a tendency to sigh with relief and say, "Thank Heaven things like that don't happen any more, in our times." Unfortunately, as the French put it, the more things change, the more they are the same. In the days of the Nazi inferno, a great many Jewish children found safety by being placed in convents. After the Second World War, when surviving inmates of the concentration camps were being restored to health and normalcy, strong attempts were made to have those children released from the convents, so that they could be restored to their families and their people. Nothing was of any avail. The late Dr Isaac Herzog, then the chief rabbi of Israel, was always a pleasant, even-tempered man. When he went to Rome about this and all his efforts failed, for perhaps the only time in his life he gave way to rage, in his utter frustration.)

On a dark night in our ancient history, Esau's demon angel appeared to Jacob as a heathen priest, for a mortal wrestling match. Closer to modern times the approach grew truly subtle and refined. In the early decades of Jewish mass immigration to America, when parents worked long and hard to earn their meager living, with no time or patience to think of their children, the little youngsters played freely on the streets — and there were "very nice people" in certain stores ready to invite them in, just to have a piece of striped candy, hear a story or two, and sing carols. And the children were always invited to come back and bring their friends.

When the techniques were refined still further, every so often in early September you might find a man standing on the street-corner, a *magén david* (six-pointed Jewish star) hung about his neck, carrying a sign that announced religious services, to be held at their quarters, on the High Holy Days. Services were held there all right, but not exactly the kind that served the God of Abraham, Isaac and Jacob. A little twist took those services off in a different direction, out of the Jewish faith.

Before Passover they would blossom again with their signs: A lovely *séder* woull be held a their quarters on Passover eve. A lovely *séder* — but instead of telling about the miraculous liberation of the Israelites from ancient Egypt they would carry on about "a human lamb" that became a "Passover sacrifice." The result was that the souls of innocent children became *their* lambs, to sacrifice on the altar of their missionary zeal.

In our times they have concentrated their zeal in Israel. At an international book fair in Jerusalem they set up a booth to display their publications. Unless you had a good sense of smell, and could draw conclusions from the contents of their publications, you would never supsect who they were. They smiled sweetly at the Israeli visitors, especially school-children, and spoke a fluent Hebrew. Unlike Esau's demon angel, none of them would even appear *openly* as a priest.

But this is only a minor incident. The important point is that for their main work they find ideal conditions in Israel: families in dire poverty, overburdened with numerous children, who have no awareness of the poison that the "dedicated social workers" bring. They come with food into a home of undernourished children and chirp brightly, "The Messiah sent us!'" Then they say, ever so sweetly, "Why don't you let some of your children eat and sleep at our place?" Soon afterward these children wear a decoration made of a horizontal and a vertical bar, and they learn (in Hebrew) the shorter catechism.

You know, a good fighter or wrestler always goes for his opponent's weak spot, where he is vulnerbale. In the epics of Homer we read of Achilles' heel. When the satanic guardian angel of Esau wrestled with Jacob in the dark before dawn, *he touched the hollow of his thigh* (Genesis 32:26). The Hebrew for thigh is *yerech;* but further on the Torah refers to his children, grandchildren, and so on, as *yotz'ey yerech Yaakov,* "those who were descended from Jacob's loins" (Exodus 1:5). So *yerech* refers to the children of Israel, the Jewish youngsters, in every generation.[64] As Esau's demon angel dislocated Jacob's *kaf yerech,* so the children in their trusting innocence can be tragically "dislocated" from the Jewish faith when the "angels" of another faith appear with their honeyed words and pious carols.

Jacob himself would not yield. He battled, and emerged victorious, forcing that dark angel to bless him. What happens in our time, though? We have something called dialogue. Men of different shades and grades and types of faith get together and talk about everything but the crucial differences in their religions. As the vapor (or, if you will, hot air) of their symposiums fills the enviornment, the vision is blurred and the differences begin to appear vague and hazy. Suddenly an annual volume appears under the name *The Bridge* — essays by "leaders" of the different faiths (including Jews, to our misfortune) that supposedly help build a "bridge of understanding."

Such a bridge we do not really need, because it can only become a one-way street, helping Jews *out*. An old Yiddish folksong tells of a bridge that *we* will build — a paper bridge, made of the paper on which the great teachings of Torah by scholars in every age have been written and printed. And on this bridge, the song continues, the Messiah (ours) will come. If we want to go straight, in the way of our Divine heritage, this one bridge is enough for us. We don't need any traffic directions from Esau's angel appearing as a heathen priest.

A second view of our Sages is that this satanic angel showed up as a scholar. This too we have experienced in our time. The world's universities have produced great scholars, honored and proclaimed. In England there was a Professor Toynbee, a world authority on history (except that when some historians looked at his precise knowledge in their particular fields, they found him not too accurately informed). He viewed the vast expanse of human history, and produced his conclusion: History demonstrates that the Jewish people and their faith are a fossil. It was time for us to wake up and realize that we had been dead for ages. As of now Toynbee's theory may resemble a fossil much more closely than Jewry and its faith.

Germany had professors — the kind who wrote "Notes toward a brief introduction" to their subject material, and the material ran to four volumes, very scholarly. And when the Nazi leaders needed "scientific theories" and "learned conclusions" as a basis for their official policy of virulent anti-semitism, the German professors obliged, with very erudite lengthy footnotes included.

In the universities of America there are also professors, dressed so tastefully and speaking in such modulated (pear-shaped) tones, in impeccable English. They teach philosophy or comparative religion, or the history of religion. We have a *tanach,* sacred Hebrew Scripture? Of course. But the Swahili (or something) also have what they regard as sacred scriptures. Yours came from a Divine revelation at Sinai? Really? You believe that?

In my day as a college student I encountered this. And what answer is a young, inexperienced student to give a "distinguished" professor (or instructor) in a case like that?

When the Israelites left Egypt and went travelling through the wilderness, the people of Amalek (descendants of Esau) attacked them without warning. Scripture says of this people, *asher kor'cha ba-derech,* "how he attacked you on the way" (Deuteronomy 25:18). But in *kor'cha* we have the word *kor,* "cold": The Israelites were ablaze with loyalty to God in their new-found faith — and the people of Amalek "cooled" them with their icy heathen hostilty.

The university professor touches nerve centers of the Jewish faith with his polished phrase, and once again *asher kor'cha ba-derech.* The blazing fervor and grandeur in the Divine word is gone. It's all cold "literature" from primitive or comparative religions. Amalek has attacked again — but ever so subtly now, just planting little seeds of doubt. Only, the seeds can grow bitter fruit.

Esau's satanic angel appeared as a scholar, says one of the Sages. In that guise he could injure our father Jacob, by touching the young innocent descendants of the Patriarch.

211

A third view among the Sages is that he appeared as a shepherd. Jacob had flocks of sheep and camels, and so did he. "What? You're taking your live-stock across the stream? So am I. Let's go together." He was an equal, a business colleague, ready to cooperate and be helpful, ready to show Jacob how to do things. . . .

Our immigrant Jews in America also found colleagues ready to be helpful and show them how to do things. "What? You keep your shop closed on Saturday? How can you compete? Do you know how much I make over the year by running my shop that one extra day a week? . . . Look: right now I can give you all the work you want, if you can meet the deadline and deliver the goods on time. Don't be a fool. . . ."

They came as colleagues, cooperative and helpful. But they set the pace and invited you to keep up. "I have a wonderful bargain for you; but you must come over Saturday morning. By Saturday night it might be too late." (When are auction sales held in New York? — generally on Saturday afternoon. You can pick up charming antiques, beautiful pieces of furniture. You just have to drop *sh'mirath shabbath* in the process.)

In the Diaspora we observe *yom tov*, the religious festivals, for two days. Sometimes it happens (as it happened to me) that an important buyer comes to town for the second day of *yom tov*. He wants to see your line of goods and give you a big order. Don't run your whole plant that day. Just come down and open the place, show the buyer your spring line, and take his big, handsome order . . . . I went through this temptation. Thank Heaven I resisted, and as it turned out I lost nothing by it.[65]

Again, as you associate with business colleagues, likely as not you will have to have lunch with them occasionally. Where do you go? — to a non-kosher reataurant, most probably. The first time you eat nothing. The second time you nibble something inconsequential. The third time you decide to have lettuce and tomatoes. And so it goes. You keep cutting corners until there are no more corners left to cut and you have gone round the bend and arrived — at non-kosher food (Heaven forfend).

So the demonic spirit of Esau has inflicted another wound on Jewry.

There is one more view of the Sages: that Esau's angel of hate appeared as an arch-bandit, a leader of outlaws. Sometimes the subtle and refined approaches against Jewry and Judaism fail. Then there is always the direct and brutal attack, when those who confront us turn into chief bandits and gangsters.

For their amusement the Romans (identified by the Sages as descendants of Esau) sent countless numbers of our people into the arena of the gladiators, to certain death. When the advocates and defenders of "the true faith" in Spain and Portogal tired of trying to persuade Jews to convert, they could always burn them at the stake. Perhaps in the "good old days" before Castro, you might have taken a vacation trip to Havana. Right by an enchanting castle, as picturesque as anything in Spain, you could have seen bones lying on the ground. What bones were they? The guide would explain in his accented English, "It was the infidels. This is where they hanged them." With a shock you might realize that he was talking about your people, Jews from Spain who braved unimaginable dangers and fears to travel halfway 'round the world to seek safety on this continent, in the bitter decades after the expulsion — only to find Cuba ruled by the same "defenders of the faith" as Spain itself.

In one country after another in the earlier centuries, when hostile rulers and neighbors tired of restricting and persecuting the Jews, telling them where they might live and what they might do for a living, taxing them beyond all reason — they could always make a pogrom, to pillage and burn everything in sight. For variety there could always be another expulsion. (Jews were expelled from England in 1290; from France in 1394; from Austria in 1420; from most of Germany by 1519; from Prague and environs in 1540; and in 1727, Catherine I banished Jews from Russia.) Of course, after an expulsion, all Jewish property left behind was there for the taking. If they appeared like arch-bandits and outlaw leaders to the Jews, they might as well profit by it.

When the "brave warriors" of the holy Crusades marched off to battle for their glorious cause, it was understood that on the way, *en passant,* they would massacre a few Jewish communities. And after long periods of covert, subtle West European anti-semitism, the Nazis brought speed and efficiency to the program of killing six million Jews, while the neighbors in Europe watched indifferently, watched happily, or helped them out. As arch-bandits the Nazis will probably never be outclassed. They made their mark in history.

When the demonic angel of Esau finished with Jacob, our Patriarch walked away limping. He was unconquered, but wounded in the thigh or the loins. As noted above, it was a symbol that the descendants of Esau would hurt particularly the children in the Jewish people. As our sages of old put

213

it, בְּרָא כְּרֵעֵיהּ דְּאֲבוּהּ a son is the "thigh" of his father.[66] And Jacob was wounded in the thigh.

However, as the sturdy limbs that support the body, the thighs also symbolize those who support the Torah, the mainstay of the Jewish people. They also become vulnerable at times to the destructive forces of satanic angels in the environment.

## ❧ HE WAITED
## FOR THE THIRD ONE

I ONCE HEARD A FINE RELEVANT THOUGHT from the renowned Talmudic scholar R. Elḥanan Wasserman (of blessed memory). He pointed to a puzzling question: Why did this demon angel wait until that dark night, to attack none but Jacob? He was no mortal human being who had to wait till he was all grown up and strong enough to attack and grapple with someone. In the words of *Midrash Tanḥuma* (*va-yishlaḥ* 8) this patron or guardian angel of Esau was none other than Samaél — a name that the Sages use for Satan — chief of all the devils, as another Midrash describes him.[67] Esau was such an important source of future evil in the world (the Sages called Rome the people of Esau, and there is reason to consider him also the ancestor of the natives of the Soviet Union) that Satan sent no agent or assistant to be his guardian angel. He took the job himself.

Then if this was the chief devil and no other, why did he wait through the lifetimes of Abraham and Isaac, until Jacob was alone at night by the stream? He clearly came for a fight to the finish because he wanted to destroy the people that would proclaim and spread their faith in the Creator. When we read in the Torah that *he* [the demon angel] *saw he could not prevail against him* (Genesis 32:26) the commentary *Lekaḥ Tov* explains that he saw he couldn't pull Jewry away from its faith in the one and only God. So this, originally, was his purpose and goal. Then why did he wait for Jacob? He could have attacked Abraham, and had he won he would have gained the same goal: no Jewry living in the faith of the Torah. If for some reason he could not make contact with Abraham, he could surely have let go at Isaac, the one and only son of the first Hebrew father and mother in the world. With Isaac eliminated, Satan's victory would have been just as complete. Why did his attack have to be against Jacob?

R. Elḥanan Wasserman gave an intriguing answer: Our first Patriarch, Abraham, personified גמילות חסדים the quality of doing kindness. This was his way of serving the Almighty and teaching others about Him. Abraham sat by his tent, its doors open in every direction, waiting for travelers in the desert passing by. When they came he fed them royally, then taught them to know the Almighty and to thank Him for the food.[68] When once no travelers came, he was so distressed that the Almighty had to send three angels disguised as Arabs, so that he could be happy giving them hospitality.[69]

Samaél the arch-devil took a gook look at Abraham, and he did not get excited. The quality of kindness גמילות חסדים is not the *heart and soul* of Jewry as God's chosen people, fulfilling His purpose in the world. As it happens, the Jewish record in philanthropy is phenomenal, and nowhere more so than in America. In New York there is a magnificent federation of Jewish charities. But sometimes one wonders what there is about it that is particularly Jewish. Its founders and patrons may have been observant and loyal to tradition, but their children generally drifted from our authentic faith. Resplendent Jewish hospitals were built and maintained, but in the course of time, one way or another, they became non-sectarian (if they were not so from the start). There is nothing very wrong with that, of course. Medical care is a wonderful and vital thing, no matter how or for whom. Only, there is nothing in it to arouse Samaél, the arch-devil opposed to the God of our faith.

This federation supported first-rate settlement houses in the neighborhoods of New York. And when the neighborhoods changed, they had to choose between serving other groups or going out and looking for Jewish customers. Again, this is all commendable, but nothing for Samaél to get excited about. After all, Reform Jews also have philanthropy and charity. Everyone recognizes how necessary and beneficial it is. America as a whole has such a dynamic program of charity that (as you might say) it even makes our dimes march. And even China and the Soviet Union must have some forms of charity. All over the world you can find social security, unemployment insurance, welfare programs. . . .

215

So Samaél watched Abraham doing גְּמִילוּת חֶסֶד acts of kindness, as his way of serving the Almighty — and he saw no reason to get up and attack our first Patriarch.

Isaac personified *avodah*, the way of prayer and worship. That was *his* main method of serving the Almighty. We read in the Torah, *And Isaac went out to meditate* (lasu-aḥ) *in the field toward evening* (Genesis 24:63). The word *lasu-aḥ* means to talk, though; and the Sages explain that he simply went out to pray; Isaac started the practice of *davening minḥah,* saying the afternoon prayer (TB *B'rachoth* 26b).

Prayer is a wonderful and necessary thing. As far back as we can remember, we have had devout Jews going to the synagogue morning and evening for prayer. Every morning the pious Jew wraps hismelf in his *tallith,* puts on his *t'fillin,* and pleads with the Almighty for Divine aid in the frail and vulnerable life of his people. All this Isaac personified in his way of faith.

Through the generations there have been those who repeated the age-old words of our prayer-book by rote, by drilled-in force of habit; and there have been those who prayed earnestly, finding meaning, comfort and strength in the words. Unfortunately, to the young the difference was not always clear. How often it happened that an old man stood in his corner at every religious service, the *tallith* over his head, tears falling from his eyes as he prayed in rapt devotion... and his son would not even come to the synagogue. The son was caught up in new causes, new winds of misguided idealism, new goal of the times. The son was not tied to the father's *tallith.* The father prayed, and the son strayed.

A number of years ago there was a hit play on Broadway called *The Tenth Man* (by Paddy Chayefsky). In one fascinating scene a group of well-trained actors (evidently with backgrounds in the defunct Yiddish theater) imitated a typical weekday morning prayer-service (*shaḥarith*) in a small *shul* in some Jewish neighborhood. One man (a *yidl*) with a short grizzly beard came in wearing a football-team sweater, with a large number on the back, and calmly proceeded to put on his *tallith* and *t'fillin.* That indeed was a key symbol, as it were. It was more like a football game than a religious service. The prayers (in perfect English translation) came flying out like a football, shuttled between reader (*ḥazzan*) and worshippers. The important thing seemed to be to rush through, as though to make a goal. It was obviously a routine, done as it had been done so many thousands of times before and would be done thousands of times again.

216

As you sat back in your theater seat and watched, you could almost be struck across the face by a blow of recognition, a moment of truth: "My God, this is how the *davening,* our sacred prayer-services, must always look to the young generation — ludicrous, bewildering, or meaningless!" If you had not known it before, you could realize then and there that if our ancient tradition of prayer could be reduced to this, no wonder generations of American Jews didn't follow their parents into the synagogue.

So Samaél the arch-devil could watch Isaac praying beautifully, in heartrending sincerity — and he would feel no urge or itch to attack our second Patriarch and finish him off. (Even the KGB, the dreaded secret police in the USSR, could understand that. When a small group of old retired Jews goes to one of the few synagogues still left in the Soviet Union, the KGB does not mind at all. They don't get excited. "So what if they go?" Only when young folk want to join in, out of curiosity or in search of a link with their historic people — then the KGB gets busy. Or if one of the old retired Jews takes a prayer-book and sits down with a little grand-child to teach him the Hebrew alphabet, they don't like that at all. And they get up and do something about it.)

Let us look back at early American Jewish history, and we will find more of the same thing. The earliest Jews to reach the New World were of Spanish and Portuguese origin. They maintained their *avodah*. They established congregations and synagogues that glory in their history today. When a congregation organized itself in Newport, Rhode Island, the Spanish-Portuguese synagogue of New York (Shearith Israel) sent it a *séfer torah*. They maintained their prayer-services faithfully in the Spanish-Portuguese rite or *minhag*. (In fact, through the years they kept the *minhag* more faithfully than kashruth and the Sabbath.)

What influence did they have on the course of our faith in American Jewish history? Where, in the ranks of observant Jewry today, will you find any descendants of those early settlers? The synagogue in Newport was declared a national, historic landmark. But no one prays in it today. The *minhag* in Shearith Israel, the Spanish-Portuguese synagouge of New York, is faithfully sephardic. But both the rabbi and the great majority of congre-gants are ashkenazic.

Go through the Jewish communities of America today, and you will find enough devotion to *avodah*. So many splendid synagogues have been built: magnificent specimens of modern religious architecture. Yet when is a word of honest prayer uttered there to the God of our fathers? They

217

become Jewish centers, attracting people to their swimming pools, sports facilities and garages.

Samaél the arch-devil watched Abraham, and he watched Isaac. And he let them alone. In their ways of life there was yet no guarantee of an eternal people, a Jewry that would last through every vicissitude of fate in its devotion to the Almighty.

Then Jacob came, איש תם יושב אהלים *a simple, whole-hearted man, dwelling in tents* (Genesis 25:27). The Midrash noted that "tents" is plural, meaning at least two — i.e. the tents of Shem and Ever, where these two men ran schools of Torah study. In those tents Jacob dwelt, going back and forth from one to the other.[70] What he did not learn in one place he learned in the other. Moreover, his father Isaac and grandfather Abraham also had much to teach him, and he learned Torah from them too.[71] When he had to leave home and stay a long while with his uncle Laban in Aram, to escape Esau's fury, he went first to the academy of Ever and spent fourteen years there, hidden, immersed in his favorite occupation of sacred study.[72] In short (says the Midrash) from his early years to his old age he dwelt in the *béth midrash,* the house of study, till he was versed in every division and aspect of Torah.[73]

So a new phase began in our ancient history. Jacob's way of faith in one God, the Creator of heaven and earth, was through Torah — the solid teaching of specific belief and definite laws: what we must do, what we may do, what we may not do. Abraham's way of kindness was fine. But you can either accept kindness and respond to it, or not. His son Isaac accepted Abraham's belief; his son Ishmael did not; he went off on his own way. For Jacob, though, the way of kindness became a part of the way of Torah. The Torah's approach includes doing kindness; it is a main principle; but the Torah goes further, leading man to serve the Almighty in every part of his life.

Isaac's way of faith was in prayer. But you can be moved by prayer or not. You can either have the inner ability to pray, or not. Isaac's son Jacob learned to pray. (Faced by the threat of Esau and his army when he returned at last from Aram to Canaan, he implored the Almighty's help.) Isaac's son Esau never took to prayer. Yet Jacob knew that prayer alone is not enough. מסיר אזנו משמע תורה, גם תפלתו תועבה *He who turns his ear away from hearing Torah, even his prayer is an abomination* (Proverbs 28:9). The channel of communication between man and God cannot be a one-way street, where we go only to ask Him to hear what we want and grant it to us. We must hear what He wants, and we must obey. Prayer is man's word to God. Torah is God's word to man.

In his devotion to Torah, Jacob was to raise twelve sons; and not one would leave his faith. They were to found the twelve tribes of Israel, the people destined to serve the Creator till the end of human history.

As one might say, Samaél the arch-devil took a good look at Jacob, and he rubbed his eyes: "What's going on here? That fellow is dangerous. He means business!" So when Jacob was alone in the still of the night, frightened of Esau whom he would have to face the next day, Samaél the demon angel of Esau had his opportunity, and he attacked. He pitted all his strength against our third Partiarch, in a conflict to the death, in one all-out effort to nip in the bud the rise of the people of the Torah in the world.

He inflicted his wound, but he could not win. Jacob prevailed, and forced a blessing out of him. This has been the underlying pattern of much in our ongoing history.

## BETWEEN EATING
## AND BREATHING

CONSIDER ANOTHER SIGNIFICANT POINT in this symbolic incident of Jacob's fight with the demon angel or arch-devil — a point that I also heard from the sainted R. Elḥanan Wasserman. As the two writhed and grappled together, what do you suppose this dark angel tried rather to do: choke the breath out of Jacob or starve him to death? Of course the answer is plain and obvious. Suppose we find a person trapped in a mine or a cave. He has had no food or water for three days; but in addition, for a short while his air supply has been cut off, and he is slowly turning blue from asphyxiation. What would you give him first: bread, water or air? Again the answer is obvious. Without food and water he can live on another while, perhaps even another day. Without air, he can lose his life in a matter of minutes.

219

A most important lesson lies here. As we moved out of the dark ages into modern times, so much of Jewry's struggle was (as we might say) for *lehem*, "bread" — food for the spirit. In the word *lehem* (לחם) are the letters *la-med, heth, mem* — denoting, if you will, *leumi-uth,* nationalism; *héruth,* freedom; *maor,* light. Europe underwent a great upsurge of nationalism, when every land and people strove to be recognized as a nation, with its own identity and destiny. In our time we saw a remaining echo of this when Charles de Gaulle, looking off grandly into the distance, murmured *La France* with a sense of grandeur and reverence, and he based his entire program on his goal of making France an important nation in the world.

When the great wave of nationalism was in full swing, Jews in Europe yearned for the same recognition. *We are a nation like all nations,* they clamored to anyone who would listen, amid debates on whether we were really a race, a religion, or a phenomenon. The driving thought behind Herzl and the Zionist program was that with a land of our own we would be recognized as a nation among the nations, and then everything would be all right. (Hence Herzl was willing to settle for Uganda instead of Palestine.)

The American revolution brought its citizens a precious freedom from British tyranny. Soon afterward the French revolution proclaimed its blazing motto: Liberty, fraternity, equality. In the American city of Philadelphia a phrase from our sacred Scripture was engraved on the Liberty Bell: *Proclaim liberty throughout the land*! (Leviticus 25 :10). And the people that brought the holy Scripture to the world sought freedom also, on a par with all the citizens of the advanced countries.

Europe underwent a period of enlightenment, to let the light of knowledge and culture chase away the cobwebs and shadows of ignorance that remained from the dark ages. So naturally, under the impetus of *haskalah,* we Jews also strove for enlightenment. We wanted to learn European culture and share in it. We battled for worldly education and entrance to the universities.

We wanted our share of *leumi-uth* (nationalism), *héruth* (freedom), and *maor* (enlightenment) — our share of *lehem,* bread, food for the spirit.

Yet we lived for hundreds upon hundreds of years without these three dubious delights. Take the matter of a flag. Toward the end of August 1898, David Wolffsohn, a *litvak* (from Lithuania) and a successful timber merchant, came to Basle, Switzerland, being a devoted friend of Theodor Herzl. "At the command of our leader Herzl," he wrote some eleven years afterward, "I came to Basle to make all the necessary preparations for the [second]

Zionist congress.... Among all the many problems that occupied my attention then, there was one — not a big problem but not an easy one.... With what flag should we decorate the congress auditorium?... We had no flag! This thought pained me greatly.... Suddenly an idea flashed into in my mind: But we do have a blue and white flag — the *tallith* in which we wrap ourselves during our prayer! This *tallith* is our banner. Let us just take it out of its cloth bag and unfurl it before the eyes of Jewry and the eyes of all the nations. So I ordered a flag of blue and white, with a *magen david* at the center.... Thus our national ensign came into being.... No one wondered, no one asked, *Where did it come from?*"[74]

As others recalled, Wolffsohn was actually walking through the streets of Basle with a friend, with this problem on his mind, when he saw a pious Jew walking with his *tallith* (with stripes of blue) in his hand. "There," said Wolffsohn to his friend, "there is our flag!" Be that as it may, one thing is clear: There had to be a flag. How could you have a nation fighting for status and recognition without a proper flag?

Yet for almost 2,000 years of exile we lived without one. We used the original: the *tallith*. Instead of wrapping himself in the flag of rampant vaunted nationalism to trumpet his rights and demand his liberty and cultural enlightenment, the Jew enveloped himself in his *tallith* and prayed to his Maker. And he knew that as the Almighty's people, Jewry was stronger, more durable than any nation; it would outlive them all. He knew that in his house of prayer and house of study, and above all in his spirit, he had more freedom than the most advanced peoples of the West. As the Sages put it, you will find no one free except a person who makes the Torah his occupation (*Avoth* vi 2). That way lies inner freedom from the evil inclination and the passions, mastery of the self. And wrapped in his *tallith,* the devout Jew knew that his volumes of Torah learning gave him more enlightenment than the cultured gentlemen of the enlightened West would ever attain. His life of the spirit was rich and satisfying.

Through the long centuries of exile, Jewry with its *tallith* and *t'fillin* had no army, no navy, no air force, no seat at the United Nations. Our people lived in dark restricted ghettos. They did not have the right to vote or to speak up in governing councils. In certain countries they could not own real estate. Many occupations were forbidden them. They were told where they might live, what they might do, and how much tax they would have to pay. They did not eat the bread, the *leḥem,* of *leumi-uth* (nationality), *ḥéruth* (freedom) and *maor* (enlightenment). כי אפר כלחם אכלתי *For I ate*

221

*ashes like bread* וְשִׁקֻּוִי בְּבְכִי מָסָכְתִּי *and mingled my drink with tears* (Psalms 102:10). This was the fare we were fed in the centuries of exile. *My tears were my bread day and night* (Psalms 42:4).

Yet we lived, with an inner strength and pride in our unquenchable Torah faith. The homes may have looked shabby and woebegone on the outside, in the squalid streets of the ghetto. Inside there was warmth and strength, because they grew and thrived in learning and observing the Torah.

Go to the Mé'ah She'arim section of Jerusalem today, and you will find a remaining echo of this. The houses might be called slums, if you insisted. Many groups in America would clamor how underprivileged they were if they had to live in houses like those. They would tell you that crime *must* breed in such conditions. . . . So walk through Mé'ah She'arim on a Friday night and drink in the blessed tranquillity. Watch the Sabbath candles glimmering through the windows and listen to the *z'miroth* wafting softly through the air. And you will wonder how anyone could call those houses slums. They seem more like a piece of paradise set down on earth.

Without the "bread" of *leumi-th, ḥéruth* and *maor* our people could live, and did. But you cannot live without air, without inhaling precious oxygen. And Jewry's oxygen is the Torah.

Stalin shut the Jewish schools in the USSR; a generation grew up without any Torah. And you had to look far and wide through the homes of Moscow to find a child who could recite the Hebrew sentence of *sh'ma yisraél*: "Hear, Israel: the Lord is our God, the Lord is one." These were always our most sacred words, recited by Jews everywhere (especially martyrs) as their last words on earth. One generation was raised without Torah, and the words disappeared.

Decades earlier, Reform and enlightenment captured the heart of German Jewry. There again a generation grew without Torah — and half of German Jewry converted out of the faith. It took Hitler to bring them back to the Jewish fold — in the concentration camps. In the mass immigration to America, another generation grew without Torah; the parents were too busy struggling for a living to establish proper schools; and how many souls Jewry lost as a result.

In an earlier chapter we mentioned R. Akiva's famous parable of the fish in the water that were advised to come out on dry land to find safety from the fishermen's nets.[75] What made the advice ridiculous is the fact that fish have gills, and so can draw oxygen only from water. We draw the oxygen for our spirit from the Torah. Whatever program of security we find that leaves out the Torah, however safe it makes our physical life, it will make the Jewish spirit die. Without Torah we are no longer part of the Almighty's own people, indestructible as we fulfill His purpose on earth.

Well, what puts oxygen into the air? It comes from the green leaves of tender plants and blossoming trees. They gather energy from the sun and put pure oxygen into the air, to let us go on breathing and living.

Our tender plants and blossoming trees are our children. The "solar energy" that they absorb is the Torah they study in their innocence and purity, fresh and eager in their zest. The Torah that comes from their lips is our sweetest ozone, if you will. The Sages knew this well: Said Resh Lakish in the name of R. Judah haNassi: The world exists only for the sake of the breath of the school children studying Torah. . . . That cannot be equalled in its innocence. . . . And this I received as a teaching from my forefathers: Any city without little children learning Torah will be devastated! (TB Shabbath 119b).

How do you build a Jewish home in America (or anywhere)? No pictures of pious rabbis, no shelves lined with volumes of learning, no record collections of ḥassidic melodies are enough. You need children receiving a sound, thorough education in a good Torah day school, so that their chatter at home, their very breath, will be of Torah. With these tender green plants growing into blossoming trees through the years, to fill your home with the oxygen of the immortal Jewish spirit, you will know you are raising a family linked into the ongoing history of the Almighty's people.

223

# *Notes* TO PART THREE

1. TB Bava Bathra 16b.
2. Genesis 25:27, B'réshith Rabbah 63, 12.
3. Tanna d'vé Eliyahu (6) 7 — ed. Friedmann p. 32.
4. *Daath Z'kénim;* so also Midrash Aggadah, and following them, Malbim.
5. The Midrash makes the point explicit: "Israel is My firstborn son" — i.e. the sons of the one **who** took the birthright (Sh'moth Rabbah 15, 27). Midrash Aggadah, Genesis 25:34, relates: How do we know the Holy One confirmed Jacob's deed? — because Scripture says, "Israel is My firstborn son."
6. Cited in L. Abraham, *Midrash Rivash Tov,* Kecskemet 1899, p. 49.
7. Similarly B'réshith Rabbah 87, 8 and Mechilta, *va-y'hi* 3: that it was by the merit of Joseph's mortal remains that the sea was divided for them.
8. TB Horayoth 10a (so too Sifra, *m'tzora, parashah* 5, 4; but the version in Midrash haGadol, which is quite different, may reflect the original text).
9. On Leviticus 14:34, evidently from a different version in the Midrash (lost to us).
10. "A man thinks, and God laughs"; Ignacz Bernstein, יידישע שפריכווערטער און רעדענסאַרטען (Warsaw 1908) p. 166 § 32.
11. British proverb from the 14th century, derived from Proverbs 16:9, *A man's heart plans his way, but the Lord directs his steps.*
12. So R. Jacob b. Asher, פירוש הטור הארוך (his longer commentary).
13. R. Abraham Menaḥem Rapaport, *Minḥah B'lulah,* Verona 1594. Note also the cogent explanation of Ralbag (R. Lévi b. Gershon): A Canaanite house might be on the point of collapse, and the Israelite occupying it would be unaware of the imminent danger; hence the *tzaraath* infection, making him demolish and rebuild it, was sent to save him. This too lends itself to interpretation in keeping with our theme.
14. William Shakespeare, *Macbeth,* act V scene v line 16.
15. This is evident from the Mishnah, Sukkah v 7-8 and Tamid v 1; and so explicitly in a responsum of R. Hai Ga'on, in *Otzar haGe'onim,* VI B 73.
16. R. Jonathan of Lunel adds most pertinently in his commentary that the departing *mishmar* stood at the southern end for its division of the *leḥem ha-panim* "so that it should be clear to all that they were leaving, and they should not take a hand in the service of the daily *olah* (burnt-offering) of the late afternoon" (for on the Sabbath the outgoing *mishmar* had to offer up the morning *olah,* and the incoming *mishmar* the afternoon *olah*) "so that those arriving would not have to quarrel with them" (*Ginzé Rishonim,* Sukkah p. 233).
17. So Rashi (TB Sukkah 56a); R. Jonathan of Lunel (*op. cit.* 234) writes that as a result they were reduced to the laborious procedure of having two *kohanim* hold each animal's head to keep it from moving, while a third did the ritual slaying.
18. So TJ (Jerusalem Talmud) Sukkah v 8; R. Ḥananél on TB writes that it was for storing both trousers and knives. The Hebrew for niche or cubbyhole here is *ḥalon,* which

generally means a window. R. Jonathan of Lunel's explanation (*loc. cit.*) is that there were windows in the walls of the Temple forecourt, which had to be opened to let in light, since the walls were very high; but for this *mishmar* they were left shut.

19. According to R. Ḥananél, the Talmud means only that she was of the clan or *mishmar* of Bilgah; but from Rashi it seems that this was also her father's name.

20. This follows readings in *Dikduké Sof'rim.*

21. So *Tosefta Kif'shuta,* IV 909.

22. So writes R. Jonathan of Lunel: and when the *Ḥashmonaim,* the *kohanim* of the Lord, gained the upper hand and they purified the Sanctuary and restored the Divine service to its proper state, etc. (*Ginzé Rishonim,* Sukkah 233).

23. Literally, as people say.

24. II Maccabees 4:12.

25. So Rashi indicates; but R. Jonathan of Lunel (*op. cit.* 234) writes that they stayed on to attend to the daily *olah* of late afternoon (after which the *mishmar* of Bilgah evidently showed up and took over). Actually, there may well have been far more to these two answers (Miriam's act and the clan's latecoming), which the Talmud did not record (perhaps so as not to shame descendants of the clan). There seems good reason to believe that the brothers Simon, Menelaus and Lysimachus, arch-leaders of the hellenizing movement to make Jerusalem a Greek-style city, subordinating authentic religious observance to it — which led directly to the revolt of the Maccabees — were members of this clan of Bilgah! (Tcherikover, *Hellenistic Civilization and the Jews,* appendix II, p. 404).

26. As noted above, the Tosefta (Sukkah iv 28) makes this point; so too R. Jonathan of Lunel (*loc. cit.*).

27. *M'lecheth Sh'lomo* on the Mishnah, citing R. Yehoséf Ashkenazi.

28. So Rambam, commentary on the Mishnah: since an incoming *mishmar* marked its arrival by loosening its ring and opening up its niche.

29. For those interested in tracing possible instances where Divine Providence acts in human history, the following should be quite absorbing. It appeared in an article titled "Germany's highway to romance" by William Birnie, in the *Reader's Digest* of August 1970:

"In 1631, during the Thirty Year War, General Johann Tilly, commander of the Catholic League forces, was closing in on the beleaguered town [of Rothenburg]. The future looked grim until the general, in a bizarre burst of whimsey, offered to spare the town if one of its inhabitants could finish off a four-litre beaker of wine in a single quaff. A former burgomaster stepped forward and pulled off the trick.

"At this point the zigzagging course of history becomes truly fascinating. Tilly turned out to be not so whimsical after all: he exacted rights to three days of plunder and a ransom of 20,000 talers, 6,000 ells of cloth, and 3,000 pairs of shoes. This helped to keep the Rothenburgers so impoverished for generations that they were unable to undertake any new building ..."

Against the tragic fate of R. Meir of Rothenburg, "the zigzagging course of history" in the town "becomes truly fascinating" indeed: A few centuries after R. Meir, the town found itself at the mercy of a man's capricious whims (not always whimsical) and was subjected to a ruinous "ransom." If in the time of R. Meir the town exulted and benefited from the plight of this sage and his community, the account was settled measure for measure.

30. Logically this should not have been, since the religious holiday of the neighbors celebrated the supposed return to life of the founder of their faith whom our people supposedly

murdered long ago. Then this should perhaps have been a time to forgive and forget, and let bygones be bygones. But logic was never a strong point of those hate-filled neighbors, prelates or laymen.

31. Hence one of the *kinnoth* (poems of lament) recited on the morning of the ninth of Av begins שַׁאֲלִי שְׂרוּפָה בָאֵשׁ לִשְׁלוֹם אֲבֵלַיִךְ "Ask, thou [Torah] burned by fire, after the welfare of those who mourn thee" — referring to a public burning of the Talmud (*Seder haKinnoth l'Tish'ah b'Av,* ed. Goldschmidt, § 42). It was written (interestingly enough) by the above-mentioned R. Meir of Rothenburg.

32. Literally, his provisions or sustenance; but Rashi explains that it means all a man will earn during the year, from which he will maintain himself (and his family).

33. Version of R. Isaac Alfasi (*Rif*) and R. Asher (*Rosh*).

34. In this connection we can note an interesting passage in the Midrash: Said R. Abbahu: If you see a man giving his money generously to charity, know that he will increase [his income]; as Scripture says, *There is one who gives freely, and he increases his wealth* (Proverbs 11:24). Said R. Naḥman: If you see a man holding back from giving charity, know that he will find his income diminishing; as Scripture says, *and there is one who withholds improperly, and he only suffers want* (ibid. Midrash Mishlé xi 26).

35. I.e. if or when they failed to collect enough in the community. (A *denarius,* or *dinar,* weighed and was worth 4.8 grams of silver.)

36. It was evidently a trade restricted to licensed dealers, or it was highly taxed.

37. Mainly from ed. Margulies. Similarly TB Bava Bathra 9a: Rava told the people of Maḥoza, "I beg you: do kindness for one another, so that you will have peace from the government." And R. Elazar said . . . Now that the Sanctuary no longer exists, if people give charity, good; if not, the heathen come and take it by force. . . ." In *ibid.* 10a we find: Just as a man's income is allotted [by Heaven] from one *Rosh haShanah* to the next, so are a man's losses determined in advance from one *Rosh haShanah* to the next [the amounts that have to come out of his income for the year]. If he is meritorious, he will fulfill the verse, *Are your not to share out your bread to the hungry?* (Isaish 58:7); if not, he will fulfill the verse, *and bring the outcast poor to your house* (ibid.) [meaning heathen who will take these amounts by force] — as in the case of the sons of Rabban Yohanan b. Zakkai's sister:

He saw in a dream (the Talmud continues) that they had to lose 700 *denarii* that year. He applied pressure to them and took money from them for charity, until only seventeen *denarii* remained with them [of the total of 700]. When the day before *Yom Kippur* came, the imperial government sent and took that from them [as a fine]. Said Rabban Yoḥanan b. Zakkai to them, "Have no fear [that you will be troubled further]. You had seventeen *denarii* left with you [that you had to lose] and this they have taken."

"How do you know?" they asked. "I saw it in a dream," he replied. "Then why did you not tell us [in advance]?" they demanded. He answered, "I wanted you to do the mitzvah [of giving charity] for its own sake."

38. For the record, though, this should be noted: When the *t'fillin* from Qumran came into the possession of Yigael Yadin, he took them (carefully wrapped) by bus to the expert who would gently unravel and open them so that their contents could be studied. On the way he was approached by Ḥabad ḥassidim (devoted followers of the *rebbe* of Lubavitch) who urged him to put on *t'fillin.* They were then on a general campaign to get as many in Israel as possible to observe this mitzvah. Ordinarily, Yadin told the young ḥassidim, he would not yield to such a

demand; he was not *dati* (religious); but that morning, moved by the precious find he was carrying, he yielded. (Perhaps this is the exception that proves the rule.)

39. The Midrash itself makes this clear:

‎. . . אל תקרי מורשה אלא ירושה; ירושה היא לישראל לעולם. [נ״א אל תקרי מאורשה אלא מורשה; מלמד שהתורה מורשה לישראל.] משל לבן מלכים שנשבה כשהוא קטן למדינת הים: אפילו לאחר כמה שנים אינו בוש לחזור, מפני שהוא אומר ״לירושת אבותי אני חוזר״. כך תלמיד־חכם שהוא פורש מן התורה והלך והתעסק בדברים אחרים, אפילו לאחר כמה שנים הוא מבקש לחזור אינו בוש, מפני שאומר ״לירושת אבותי אני חוזר״. (שמות רבה לג ז; ספרי דברים § שמה)

. . . Do not read it as *morashah*, a heritage, but as *y'rushah*, an inheritance: it is an inheritance for Jewry forever. [Another version: Do not read it *me'orasah*, betrothed, but *morashah*, a heritage — which teaches that it is a heritage for Jewry.] To give a parable: A royal prince was kidnaped as a little boy and taken to a land overseas. Even after many years he would not be ashamed [bashful or hesitant] to return, because he would say, "I am returning to my father's patrimony." So too if a Torah scholar leaves the Torah and goes and becomes occupied with other matters, even after many years he need not be ashamed or hesitant to go back to it, for he can say, "I am returning to the inheritance that my forefathers left me" (Sh'moth Rabbah 33, 7; Sifre, Deut. § 345).

In another version, this applies not only to a Torah scholar:

‎ד״א מורשה: אפילו יחיד שבישראל שלמד דברי תורה ופירש למקומות אחרים אינו בוש שיחזור, שכן הוא אומר ״לירושת אבותי אני חוזר״. (מדרש תנאים, לג ד)

Another meaning of *morashah*: Even any individual in Jewry who learned words of Torah and departed for other areas need not be bashful (hesitant) to return, for he can say, "I am returning to the inheritance bequeathed by my fathers" (Midrash Tanna'im 33:4).

So the Torah is not an inheritance that we can squander away or forfeit by neglect beyond recall. It is always there, waiting for us. Note this further passage in the same Midrash:

‎ד״א מורשה ולא ירושה: שלא יאמר בן עם הארץ ״הואיל ואין אבי תלמיד חכמים, מה אני מועיל אם אני אלמד תורה?״ (שם)

Another meaning: It is a heritage and not an inheritance [from father to son] — so that the son of an ignorant, unlettered man should not say, "Since my father was not a disciple of Torah scholars, what can I accomplish if I study Torah?" (*ibid.*)

As a heritage, it is the God-given birthright of every Jewish child. To quote once more from the same Midrash: R. Judah said in Rav's name: Whoever withholds a *halachah*, a definitive law, from a student, it is as though he robbed him of his inheritance from his forefathers: For Scripture says, *Moses commanded us the Torah, the heritage* — it is a heritage for you bequeathed by your forefathers since time immemorial.

40. How remarkably tradition has been kept through the centuries in the mitzvah of wearing *tzitzith* — even regarding an insignificant detail — may be seen from the *ḥaluk*, the type of tunic, discovered in the Cave of Letters from the time of Bar Kochba (about 130 CE). Two parts (sheets) were sewn together, with the middle section left open, unsewn, so that it could go over the head (whereupon the stitches lay on the shoulders). Along the length of each part (running along the height of the wearer) were two bands of darker color. When the two parts were sewn together well, the bands met exactly, and thus seemed to run the whole length of the

227

tunic. As Yigael Yadin notes, those bands are quite certainly the ancestors of the dark stripes that adorn the *tallith* (prayer cloak) today, as well as the traditional woolen *tallith katan*. (See Yigael Yadin, *Bar Kokhba*, pp. 69–73.)

41. R. Tovyah b. R. Eliezer, *Lekah Tov*. Similarly Sifre on the verse (Deut. 33): Let them not be, in your eyes, like an old proclamation, which no one reads any more with respectful attention, but rather like a new decree, which all run to read (similarly Rashi to Deuteronomy 26:16).

42. Hebrew, *livnath;* while Rashbam renders it "whiteness" from *loven,* for Ibn Ezra (and the Targum PsJonathan, cited below) it means a brick, from *l'vénah*.

43. John Suckling, *Against Fruition* (c. 1640).

44. The text which follows is according to the edition of David Rieder.

45. There is a fuller version in Pirké d'R. Eliezer, chapter 48 (115b), given also in the commentary of Ḥizkuni (whose readings are cited here in brackets): R. Akiva said: Pharaoh's servants would [harry and] beat the Israelites so that they should make the [doubled] tally of bricks for them — as Scripture says, *the number of bricks you shall impose on them* (Exodus 5:8) [*yet shall you deliver the number of bricks* (ibid. 18)] — although the Egyptians would not give the Israelites straw; as it says, *Straw is not given to your servants, and they tell us: Make bricks!* (ibid. 16). The Israelites had to gather straw in the wilderness, and they would tread and trample on it with their donkeys and with their sons and daughters. The straw of the wilderness [was full of thorns and nettles, and it] pierced the heels of their feet, till blood issued and mingled with the mortar. Rachel the granddaughter of Shuthelach (Numbers 26:36) was close to giving birth, and she was treading the mortar together with her husband, when the child emerged from her womb and became mixed into the brick mold. She wailed for her child, and her outcry ascended before the Divine throne of glory. Then the angel Michael came down and took the brick mold with its clay [and took it and formed it into a brick], and he brought it up before the throne of glory [and placed it beneath the Holy, Blessed One's feet. Hence Scripture says, *and under His feet there was as a form of a sapir brick*: It was a brick made from the *shafir,* the embryo, of the young woman who had been about to give birth].

Shorter, different versions are to be found in two commentaries deriving from the *baaley tosafoth*: *Hadar Z'kénim* and *Paané-ah Raza*.

46. See the passage in the preceding note.

47. Pirké d'R. Eliezer 48 (115b), directly after the passage cited in note 45.

48. Note also the words of *Hadar Z'kénim*: The Holy, Blessed One took it [the brick with the embryo] and placed it before Him for a remembrance. As long as the Israelites were in Egypt, that brick remained before Him for a remembrance; and when they were rescued and delivered, the Holy, Blessed One set it beneath His feet, and there was light and joy in His presence.

49. Ignacz Bernstein, יידישע שפריכווערטער און רעדענסארטען p. 167 s.v. מעשה 1.

50. Tosefta, Avodah Zarah i 20; TJ Pé'ah i 1.

51. TB Yevamoth 64b; TJ vi 6.

52. Rambam, *Mishneh Torah, hilchoth milah* i 18.

53. It is cited in Yalkut Shimoni I § 560, end of *sidrah nitzavim*, in a slightly different version, which has generally been followed in the translation below.

54. Marlon Brando in *On the Waterfront*.

55. As noted earlier in this work, the Talmud tractates *Bava Kamma, Bava M'tzia* and

*Bava Bathra* are actually three sections of one large tractate, *massecheth n'zikin,* as the Talmud itself attests in TB Bava Kamma 102a.

56.   In the Tosefta, the tractate *kélim* is likewise divided into three sections — *bava kamma, bava m'tzia, bava bathra* — on account of its length.

57.   E.g. in Exodus 22:6,27.

58.   Targum Jonathan to verses 25 and 29; Targum Onkelos to verse 31; B'réshith Rabbah 77, 3; 78, 3; Shir haShirim Rabbah 3:10; Tanḥuma, *va-yishlaḥ* 7.

59.   Tanḥuma, *va-yishlaḥ* 7.

60.   Midrashim in note 58.

61.   See e.g. Pirké d'R. Eliezer 27; Mechilta *shiratha* 2; Sh'moth Rabbah 21, 5; D'varim Rabbah 1, 22; Tanḥuma, *mishpatim* 17; Midrash Sh'muél 18.

62.   Following *Dikduké Sof'rim.*

63.   B'réshith Rabbah 77, 2; Yalkut Shimoni I § 132; Shir haShirim Rabbah 3:10.

64.   The commentary *Lekaḥ Tov* actually interprets *kaf y'récho* (the hollow of his thigh) as a reference to the organ of procreation. R. Sh'muél Yitzḥak Reggio writes explicitly in his commentary that it denotes the descendants of Jacob.

65.   It was noted (or quoted) above that "the more things change the more they are the same." A similar event was recorded by R. Meir Lehmann (of the school of Samson Raphael Hirsch) as a true incident, that actually happened in late-nineteenth century Germany. It is given here from the Hebrew, as it appears in *Mivḥar Sippurey Massoreth,* ed. David Zaretsky, Tel Aviv [1958]:

When I spent last summer at Schweningen, I came to know the old man who is the hero of this short but true story.

In the past, Mr P. was the owner of the largest and most prominent stores (shops) in the Hague. Recently, however, he gave it over to his sons. He was close to eighty, but still strong and active, and he was blessed to have his aged mother still living, with him.

One Friday evening in the winter, the large family was seated at the beautifully bedecked and tastefully laden Sabbath table, enjoying the traditional meal. They had already eaten some of the savory dishes, and the sounds of *z'miroth,* the Sabbath table hymns, now filled the house. Suddenly the domestic servant entered with a message: An official from the royal court wished to speak with Mr. P.

"I am sorry to disturb you," said the official as he entered the room. "But I come on an errand from his excellency, Duke Hendryk. His excellency requests Mr P. to send immediately the carpets listed here, to the royal palace. His excellency must have these carpets at once, as they are needed to decorate the banquet hall for a festive performance to take place this very evening."

"To my deepest regret," replied Mr P., "it is impossible for me to fulfill the request of his excellency the duke. The Sabbath began some two hours ago. To carry out his excellency's wishes would mean my violating the Sabbath, and this I cannot do. It will be necessary for his excellency to wait until tomorrow evening."

"What a strange demand you make," said the royal court official, laughing. "The performance is in honor of distinguished guests who must depart on their way tomorrow morning. It is to take place tonight. We cannot possibly wait with the decorations until tomorrow evening."

"Yet I cannot do business on the Sabbath," said Mr P. evenly. "Please convey my profoundest apology to his excellence. If only you had come three hours ago!"

The official bowed courteously and left; and the sounds of the interrupted *z'miroth* started again from the beginning. Thus the family was still sitting around the table when the messenger of the duke appeared again.

"Mr P., his excellency asks that you send the required carpets at once. They are not to be gotten at any other store, and they are essential for this occasion. If we do not get them immediately, our entire evening program will be disrupted."

"Yet I can only repeat what I said before. It is the Sabbath now, and to my deepest regret it is impossible for me to fulfill his excellency's wish."

Just after the family finished saying the grace after meals, the messenger came a third time, bringing with him now a handwritten note from the duke:

*Dear Mr. P. —*

*I absolutely must have the carpets I requested, without delay. If necessary, I am prepared to pay two or even three times their price. But if despite this you refuse to grant my request, you can imagine the consequences. Please consider the matter carefully.*                                *Yours, Hendryk*

After reading the note, Mr. P. spoke: "As it is the holy Sabbath, I cannot answer in writing. Be so kind as to tell him that he is indeed a noble and powerful ruler among us. It is my duty to obey him and always fulfill his wish. Yet above us all there is the supreme King of kings, our Creator; and He commanded me to rest from work on the Sabbath. It grieves me to lose so distinguished a client as his excellency. But I cannot act otherwise."

Once the messenger left, the grown sons, who were active in the business, spoke up: They should have sent the carpets, without mentioning any price. What a blow it would be to lose the duke as a customer. . . . But the aged mother of Mr. P. retorted, "Don't you vex your father. We should be thankful to the blessed Lord that we've had this chance to make a sacrifice for Him. Whatever we lose, He can make up to us . . ."

On Saturday night Mr P. received another message from the duke: He was to come and see the duke Monday morning at ten.

There was a troubled mood in the family till Monday arrived. True, it was a free country. Even the duke couldn't punish Mr. P. for refusing his request. Yet he felt apprehensive as he entered the duke's chamber at ten o'clock. The duke, however, was cheerful and smiling:

"My dear Mr P., I must ask you to forgive me for the unpleasantness I caused you this Friday night. Baron L. came to visit me, and our conversation covered many topics, until we began talking about the Jews. The Baron insisted that the Jews are the most materialistic of all people, ready to sell anything and everything for a price. I disagreed — and we decided to put *you* to the test. You were to show us if a Jew would really sell anything and everything for a price. Well, I am happy that I turned out to be right. . . . Needless to say, I intend to buy from you as in the past; and I will try to have his majesty the king join your list of customers."

A few weeks later, Mr P. received a certificate appointing his firm as one of the "suppliers to the royal court."

(Not always do tests of this kind bring such happy results so soon. Yet the believing Jew regards every incident of this nature as a test by Heaven; and he knows that if he meets the challenge, one way or another he won't lose by it.)

66.    Tosafoth to TB Yevamoth 3a, s.v. *m'kami;* similarly TB Eruvin 70b and B'rachoth 52a.

67.    D'varim Rabbah 11, 9. He is called Satan in Pirké d'R. Eliezer, and is so regarded throughout the Zohar; see R. Reuben Margulies, מלאכי עליון pp. 248-270.

68. Midrash T'hillim 37,1; TB Sotah 10b; B'réshith Rabbah 49, 4.
69. B'réshith Rabbah 48, 7; TB Bava M'tzia 86b-87a.
70. B'réshith Rabbah 63, 11; Tanḥuma ed. Buber, *va-yishlaḥ* 9.
71. Tanḥuma, *sh'moth* 1; Midrash haGadol, Genesis 25:27.
72. Séder Olam 2; B'réshith Rabbah 68, 11; Midrash haGadol, Genesis 28:10.
73. Séder Eliyahu Rabbah (5) 6 — ed. Friedmann p. 29.
74. Written in Hebrew for *haTz'firah* before the Zionist congress of 1911, and reprinted in M. Nimtza-bi, *haDegel,* Tel Aviv 1948. The copy in the Jewish National Library, Jerusalem, bears a handwritten marginal note, evidently by the author, that this flag was originally unfurled at the second congress, not the first, as Wolffsohn indicated in his article. Wolffsohn erred in recalling the event some eleven years later.
75. TB B'rachoth 61b.

# 4

## Land of milk and honey

אֶרֶץ אֲשֶׁר ה׳ אֱ־לֹהֶיךָ דֹּרֵשׁ אֹתָהּ, תָּמִיד עֵינֵי ה׳ אֱ־לֹהֶיךָ בָּהּ
מֵרֵשִׁית הַשָּׁנָה וְעַד אַחֲרִית שָׁנָה (דברים יא, יב)

*It is a land which the Lord your God cares for; the eyes of*
*the Lord your God are always upon it, from the beginning of*
*the year to the end of the year.*      (Deuteronomy 11:12)

E HAVE A HOMELAND; THIS WE ALL KNOW. Not all of us may be ready to go home yet, perhaps. As the Ḥafétz Ḥayyim (the pious sage of Radun) once wrote, if the Messiah were to really, truly come tomorrow, he would surely find a great many Jews caught short, not at all ready for him. They would then excuse themselves to the Almighty, "Of course we believed he was coming. We never doubted it for a moment. We just weren't certain it would happen so soon. We thought the Diaspora could continue another few years at least . . . "[1]

In the same way, we know we ought to go there, but not all of us are ready. Yet at least we know the homeland is there, ours, with some three million Jews living in it (*kén yirbu*).

Now, just what makes it ours, though? Exactly how do we own it?

If you asked someone in Israel's foreign office, you would likely get a long involved (printed) answer going into details about the Balfour Declaration (issued by England in 1917, that it views with favor the wish of the Jewish people to have a national home in Palestine), the British rule of Palestine under the mandate of the League of Nations, and the recognition of the State of Israel by the United Nations in 1948. It is a fine answer, full of first-rate international law, very legal, very scholarly.

Ask a pious bearded Jew in Jerusalem the same question, and you'll get a different answer altogether: What makes the land of Israel ours? — the Almighty said so. Where, when, to whom did he say so? — He gave our Patriarchs a solemn promise that this land would belong to their descendants; and we are the descendants of Abraham, Isaac and Jacob. Simple.

235

There once was a League of Nations. Today there isn't. Today there is a United Nations (which over the years has begun to resemble an instrument of some Arab League or something). Tomorrow it may not exist. To the believing Jew it makes precious little difference. The Almighty's word is durable. Once given, it lasts forever. You can depend on it. Hundreds of thousands live in Israel today because that is exactly what they depend on.

I believe it was the last time I had the honor and privilege of speaking with Reb Aaron Kotler (of blessed memory), probably the greatest Talmudic scholar of our time, when I heard a most interesting thought from him, showing how the Patriarchs trusted the Almighty's promise, and acted on it. It was about six in the evening when Reb Aaron come into my office, and as often before, he began with an original *d'var torah,* a bit of interpretation of our Torah:

In a previous chapter we dwelt on the encounter with his brother Esau that our father Jacob feared. It finally turned out well, and the brothers parted amicably (Genesis 33). Esau took off for Mount Seir; and then we read, ויעקב נסע סכתה *Jacob journeyed to Sukkoth* ויבן לו בית *and he built himself a house,* ולמקנהו עשה סכת *and for his flocks he made shacks* (or *booths*); על כן קרא שם המקום סכות *he therefore called the name of the site Sukkoth* ("shacks" or "booths"; Genesis 331:7).

There are several points to be noted here. First, if Scripture tells us this, it must have been a special, out-of-the-way trip, not something routine that he would ordinarily do in taking care of his flocks. Then the question is: Why did he make the trip?

Next, why did he build a house for himself? As the Sages reckon it,[2] he stayed there just eighteen months — two summers and one winter in between. But this was in the Middle East, where the summers are hot and the winters are mild (with occasional rain). Then why did he need a house? Surely a good sturdy tent would have been quite adequate.

A third difficulty is the part about shacks for his livestock. Why do we need to know that? What difference would it make if he kept his sheep and cattle in the cellar or the parlor? It is a clear, firm principle in our tradition that the Torah, down to the last word, is the living truth of God expressed in human language. But what Divine truth can lie hidden in this piece of information, on where he kept his flocks and herds?

One more point: Scripture tells us that because he built *sukkoth* (shacks, or booths) for the livestock, he called the location Sukkoth. If you took an area of vacant land and built a house and a garage on it, would you call it Garagetown? Then what are we to make of these words of the Torah?

I can recall Reb Aaron Kotler (of blessed memory) sitting in my office, waiting a moment for these questions to sink in. Then he began his answer:

When the Almighty promised the holy land to Abraham, saying, "to you will I give it, and to your progeny forever" (Genesis 13 : 15), He told him further, "Arise, walk through the land, in its length and in its breadth, for to you will I give it" (*ibid.* 17). As the Sages explain, this meant the land would be his (for his descendants to inherit and take) provided he went through it on his own two feet.[3] He could not sit and wait for it to be handed him on a silver platter. (As R. Israel Salanter once said, it is for us to do, to act; then it is for the Almighty to accomplish.)

So Abraham went through the land. With his servants and his flocks and herds he traveled about. But he could not cover everything. . . . One day, though, a messenger came to tell him that war had broken out, four kings against five. The messenger himself was a refugee from the battlefront who had barely escaped. To make a long story short, the four kings defeated the five; but one of the five was the sovereign ruler of Sodom, where Abraham's nephew Lot lived. So the four victorious kings took Lot captive, with all his possessions.

Abraham didn't hesitate; *he led forth his trained men . . . and gave chase as far as Dan* (Genesis 14:14). He battled the four victorious kings and defeated them, and set his nephew free. Since he had reached Dan, the land was now his, for his descendants to inherit, as far north as Dan.

How far south did he ever get? After Sodom and Gomorrah were destroyed, *Abraham journeyed from there* [from where he had been living] *to the land of the South* (Genesis 20:1). Later we find that the site acquired the name Be'er Sheba.

When Americans speak of the expanse of their land, they use the phrase, "from Maine to California." When Scripture tells of all the Israelites getting together, we read, *Then all the children of Israel went out, and the populace assembled as one man, from Dan to Be'er Sheba* (Judges 20:1). This became our standard phrase, used to this day by writers and journalists, to denote the territory of Israel proper: "from Dan to Be'er Sheba." And here we see: these were the limits of Abraham's traveling through the land.

Well, Abraham was the first Patriarch, and his grandson Jacob was the third. Abraham's blessings went to Isaac, and Isaac's to Jacob. From his

237

twelve sons the tribes of Israel would develop. Abraham, as we might say, was only the great-grandfather of the Jewish people, but Jacob was the father — and a father has to look out for his children and provide for their future.

Jacob took a look at the territory that Abraham had covered, from Dan to Be'er Sheba. It was all well and good: but where was all the farmland they would need? the corn belt for growing grain? the fertile fields for raising fruits and vegetables? rich pastureland for the flocks and herds that would supply milk, and meat too? There had to be a regular food supply for twelve tribes. There had to be a hinterland of good, fertile soil.

When Jacob first returned to the Promised Land, a married man, with eleven of his twelve sons already born and growing, he could not give the matter any thought. Esau was still intent on murdering him, and he had to deal with that first. Once Esau was pacified and away, Jacob took off for Sukkoth, on the other side of the Jordan River. There was plenty of fertile land there.

In the ages of exploration, when a voyager landed on new territory where no white man had ever trodden, he would erect a landmark or affix a sign of some kind, to establish his claim to the land. When a prospector dug for gold in the far West and he struck pay dirt, he would have *his* way of staking his claim to the site. This is what Jacob did in the fertile Jordan valley. In keeping with the Almighty's promise to Abraham, *Arise, walk through the land . . . for to you will I give it* (Genesis 13:17), he traveled through the Transjordan, and established his claim to it by building a house — not a tent or a hut for the eighteen months he would stay there, but a structure of permanence, to last through the many years until his descendants would come and take it.

Then the Torah states, וּלְמִקְנֵהוּ עָשָׂה סֻכֹּת *he made shacks for his livestock* (Genesis 33:17). Why is this important? — it shows his intention. "This particular area," he said in effect, "'is prime pasture land. I want it for farm-land for my decsendants, to raise their herds and flocks here."

Jacob the Patriarch was יוֹשֵׁב אֹהָלִים "a dweller in tents," a scholar given to sacred study in the tents of Torah. Years later, when he left Canaan with his entire family to travel down and settle in Goshen, *he sent Judah before him to Joseph* l'horoth, *to show the way before him to Goshen* (Genesis 46:28). But *l'horoth* is from the same root as the word Torah. So the Midrash (*B'réshith Rabbah* 95, 3) explains that he sent Judah ahead to set up a school, a place of study for all the sons and grandsons. Jacob epitomized devotion to sacred learning.

Here, however, he wanted it understood that the land was for sheep and cattle and farming, and not for a network of religious schools. Important as sacred study is, אם אין קמח אין תּוֹרה "if there is no flour [food] there is no Torah study" (*Avoth* iii 21). His descendants would need a regular supply of milk and dairy products, beef and wool (to say nothing of grains, fruit and vegetables, from the rest of the Jordan valley). So Scripture continues, על כן קרא שם המקום סוכות *therefore he called the site's name Sukkoth* — the name of the shacks (or booths) that he built for the livestock. The name would indicate the purpose of the area beyond dispute.

The time came when Moses led the Israelites out of Egypt and through the wilderness, all the way to the Transjordan (which they conquered). They reached (and took) the territory that Jacob had traversed going to Sukkoth. Then we read in the Torah that the tribes of Reuben and Gad came to ask Moses for this territory as their share of the Promised Land, because they had very large flocks of sheep and herds of cattle (Numbers 32:1–5).

Moses did not take kindly to their request. The Israelites still had to cross the Jordan and battle the nations of Canaan in order to conquer the land. If two tribes stayed behind, safe and sound in the Transjordan, not only would the Israelites have a smaller fighting force; they would have a discouraged and disgruntled fighting force (*ibid.* 6–7).

The tribes of Reuben and Gad answered manfully, "We will build sheepfolds for our flocks and cities for our little ones; but we — we will take up arms, ready to go before the children of Israel ... " They were prepared to battle for the land of Canaan, in the forefront of the Israelite army, once they could leave their families safe in fortified cities. But, they insisted, they wanted this land east of the Jordan as their territory (Numbers 32:16–19).

Moses was pleased with their answer. If they did as they promised, he said, all would be well and they could have the territory (*ibid.* 20–23). But as the Midrash notes,[4] he tried to set them straight on one point: They had said, "We will build sheepfolds here for our flocks, and cities for our little ones" (*ibid.* 16) — sheepfolds first, then cities, as though they cared more for their livestock than for their children. So Moses told them, "Build yourselves cities for your little ones, and sheepfolds for your flocks..." (*ibid.* 24). They might be sheep farmers or cattle barons till the cows came home, but the fortified cities should come first, to keep the women and children safe. The humans were more important than the animals.

239

The tribes of Reuben and Gad took the hint. Now they replied, "Our little ones, our wives, our flocks and our cattle shall remain there in the cities of Gilead" (*ibid.* 26) — the women and children first.

Yet (as R. Aaron Kotler pointed out) there was good reason why originally they spoke first of protecting the sheep and cattle: This was the whole basis of their claim. 'The land here belongs to us,' they said in effect, 'because we have all these flocks and herds to raise and protect and care for. We have a first claim here — because when our ancestor Jacob took possession of the land for his descendants, he marked it for grazing. He built *sukkoth* (shacks) for his livestock and called the site Sukkoth! So we ask it for ourselves.'

Moses consented, provided they joined in the fighting for Canaan across the Jordan, under Joshua's command — which they later did. In the *Book of Joshua* (chapter 13) we read how Moses had apportioned this territory east of the Jordan among the tribes of Reuben and Gad (and half the tribe of Manasseh, since it too needed farmland). What happened to the city or town of Sukkoth itself? — it went to the tribe of Gad (Joshua 13:27).

Yet isn't this a bit strange? Reuben was the firstborn, Jacob's oldest son. Surely it should have gone to his tribe? — The answer lies in the Torah's words. We read ומקנה רב היה לבני ראובן *The children (people) of Reuben had a great stock of cattle,* ולבני גד עצום מאד *but the children of Gad had a very immense stock* (Numbers 32:1), evidently far more than the tribe of Reuben. Since Jacob had designated Sukkoth as a center for grazing and Gad had more livestock, that tribe had a stronger right to it.

This, you see, is how we learn our brand of Zionism — from the immortal words of the Torah. This is how we understand our claim, our right to the holy land. When England issued the Balfour Declaration in 1917, a great many people were impressed, heartened, and even overjoyed. The observant learned Jew was aware of other Declarations, issued by the Almighty to our Patriarchs and recorded in the Torah. However you look at it, placed beside those Divine statements, the Balfour Declaration pales by comparison.

When the United Nations did us a favor in 1948 and recognized the State of Israel, a great many were even more impressed, heartened and overjoyed — so much so that an annual prayer-service was formulated to mark the day in our synagogues. People everywhere felt grateful to such personages as Theodor Herzl and Chaim Weizmann and the whole pantheon of Zionist luminaries. The general feeling was that Zionism had succeeded; it had achieved its goal.

The observant Jew bore in mind that all this was not exactly how the Almighty promised to make the land of Israel ours. The events of 1948 might be at best the outer trappings of a more profound, underlying process. The Almighty told Abraham, קוּם הִתְהַלֵּךְ בָּאָרֶץ לְאָרְכָּהּ וּלְרָחְבָּהּ *Arise, walk about in the land, through its length and its breadth,* כִּי לְךָ אֶתְּנֶנָּה *for to you will I give it* (Genesis 13:17). A single simple principle: let Abraham go through it, and wherever he went, that part of the Promised Land would be his, to bequeath to his faithful descendants. He covered Israel proper, west of the Jordan, "from Dan to Be'er Sheba"; as his grandson, heir to the same Divine promise, Jacob went through the Transjordan. So these Patriarchs might rightly be called our true "Zionist leaders and founders."

But now, this Divine rule was not given to the Patriarchs alone. On the banks of the Jordan, Moses told his people, "For if you will keep this entire *mitzvah,* which I command you to do, to love the Lord your God, to walk in all His ways and to cling to Him, then the Lord will drive out all these nations before you, and you shall dispossess nations greater and mightier than yourselves. *Every place where the sole of your foot shall tread shall be yours*: from the wilderness and the Lebanon, from the river — the river Euphrates — and up to the further sea, shall be your territory" (Deuteronomy 11:22–24).

The same principle holds for the heirs of Abraham and Jacob: Go with faith in the Almighty, and wherever you walk in the holy land it will become yours — with or without the blessing and consent of the United Nations. And perhaps this is why the Talmud says כָּל הַמְהַלֵּךְ ד' אַמּוֹת בְּאֶרֶץ יִשְׂרָאֵל מֻבְטָח לוֹ שֶׁהוּא בֶּן עוֹלָם הַבָּא *Whoever* walks four cubits in the land of Israel can be assured that he will live in the world-to-come (TB *Bava Kamma* 110b). The reason might be that as an heir of Abraham and Jacob, a Jew thus does his share to make sure that a piece of Israel will be ours.

What was the Zionist program compared to this? From Herzl to Weizmann the assumption was that the land belonged to others, and we had to get it from them. We know the land is the Lord's very own (this is why we call it the holy land), and He gives it to us in His way, on His terms.

241

## DEM BONES
## SHALL RISE AGAIN

THE LAND IS THE LORD'S, and He promised it to us; but it cannot be given to our people unless Jews live and work in it, to make it blossom and thrive. *The dead do not praise the Lord* (Psalms 115:17). Seen in perspective, then, the state of Israel is indeed a double miracle: Not only did the land have to become ours again, but live people had to come and settle there — live people who had become accustomed to the conditions of *galuth* (the Diaspora), finding some security in it along with all its troubles and *tzores*. They had to be willing to uproot themselves from the world they knew, to come to a new land, ready to face the hardships and the dangers.

In a sense it brings to mind the vision of the prophet Ezekiel: He was taken and set down in a valley of very dry bones, and the Almighty asked him, "Can these bones live?" (Ezekiel 37:1–3). As he stared at the sight, the Almighty told him to prophesy over them, "Behold, I shall bring breath into you, and you shall live" (*ibid.* 5). Ezekiel watched, and he saw the bones coming together amid great noise and commotion, till they fitted together into complete skeletons. They took on sinews and flesh and skin, and he saw whole human beings; but they were not alive yet. So the Almighty told him, "Prophesy to the air ... Come from the four winds, O air, and breathe upon these slain ones, that they may live" (*ibid.* 9). So, as we read, *breath came into them and they lived, and stood upon their feet, a very very great multitude. Then He said to Me: Son of man, these bones are the whole house of Israel. Behold, they say: Our bones are dried up and our hope is lost; we are utterly cut off. Therefore prophesy and say to them: Thus says the Lord God: Behold, I will open your graves and make you come out ... and I will bring you into the land of Israel* (Ezekiel 37:10–13).

A most gripping vision and prophecy it was. And let me say that to connect it with the return of our people to our homeland in this century is by no means an original idea of mine. In the early years of the British mandate, as Jewish migration to Israel increased, the British government decided to invest a large sum of money in developing the land, counting on the increasing Jewish population to make it profitable. The lords of London had to approve the decision, and they set about debating the matter with typical British caution. The head of the Bank of England knew, however, that it was a sound move financially; and to drive the point home to the conferring gentlemen, he took out an English Bible and quoted this chapter to them from the *Book of Ezekiel*. "There," he said, "do you see? God promised the Jews they would come out of their graves and rebuild the land. With this investment we shall help them. You need have no fears. Dead and inert as these people may seem, they are coming rapidly to life. It will be a wise investment that we make."

Yet what did Ezekiel really see here? Was it a dream? Was it the vivid image of prophetic vision? Or did human beings actually come alive from very real bones? And if it was a true happening, who were those human beings, and what happened to them afterward?

These are questions that the Talmud takes up:

רַבִּי אֱלִיעֶזֶר אוֹמֵר: מֵתִים שֶׁהֶחֱיָה יְחֶזְקֵאל עָמְדוּ עַל רַגְלֵיהֶם וְאָמְרוּ שִׁירָה וּמֵתוּ. מַה שִׁירָה אָמְרוּ? ה' מֵמִית וּמְחַיֶּה, מֵמִית בְּצֶדֶק וּמְחַיֶּה בְּרַחֲמִים רַבִּים. רַבִּי יְהוֹשֻׁעַ אוֹמֵר, שִׁירָה זוֹ אָמְרוּ: ה' מֵמִית וּמְחַיֶּה, מוֹרִיד שְׁאוֹל וַיָּעַל (שמואל א' ב ו). רַבִּי יְהוּדָה אוֹמֵר, אֱמֶת מָשָׁל הָיָה. אָמַר לוֹ רַבִּי נְחֶמְיָה: אִם אֱמֶת לָמָה מָשָׁל, וְאִם מָשָׁל לָמָה אֱמֶת? אֶלָּא בֶּאֱמֶת מָשָׁל הָיָה. רַבִּי אֱלִיעֶזֶר בְּנוֹ שֶׁל רַבִּי יוֹסֵי הַגְּלִילִי אוֹמֵר: מֵתִים שֶׁהֶחֱיָה יְחֶזְקֵאל עָלוּ לְאֶרֶץ יִשְׂרָאֵל וְנָשְׂאוּ נָשִׁים וְהוֹלִידוּ בָּנִים וּבָנוֹת. עָמַד רַבִּי יְהוּדָה בֶּן בְּתֵירָא עַל רַגְלָיו וְאָמַר: אֲנִי מִבְּנֵי בְנֵיהֶם, וְהַלָּלוּ תְּפִלִּין שֶׁהִנִּיחַ לִי אֲבִי אַבָּא מֵהֶם. (בבלי, סנהדרין צב ע"ב)

R. Eliezer said: The dead whom Ezekiel brought to life stood up on their feet and uttered praise-song, and then died. What praise-song did they chant? *"The Lord puts to death and brings to life* (I Samuel 2:6). He puts to death in righteousness and brings to life in abounding mercy." R. Joshua said this was their hymn of praise: *The Lord puts to death and brings to life. He brings [one] down to the grave and brings [him] up (ibid.)* R. Judah said: It was a truth-parable. So R. Neḥemiah asked him: If it was truth, why was it a parable? and if it was a parable, why was it truth? — Indeed, in the truth there was a parable. R. Eliezer the son of R. Yosé the Galilean said: The dead whom Ezekiel brought to life went up to the land of Israel, married and had children — sons and daughters. At that R. Judah b. Bathyra stood up on his feet and said, "I am one of their descendants, and these

243

are the *t'fillin* (phylacteries) that my grandfather left me from them" (TB *Sanhedrin* 92b).[5]

Was it parable or truth, vision or reality? Debating the question, the Talmud decides it was true enough; it actually happened; but it was only a parable or symbol of a greater truth in the future. As R. Eliezer b. Yosé the Galilean said, those resurrected people went to Israel and thrived. In the future too, like a dead man returning to life, the Jewish people would come from the exile into the holy land.

So the head of the Bank of England (mentioned a few paragraphs back) was on the right track when he applied this vision of Ezekiel to the Jews migrating in numbers to Palestine (as our land was then called).

R. Eliezer, though, gave those resurrected persons a very short life-span. As he saw it, when Ezekiel revived them they rose to their feet, chanted their hymn of praise, and died.

Well, the Talmud said it was a symbolic prevision of the future. Through the early centuries of our exile in Europe there was a small slow trickle of pious Jews to the holy land, mostly old folk coming to live out their last years in the hallowed aura of Jerusalem. If this is what R. Eliezer saw in his conception of the future, he could hardly be blamed for saying they arose from death, chanted their hymn of praise, and died. Of advanced age (as a rule) when they arrived, those early settlers came to build or establish nothing more than lives of personal piety. They left the spiritual death of the exile for renewed life in Israel's holiness, till their life ended.

Through the 18th and 19th centuries, however, the number of such immigrants to Israel increased. There was the impetus of the disciples of the Vilna Gaon. There were ḥassidic rabbis, especially R. Mendl of Vitebsk, who came about the middle of the 18th century with over 300 souls, including women and children. Is short, there was a steady *aliya* to the holy land — except that no one called it that. There was no major Jewish organization or agency to sound a trumpet of publicity over those simple, unassuming immigrants with their quiet courage. No Herzl or Weizmann inspired them to come, but only the Divine promise and the Divine commands in the Torah. God said the land is for us, and it is a mitzvah to live there.

They generally left family behind, brothers and sisters, perhaps grown children and grandchildren, and braved the hardships and dangers of the long ship journey, so that they could spend the rest of their lives in Israel.

It mattered little to them which Turks or Arabs might be in control of the land. Whatever dark hovel or bit of a dwelling they had, they cherished more than any mansion that the Diaspora might offer. In the holy land they were closer to the Creator.

This was their resurrection. So they came alive out of a long spiritual death-like sleep. How did they subsist? — the communities "back home" sent money. Every devout home had a *pushke,* a charity-box with a slot for coins. As a good Jewish homemaker went to light her Sabbath candles late Friday afternoon, she put a few coins into the *pushke.* The money was collected and sent regularly to Israel, to be distributed among the pious people.

The great majority of "modern" Jews, however (especially the followers of Herzl and Weizmann) shrugged their shoulders and hardly took any notice. "What? You would call that a resurrection, a return from death to life? — religious Jews who came to live out their lives in Torah study and prayer? How long can it last? They will soon be dead again" — just like those whom Ezekiel brought back to life in the valley of the dry bones, in R. Eliezer's view. They arose, hymned their praise-song, and went back to their eternal sleep. What significance can all those settlers have in the holy land? They are just the old *yishuv* (the old settlement), stagnant and meaningless.

There is another view in the Talmud, however. R. Eliezer b. R. Yosé the Galilean said those resurrected people went up to Israel, and they married and had children and grandchildren. The old *yishuv* began with older Jews who came to retire in the Creator's vineyard. But young folk came too. They built housing, schools and a hospital. They built a community, and new life took root. They married and raised families that lasted.

At the Talmud's discussion, when R. Eliezer b. R. Yosé the Galilean gave his view, R. Judah b. Bathyra stood up in the *beth midrash* (the house of study) and announced himself as living proof: He was one of the descendants of those who came back to life long ago in the valley of the dry bones. We know he came from a family line of *n'si'im,* patriarchs, religious heads of Israel. Yet this noted scholar from a distinguished family line traced his lineage back to the dead whom Ezekiel had resurrected. And he held up evidence for all to see: a pair of *t'fillin* that had been used by one (or some) of those resurrected men, and then handed down from generation to generation.

Evidence it certainly was — not only that those people resurrected in the valley had been real, but that they had been devout and observant Jews. In our time, to our misfortune, there are some who migrate to Israel with the idea that living in the land is enough to provide a Jewish identity and way of life. Once in Israel, they say, there is no need for Torah and *mitzvoth*; enough to be Israelis. They forget (or perhaps never learned) the Almighty's clear warning, *You shall therefore keep all My statutes and all My laws, and observe them, so that the land where I am bringing you to dwell therein shall not vomit you out. And you shall not walk in the customs of the nations which I am casting out before you; for they did all these things, and therefore I abhorred them* (Leviticus 20:23). The people whom Ezekiel brought back from death to life remembered the warning. They put on *t'fillin* every day for their prayer. So the community endured and thrived, until, generations later, a noted scholar like R. Judah b. Bathyra could arise from them.

In the old *yishuv* you could also find pairs of *t'fillin* prized and treasured, and handed down reverently through the generations. They have *t'fillin* made by pious craftsmen of high repute out of first-rate material, the *parshioth* (portions of Scripture on parchment, placed inside the boxes of the *t'fillin*) written by *sof'rim* (scribes) who were revered. The *t'fillin* are there because the Heaven-blessed way of life is there, cherished and transmitted through the generations. So in Israel's old *yishuv,* you can also find outstanding Torah scholars from distinguished families, who can trace their lineage to early settlers in the 18th and 19th centuries.

As the 19th century gave way to the 20th, immigration to Israel increased by leaps and bounds. Religious Jews came, both within and outside the Zionist movement. And the way of life of the old *yishuv* spread its influence to other areas and communities in the land. It was a matrix of help, guidance and inspiration. In short, Israel stopped being a place for the old to go and die there, embraced by holiness — in keeping with R. Eliezer's view that the resurrected men in the valley revived, chanted their praise-song, and returned to death. The second view became reality: Those who left the spiritual death of exile for renewed life in the holy land established a viable flourishing Jewish community, where *t'fillin* rather than artistic masterpieces become family heirlooms.

# THE QUESTION
# OF IDENTITY

IN THE VALLEY OF THE DRY BONES Ezekiel spoke his unforgettable words of prophecy; a mighty wind blew, and the bones were gathered and transformed into human beings, risen from death to live again. It remains for the Talmud to consider: Who were they? What and where had they been before they died and became reduced to a mass of bones?

וּמַאן נִינְהוּ הַמֵּתִים שֶׁהֶחֱיָה יְחֶזְקֵאל? אָמַר רַב, אֵלּוּ בְּנֵי אֶפְרַיִם שֶׁמָּנוּ לַקֵּץ וְטָעוּ, שֶׁנֶּאֱמַר, וּבְנֵי אֶפְרַיִם שׁוּתָלַח וּבֶרֶד בְּנוֹ וְגוֹ׳ וַהֲרָגוּם אַנְשֵׁי גַת הַנּוֹלָדִים בָּאָרֶץ כִּי יָרְדוּ לָקַחַת אֶת מִקְנֵיהֶם וְגוֹ׳ ‎(דה"א ז כ—כא). וּשְׁמוּאֵל אָמַר, אֵלּוּ בְּנֵי אָדָם שֶׁכָּפְרוּ בִּתְחִיַּת הַמֵּתִים, שֶׁנֶּאֱמַר, וַיֹּאמֶר אֵלַי, בֶּן אָדָם, הָעֲצָמוֹת הָאֵלֶּה כָּל בֵּית יִשְׂרָאֵל הֵמָּה; הִנֵּה אֹמְרִים יָבְשׁוּ עַצְמוֹתֵינוּ וְאָבְדָה תִקְוָתֵנוּ נִגְזַרְנוּ לָנוּ ‎(יחזקאל לז יא). רַבִּי יִרְמְיָה בַּר אַבָּא אָמַר, אֵלּוּ בְּנֵי אָדָם שֶׁאֵין בָּהֶן לַחְלוּחִית שֶׁל מִצְוָה, שֶׁנֶּאֱמַר, הָעֲצָמוֹת הַיְבֵשׁוֹת שִׁמְעוּ דְּבַר ה׳ ‎(שם ד). רַבִּי יִצְחָק נַפָּחָא אָמַר, אֵלּוּ בְּנֵי אָדָם שֶׁחִפּוּ אֶת הַהֵיכָל כֻּלּוֹ בְּשִׁקְצִים וּרְמָשִׂים, שֶׁנֶּאֱמַר, וָאָבוֹא וָאֶרְאֶה וְהִנֵּה כָל תַּבְנִית רֶמֶשׂ וּבְהֵמָה שֶׁקֶץ וְכָל גִּלּוּלֵי בֵּית יִשְׂרָאֵל מְחֻקֶּה עַל הַקִּיר סָבִיב סָבִיב ‎(יחזקאל ח י); וּכְתִיב הָתָם, וְהַעֲבִירֵנִי עֲלֵיהֶם סָבִיב סָבִיב ‎(שם לז ב). רַבִּי יוֹחָנָן אָמַר, אֵלּוּ מֵתִים שֶׁבְּבִקְעַת דּוּרָא... שֶׁבְּשָׁעָה שֶׁהִגְלָה נְבוּכַדְנֶצַר הָרָשָׁע אֶת יִשְׂרָאֵל הָיוּ בָּהֶן בַּחוּרִים שֶׁהָיוּ מְגַנִּין אֶת הַחַמָּה בְּיָפְיָן, וְהָיוּ רוֹאוֹת אוֹתָן כַּשְׂדִּיּוֹת וְשׁוֹפְעוֹת דַּם זִיבָה. אָמְרוּ לְבַעֲלֵיהֶן וּבְעַלֵיהֶן אָמְרוּ לַמֶּלֶךְ; צִוָּה הַמֶּלֶךְ לְהָרְגָן וַהֲרָגוּם; וַעֲדַיִן הָיוּ שׁוֹפְעוֹת דַּם זִיבָה, וְצִוָּה הַמֶּלֶךְ וּרְמָסוּם. ‎(בבלי, סנהדרין צב ע"ב)

Now, who were the dead that Ezekiel revived? Rav said: They were the people of Ephraim who calculated the end [of the Israelites' enslavement in ancient Egypt] and made an error. For Scripture says, *And the sons of Ephraim: Shuthelah,* etc. *whom the men of Gath that were born in the land slew, because they came down to take away their cattle,* etc. (I Chronicles 7:20–21). Sh'muel said: These were people who denied that the dead are ever to be resurrected; for we read, *Then He said to me: Son of man, these bones are the whole house of Israel who say herewith, "Our bones are dried up and our hope is*

247

*lost; we are utterly cut off*" (Ezekiel 37:11). R. Yirmiah b. Abba said: These were people who had in them no vitalizing moisture of *mitzvah*, religious good deeds; as it says, *O dry bones, hear the word of the Lord* (*ibid.* 4). R. Yitzḥak Nappaḥa (the smith) said: These were the people who covered the entire Temple with abominable and creeping things; for it says, *So I went in and saw, there, every form of creeping thing and detestable beast, and all the odious idols of the house of Israel, portrayed on the wall* saviv saviv, *round about* (Ezekiel 8:10); and there it is written, *He took me by them* saviv saviv, *round about* (*ibid.* 37:2). R. Yoḥanan said: These were the dead of the valley of Dura . . . For when the wicked Nebuchadnezzar drove the Israelites into exile, there were young men among them whose beauty put the sun to shame. When the Chaldean women saw them, they suffered dysmenorrhea [so distraught with longing were they]. They told their husbands, and their husbands told the king, whereupon he ordered them [the young men] executed. Yet the dysmenorrhea continued [at the sight of the slain young men]; and so by the king's order they were trampled [beyond recognition] (TB *Sanhedrin* 92b).[5]

The first view about their identity is that they were from the tribe of Ephraim. In other sources we find the details: While all the Hebrews were still cruelly enslaved in ancient Egypt, before Moses appeared to liberate them at last, the tribe of Ephraim made a calculation. They evidently had accurate chronological records, and by their reckoning it was exactly 400 years since the Almighty had told Abraham in making a covenant (a solemn pact) with him, *Know, O know that your progeny will be alien in a land not their own, and they shall serve them; and they shall afflict them 400 years; but also that nation, whom they will serve, I will judge; and afterward they shall come out with great wealth* (Genesis 15:13–14).

From the plain meaning we would have expected the Israelites to have been actually enslaved in Egypt 400 years, from the time Pharaoh first put them to work making bricks and building store-cities for him. But the Sages teach that in His kindness the Almighty began counting the years from long before, so that the actual enslavement of the Israelites lasted only 210 years.[6] Evidently the tribe of Ephraim knew something of this tradition, and they assumed that the Almighty had meant 400 years from the very time He foretold this to Abraham. By their reckoning exactly 400 years had passed. It was time to leave.[7]

The next day or so, one bright Ephraimite appeared and announced, "The Almighty manifested Himself to me, that I should take you out of

Egypt!" The other tribes shrugged their shoulders and went back to making bricks and doing their construction work. The Ephraimites, though, considred themselves aristocrats, being descended from Joseph the ruler of Egypt; and they thought themselves mighty warriors.[8] Some 200,000 of them took their wives and children, and armed with weapons they left.[9]

They had made a small mistake in their calculation, though. The Almighty told Abraham, "your progeny, *zera*, will be alien," etc. — and by this He alluded to Abraham's son Isaac. Decades later, after Isaac was born, the Almighty told him. "for through Isaac shall progeny, *zera,* be called yours" (Genesis 21:12). From the birth of Isaac, Abraham's true progeny or descendants began to exist in the world; and from that moment the Almighty calculated the 400 years of enslavement in an alien land.[10]

According to *Séder Olam* (chapter 1) Abraham was seventy when he received this prophecy about the 400 years; when Isaac was born, he was 100 (Genesis 21:5). This is why Scripture states, that "the time the children of Israel dwelt in Egypt was 430 years" (Exodus 12:40): 400 reckoned from the birth of Isaac, 430 from the time of the Divine covenant with Abraham, when this slavery was foretold to him.

The Ephraimites made a small mistake and went out thirty years too soon — and it cost them their lives. They went blithely down to Gath in the land of the Philistines; and seeing cattle, they wanted to take the beasts. They had their reason: Didn't the Almighty promise Abraham that when the long period of slavery would end, *afterward they shall come out with great wealth* (Genesis 15:14)? If this was the time for the great release from bondage (as they reckoned), they were entitled to take the wealth of the heathens. So the Philistines in Gath came out and slew them (I Chronicles 7:21).[11]

Well, in modern history we have had our share of Ephraimites. Perhaps there was Theodor Herzl himself to start with, shuttling feverishly among the imperial palaces of Europe, and finding all his efforts doomed, till he died at an early age, and his sons converted out of the faith.

There were countless uncelebrated visionaries who went directly to Israel to take possession of the land far ahead of anything like the proper time, tragically ill-equipped for the harsh realities of malaria, hostile neighbors and corrupt officials. There were the Revisionists who thought that as the chosen people they were entitled to go parading to Israel in aristocratic fashion, organized into fighting units, bearing arms and marching with military pomp and bravura. They would simply but imperiously take all that the Almighty promised us, with small concern for anyone who stood in their way.

For all this a price had to be paid. They mobilized reactions of hostility and aggression in the peoples and nations about them. Hatred came to the fore, and Jews were attacked. When the British ruled the land under the mandate, trying to do the job as best they could, in their own mutton-headed bumbling way, we had the fruits of Revisionism: impatient "Eph-raimites" who thought to speed up the approach of the *ge'ulah,* our national liberation and sovereignty, with bombs, murder and sabotage. Young Jews sacrificed themselves, going bravely to the gallows when caught, be-lieving they were acting in a holy cause. We have lived to see (to our sorrow) Arab infiltrators come into Israel just as convinced that theirs is a holy cause, and just as ready to sacrifice themselves.

Hasty imperious conquest by violence and bloodshed (where it is not in self-defense and not clearly sanctioned by Heaven) can never be the way to realize the Divine promise of the land to the heirs of Abraham, Isaac and Jacob.

Sh'muel gives another view in the Talmud: In the valley of the dry bones, Ezekiel brought back to life people who had refused to believe that the dead *can* come back to life.

In our modern history we have had our share of those as well. The founders of the *haskalah* movement believed that authentic Judaism was a doomed and dying thing, with which Jewry must wither and lose its spiritual life — and this death (they insisted) would be final: no resurrection ever. So they clamored for us to "mix and match" with our non-Jewish neighbors: Mix with their cultural life by sharing in it; learn their language and literature, their music and art, and join in. And match our culture to theirs. Instead of a "narrow, insular" Torah life, develop a Jewish culture — literature and art and music — and bring it to them to enjoy. Be a man among men.

As mentioned in an earlier chapter, Moses Mendelssohn was a foremost pioneer (if not *the* foremost pioneer) of *haskalah.* His children converted out of the Jewish faith.

Many others believed that the traditional Jew, in his world of Torah, was doomed — and there is no life after death. So they simply assimilated, or they turned socialist or bundist or communist. Even the core Zionists who built up our land into the State of Israel were radical left-wingers.

The wanted no part of the *golus yid* (Diaspora Jew) and his Torah (except for his UJA contribution). After all, when they saw six million killed by the Nazis like sheep — docile, unresisting — they felt such a deep shame at those "relatives" of theirs that they wanted nothing more to do with them. They became Israelis in the sense of Canaanites (a good number of them actually called themselves so). Diaspora Jewry, as far as they were concerned, was in three stages: doomed, dying, dead. In their new Canaanite spirit they raised a generation of Hebrew-speaking Israelis that could easily be taken for Frenchmen or Italians if they changed their language.

What did the Almighty do in the valley of the dry bones? Says the Sage named Sh'muel: He brought back to life the very people who never believed the dead can be revived. What has been Israel's history in the short period since it proclaimed its existence? — three wars for survival, when by every logical calculation *it* was doomed, with no glimmer of hope to be resurrected. And the country is still there, alive and growing.

How did it happen? What let the young small country not only survive but achieve stunning victories on the battlefields? The official answer used to be *tzahal,* Israel's defense forces, in which the Israelis believed far too strongly, to the point of idol-worship. Since the setbacks and losses in the Yom Kippur War, however, that answer is not given so emphatically any more. We are more in a mood to listen to the clear single answer of R. Nahman of Bratzlav, one of the most incisive and inspiring spirits of *hassiduth.* Consider well these words of his:

"Prayer is interlinked with miracles, that are not natural. For at times by the laws of nature there is something that must happen, and prayer overturns nature. The main miracles, which means (in effect) the main core of prayer, are nowhere but in the land of Israel. . . . Egypt is the opposite of the land of Israel . . . the opposite of miracles; and for this reason there is no room for prayer in Egypt. . . ."[12]

We might rub our eyes as we read this and wonder if it was really written around the beginning of the 19th century, and not yesterday or the day before.

Then what made Israel come out alive and kicking from three impossible wars for survival? — prayer, says R. Nahman of Bratzlav. Whether in Israel's synagogues or in the hearts of anxious, anguished Jews the world over, glued to their radios, there was certainly prayer enough, with yearning and hope, for Israel to emerge from its battles intact and undefeated. Perhaps never before or after was Jewry so united as in its hope and prayer for

Israel at war. And talking of miracles, the whole world has still found no other way to describe the events of the Six-Day War.

In the Yom Kippur War there was one miracle just as obvious and spectacular, when, with its own side of the Suez Canal invaded, the soldiers of Israel crossed the Canal into enemy territory and soon brought Egypt to the brink of defeat. (Thanks only to the Soviet Union and its threats, Israel could not achieve full victory. The whole thing was hushed up afterward, so that to this day Egypt takes pride in its "victory.")

So in our newspaper headlines and television reports we have witnessed miracles as astounding (in their way) as anything Ezekiel saw in the valley of the dry bones. The dead who came to life in that valley were (according to Sh'muel) people who had never believed that a human being can live again after his life ends. Just why were *they* resurrected? The early commentary *Yad Ramah* on the Talmud explains: The Almighty treated them with kindness beyond the letter of the law. By law they did not deserve to return to life (since they had always denied that such a thing could happen). Why did He do it? — to let them know that their denial was all wrong and unjustified. But above all (Rashi and *Yad Ramah* add) it was a symbolic act, so that all Jewry should understand that a return to life awaits them too after passing on. For if it happened to those men in the valley, it would surely happen with everyone else.

This is what we are witnessing in Israel's short but eventful history. Before the Six-Day War, many there expected the country to be wiped off the globe, beyond any doubt, right into the Mediterranean. Listening to the Arab threats, calculating the Arab strength, they were certain that Israel was as good as dead, past any chance of survival or revival. When the Yom Kippur War broke out, odds were given in Europe to "sporting types" willing to bet on the outcome (who watched it all with fascinated interest, like the ancient Romans looking at gladiators and wild animals); and believe me, the odds were heavily against Israel. To this day one head of Europe's Nato cannot understand why and how the Jewish homeland is still on the map.

Yet survive the Israelis did, and very well, thank you. Why? As R. Naḥman of Bratzlav would say, the focused prayer and hope of Jewry produced some miracles, because Israel is by nature all miracles. Behind it, though, if we read our Talmud correctly, is the Almighty's will and purpose. The blessed Lord had His own way of teaching us faith that our land and our people will live, beyond every calculation, prediction or expectation. To paraphrse Rashi, if this land could survive, with its predominantly non-religious or atheistic population that believed itself doomed for good, with founding fathers and leaders who believe the Torah and Jewish faith of the *galuth* doomed beyound recall, then it proves that the God of Israel is alive and healthy, and all He holds dear, including religious Jewry and its Torah, will always endure and return to life.

A simple thought, no? You don't have to be a great scholar or mystic to see the point. Yet alas, there are still many *farshtopte kepp* (blockheads) among our people to whom this thought has not penetrated.

That, at any rate, was Sh'muel's answer. R. Yirmiah b. Abba, however, was not satisfied with it. *What?* said he; those people only denied that the dead will be resurrected? Oh no: they were far worse. Do you know why their bones, that Ezekiel saw piled in the valley, were so very dry? — because while they lived they never did a single mitzvah, a single religious good deed, to refresh their spirit as moisture refreshes and vitalizes a plant. As a parched throat needs water, as dry soil waits for rain, so the Jewish spirit needs the *mitzvoth* of the Torah. Yet while they lived, those people rejected and spurned every last mitzvah. And still they were brought back from death to life — as a sign to the whole of Jewry that no one need despair. In His great kindness, *all* will return to life (for who can be worse than they?).

This too echoes Israel. If the Israelis had rejected life in the Diaspora as a doomed, lost cause and decided to establish a religious, observant life in the holy land, that might have been commendable and valuable. But the fine minds of Labor Zionism and their followers rejected the Torah along with the religious life of the *galuth*. They threw out the baby with the bath, refusing to see any mitzvah, any fulfillment of the Divine will, in their very return to the land.

Long ago Israel had a king named Aḥab. In the words of the Talmud (*Sanhedrin* 102b) he once proclaimed publicly that he wanted no part of the God of Israel. Unfortunately, Israel's former leaders sometimes gave the impression of being his successors, following in his footsteps. When a high American official is sworn into office, he generally invokes the name of God, prayerfully, in his acceptance speech (or inaugural address). Not so formerly in Israel — because God belonged to some of the opposition parties.

And yet, says R. Yirmiah b. Abba, there is no need to despair or lose hope. It was this very kind of people who were returned to life in the valley

253

of the bones — as a lesson to us all. Such people will go on living in Israel;
and through the continuing events of its young history the Almighty will
go on teaching them that (as R. Naḥman of Bratzlav said) Israel is firmly
interlinked with miracles and is under His own constant watchful care,
above the rules of nature, military strategy, and international politics.

As R. Yirmiah b. Abba quoted, Ezekiel exclaimed in the valley, *O dry
bones, hear the word of the Lord!* (Ezekiel 37:4). This was all those old heretics
had to do, and at Ezekiel's prophecy they returned to life. This is all that the
leaders of Israel and their followers have to do, and the country can return
to a spiritual life that will bring untold blessing.

R. Yitzḥak Nappaḥa had a fourth answer: The resurrected people in the
valley were those who had brought *sh'katzim ur'masim* to the holy Temple
in Jerusalem, all kinds of abominable forbidden insects and crawling creatures, until they covered the Temple walls.

In the Yiddish folk-idiom, though, *sh'katzim ur'masim* connotes non-
kosher food. One emphatic way that out grandafthers had of declaring
something non-kosher was to say it was *treyf vi sh'kotzim ur'mosim.*[13] And
this too, alas, we have today in our Jewish life linked with Israel, our land
of milk and honey. American Jews, especially of the Reform variety, have
a way of building fancy synagogues and calling them temples. How many
dinners have been held in those temples to raise funds for Israel, where the
food has indeed been *treyf vi sh'kotzim ur'mosim*!

Of course, any red-blooded American Jew stung by this accusation
would immediately retort by pointing out how good and splendid the
cause is: supporting Israel. True; but then it is what our Sages call *mitzvah
ha-ba'ah ba'avérah* — a *mitzvah* that comes about through a sin; and sad to
say, our Sages teach that it is of no value at all.[14] In other words, on balance
the Almighty is not pleased by it. A person who has stuffed himself on a
good non-kosher dinner at his temple, and made his sizable contribution
(or pledge) to the United Jewish Appeal, need not go home feeling pleased
with himself. For all we know, the people mentioned in the Talmud who
filled the Sanctuary in Jerusalem with unclean vile crawling creatures might
also have believed that with this they were serving the Lord, and they too
may have felt very pleased with themselves. Yet the prophet Ezekiel
thundered that the Almighty found it detestable.

And still, says R. Yitzḥak Nappaḥa, those people were brought back
to life — again, as an object lesson for our people, so that all Jews, of

whatever kind and sort, can take heart, assured that they too will return on the great day of resurrection.

Remember, though, the two views in the Talmud that were given above: One Sage holds that the people whom Ezekiel revived rose on their feet, hymned their song of praise to the Almighty, and died again. Another says that they went to Israel, married, and raised families that endured.

If the revival is linked with the land of Israel, it will last.

We know what is happening to American Jewry outside the ranks of the fully observant. We see the alarming rate of increase in intermarriage everywhere. From one generation to the next, Jewish identity, involvement and commitment has been dwindling and dying; and it can be safely predicted that once dead, a proud affirmative sense of Jewish identity does not return to life.

Our state of Israel, though, has had the power to galvanize and mobilize such a sense of belonging and commitment. Around Israel and its needs our people unite and respond as for few other causes in Jewish life.[15] To quote again from the trenchant words of R. Naḥman of Bratzlav: "By giving charity to Israel we become included in the atmosphere of Israel, which is in essence like holy breath without sin;[16] and through that, stern judgment and darkness, etc. are nullified (removed) in the world."[17]

Perhaps then the great revivifying power of Israel (which, as R. Naḥman said, is pure miracle) does and will reach even to those who support it amid the abominations of their non-kosher dinners in their temples. For many of them it has certainly given a new lease of life to a good sense of Jewish identity and pride, that might otherwise have died long ago. With many of them, too, we find their grown children going to Israel for a period of study or service, where they have a chance of becoming interested in authentic observant Judaism and embarking on a program to learn it.

We must never underestimate the power of k'dushah, holiness. And to quote R. Naḥman of Bratzlav once more, "the land of Israel is the sum total of all holiness."[18]

The Talmud has one more answer about the people resurrected in the valley of the bones. R. Yoḥanan reminds us that over 2500 years ago Nebuchad-nezzar invaded Israel, destroyed the first Sanctuary in Jerusalem, and exiled our people to his country of Babylonia. Among the exiles there were incredibly handsome youths, with a dazzling masculine beauty that could put the sun to shame. So attractive were they that when the Chaldean women of Babylonia saw them, they grew physically sick with longing. Naturally, their husbands were not pleased, and they complained to their king. They probably asked him, "What did you go and import into our land? breathtakingly handsome young Hebrews? Do you know what is happening to our home life?

Like a certain *fuehrer* in our century, Nebuchadnezzar had a simple (final) solution: The Hebrew youths were take to the valley of Dura and put to death. It didn't help, though. The Chaldean women could still go and gaze at their features, and they still swooned. So their husbands probably complained again to their king. At his order the bodies were trodden and trampled over, till they were mangled beyond all recognition.

Does the story sound far-fetched? Read the history of such "stars of the silver screen" as Rudolph Valentino and Clark Gable (if they weren't in your time). Read about the effect they had on the millions of women who saw their films — the fan clubs and the mob scenes at their personal appearances. Read what happened at Valentino's funeral, when the man was already dead. All along, crooners and pop-singers have been able to exert such a powerful, mesmeric effect on their female audiences.

But what lesson lies in this for us? Well, through all the phases of our exile, where and when opportunity offered, there were Jews of youthful energy and determination, ready to prove how handsome and attractive they could be in their achievements. What spells success in the surrounding milieu? Is it grades and marks in the classroom, all the way through a university education, by showing brilliance in classical fields of study? We had our boys, determined to do better, to carry off the honors and awards, to outshine everyone. They came to a setting where success was measured by achievement and profits in business, and there were those who resolved to build bigger and better empires of commerce, out of their imagination and daring. Was it a mark of success to belong to the country club? No matter how, they would gain admittance. Come what might, their stars would shine brighter in the firmament of their adopted land — brighter even than the sun.

Could one achieve fame and fortune in politics? Members of our people were off, running for office faster and better than their opponents. Wherever, whenever a new "style of living" developed for those who called themselves "the beautiful people," there were always some few from our ranks only too eager to join them, heedless of the consequences. (One recalls the late but unlamented Senator Joe McCarthy shown on television, as the

Senate's committee worked to decide if he should be censured for his activities in slander and character assassination. As he appeared on the television screen, there was always his trusty lieutenant or henchman whispering sleazily into his ear. And there was an ache in the heart at the knowledge that not only was that young man Jewish, but he had one of the most glaringly obvious Jewish family names in the world.)

Unwisely, blindly, there have always been those who aroused resentment and hostility by their fierce competition, their resolve to achieve and join and outshine — to fly with the jet set, to be more dazzling than the sun in their success. And they were stunned when they were rewarded not by admiration and applause but by resentment and hatred. Of course they immediately labeled it anti-semitism and set up organizations to counteract it, to convince all the neighbors that they were really splendid charming people at heart.

In the valley of Dura, says R. Yoḥanan, the exquisitely attractive youths were killed, then mangled beyond recognition. To our eternal sorrow, this has been the fate of the *n'shamah*, the Jewish heart and soul of everyone who resolved at all costs to be a super-success in the Diaspora, to outdo and outshine all the competition. By birth such a person remained Jewish (as Hitler proved). Any spiritual Jewish identity he may have had was trampled and mangled out of any recognizable shape in the process.

So we read of resurrection in the Torah, of people resurrected from dry bones and returned to life. They had lived before. Now they would live again.

Who were they? As we saw, the Talmud gives five answers. Yet if we may say so, the history of our time has given its own answer, with the unmistakable ring of metaphysical truth. For our time produced its own "valley of dry bones" when six million Jews were exterminated in the gas chambers of Europe.

Strangely enough, this thought finds an echo in a passage of the Midrash: "Just as there [in ancient Egypt] there were sixty myriads, so here [in the valley of the dry bones] there were sixty myriads" (*Pirké d'R. Eliezer* 33). Like the word "myriads," the Hebrew original, *ribbo*, can mean either 10,000 (as it is generally understood) or simply a vast multitude (from the root *rav*, "a great many"). The Hebrews who left ancient Egypt with Moses numbered 600,000 (Exodus 12:37) — sixty myriads, a myriad meaning 10,000. In the valley that Ezekiel saw, the Midrash says there were (likewise) sixty myriads of deceased persons reduced to a mass of bones. This might mean sixty multitudes of 100,000 each : six million. (Remember too that when the Allied forces took Germany and our people could enter the concentration camps, we found the survivors no more than skin and bones — dry haunted living skeletons.)

In the valley, at the Almighty's word, Ezekiel lifted his voice in prophecy. A great wind came blowing from the four directions of the world, and stirred the bones into life. They were transformed back into human beings.

The miracle of our time was not that direct and obvious. We could not bring the six million themselves back to life. For them we could only mourn and vow to remember. But the survivors, the haunted living skeletons, could be slowly restored to human form and normal life. With patient care they were able to live again, to plan and build and achieve. Hitler had decided to exterminate the Jews of Europe. Though sharply reduced in number, the Jewry of Europe survived him and returned to life.

What happened to the people that Ezekiel revived? R. Eliezer said they stood up, uttered praise-song, and died again. This too we saw. Whoever survived the cruel nightmare of the holocaust surely felt a great surge of joy and gratitude to his Maker at being alive, at being able to move and act, subject to no more persecution by murderers. But then some simply came to America to make money. Or they stayed in Europe, even in Germany itself, determined to get rich and live in style. A good number of them never married, never raised families. They only wanted the security of wealth after the Nazi nightamare. Some even had to have their homes filled with loaves of bread or piles of food, which they could never eat because there was too much. When it spoiled, they threw it out and bought more food in excess.

Above all, they never built any Jewish lives of significance or worth. To all intents and purposes, they became Germans, Poles, Hungarians, etc. They lived on as if there had never been a Hitler and they had never been Jews. Spiritually, they died under the Nazis, returned to life, and died again.

But there is another view in the Talmud. R. Eliezer b. R. Yosé the Galilean says that the people whom Ezekiel revived went to the land of Israel, married and raised families that endured.

Did this also happen in our time? — *Yes indeed!* This was the true miracle that we witnessed, as stunning in its way as anything Ezekiel saw. The six million perished, but it was as if they bequeathed their spirit, their silenced will to live, to the rest of their people. In the aftermath of the second World War came a determination of steel, forged in the crucible of the holocaust, that whatever the price, there must be a Jewish homeland, a country that Jews can call their own, from which they can never again be sent in cattle cars to concentration camps. American Jewry awoke, after decades of a death-like sleep of indifference, to a new sense of responsibility and purpose, ready to "lend a hand" of material and political support, as the state of Israel was born.

"Son of man," said the Almighty to Ezekiel in the valley, "these bones are the whole house of Israel. Behold, they say: *Our bones are dried up and our hope is lost; we are utterly cut off.* Therefore prophesy and say to them . . . Behold, I will open your graves . . . O My people, and I will bring you to the soil of Israel . . . And I will put My spirit in you, and you shall live; and I will settle you on your soil . . ." (Ezekiel 37:11–14).

This was the original prophecy for the great pile of dry bones. They were to become human beings again — on Israel's land. There they would endure. So in the one decade of the 1940's we went from frantic dismay and anguished mourning over six million dead to joyous exultation over the rise and survival of the state of Israel: an independent homeland after almost 2,000 years of exile.

It was the resurrection of the *house* of Israel. A house as a rule is a place where a family lives, with growing children. The settlers of Israel in our time have raised families that are raising their own families in turn. As R. Eliezer b. R. Yosé the Galilean said, those who came back to life in the valley went to Israel, married, and lived to see children and grandchildren. The miracle of resurrection was not meant to be a flash in the pan, a coruscation of fireworks that would die in the night, leaving darkness and silence. Thank Heaven, the generations in Israel continue.

We have witnessed a miracle. Yet how truly R. Naḥman of Bratzlav spoke when he said (around the start of the 19th century) that *everything* about the land of Israel is supernatural. Since its birth, Israel's miracles have only grown bigger and better.

Immediately after the Six-Day War, I recall, someone asked me, "What will happen now in Israel?"

"If you can explain what happened in the past six days," I told him, "I can explain what will happen in the next six days."

The miracles have continued; and Israel needs still more supernatural help from our Father in heaven. In the natural order of things, the forces

259

massed against our homeland are far beyond her. Then let us remember what R. Naḥman said: that Israel, miracles and prayer are all one, all interlinked together. It will take our hope and longing and prayer, our focused care and concern, to make the vitally needed wonders keep happening. "These bones," said the Almighty to Ezekiel in the valley, "are the whole house of Israel." The great revival of spirit, from the death and despair of the holocaust to the creation of Israel, did not happen for the Israelis alone. It was a profound spiritual revival for "the whole house," *di gantze mishpocheh* of Jewry, the world over.

It affected Jews who had long turned to various kinds of assimilation, convinced that historic Jewry and its authentic faith were doomed, dying and dead beyond recall; and after this death, they were convinced, there could be no resurrection. It affected Jews who had long forgotten what a mitzvah was, a religious good deed for God and his people. It affected those who blithely held non-kosher dinners in their temples, slowly losing all contact with their people. It affected even the "beautiful people" who basked in the dazzling glory of their successes, never realizing how mangled beyond recognition their Jewish souls, their Jewish identity, had become.

In the ancient Sanctuary of Jerusalem, the only place that could rightly be called our Temple, the *kohen gadol* (chief of all the *kohanim*) entered the holy of holies, its most sacred chamber, only once a year: on *Yom Kippur,* the Day of Atonement. Before he left, he prayed there briefly for his people. So we read: And for the people of Sharon he would pray, "May it be Thy will, O Lord our God and God of our fathers, that their homes should not become their graves."[19] The simple meaning is that the ground in the plains of Sharon was not solid enough for building houses. There was always danger that on account of heavy rain the houses might collapse; and at least twice in seven years the houses always had to be rebuilt.[20]

What could better symbolize "the house of Israel" in the Diaspora? In one country after another our people settled and built houses, careers and lives, only to discover to their misfortune how unsolid was the "soil" beneath them: the land where they lived, and its people. From one country after another there was expulsion. In one country after another there were pogroms — until the biggest pogrom of all came along: the Nazi holocaust. How many times in our history we needed that sacred fervent prayer of the *kohen gadol*: "May it be Thy will . . . that their homes should not become their tombs" — that driven or ravaged in one place, our people should find a haven elsewhere.

Yet that prayer might have had another meaning. The plain of Sharon was lush fertile soil warmed by the sun. Farming there was easy and profitable. The people living there could easily feel they had found a private little paradise on earth. They could forget that there was any higher purpose in life — a God in heaven, with His Sanctuary in Jerusalem. In their affluence and comfort, from the spiritual viewpoint their homes could become their tombs, where they could spend their life in one long sleep. So the *kohen gadol* prayed for them on *Yom Kippur* in the most sacred part of the Sanctuary.

Who ever counted the American Jews who felt they had achieved their dream (the great American dream) when they acquired a beautiful home in a prestigious suburban neighborhood, that could be shown with pride to all and sundry? As for any awareness of Jewish causes and ideals, obligations and commitments, all that tended to fade into oblivion in the comfortable death-like sleep of the spirit in its comfortable home. Those houses too could turn into graves for the living.

"Son of man," said the Almighty to Ezekiel, "these bones are the whole house of Israel ... Therefore prophesy and say to them ... Behold, I will open your graves and make you come up out of your graves, O My people; and I will bring to you the soil of Israel" (Ezekiel 37:11–12).

In his commentary, R. David Kimḥi states that this refers specifically to Jewry in the exile. Those who knew that their homes in the Diaspora were built on poor, shaky soil — those who experienced or learned the lesson of the holocaust — picked themselves up and went to Israel. For many an American Jew whose home had become, spiritually speaking, his grave, the birth of Israel in 1948 "opened up his grave": He found a new sense of identity with the Jewish homeland, supporting it with pride and joy.

Such was the great resurrection in the 1940's. But what happens now? In Israel itself they have begun to realize that for this land, natural laws don't work. For a while they had an adage: Whoever doesn't believe in miracles in Israel is no realist. Yet there was also a taxi-driver there whom I recall, who was able to recite whole chapters of the prophecies of Isaiah as he drove his cab bare-headed; and he flatly denied that anything miraculous had occurred at all in the Six-Day War. "We did it," he insisted. "We fought back, and we won."

What course will *we* take? Will we let our homeland continue with "business as usual," trusting that all will be well (Heaven will take care of

261

everything) while we sleep in our beautiful homes? Shall we be among those who revived at the resurrection, sang a great hymn of praise and exultation, and went back to the sleep of death? Or do we realize the full truth of R. Naḥman of Bratzlav's words, that the land can only be all miracle and prayer? that Heaven's supernatural help must continue if the land is to have a future, and it will continue only if we add our prayers and fervent support?

Seen in entirety, the people of Israel can be conceived as one human being.[21] The hands, beyond any questions, are the fine dedicated soldiers of Israel's defense forces. They "bear arms" and use their hands most effectively when necessary. The feet, we might say, are the infantry. The eyes and ears are perhaps are perhaps Israel's excellent intelligence service (*shin beth*). About the head there would be two opinions. For the secular, non-religious Jew there are the heads of government, starting from Israel's president and prime minister. For the religious Jew there are the *roshey yeshiva*, the heads of Israel's Torah schools and academies, to whom we look for guidance and by whose word we live.

But now, what is the heart? To my mind there is little doubt that it is the devoutly religious Jews of Israel, especially the students of Torah, who spend night and day in learning our sacred heritage. When our Sages wanted to indicate the main thing in Jewish religiosity, they said רחמנא ליבא בעי "The merciful God wants the heart."[22] The heart must be aware of the Almighty's presence and wishes, and must respond. It is the devout, pious Jews of Israel, steeped in Torah study and worship, who live with this awareness of Him and this response. So they are indeed Israel's heart. It is they above all who need our support and concern.

For nineteen years, from 1948 to 1967, a good part of Israel, including the old city of Jerusalem, was in the hands of Jordan. So advertisements appeared in American magazines: "Visit Jordan, the holy land." If that makes us smile, let us stop and think: What makes Israel the holy land? Is it the secular Israeli who lives as a Hebrew-speaking Italian or Rumanian? Is it a so-called socialist government that gave missionaries a free hand because the country has to be a democracy?

When R. Eliezer b. R. Yosé the Galilean said that the people whom Ezekiel revived went to Israel, married, and raised families that endured, R. Judah b. Bathyra stood up and said he was the living proof of it: He was descended from those very people. And he held up a pair of *t'fillin* as further proof: It had been handed down from those same people, through the generations.

262

Do we want *our* miracle of resurrection to last? Then as much as we can, we must make sure it remains the holy land, raising scholars who can rank in our time as R. Judah b. Bathyra ranked in his. We must support the kind of Jews who will pass on the mitzvah of *t'fillin*, with all that it means, down the generations.

The Talmud teaches that the Almighty said about the destruction of the holy Temple and the city of Jerusalem some 1900 years ago, "I set fire to Zion, and I will yet rebuild it with fire." What kind of fire does this mean? Consider what R. Sh'néor Zalman of Liady, the great founder of the *ḥabad* ḥassidic movement (of Lubavitch), wrote to his followers over two centuries ago, to urge them to support the ḥassidic settlers in Israel: "Let the old love and affection for the holy land be aroused and renewed, as in the olden days, so that it burns like flames of fire within a person, deep in the heart . . ."[23]

With this kind of fire in our hearts, with our passionate prayerful concern for Israel's welfare, the Almighty can rebuild Zion, our holy land.


# ❧ OUR FOREIGN AND OTHER RELATIONS

THE RABBI OF LUBAVITCH ONCE SAID: if you want to be up-to-date in the world, always read the *sidra*, the Torah portion of the week. Pay attention when it is read in the synagogue Saturday morning, and you can often find it shedding light on current events to a startling degree.

Take a simple story in *B'réshith,* the Book of Genesis, that happened several thousand years ago, in the pastoral nomadic setting of the ancient Middle East, long before the age of superpowers and atomic arsenals. Abimelech king of Gerar saw that Abraham was successful and prospering: *God is with you in all that you do. Now therefore swear to me here by God that you shall not deal falsely with me . . .* (Genesis 21:22–23). *And Abraham said: I will swear. Then Abraham reproved Abimelech about the well of water that*

*Abimelech's servants had taken by violence. And Abimelech said: I do not know who has done this thing; moreover, you did not tell me; and furthermore, I did not hear of it until today (ibid. 24–26).*

So Abraham gave the Philistine king sheep and oxen, and they made a covenant, a solemn agreement (*ibid.* 27). Then our generous Patriarch gave the king seven ewe-lambs in addition. What, asked Abimelech, were *they* for? *And he said: These seven ewe-lambs you will take from my hand, that it may be a witness for me that I dug this well (ibid. 28–30).*

So it was just a small simple agreement in the ancient Middle East between a local king and a prosperous sheep and cattle farmer. If it is in the Torah, though, we know the good Lord put some timeless, abiding truths into it. It is worth studying, because as the Sages say (TB *Sotah* 34a), מעשי אבות סימן לבנים any incident with the Patriarchs is a sign for their children, an augury showing a pattern that will recur in the later history of our people.

Abimelech saw Abraham alive and prospering. And that, says the Midrash, impressed him. Sodom had vanished in smoke — if you will, in a Divine version of atomic annihilation. Not a soul went there anymore. And here was Abraham, with all his wealth intact.[24] Sodom had been hostile to strangers. In Sodom it had been a crime to give hospitality to anyone passing through. The people there wanted to conserve and hoard their wealth.[25] And they were wiped off the map. As a result, no one came traveling to that part of the world any more; and Abraham, who lived in the vicinity and had thrived all his life on providing hospitality to wayfarers, found himself without a soul in sight whom he could give a square meal. So he pulled up stakes (says the Midrash)[26] and came to Gerar, Abimelech's bailiwick, where he could resume his generous hospitality business as usual.

Abimelech saw Abraham giving and giving, and still doing better than ever. It was uncanny, he felt. A twinge of awe moved him: This man was more than simply lucky. *God is with you,* he said, *in all that you do.* As the Midrash puts it,[27] he saw miracles happen for Abraham, and he grew frightened of the man. So he said, "Swear to me," etc. It would be better to have Abraham on *his* side, a friend and not a foe.

Thus the Midrash quotes the words of the wise king Solomon: *When the Lord finds a man's ways pleasing, he makes even his enemies be at peace with him* (Proverbs 17:7).[28]

We could surely sum up Jewish history, from ancient Rome's rule of our homeland until our day, with this brief sentence: We gave and gave, and we are still alive and very much in existence. To every power that ruled over us, from ancient Rome and on through Europe's lands of our exile, we were always important and valuable as a source of income. Our lords and masters were good at devising taxes: direct and indirect, open and concealed, regular and special. In 1277, when the ruler in England could squeeze no more money from his Jews, he expelled them.

Yes, we gave and gave . . . and we are still on the map. When the Nazis needed victims for their crematoria and gas ovens, we gave them six million; and our people still exists (with a state of its own). And always we took care of our own, with systems of charity for the poor, medical care for the sick. Given freedom and opportunity in the lands of democracy, we gave again, over and over, contributing solidly to commerce and industry and national growth. We built hospitals for all, and provided doctors to staff them. It is openly acknowledged that life in America would be immeasurably poorer without the contribution of its Jews . . . And in recent decades we give sizable sums annually for Israel. Like Abraham, we have always given and given more, and we are still alive and well, thank you.

So like Abraham, we sometimes gained a surprising ally.

Go back in history and you will find that England was no friend of the Jews. It was the first to produce a blood libel against the Jews (Norwich, 1144) and the first to expel them (1277). Go forward in history to the land of Israel's years under the British mandate, and you find again that it could not possibly be called friendly. Yet in 1917 England saw that the Jews were very much around. It was the First World War, the first blazing armed hostility on a global scale, and England wanted every friend it could get. And the Jews were around — in Germany, Russia and America. You could almost call them a world force. In fact, suave, cultured, polished Chaim Weizmann did so, posing as their spokesman.

So in 1917, believing it needed the Jews as friends and not foes, England issued the Balfour Declaration, "viewing with favor the establishment in Palestine of a national home for the Jewish people." Thus the ball was set rolling that would eventually snowball into the State of Israel.

In 1948 Israel needed recognition at the United Nations in order to enter the annals of modern history as a state. If England was then no friend of the Jews, how should we describe the attitude of Stalin's Soviet Union? like the feeling, perhaps, of a rabid dog in the skin of a Russian bear? Yet in 1948 it wanted influence in the Middle East, and there was the rebuilt Jewish homeland, alive and growing, and ruled by a strongly socialist group. With the charm of a Russian bear, the USSR wanted to endear itself to Israel with a bear hug — and it voted in the UN to recognize the newborn Jewish state. With America's President Truman already favorable, Israel received formal recognition.

As with Abraham so with his descendants: *When the Lord finds a man's ways pleasing, He makes even his enemies be at peace with him.*

That is fine, you might say; really splendid. England started us on the way to a rebuilt homeland, and the Soviet Union helped it gain recognition as a state.

Wait, though. There is more in the Torah's story: *And Abraham took sheep and oxen and gave them to Abimelech, and the two of them made a covenant* (Genesis 21:27). Jewish wit and humor has always been known for its irony, its sardonic ability to laugh at our treatment in the lands of our exile. Very possibly our people was taught this irony, touched with sarcasm, by this passage in the Torah: For here Abimelech came to Abraham asking for a treaty of friendship — and Abraham gave Abimelech a substantial gift. A simple augury, foreshadowing a pattern in the Jew's "foreign relations": whether we come to them or they come to us, we pay.

For the Balfour Declaration, there was a Jewish Brigade fighting in the British army; and Weizmann gave England the benefit of his chemical research. For its recognition of Israel at the UN, the Soviet Union expected Israel to help it gain a foothold of influence in the Middle East. When its hopes failed to materialize, it turned viciously anti-Israel.

By *kal va-ḥomer* (*a fortiori*), reasoning from the less to the more, it was only to be expected that when Israel sought agreements with others, it certainly had to give. In the hope of having allies and friendly votes at the UN, the Jewish state plied developing countries in Africa with expert advice and help.

Unfortunately, though, there is another little point in this passage of Scripture: ויכרתו שניהם ברית literally, *and they made, the two of them, a covenant.*

There is an old ḥassidic tale that one day R. Simḥa Bunem of P'shis-cha hired a man with a coach and horses to take him, with some of his ḥassidim (pious devoted followers), to Warsaw. Arriving in the big city, the men asked him where they should stop, and the ḥassidic rabbi said to drive

266

on through the streets. Suddenly he told the driver to stop at a certain tavern, and the men got off and went inside. There they found two porters at a corner table, plain Jews who made their living by carrying heavy burdens. The two sat, each with his glass of whiskey, talking.

As R. Simḥa Bunem listened, he heard one ask the other, "Have you already studied the *sidra*, the Torah portion of the week?"

"Yes," the other replied.

"I've also learned it through," said the first porter, "and I found one thing hard to understand: It says, *and they made, the two of them, a covenant.* How could our father Abraham make a solemn agreement with the idol-worshipping Abimelech?"

Replied the other man, "I too couldn't understand why it is written ויכרתו שניהם ברית *and they made, the two of them, a covenant.* It would surely have been enough for Scripture to say ויכרתו ברית *and they made a covenant.* But now I see that your question answers mine. The meaning here is that even though they made a solemn agreement, they remained nevertheless 'the two of them'; they achieved no unity, to become as of one mind."

Once R. Simḥa Bunem heard that he returned to his horse-driven coach, followed by his *ḥassidim*, and told the driver to head back for P'shis-cha. "I had no other need to be in Warsaw," he told his devout followers, "but to hear these words of those two concealed *tzaddikim* (men of piety)."[29]

If this bit of interpretation gave the renowned ḥassidic rabbi vital food for thought, it should certainly be enough for us to ponder. Only a few centuries after Abraham and Abimelech, a one-eyed heathen soothsayer (Balaam) said of us, *Behold, this is a people that shall dwell alone, and shall not be reckoned among the nations* (Numbers 23:9). Refusing to accept it, Israel's heads of state are learning this lesson over and over in the harsh and expensive school of experience. The Jewish state gave and gave to develop, ing countries in Africa. Not one remained a true ally, of one mind with Israel.

As for England and its Balfour Decalration, any hopes for unity on its part with the Jewish people in their yearning for a homeland evaporated rapidly in the years after 1917. England was very much a separate power, with its own interests and motives. As it took control of the holy land after the first World War, the Balfour Declaration was conveniently forgotten. For years it was never mentioned in any official papers, until it was finally given a new "interpretation" — because the British were busy currying Arab favor.

England and Israel remained two, not one: distressingly apart, tragically at loggerheads.[30]

Closer to our time, we have seen good old Uncle Sam become Israel's "true ally." It was only natural, you might say. After all, Israel is a shining outpost of democracy and Western civilization in a backward, stagnating Middle East that is generally prey to Fascist and Communist ideologies. Of course, we would think, America and Israel *should* be allies.

They have remained two, however, not one. America has developed ambitions and wishes of its own, to gain influence (and oil) among the Arabs. And as Abraham gave Abimelech sheep and oxen because Abimelech wanted a pact of friendship, so the little land of Israel has been asked, cajoled and pressured to give and give and give. Moreover, if Scripture here teaches us to expect irony in Israel's foreign relations, we have surely witnessed the very height of irony when a Jew (a refugee from Nazi Germany) became America's secretary of state and took the initiative in demanding that Israel continue giving and giving and giving — as never before . . .

But perhaps the most striking lesson of the Torah here lies in the "extra little detail" of the well, apparently a minor side-issue.

After Abraham and Abimelech make their covenant or agreement, the Patriarch gives the Philistine king seven ewe-lambs. What, asks the little king in surprise, is this? — presents? Abraham explains: Since the king's servants seized a well from his servants, which Abraham's men had dug originally, he is giving him these seven lambs to help make it clear (or to help Abimelech remember) that the well is his and is not open to dispute.

If anyone asks what relationship *this* has with Jewish history, he must be joking. Here is a prime example of the mordant irony that has been so characteristic for our people's fate. Abraham tells Abimelech that he dug the well (Genesis 21:30). Then how could it belong to anyone else? Yet along came the king's servants and took it by force. "It is ours," they said.[31] So to get his property back and retain it, the Patriarch paid. Today we call it a protection racket ("Pay so that we will protect you from harm — by us"). For the Jewish people, descended from Abraham, it became almost standard treatment.

Who can count the number of times our people paid heavy sums to government officials in the lands of our exile, simply not to be expelled? to be able to continue running a shop? to be allowed to buy or build a home? perhaps even to breathe regularly?

And what else has characterized the entire story of our return to our homeland, through the centuries and on into the decades that produced the State of Israel? Others seized the land that was ours by the Divine promise, where our ancestors had lived for centuries. For every bit of it that we wanted back, we had to pay dearly, over and over.... (At the very least, *Keren Kayemeth* had to pay Arab landowners fat prices.)

Yet the *most* poignant point in the passage lies in Abimelech's answer when Abraham berated him because the king's men had seized the well. *And Abimelech said: I do not know who has done this thing; moreover, you did not tell me; and furthermore, I did not hear of it until today* (Genesis 21:26). Here is a really full three-part answer (reminding one for a moment of the reply a woman gave, in a story by Sholom Aleichem, when a neighbor accused her of having borrowed a whole, perfect pitcher and having returned it to her cracked: "First of all, it was whole when I gave it back to you. If it is cracked now, that must have happened afterward, in your house. Secondly, if it was cracked when I returned it, it must have been so when I took it from you. And finally, I don't remember ever borrowing it from you in the first place.")

With the very first part of his answer, "I do not know," Abimelech set a pattern that has remained almost classic. Ever the victim of injustice, the Jew cries out for elementary human rights. Through our long and bitter history, from those who were supposed to uphold the law and maintain order, the answer always came, "We do not know about this. Are you sure you were wronged?"

Read the histories of the Crusaders, and you will find barely a mention of the entire Jewish communities in France and Germany that the "holy warriors" massacred on the way to their "holy wars." The historians "do not know" about it. No one told them.

Many Jews living today can recall the anguish of writing to relatives in Europe in the late 30's and early 40's, and sending them packages, as they had done for years, only to have the mail come back marked "Address unknown". How much misery and despair those two words brought to hundreds of thousands of Jewish hearts. As the Nazi machine achieved its satanic efficiency, the post offices of Germany, and then of East European countries, no longer knew the whereabouts of Jewish residents. "Address unknown" — לא ידעתי *we do not know.*

In the Soviet Union of our day, someone trying desperately to get an exit visa, so that he can go to Israel, may find himself beaten up on the street.

The police watch (or they do not) and do nothing. לֹא יָדַעְתִּי *Ya n'ye znayet*: "Don't know nothing."

Take again the land of Israel under Britain's mandate. The Arabs seemed to have learned *their* lesson from this passage in Scripture. When Abimelech's servants seized Abraham's well, the Patriarch gave a handsome gift to have it left in his possession. It was a policy that paid off. So whenever the Arabs felt the urge, they rioted, leaving dead and wounded Jews in their wake. And the British, with their "impeccable" sense of fair play, always decided it was necessary to compromise. Thus the Jews had to pay and yield; they had to go and give up something, accept restrictions and limitations.

In April 1920, the Jewish settlements in Upper Galilee were attacked; Tel Ḥai was destroyed and Joseph Trumpeldor killed. In March 1921 there were anti-Jewish riots in Jerusalem. In May 1921 there was violence in Jaffa, and large-scale attacks occurred in several Jewish settlement towns. Came August 1929 and there was violence again in Jerusalem (in connection with the *kothel maaravi*, the Western Wall). On August 24 some seventy Jews of the pious, devout community were slaughtered in Hebron. Tel Aviv and Haifa also felt the effects of Arab tumult; and in Safed eighteen were killed as Arabs ransacked and burned the Jewish quarter. April 1936 brought still more riots, in Jaffa and Tel Aviv.

What was the British response? לֹא יָדַעְתִּי מִי עָשָׂה אֶת הַדָּבָר הַזֶּה *I do not know who did this*. "We need an inquiry commission." וְגַם אַתָּה לֹא הִגַּדְתָּ לִּי *Moreover, you did not tell me*. וְגַם אָנֹכִי לֹא שָׁמַעְתִּי בִּלְתִּי הַיּוֹם *And furthermore, I did not hear of it until today*. They knew nothing and heard nothing "until today": no one could tell them a thing until their group of officials, specially appointed, came to take testimony (including Arab propaganda and mistruths). They had to be officially told. Only then did they learn "the facts" at last. So England became famous (or infamous) for its inquiry commissions, leading to official reports and white papers.

If Abraham wanted to keep the well that his servants had dug, he had to give away lambs. In the land of Israel, if we wanted to keep what was ours by Divine right, what the Almighty solemnly promised the children of Abraham, Isaac and Jacob, we had to give plenty in turn. The Transjordan was forbidden to Jewish settlement. Immigration in the crucial 30's and 40's was cruelly limited and forbidden. And when Israel became an independent state, there had to be "partition": we had to give a major portion of the land to the Arabs, so that we could have the rest.

Time and again, Arab infiltrators came into Israel and murdered innocent Jews, including women and children. In response, Israel's defense forces attacked their bases in Lebanon. And behold, Israel was condemned at the United Nations for its aggression. "Wait a minute. What about *their* aggression—what they did to us?" לֹא יָדַעְתִּי "We do not know about that."

For nineteen years Jordan had in its possession the *kothel maaravi*, the Western (or Wailing) Wall, the place most sacred in all the world for the Jews. According to UN orders, to which Jordan had agreed, Jews were to have access to it. And for nineteen years the Wall remained barred to us. Did any protest ever come from the UN? לֹא יָדַעְתִּי "We do not know about it." When the Six-Day War gave us back the Old City of Jerusalem, we found precious historic synagogues in ruins; sacred old gravestones had been used for building materials. Did the UN ever take notice? לֹא יָדַעְתִּי "Sorry: we have no knowledge of that."

Before June 1967 Nasser of Egypt never let an Israeli ship through the Suez Canal. Then he sought to bar Israeli shipping altogether at the Bab-el-Mandev strait. And the world spun on its course. לֹא יָדַעְתִּי "We know nothing about it." Finally Nasser screamed his determination to drive Israel into the Mediterranean Ocean. וְגַם אָנֹכִי לֹא שָׁמַעְתִּי No one in the world seemed to have heard a word.

In general, it might be added that the last two parts of Abimelech's answer form a unit: *Moreover, you did not tell me; and furthermore, I did not hear of it until today.* We always tell the world, over and over. We have Jewish organizations whose sole purpose seems to be to "tell the world." Yet the world seems to have a convenient deafness for longer or shorter periods, where Israel and Jewry are concerned. (At the UN, of course, it is all official. They know nothing until we file a complaint.)

So we give and give and give again, like Abraham. What do we want in return? Read the Midrash:

מְלַמֵּד שֶׁהִפְרִישׁ אַבְרָהָם אָבִינוּ שֶׁבַע כְּבָשׂוֹת כְּנֶגֶד שֶׁבַע מִצְווֹת שֶׁנִּצְטַוּוּ בְּנֵי נֹחַ, שֶׁנּוֹהֲגוֹת בְּאוֹתוֹ דוֹר. (מדרש הגדול, בראשית כא ל; שמג)

This teaches that Abraham set apart seven ewe-lambs in correspondence to the seven commandments for the children of Noaḥ, that were in effect for that generation (*Midrash haGadol*, Genesis 21:30—343).

For the Jews there are 613 commandments (*mitzvoth*) in the Torah. As the Sages explain, however,[32] seven commandments in the Torah are

271

also binding on the children and descendants of Noaḥ (meaning all man-kind, since only Noaḥ, with his sons and their wives, survived the flood). So this, you see, was all Abraham wanted: to keep Abimelech reminded of the seven Divine laws and moral obligations that were obligatory for him — which included prohibitions against robbery and murder and things like that.

This is all we ever ask of the world: simple justice for all, without violence, banditry or murder. Yet is it simple? When an individual robs and kills, he is called a criminal and is punished. When a professional hooligan makes the brutal murder of women and children an "Arab policy," he is received, heard and applauded at the UN.

When the Arabs mounted their "oil offensive" in full force, Israeli diplomats sought to appeal to a sense of justice among European officials. In a sense, you might say, some descendants of Abraham tried to remind some people in the Western world of the seven commandments for Noaḥ's descendants. At last one high-ranking officer said, "The trouble with you Israelis is that you expect morality and decency in international relations." (Then what *should* we expect? — good old-fashioned horse trading, to find ourselves sold under the table? We have a simple sentence in our Friday evening prayers, from the Book of Psalms, 98:5–9: *Sing praise to the Lord*... *He will judge the world with righteousness, and the peoples with straight-forward justice*. We pray and await one plain kind of justice, morality and decency, whether it concerns an individual, a nation, a superpower, or a solid block of nations with a majority of votes at the UN.)

Disheartening as the subject may seem, remember how this passage in the Torah ends: After Abraham and Abimelech finished their business, *Abraham planted a tamarisk tree in Be'er Sheba, and called there in the name of the Lord, the everlasting God* (Genesis 21:33). As the Midrash teaches, the Hebrew for tamarisk tree, אֵשֶׁל *éshel,* can be taken as an abbreviation for אכילה, שתיה, לויה *achilah, sh'thi-ah, l'vayah*: food, drink and escort. He planted an orchard with all types of fruit trees, and opened a kind of inn with every sort of food, to provide free meals for all who came traveling by — so as to teach them to acknowledge God and thank Him.[33] Let the world spin on its axis and agitate as it wished. He went back to his old business of hospitality and teaching the true faith. This was his job, his God-given destiny.

And why not? Look at this striking passage in the Midrash, about the well that Abimelech's servants had taken away by force:

רַבָּנָן אָמְרִי: רוֹעָיו שֶׁל אַבְרָהָם הָיוּ מְדַיְּנִים עִם רוֹעָיו שֶׁל אֲבִימֶלֶךְ. רוֹעֵי אַבְרָהָם אוֹמְרִים,
לָנוּ הַבְּאֵר; וְאֵלּוּ אוֹמְרִים, לָנוּ הַבְּאֵר. אָמְרוּ לָהֶם רוֹעֵי אַבְרָהָם: כָּל מִי שֶׁהַמַּיִם עוֹלִים
לְהַשְׁקוֹת אֶת צֹאנוֹ, שֶׁלּוֹ הִיא הַבְּאֵר. כֵּיוָן שֶׁרָאוּ הַמַּיִם צֹאנוֹ שֶׁל אַבְרָהָם אָבִינוּ מִיָּד עָלוּ.
אָמַר לוֹ הַקָּדוֹשׁ־בָּרוּךְ־הוּא: אַתְּ סִמָּן לְבָנֶיךָ. מָה אַתְּ, כֵּיוָן שֶׁרָאוּ הַמַּיִם אֶת צֹאנְךָ מִיָּד
עָלוּ, אַף בָּנֶיךָ כֵּיוָן שֶׁהַבְּאֵר רוֹאָה אוֹתָן מִיָּד תְּהֵא עוֹלָה... אָמַר לָהֶם ר׳ יִצְחָק בֶּן
חֲקוֹרָה: עוֹד מִן אַתְרָה לֵית הִיא חֲסֵרָה. בַּעֲבוּר הָיְתָה לִי לְעֵדָה, אֵין כְּתִיב כָּאן, אֶלָּא,
בַּעֲבוּר תִּהְיֶה לִי לְעֵדָה. (בראשית רבה נד ה)

The Sages said: The shepherds of Abraham quarreled with Abimelech's shepherds. Abraham's shepherds said, "The well is ours," and the others said, "The well is ours." Said the shepherds of Abraham to them, "Whoever [of us] finds that the water rises to give *his* sheep to drink, the well is his." Once the water saw Abraham's sheep, it rose instantly. Said the Holy, Blessed One, "You are an augury for your children. Just as with you, once the water saw your sheep it rose instantly, so with your children: Once the well sees them it will rise up directly."... Said R. Yitzhak b. Hakorah: The proof [for this] is not lacking here either. It does not say, "that it *was* a witness for me," but *that it shall be a witness for me* (Genesis 21:30) (*B'réshith Rabbah* 54, 5).

Water is the most vital and precious commodity in the Middle East. With it, land can flourish and life can thrive. Without it, you have desert land, and a barren miserable nomadic existence. For Abraham, says this Midrash, the water of the well rose of itself. It was his destiny to find this vital life-sustaining ingredient. So he planted trees, grew food, and provided hospitality for all, to teach the world the only faith by which it can survive: faith in the Creator.

Just as two groups of servants quarreled over the well in ancient times, so today a quarrel goes on over major parts of the land of Israel. We Jews claim it, as the descendants of Abraham, Isaac and Jacob. The Arabs claim it because they lived on it for some period of time. So, says the Midrash, there is a simple test, which Abraham's servants used about the well: "Let us see for whom the water comes up."

Who was able to bring water into the land, digging in the hot sun, fighting malaria, connecting pipes, building conduits and systems of irrigation? Who made the land flower and blossom — the Arabs in their miserable squalor, living with their few sheep and goats in their hovels? or the Jews who worked with a matchless devotion?

Says the Midrash further: The Almighty promised Abraham that this would happen for his descendants too: for the Hebrews who left Egypt and journeyed forty years through the wilderness. They also would always find a well ready to send its water coursing up for them. Then another Sage adds: When Abraham gave Abimelech the seven ewe-lambs, "*so that it shall be a witness for me that I dug this well*" (Genesis 21:30), he did not mean the seven animals. They were only a bribe, to help Abimelech accept the truth. The "witness" or proof that the well was his was the fact (as the Sages said) that the water came up for his sheep. And he said, "it *shall be* a witness." It was to happen again in Jewish history.

And this, past any doubt, is the destiny of our land of Israel: to find the water rising up for it, to be able to thrive and flourish as an oasis of hospitality amid the desert lands all about. We have seen Israel blossom almost miraculously in the physical, material sense. And to the pious Jew this is of immense significance: You can have no clearer sign of the approaching Messianic end, says the Talmud (TB *Sanhedrin* 98a), than this verse in Scripture: *But you mountains of Israel, you shall send forth your branches, and yield your fruit to My people Israel; for they are soon to arrive* (Ezekiel 36:8). In the water rising for our people, to irrigate the land and make it flourish, lies the proof that we are the rightful heirs of Abraham, returning to the land the Almighty gave him.

Yet it is certainly not Israel's destiny to provide food or any material goods to a world pursuing its heathen goals. At the moment the only material commodity that the world wants from the Middle East is oil, and nature has not endowed Israel richly with that.

It is Israel's indomitable destiny to supply "water" to the world passing by, the "water that rises by itself for Abraham's sheep" — for water, as the Talmud explains (TB *Bava Kamma* 17a), means nothing but Torah, which alone can slake the growing thirst in the world for Divine knowledge and spirituality. *Behold, the days are coming ... when I will send a famine upon the land: not a famine of bread nor a thirst for water, but only to hear the words of the Lord* (Amos 8:11). Unlikely as it may now seem, scornful as the irreligious may be, we know this is Israel's future. *On that day, living waters shall flow out from Jerusalem* (Zechariah 14:8).

After the first Zionist Congress, Herzl wrote feverishly in his diary (he seems to have done everything feverishly), "Were I to sum up the Basel Congress in a word ... it would be this: At Basel I founded the Jewish state. If I said this out loud today, I should be answered by universal laughter. Perhaps in five years, certainly fifty years, everyone will know it."[34] Because it suited the Almighty's purpose, even that prophecy (or boast) of a non-religious Jew was fulfilled in a sense, and in 1948 the Jewish State was proclaimed. How much more certainly will the Divine promise of Scripture, given by His prophets, come true in its time: Israel will become the focal point of spirituality in the world, so that *they shall not hurt nor destroy in all My holy mountain, for all the earth shall be full of the knowledge of the Lord, as the waters cover the sea* (Isaiah 11:9).


## ❧ ISAAC'S TURN

HOW DOES THE OLD SAYING GO? "Like father, like son." Abraham found Abimelech at his doorstep one fine day, accompanied by a royal retinue, wanting to make a friendship pact. When Isaac was a grown man, his turn came. One fine day he found Abimelech at *his* doorstep, accompanied by a royal retinue and wanting a friendship pact. (Likely, though, it was not the same Abimelech but a son of the first one. The name was probably the title of every king of Gerar, just as every king of Egypt was called Pharaoh.)[35]

Well, if Abraham in his time had been surprised at his royal visitor, Isaac was now astounded: *And Isaac said to them: Why have you come to me, seeing that you hate me, and you sent me away from you?* (Genesis 26:27). He may have said "sent," but he meant "chased." A famine in his own land (Canaan) had made him come to Gerar (*ibid.* 1). There he became a farmer, planting wheat and raising cattle; and he prospered. So his dear sweet Philistine neighbors became envious (*ibid.* 12–14). First they stopped up all his wells, which his father's servants had originally dug; they filled them up with earth. Then, just in case he failed to take this "subtle" hint, they told him, *Go away from us, for you have taken much strength from us* (*ibid.* 15–16).[36] As the Midrash explains, they told him, "All the mighty wealth you have amassed — has it not come to you from us? In the past you

275

had one flock of sheep, and now you have so many!" (*B'réshith Rabbah* 64, 7).

Was it logical? They had their landed property, and he had his; and his wealth came from the workings of nature, from raising crops and sheep. How did this cost them anything? But logic was never a heathen's strong point.

One fine *maggid* (preacher) of an earlier generation made the point quite well: Look (he said). Isaac did not open a store or shop of any kind, to sell merchandise: no neighbors could complain of any competition (cut-throat or otherwise) that was killing their trade. He did not open a tavern in the village (as many a Jew in Eastern Europe had to do decades ago, for lack of any other way of earning a living): no one could complain that he was impoverishing and demoralizing the poor villagers by enticing them into the pleasures of strong drink. He did not even open a pawn shop or loan company: no one could argue that he was growing fat and sleek through usury, by taking interest. He was a plain farmer, earning an honest living by the sweat of his brow. Yet that did not prevent the natives from rising up against him and throwing him out, insisting that he had grown wealthy at their expense.[37]

So here we have an early example of "anti-semitism" — and Isaac left them, wanting no part of any quarrels.[38] He pulled up stakes and moved on. Then, in parallel with his father's experiences, his servants dug precious wells, only to have the Philistines argue and claim them. Finally, to "get away from it all," he moved away to Be'er Sheba.

After Abraham had moved from Gerar to Be'er Sheba, he received a royal visitor named Abimelech, seeking to make a treaty of friendship with him. Now the same thing happened to Isaac; and he asked for an explanation: If they hated him and could not tolerate him in their area, what did they want with him now? With a kind of sweet (treacly and hypocritical) innocence they answered: *We saw plainly that the Lord is with you; so we said: Let there be an oath between us, between us and you, that you will do us no harm, just as we did not touch you, and we did you nothing but good, and sent you away in peace* (Genesis 26:28–29).

As a lesson in Hebrew or Jewish foreign relations, this is surely a gem. His ex-neighbor comes to tell the Jew of the great kindness he showed him. "What kindness was that?" the puzzled Jew asks. Oh, replies the former neighbor, he could have punched him in the nose, blackened his eye, broken his jaw, or at least smashed a few windows. "But you see," he concludes, beaming with pure friendship, "I let you go in peace." Was that not sweet of him?

As a dry comment on this incident in the Torah, the Midrash tells a story:

In the days of R. Joshua b. Ḥananyah, the wicked [Roman] empire decreed that the holy Temple [destroyed in the year 70 CE] might be rebuilt. Pappus and Lulianus set out tables from Acco to Antioch, and they thus provided those coming up from the exile [to Jerusalem, to do the construction work] with all their needs. So those Cuthites [Samaritans] went and said [to the Roman emperor], "Let it be known to the king that should this rebellious city [Jerusalem] be built up and its walls finished, they will not pay *minda, b'lo* or *halach*" (see Ezra 4:13). The word *minda* means the land tax; *b'lo* means the poll tax; and *halach* is the period of required free labor for the empire.

Said [the Roman emperor] to them, "What can we do, after I have given the decree?" They answered him, "Send word and tell them: they must either move it from its place [build the holy Temple elsewhere] or enlarge it by five cubits or shorten it by five cubits — and by themselves they will withdraw from it."

Well (the Midrash continues), large crowds [of Jews] were gathered then in the plain of Beth Rimmon. When these written decrees arrived, they burst out weeping and wanted to rebel against the [Roman] empire. Said [the Sages], "Let a wise man go and calm the populace down"; and they decided, "Let R. Joshua b. Ḥanayah go, since he is a consummate master of the Torah." He went up and declaimed:

A lion once killed and ate an animal as its prey, and a bone stuck in his throat. So he announced, "Whoever comes and pulls it out, I will reward him well." Along came an Egyptian heron, whose beak is long; he inserted his beak and pulled it out. Then he said, "Give me my reward." Replied [the lion], "Go about proudly and boast that you entered a lion's mouth in peace and you left in peace."

[This is what R. Joshua b. Ḥananyah told the excited populace. Then he said] "Even so, it is enough that we have entered into this [Roman] people's midst in peace and have left in peace" (*B'réshith Rabbah* 64, 10).

This is the comment of the Midrash on Isaac's experience. Strangely enough, the story of the lion and the heron can be found in Aesop's fables, with only a slight change in the cast of characters: a wolf instead of a lion.[39] Evidently it was a popular tale, known all the way from Greece to the land of Israel. Only, there was a difference between the two countries: To the Greeks it was just a fable, with a nice little moral: Beware of helping evil men. The only reward you can hope for is that they won't add injury to ingratitude. To the Jews in Israel it was an enduring lesson from the Torah, taught us initially by the interaction between Isaac and Abimelech.

No: to the Jews it was no fable, but a central pattern of reality. We interact with neighbors, whether in the land of Israel or in the centuries of exile. And if we come out alive and well, we have reason to be thankful. It might be funny if it weren't so sad and true. The Midrash notes:

מְלַמֵּד שֶׁהֶחֱזִיקוּ טוֹבָה לְאָבִינוּ יִצְחָק שֶׁלֹּא נָגְעוּ בּוֹ לְרָעָה, לוֹמַר לְךָ שֶׁנַּפְשָׁם מִתְאַוָּה לָרַע

(מדרש הגדול, בראשית כו כט)

"This teaches that they considered it a favor to our father Isaac that they had done him no injury — which tells you that their spirit yearns to do harm" (*Midrash haGadol*, Genesis 26:29—456). Indeed, says the commentary of the *baaley tosafoth*, Abimelech told Isaac in effect, "We did you a great kindness by sending you away in peace, because it is our way to harm anyone who comes along."

Laugh or cry, grow angry or resigned, it is the bitter truth. There were rich Jews who had to leave Nazi Germany in the 30's with hardly a penny to their name — and they remained grateful for the rest of their lives that they had found a way out. Jews in the Soviet Union get thrown out of work once they apply for an exit visa to be able to go to Israel. They live a hand-to-mouth existence for months, even years. If they annoy the KGB (secret police) — and nobody knows there from one day to the next just what may suddenly annoy them — they may spend a few years first in a prison cell or a Siberian labor camp. When and if they get their precious exit visa at last, they may have to pay heavy fees before they can leave. Yet when they finally get out they know they are members of a fortunate minority.

Not too long ago, the State of Israel found itself very much in the midst of long-drawn-out negotiations (thanks largely to American foreign policy), trying to get from Egypt some kind of promise of non-aggression — no war — in return for conquered territory that Egypt demanded back. And dear old Henry K. did his best, from the depths of his deep voice, to explain to Israel why it was impossible for Egypt to give such a promise. It was worthwhile for Israel (we were assured) to yield territory in return for the simple fact that for a while Egypt would not actually boil over in its frenzy and make war.

Of course, this took Israel right back into the good old protection racket; but it was also Isaac's experience with Abimelech come back to life, only on a larger canvas: See how strongly and instinctively the Arabs are given to belligerency. So if they will sit still and spare you, be grateful, dear Israel, and pay through the nose.

The nature of the world, as our Sages saw, is evil. Given power, people seek to harm and injure others, always imagining it necessary or profitable for their own welfare. In such a world the Jew has lived for hundreds and thousands of years, moving on his own God-given odyssey. And the Jewish people survives.

What weapons have we had for our defense? There is a story told of a pious young Jew who was drafted into the czar's army in Russia, during a war. As he prepared to go off to the army camp, his best friend asked him, "Zanvel, aren't you afraid? Plenty of people get killed in a war." Zanvel shrugged his shoulders: "I rely on the Almighty."

"Listen," said his friend: "don't just rely on the Almighty . . . Make sure to say *t'hillim*" — the prayerful chapters of the Book of Psalms.

For a while the non-religious Jews in Israel had an absolute trust in the power of their defense forces to deal with anything that came along. Since the Yom Kippur War their trust remains a little dented. Even they are starting to glimpse what the devout Jew has known since time immemorial: that the supreme Jewish weapon through history has always been prayer in faith. And it has given us the miracle of survival.

The Talmud makes the point well: Moses came and said, *the great, mighty and awesome God* (Deuteronomy 10:17). Came Jeremiah and said, "Aliens are crowing in triumph in His holy Temple. Where is His awesome majesty?" — and he would not say the word "awesome" [about the Almighty, in his prayer] . . . Then they [the men of the Great Assembly] came and said, "On the contrary . . . These are his awesome deeds: if not for fear of the Holy, Blessed One, how could one people endure among the nations?" (TB *Yoma* 69b).

If everything that occurred with the Patriarchs set a pattern for Jewish history, let us remember what happened to Laban when Jacob left him and he went chasing after him. When he finally caught up with Jacob, Laban said, *It is in my power to do you harm, but the God of your father spoke to me*

279

*last night*... (Genesis 31:29). As we read a bit earlier, *God came to Laban the Aramean in a dream by night and said to him: Take heed that you do not speak to Jacob, either good or bad* (*ibid.* 24).

Whether the nations of the world have had pleasant dreams or nightmares, we do not know. As Abimelech of Gerar and Laban of Aramea indicated, there is a strong natural drive among them to do us harm. Anyone who doubts it must be blissfully unaware of Jewish history and must manage to live in ignorance of Israel's current history. As the prophet said poignantly, *Israel is a scattered, driven sheep* (Jeremiah 50:17). And the Midrash states: Said David: What can one sheep do amid seventy wolves? What could the people Israel do amid seventy mighty nations — if Thou didst not stand by them every single moment? (*P'sikta Rabbathi* 9 — 32a–b).

This is the mark of His awesome majesty — that as His people we go along, one lamb among seventy wolves, and yet we emerge intact.

Herzl and his cohorts thought a Jewish state would end all that. We would be a nation among the nations, our flag getting equal space at the UN. Israel remains one small lamb amid seventy snarling wolves, many of whom form a solid voting bloc at the UN.

אַדְרִיָאנוּס קֵיסָר אָמַר לְרַבִּי יְהוֹשֻׁעַ: גְּדוֹלָה הִיא הַכִּבְשָׂה הָעוֹמֶדֶת בֵּין שִׁבְעִים זְאֵבִים.
אָמַר לוֹ: גָּדוֹל הוּא הָרוֹעֶה שֶׁמַּצִּילָה וְשׁוֹמְרָה וְשׁוֹבְרָן לְפָנֶיהָ.

Said the emperor Hadrian to R. Joshua, "How great is the sheep that endures among seventy nations." The Sage replied, "How great is the Shepherd who rescues her and keeps her safe, smashing them before her" (*Esther Rabbah* 10, 11; *Tanḥuma, tol'doth* 5).

Like Hadrian the emperor of ancient Rome, the world is amazed and awed at the miracle of Jewish survival; and it begins to regard the Jew as some supernatural creature. It begins seeking to know the "Jewish mystique." The pious Jew, however, who knows himself quite well, is aware of no mystique about him. He lives his life of prayer, Torah study, and religious observance of the mitzvoth. Whatever mystique there is about his life and his endurance, lies in the unseen and unsuspected workings of a Divine power in the world. The lamb among the wolves knows its Shepherd.

So the Jew stands in prayer three times a day, and as he negins *sh'moneh esréh*, the central part of the prayer, he calls on his Maker as *the great, mighty and awesome God*. He knows that this is how the Almighty shows His awesome power: by the enduring, ineradicable existence of the Jewish homeland, and with it the existence of Jewry.

280

## THE LESSONS
## IN DESTRUCTION

In ONE IMPORTANT RESPECT people are very obviously superior to animals: Human beings can learn from the past; animals cannot. No dog or cat can profit from the experiences of an ancestor. A household pet lives the same kind of life today, with the same instincts, abilities and limitations, as a pet thousands of years ago. Human beings can listen, read and learn. זְכֹר יְמוֹת עוֹלָם, בִּינוּ שְׁנוֹת דֹר וָדֹר *Remember the days of old,* Scripture tells us; *understand the years of every single generation* (Deuteronomy 32:7).

Thus we Jews study the Torah left us by the generations before us. We try to understand and live up to the religious rules, piety and worship of our forebears. They left us standards of faith to achieve, goals of devotion to reach. And we try to live by their historic, time-honored guidelines.

Our bitter enemies, says the Midrash, also kept trying to learn from the past — but in a different way, and for a different purpose:

אָמַר ר' לֵוִי: אוֹי לָהֶם לָרְשָׁעִים שֶׁהֵם מַעֲמִיקִים עֵצוֹת עַל יִשְׂרָאֵל. כָּל אֶחָד וְאֶחָד אוֹמֵר, עֲצָתִי יָפָה מֵעֲצָתְךָ. עֵשָׂו אָמַר: שׁוֹטֶה הָיָה קַיִן שֶׁהָרַג אֶת הֶבֶל אָחִיו בְּחַיֵּי אָבִיו. וְלֹא הָיָה יוֹדֵעַ שֶׁאָבִיו יִפְרֶה וְיִרְבֶּה? [וַהוֹלִיד אֶת שֵׁת]. אֲנִי אֵינִי עוֹשֶׂה כֵן, אֶלָּא, יִקְרְבוּ יְמֵי אֵבֶל אָבִי וְאַהַרְגָה אֶת יַעֲקֹב אָחִי (בראשית כז מא) [וְאִירַשׁ חֶלְקוֹ]. פַּרְעֹה אָמַר: שׁוֹטֶה הָיָה עֵשָׂו, שֶׁאָמַר, יִקְרְבוּ יְמֵי אֵבֶל אָבִי. לֹא הָיָה יוֹדֵעַ שֶׁאָחִיו יִפְרֶה וְיִרְבֶּה בְּחַיֵּי אָבִיו? אֲנִי אֵינִי עוֹשֶׂה כֵן, אֶלָּא עַד דְּאִינּוּן דַּקִּיקִין תְּחוֹת כַּרְסֵי אִמַּתְהוֹן, אֲנָא מְחַנֵּק לְהוֹן. הָדָא הוּא דִכְתִיב [הָבָה נִתְחַכְּמָה לוֹ (שמות א י) – נִיהְוֵי חֲכִימִין יוֹתֵר מִן קַדְמוֹי. מִיָּד] כָּל הַבֵּן הַיִּלּוֹד הַיְאֹרָה תַּשְׁלִיכֻהוּ (שמות א כב). הָמָן אָמַר: שׁוֹטֶה הָיָה פַּרְעֹה שֶׁאָמַר, כָּל הַבֵּן הַיִּלּוֹד ... [וְכָל הַבַּת תְּחַיּוּן]. לֹא הָיָה יוֹדֵעַ שֶׁהַבָּנוֹת נִשָּׂאוֹת לַאֲנָשִׁים וּפָרוֹת וְרָבוֹת מֵהֶם? אֲנִי אֵינִי עוֹשֶׂה כֵן, אֶלָּא, לְהַשְׁמִיד לַהֲרֹג וּלְאַבֵּד אֶת כָּל הַיְהוּדִים מִנַּעַר וְעַד זָקֵן טַף וְנָשִׁים (אסתר ג יג). אָמַר ר' לֵוִי: אַף גּוֹג וּמָגוֹג לֶעָתִיד לָבוֹא עָתִיד לוֹמַר כֵּן: שׁוֹטִים הָיוּ הָרִאשׁוֹנִים שֶׁהָיוּ מַעֲמִיקִים עֵצוֹת עַל יִשְׂרָאֵל. לֹא הָיוּ יוֹדְעִים שֶׁיֵּשׁ לָהֶם פַּטְרוֹן בַּשָּׁמַיִם? אֲנִי אֵינִי עוֹשֶׂה כֵן, אֶלָּא בַּתְּחִלָּה אֶזְדַּוֵּג לְפַטְרוֹנָם וְאַחַר כָּךְ אֶזְדַּוֵּג לָהֶם. הָדָא הוּא דִכְתִיב, יִתְיַצְּבוּ מַלְכֵי אֶרֶץ וְרוֹזְנִים נוֹסְדוּ יָחַד עַל ה' וְעַל מְשִׁיחוֹ (תהלים ב ב). אוֹמֵר לוֹ הַקָּדוֹשׁ־בָּרוּךְ־הוּא: לִי אַתָּה

281

מִזְדַּוְּגֵ? חַיֶּיךָ שֶׁאֲנִי עוֹשֶׂה עִמְּךָ מִלְחָמָה – שֶׁנֶּאֱמַר – ה׳ כַּגִּבּוֹר יֵצֵא, כְּאִישׁ מִלְחָמוֹת (ישעיהו
מב יג). וְאוֹמֵר, וְיָצָא ה׳ וְנִלְחַם בַּגּוֹיִם הָהֵם כְּיוֹם הִלָּחֲמוֹ בְּיוֹם קְרָב (זכריה יד ג). (תנחומא
הקדום, אמור יח; מדרש תהלים ב; ויקרא רבה כז יא)

Said R. Lévi: Woe to the wicked people, who propound deep plots against the people Israel. Every one of them says, "My plan is better than your plan." Esau said, "Cain was a fool when he killed his brother Abel. Did he not know his father would be fruitful and multiply? [and he begot Seth]. I will not do so; rather, *let the days of mourning for my father approach, and I will kill my brother Jacob* (Genesis 27:41) [and I will inherit his share]."

Pharaoh said, "Esau was a fool when he thought, *let the days of mourning for my father approach.* Did he not know that his brother would beget children during his father's lifetime? I will not act like that; rather, while they are but tender infants under their mothers' birth-stool, I will snuff the life out of them." Hence it is written, [*come, let us deal wisely with them* (Exodus 1:10) — let us be wiser than those who were before us. Therefore] *Every son that is born, you shall cast into the river* (ibid. 22).

Haman said, "Pharaoh was a fool when he decided, *Every son that is born, you shall cast into the river, but every daughter you shall keep alive.* Did he not know that the daughters would get married to men and would bear them children? I will not do so, but will rather *destroy, slay and bring to perdition all the Jews, young and old, children and women, in one day*" (Esther 3:13).

Said R. Lévi: Gog and Magog too are destined to speak so in the distant future: Those early ones who hatched deep plans against the people Israel were fools. Did they not know that they [the Jews] have a protector in heaven? I will not act like that, but first I will engage their protector in battle, and afterward I will war against them." Hence it is written, *The kings of earth position themselves, and the rulers take counsel together, against the Lord and His anointed* (Psalms 2:2). Then the Holy, Blessed One will say to them, "You have come to engage *Me* in battle? As you live, I will make war with you!" — as Scripture says, *The Lord will go forth like a mighty man, like a man of war* (Isaiah 42:13); and it says, *Then the Lord will go forth and fight against those nations, as when He fights on a day of battle* (Zechariah 14:3).[40]

R. Lévi did a historical survey, if you will, of those with a desire to destroy Israel: the man, the people, the land; and he saw a line of development:

282

Each tried to learn from the mistake of the one before him, and sought to make his method more sophisticated and effective.

First there was an individual named Israel: our father Jacob. When his brother Esau developed enough hatred to kill him, he looked back to someone before him who had killed a brother — Cain; and he studied that homicide carefully. "That Cain," he decided, "was not intelligent. He could have waited till his father (Adam) was too old to have any more children. Then killing off his brother would be a profitable business: he would remain Adam's sole heir and inherit everything Adam owned."

So we read in Scripture how Esau planned, "Let the days of mourning for my father approach," let him be so old that death is in sight, and he cannot father any more children, "and I will kill my brother Jacob." Then his crime would pay. He would inherit all that Jacob stood to gain through the blessing he had received, in place of Esau, from their father Isaac.

Esau was clever, no? Along came Pharaoh (says R. Lévi) and he was astonished at Esau's stupidity. How could that man have been such a fool? He waited all those years, till his father would be at death's door — and in the meantime Jacob had twelve sons, twelve heirs; Esau would never inherit a fig from Jacob's property. What was the point, in general, in killing a man who left twelve sons to succeed him? Moreover, should Esau lift a finger then against Jacob, they were sure to defend him, or at least avenge his death if Esau achieved his purpose.

Pharaoh was going to be much more clever. He wanted to keep the Hebrews subdued and suppressed, so that they could never pick their heads up. The way to do that was to kill off all the male children right at birth. The great river Nile coursed through the land. Just throw the children in, he ordered. Of course, said he, little girls might be left alive. They were harmless; and when they grew up they could serve as slaves and concubines (to the Egyptians, immorality was a way of life).[41]

The next figure in our Hall of Ill-fame, who planned some wholesale murder for the Jewish people, was Haman. He in turn shook his head in wonder at Pharaoh's imbecility. It was such a mistake, he thought, to leave the newborn girls alive (just because the Egyptians loved their immoral pleasures). The girls would only grow up and bear children. By our normative religious law, any child born to a Jewish mother is a Jew, whoever, whatever the father may be. And if the Hebrew girls in Egypt remembered the sacred teachings of their parents and grandparents, they would rear their children to be loyal to the God of Abraham, Isaac and Jacob.

283

So, Haman sighed, what kind of a final solution to the Jewish problem was that? And he came up with the *final* final solution: wholesale total destruction; kill them all out at once — old and young; men, women and children. He sent out the king's couriers with a royal proclamation, signed and sealed by the emperor, calling on every loyal anti-semitic subject in the vast empire of Ahasuerus to rise up on the thirteenth of Adar for a great big day of fun and games — one gigantic massacre, one enormous blood-bath. And there you are, thought Haman blissfully: no more Jews.

It was such a beatiful plan; but like the best-laid plans of mice and men, it went astray. It did not work. As Haman swung from the gallows in the breeze, the Jews were still very much in existence.

Since his time, many others have tried Haman's approach. In the course of history the Jews have borne the brunt of massacre by Greeks and Romans, British and French, Germans and Russians, Lithuanians and Polacks, Rumanians and Ukrainians, Arabs and Turks. You name them — we were their victims. Heaven alone has the full record of our tragedies and our martyrs. Yet our people lived on.

In keeping with R. Lévi's teaching, each new enemy of ours tried to improve on the approach and techniques of those before him. At last Nazi Germany drew its plans in the grand manner, using the advances of science, the skills of technology, and the robot-efficiency of the Prussian Junker. We lost a third of our people — but in the aftermath a Jewish state was born, and American Jewry awoke to a newborn sense of commitment and responsibility.

Is the game over? Are we finished with satanic schemers and planners trying to find bigger and better ways to solve our problem by dissolving our existence? No, says R. Lévi. The prophet Ezekiel tells of someone named Gog from the land of Magog (Ezekiel 38:2), who will come to wage fierce battle against Israel after Jewry has returned from the exile to its homeland. Well, says R. Lévi, Gog will also seek a final solution to help us out — out of existence. He will sit and ponder why all the Jew-haters who came before him failed. Where did they go wrong? . . . And he will come to a fascinating solution:

Our Sages teach that basically, mankind was divided into seventy nations, each with its own language; and to each a patron angel was assigned, a protector in heaven to champion its cause.[42] In the entire Book of Esther, that tells of Haman and his downfall, the name of God is never

284

once mentioned. It all might seem to have happened naturally, by the turn of events. But that won't fool Gog. He will realize that the strange good fortune of Israel and the Jewish people is due entirely to its protecting patron angel in heaven. Otherwise, how could one solitary lamb really survive so long among seventy wolves?

Logical, no? Going further with his faultless logic, Gog will decide that the only way to solve the Jewish (or Israeli) problem with a really *final* final solution is to deal first with its protector in heaven — the God of Israel.

Who exactly is Gog of the land of Magog? As with most of the prophecy in Scripture, is it hard to know precisely which nation is meant. Yet if anyone could find a better candidate for the role than the Soviet Union, I for one would be greatly surprised. [43]

The Jews in the USSR are a minority group, and so are the Armenians. Yet Stalin and his cohorts never clamped down viciously on the Armenian language and schools. How else can it ever be explained logically, with cool reason, why every kind of Jewish school in the Soviet Union was shut down? why the remaining synagogues are so pitifully few in number? why it is a crime there to study Hebrew, or to learn about the land of Israel? Unless we accept the basic axiom, inscrutable and inexplicable as it may be, that in the mind of humanity God remains inextricably linked with the Jewish people, its history and destiny, how can we understand why Jewish writers and intellectuals who toed the communist line faithfully were purged? why, with no basis in fact, Jewish doctors were suddenly accused of plotting against Stalin's life, and were treated accordingly?

To this day we remain appalled at the attention that the Soviet secret police pay to every detail of the Jewish religion that someone might wish to observe: Circumcision is ruthlessly forbidden; keeping the Sabbath properly is virtually impossible; *sheḥittah*, ritual slaughter of animals to provide kosher meat, is almost non-existent. And if a retired old man tries to teach his little grandchild the Hebrew alphabet, from a page of an old prayer-book that has fallen apart, the secret police feel very offended and react sharply.

They could not really remove the Almighty from the vast empire of the USSR. His presence is everywhere. Not an iota of earthly existence is hidden from His awareness. Open your heart to Him, and He is with you. So they do their best to cut off every possible contact that a Jew might have with Him, through Torah, prayer or mitzvoth. For decades, not a single Jewish school of any type has existed in Stalin's paradise, and today

285

you would have to look far and wide to find a Jew there who can recite the Hebrew verse of *Sh'ma yisraél*, "Hear, O Israel, the Lord is our God, the Lord is one" — the most sacred sentence in our life, the affirmation of our faith that the Jew recites even on his deathbed, as his last words on earth.

The Soviet Union encourages a living Armenian culture in its Armenian republic, so that it can attract Armenian tourists from other countries. Somehow it could not find it in its Russian heart to accord the same treatment to any Jewish culture worthy the name. The Russian Orthodox church goes on its way fairly smoothly in the USSR. Only the Jewish faith receives "special treatment."

Why? What other explanation can be found than the role of the Jew, since time immemorial, as "the chosen of God," chosen to be His people in the world? As the Sages put it succinctly, סיני, שמשם ירדה שנאה לעולם The mountain where we received the Torah was called Sinai (pronounced *sin-ai*) because from there *sin'ah*, hatred, descended into the world (TB *Shabbath* 88a).

In battling the Jew and his faith, the USSR really seeks a way of action for its profound wish to battle God. Unable to find Him, they go for the jugular vein of His people's spirit. And now the battle storms about Israel, the land God promised us through our ancestors.

There is really nothing new in this. Long ago (we read in the Midrash) R. Ḥiyya said: What do the heathen nations of the world resemble? — a man who hated the king and wanted to attack him, but was unable to. What did he do? He went to his [the king's] statue and wanted to knock it over; but he was afraid of the king, that he might put him to death. What did he do? He took an iron nail and drove it in underneath it. Said he, "By making the base collapse I will make the statue topple." So the heathen nations want to attack the Holy, Blessed One, and they cannot; and they come to attack Jewry ... To give an illustration: When someone cannot strike a donkey [in his frustration] he hits the pannier [saddle]. Thus, being unable to proceed above [against the Almighty] they turn against Jewry (*Tanḥuma, p'kudé* 4).

This is what is going on in our time. Yet so immersed are we in the daily headlines and installments of televised news that few of us ever sit back and note an amazing thing. The prophet Ezekiel foresees a war that Gog will wage against the land of Israel. Similarly, the second chapter of *t'hillim*, the Book of Psalms, begins: *Why are the nations in an uproar, and the people plotting in vain?* And the Sages teach that this refers to Gog and

Magog.[44] Well, go back some seventy or eighty years in time. Could anyone possibly imagine in the late nineteenth or early twentieth century a major world power, or "nations in an uproar," rising in hostility against the land of Israel? The land was ruled by a sick, corrupt, lethargic Turkey; a small community of pious Jews in Jerusalem devoted itself to Torah study and prayer; and the great powers of the world were busy with their own affairs.

Today we see it before our eyes, and fail to realize that Scripture foretold it so long ago. Wanting power and influence in the Middle East, the great colossus of the USSR became a major factor there, encouraging the Arab nations, by the lavish supply of armament and by advice, to rise *in an uproar*, as Scripture says, against Israel. Both in June 1967 and in October 1973 the USSR was there on the sidelines, cheering them on with such encouraging advice as, "Why stop till you have moved them into the Mediterranean Ocean?" And both times it raised its mailed fist in threat to stop Israel from following its military progress to the logical conclusion of the enemy's total defeat.

Here again the question arises: Why Israel? Why is this little piece of land so important to the Arabs, and by a series of "well-oiled" involvements, to the rest of the world? It is small; it has no outstanding natural resources. The Palestinian Arabs who once lived there either sold their land to the Jews for a good price or fled because of wars started by fellow-Arabs. If there were the slightest wish in the Arab world to have them simmer down and settle down, to live decent, useful lives, their problem could have been solved long ago, for a fraction of the amount that is spent annually for armed belligerence against Israel. They could have been permanently resettled on land just as fertile or better. The Arab world can afford it.

Then why the ceaseless hostility and rancor? Why do they take the approach of certain professional "accident cases" — people who get themselves slightly hit by a car, then produce gory photographs of the wounds and come to court swathed in a mountain of bandages and hobbling on crutches, in order to collect unbelievable damages? And why do so many other countries and peoples in the world go along with them?

With no ordinary, rational explanation in view, it must be as the Psalmist said: *Why are the nations in an uproar, and the peoples plotting in vain? The kings of earth position themselves, and the rulers take counsel together, against the Lord and His anointed* . . . The real hostility is not aimed against a people or a land, but against the Almighty. It is expressed against this

287

people and this land only because they are "His anointed" — what He chose to call His own.

Now the words of the prophet and the Midrash gain a new clarity. We read, *Then the Lord will go forth and fight against the nations, as when He fights on a day of battle* (Zechariah 14:3). Today we would probably look at this prophecy as people in the last century looked at the prophecies about nations, especially the mighty Gog, rising in an uproar against Israel. Besides, we might well wonder: What need can the Almighty have to go out and fight? Surely He could arrange for the nations of the world to fight one another?

The Midrash quoted above gives the answer: The wicked of the world are history-minded. They want to make sure they learn from the past, so as not to repeat the mistakes of those who lived before them. So, says the Midrash, they keep trying to improve and refine their techniques for destroying the Jewish people — till at last they will realize that in order to achieve this goal, they must battle and vanquish Jewry's protector in heaven.

"Very well," says the Almighty, "*I* am their protector in heaven." *For the Lord's portion is His people, Jacob is His inheritance* (Deuteronomy 32:9). חַיֶּיךָ שֶׁאֲנִי עוֹשֶׂה לִי בָּאתָ לְהִזְדַּוֵּג? You have come to engage *Me* in battle? עִמְּךָ מִלְחָמָה As you live, I will make war with you. Hence the prophet proclaims, *Then the Lord will go forth and fight against the nations.*

In our time we can see the truth of R. Lévi's teaching. Yigal Allon, Israel's foreign minister in an earlier period, once reported: "In 1951, in England, I chanced to meet a well-known Arab scholar. We talked about the war of 1948 [Israel's War of Independence], and this is what the scholar, a moderate by reputation, had to say: 'You did win the first round, but in the inevitable second round the Arabs will triumph.' When I asked him on what grounds he was predicating his forecast, he said: 'In general the loser learns from his reverses and errors more than the winner learns from his victory.'"[45]

There were a few other rounds after the war of 1948, and thank Heaven, Israel fared quite well in the military aspects. Yet after every armed conflict with Israel, the Arabs keep studying the errors and shortcomings that made them lose it. So they go to the munitions markets of the world and get more sophisticated weapons and equipment. If their soldiers cannot fight, they get automatic equipment which only needs someone to push a button. And of course, dear old Gog, the Soviet Union, is always ready to supply them and oversupply them; and it even sent in experts to work the ultra-sophisticated things for them (an Arab might push the wrong button). Thus they keep planning and dreaming and boasting, "Next time we will show you."

The Midrash states so very aptly: ... The Israelites told the Holy, Blessed One, "O Master of the world, they have no other work to do but sit and hatch plans against us." ... Said the Holy, Blessed One, "But what will they accomplish? They issue decrees and verdicts against you, and I nullify and squash them" (*Tanḥuma, tol'doth* 5).

We have seen the nations huffing and puffing, baring fangs and claws against the small isolated land of Israel. Yet their real enemy and target is the Almighty; and what does the Psalmist say? *He who sits in heaven laughs; the Lord jeers at them* (Psalms 2:4).

In 1967 and again in 1973 the goal of the warring Arabs was to drive Israel into the Mediterranean Sea. They wanted (you might say) the waves of the ocean to billow up and cover the Israelis forever. Says the Midrash: A wave rises up and grows powerful, as though it is going to inundate the entire world. Yet when it reaches the shore, it flattens out in prostration before the sand. So too the nations: Whichever one takes up arms to harm the people Israel, falls before them. The actions of the world are compared to the sea, as Scripture says, *But the wicked are like the tossing sea* (Isaiah 57:20); and the people Israel are compared to the sand [the shore] as it says, *Yet the number of the children of Israel shall be as the sand of the sea* (Hosea 2:1) (*Midrash T'hillim* ii 2; *Yalkut Shimoni,* Isaiah § 350).

Any plan hatched in Arab or Soviet hatcheries to make Israel disappear under the ocean waves will come to nothing. It will fall flat. *The Lord annuls the plan of nations; He foils the schemes of peoples. The Lord's plan stands forever; the thoughts of His heart are for generation after generation* (Psalms 33:10–11). And His plan is to have Israel flood the world — with a knowledge of the Divine purpose in creation: His wishes and His blessings. To quote again the immortal words of the prophet: *They shall not hurt nor destroy in all My holy mountain; for the earth shall be full of the knowledge of the Lord, as the waters cover the sea* (Isaiah 11:9).

289

Iन the lore of the Sages another fascinating story illuminates our theme. We know the Torah's account of the binding of Isaac. Incomprehensible as the Divine command may have seemed, Abraham rose early in the morning to obey it, ready to go and sacrifice Isaac, the only son Sarah had borne him. He made all the preparations to set out, *and he took his two servant-boys with him* (Genesis 22:3). Who were the two servants? As the Midrash tells it,[46] they were Ishmael and Eliezer. And as they went along early in the morning, says the Midrash,[47] the two servants had an interesting conversation:

[בְּעוֹד שֶׁהָיוּ אַבְרָהָם וְיִצְחָק מְהַלְכִין בַּדֶּרֶךְ] נִכְנְסָה תַּחֲרוּת בֵּין יִשְׁמָעֵאל לְאֱלִיעֶזֶר [עֶבֶד אַבְרָהָם, שֶׁהָיוּ שׁוֹמְרִים אֶת הַכֵּלִים וְאֶת בְּהֶמְתָּם]. יִשְׁמָעֵאל אוֹמֵר: עַכְשָׁו אַבְרָהָם מַקְרִיב אֶת יִצְחָק לְעוֹלַת מוֹקְדָה עַל גַּבֵּי הַמִּזְבֵּחַ, וַאֲנִי בְּנוֹ בְכוֹרוֹ, אִירַשׁ הַכֹּל [כָּל הַנְּכָסִים שֶׁיִּשָּׁאֲרוּ מֵאַבָּא]. אָמַר לוֹ אֱלִיעֶזֶר: כְּבָר גֵּרַשְׁךָ כְּאִשָּׁה מְגֹרֶשֶׁת מִבַּעֲלָהּ וְשִׁלַּחֲךָ לַמִּדְבָּר; וְעַד שֶׁלֹּא נוֹלַדְתָּ אֲנִי עַבְדּוֹ [נֶאֱמַן בֵּיתוֹ] מְשָׁרֵת לְפָנָיו בַּיּוֹם וּבַלַּיְלָה, וַאֲנִי הוּא שֶׁיּוֹרֵשׁ אוֹתוֹ. וְרוּחַ הַקֹּדֶשׁ צוֹוַחַת, מְשִׁיבָה וְאוֹמֶרֶת לָהֶם: לֹא זֶה יוֹרֵשׁ וְלֹא זֶה יוֹרֵשׁ, אֶלָּא זֶה יְרֻשָּׁה לְבַעֲלָהּ עוֹמֶדֶת. (מדרש הגדול, בראשית כב ג, שנא—בב; פרקי דר' אליעזר פל"א; [מדרש ויושע]

[As Abraham and Isaac went on their way] a quarrel arose between Ishmael and Eliezer [Abraham's servant, who were guarding the equipment and their animal]. Said Ishmael, "Now Abraham is going to sacrifice Isaac as a burnt-offering in the fire on the altar; so I, his older son, will inherit everything [all the property that will remain from father]." Replied Eliezer, "He already drove you out like a woman divorced by her husband, and he sent you off into the wilderness. From before the time of your birth, however, I have been his [faithful household] servant, attending upon him day and night. I am the one who will inherit from him." And the sacred heavenly spirit proclaimed in response to them, "Neither this one will be the heir, nor that one. The inheritance remains its rightful owner's!"

It must have been boring for the two servants just to follow along behind Abraham and Isaac. Then, *on the third day Abraham lifted up his eyes and saw the place afar off; and Abraham said to his servant-lads: Stay you here with the donkey, and I and the lad will go yonder* . . . (Genesis 22:4–5). With nothing to do but watch the supplies and the animal, the two servants started talking, and got into an argument. Knowing what was in store for Isaac, each looked to a rosy future. Ishmael was Abraham's older son, born from Hagar. Soon enough, thought he, Isaac would be just a small heap of ashes; then *he* would be the heir. Abraham was very wealthy and very old. He, Ishmael, was going to be rich. Above all, there was the Divine promise to Abraham, *for all the land which you see, to you will I give it, and to your progeny forever* (Genesis 13:15). In a glorious technicolor dream Ishmael could see his descendants receiving the Promised Land, with God's timeless blessing . . .

Hold on a minute, said Eliezer; not so fast. You were born to Abraham, but he disowned you. Like a man divorcing and disowning a woman, he drove you (and your mother) out into the wilderness. You are back now only as a servant; and as a servant I outrank you. Long before you were born, I was already managing his household. He drove you away; and 'out of sight, out of mind.'[48] I have been with him all these years, day and night, attending upon him. He always sees me serving him faithfully, hand and foot. He will remember me with gratitude, and make *me* his heir.

In a way, their argument cast its shadow ahead into world history. The good Lord promised Abraham the land we call Israel; and He promised him that a single son, Isaac, would be his heir (Genesis 15:4; 17:19; 21:10–12). Their descendants who made of their faith a living, durable reality in the world, are the Jewish people. Hence, by the elementary principles of logic, they are heir to the Divine blessing and promise of the holy land.

Such niceties and fine considerations, however, never meant a fig to the mighty powers of the world. From Babylon to Rome in the ancient world, they were ready to conquer the land and enslave or exile its people. Isaac was originally supposed to go up in flames on the altar fire, as a sacrifice. Taking their cue perhaps from that, they found it no great task to sent our holy Temple up in flames, and to burn and pillage ruthlessly. They came ready to inherit what the Almighty had given Abraham to bequeath.

So the land of Israel has just as bloody and tortured a history as the people, especially because it is "holy to three faiths." It was ruled by pagan Romans and Christian Romans, Moslem Arabs and Moslem Turks. In its checkered history, the Crusaders came to "rescue it from the infidels," only to lose control, in the course of time, to other "devout" bloody warriors.

And the controversy goes on today. Who has the right to the holy land? Styling themselves the descendants of Ishmael, the Arabs claim Abraham as their ancestor. (There is no evidence or basis for this claim, however. In ancient times, as the Sages teach, a conquering king of Assyria transplanted and relocated all the peoples in the Mediterranean world, jumbling them up thoroughly.[49] Historical records have given no grounds to disprove or doubt this tenet of the Talmud.) The Moslems built a mosque over his sepulchre, the Tomb of Machpelah, and made it their holy place. For centuries they occupied the land as its owners. The Jews were gone, spread out across the world. Look, said the Arabs: God drove them out, like a husband who divorced his wife. They are dispersed, living among many peoples, mingling and assimilating. A Russian Jew looks Russian; a Yemenite Jew looks Yemenite; an Indian Jew looks Indian. They are gone, disinherited, unrecognizable. We are the heirs to the holy land, thank you very much.

So *they* became the "faithful believers." In addition to the mosque over the Tomb of Machpelah (where both Abraham and Isaac were buried, as well as Jacob, and their respective wives) they built their Mosque of Omar on the site of our devastated Sanctuary, on Mount Moriah, where once Abraham had bound Isaac on the altar.

Ishmael was only too happy and eager to become the heir.... Wait, though: there was also Eliezer. And in the course of history, there were followers of a faith that venerated a certain Jew from Nazareth. They came forward likewise, with all the beautiful humility of Uriah Heep, and very piously accepted the mantle of Abraham's inheritance.

Eliezer was indeed Abraham's devoted servant. As the Sages relate (TB *Yoma* 28b), he mastered the religious doctrines of Abraham, and taught others the Patriarch's ways of piety and faith. In fact, say the Sages, he was so close to his master through the years that he came to resemble him, and he gained an equal control over his evil impulse (*B'réshith Rabbah* 59, 8). It is easy to understand why he felt ready to become his master's heir, to take possession of Abraham's property, including the Divine right to the Promised Land. He was ready to be his master's successor by championing Abraham's faith and proclaiming it to the world.

In a sense, the worshippers of the new faith deriving out of Nazareth followed somewhat in Eliezer's path. They picked up many elements of the

Jewish faith. Basic maxims and teachings of the Sages of the Talmud turn up bodily in their "new testament," until they could give the illusion of resembling the Jews, as the carriers of a "new and better" version of Judaism. Certainly their way of faith may have seemed prettier. Desperately in need of a new, healthy, morally sound religion to replace the decadent, corrosive paganism of the Greek and Roman world, they made an amalgam of Judaism and Greek mythology (which knew of many "sons born to gods") — and they proclaimed themselves the religious successors to the Jews. They pronounced us officially disowned by God; we were no longer His chosen people, they said; *they* were. As of their appearance on the scene, they intoned, they held the keys to the kingdom of Heaven; and we could get in only by their courtesy.

Then, in the kindness of their hearts, to make sure we would get to heaven, now that we had become not God's chosen people but a bunch of damned outcasts, they were ready to take a little hint from the story of Isaac. They were ready to bind us well and set a match to us. And if the original Isaac was saved by the Almighty, they would "correct" this detail.

This was their glorious vision of piety: send the Jew up in flames, in the fires of the Inquisition, and *they* would serve God as His faithful flock. Like Eliezer, they were sure of their place under heaven. Long before the time that Ishmael's supposed descendants developed their Moslem faith, they were His faithful servants, chanting plainsong in their cathedrals and monasteries. They went on serving Him night and day, burning infidel Jews as sacrifices. Very religious, no?

Such, if you will, were the self-styled successors of Eliezer, proceeding with their claim as heir. Yet the so-called descendants of Ishmael were active too. In the years between 1917 and 1948, while Jews strove with every ounce of their strength to make a national home in Palestine as a place of refuge for those who could leave the charnel house of Europe, the "Ishmaelites" raised their hopes and their voices anew.

For centuries the Arabs lived their dormant peasant or nomad existence, domiciled with their domestic animals. Then, with cooperation enough from Nazi Germany on the one hand and British officers in Palestine on the other hand,[50] they mounted an Arab nationalist movement. Suddenly the so-called Ishmaelites had a brand-new passionate yearning to inherit the land of Israel. And what about the Jews? Well, like Isaac, they were being bound as a sacrifice: they would be sent up in flames in Hitler's crematoria, crisply and efficiently.

293

So the British decided they could admit into Palestine only as many Jews as the land could hold. They measured carefully something called economic absorptive capacity; and Lord Peel conveniently concluded that there was hardly room enough left in the land to swing a cat. Thus the so-called, self-styled descendants of Ishmael dreamed their happy dream of inheritance.

Closer to our day there has been a new chapter in the "dispute over the inheritance." The boundaries that the United Nations set for Israel differ somewhat from the Torah's boundaries — by about fifty percent, if not more. The Almighty has His own way of working things out, however; and every time the Arabs made war, Israel gained territory. Then of course the nations came and said, "Dear Israel, this is not good, refined, gentlemanly behavior. Give back the territories." Various pressures were applied over the years, and at last the Arabs saw a gleam of hope of getting back "their" land. Long before there was any suspicion of a proposal of a tangible agreement, violent arguments broke out in the Arab camp: Who would rule in Judea and Samaria? Who would control the West Bank? Once again the voices of dispute over the inheritance were loud and raucous.

To the Jew in the Diaspora it can all seem frightening at times. He watches his television screen, and grows absolutely alarmed: "Poor little Israel." Among religious Jews in the land, however, you can see one promise of the Torah fulfilled: *you shall dwell in security in your land . . . you shall lie down to sleep, and none shall make you afraid* (Leviticus 26:5–6). What gives them a feeling of safety and inner peace? It was in the holy land (near Mount Moriah) that the sacred heavenly spirit proclaimed (as we read in the Midrash), "Neither this one will be the heir, nor that one. The inheritance remains its rightful owner's!" The pious Jew in Israel still hears the echo of that Divine retort, confirmed by history. Gone are the Romans, Byzantines, Crusaders, Mamelukes, Ottomans and British — and the Jews are there — to stay.

To the claim of Eliezer's "heirs" the same retort applies. The Vatican found the State of Israel very upsetting. It might possibly mean (as many honest and decent Christian theologians acknowledged) that the Chosen People had not been replaced after all, but by Divine providence the "accursed outcast Jew" was coming back "to do business at the old stand."

The Vatican cherished perhaps a belief that what Abraham began at the altar on Mount Moriah, they would finish. From Abraham's altar Isaac returned alive, unscratched and unburnt. Minions of the Vatican did enough slaughtering and burning of their own, trying to correct Abraham's omission. Then, from their headquarters and branches, many watched placidly enough as others, and finally Hitler, made herculean efforts to finish the job.

The Christians had their own "one and only son" — another member of the Hebrews, who, they said, was crucified but returned to life three days later. With Isaac killed off and their "son" alive and waiting to reappear on stage as their messiah, they were sure of being Abraham's spiritual heirs, the foremost exponents of monotheism in the world.

In a poem that is sometimes sung among the Sabbath *z'miroth* (tables hymns),[51] the medieval scholar R. Abraham ibn Ezra put in a line, taken bodily from the Biblical story of two women who bore infants, one of which died, whereupon each claimed the live one, and they came to have King Solomon decide it. In ibn Ezra's poem it is Hagar, Ishmael's mother, who says those famous words: לֹא כִּי בְּנֵךְ הַמֵּת וּבְנִי הֶחָי *Not so: your son is the dead one, and mine the living one!* (I Kings 3:22).

Let the Ishmaels and Eliezers of our world make this claim till they are blue in the face. Our Isaacs live, content and secure in the land that God gave Abraham. To all the dramatic outbursts and thundering denunciations against Israel, the sacred heavenly spirit answers, "Neither this one is the heir, nor that one. The inheritance remains its rightful owner's" . . . *and you shall dwell in security in your land.*

## ❧ GAINING PERSPECTIVE

**A**T TIMES WE MIGHT STOP FOR A MOMENT AND WONDER: What is the underlying meaning of Israel in our time? What is the basic significance of the kaleidoscope of events that have been making the world's headlines for decades?

Bear in mind this simple sentence from the writings of the prophets: כִּימֵי צֵאתְךָ מֵאֶרֶץ מִצְרַיִם אַרְאֶנּוּ נִפְלָאוֹת *As in the days of your emergence from*

*the land of Egypt, I will show him marvels* (Micah 7:15). The history that
Israel has been making in our time, year after year, can be seen in perspective
if we consider what happened with our ancestors, the ancient Hebrews, in
olden Egypt.

Our people then had no Torah, no culture, learning or breeding. They
were slaves, building vast structures out of mortar and bricks, for the
Pharaohs. Egypt had a great civilization then, which archaeologists and
Egyptologists are still discovering, deciphering and studying. Pharaoh sat
on his throne in splendor, certain of his royal superiority. By his religious
beliefs he was beloved by his gods, and unlike ordinary mortals, he would
live after death. It was only right (he was sure) for an inferior people of no
account to serve him as slaves. He reigned in radiant majesty, receiving
homage on all sides.

Somewhere out in the wilderness, on a mountain called Ḥoreb, the
Almighty told Moses to go meet his brother Aaron, and go with him to
Pharaoh. So the two brothers duly arrived at the royal palace. Says the
Midrash:

אָמַר ר׳ חִיָּא בַּר׳ אַבָּא: יוֹם פְּרוֹזְבּטְיָא שֶׁל פַּרְעֹה הָיָה, וְהָיוּ כָל הַמְּלָכִים בָּאִים וּמְעַטְּרִים
אוֹתוֹ, שֶׁהָיָה קוֹזְמוֹקְרָטוֹר; וְהָיוּ מֹשֶׁה וְאַהֲרֹן עוֹמְדִין עַל פֶּתַח פַּלָטִין. נִכְנְסוּ אֵצֶל פַּרְעֹה
וְאָמְרוּ לוֹ: שְׁנֵי זְקֵנִים עוֹמְדִים עַל פֶּתַח פַּלָטִין שֶׁלְּךָ. אָמַר לָהֶם, וְיֵשׁ בְּיָדָם עֲטָרוֹת? אָמְרוּ
לוֹ, לָאו. אָמַר לָהֶם בָּאַחֲרוֹנָה, יִכָּנְסוּ. נִכְנְסוּ אֵצֶל פַּרְעֹה; אָמַר לָהֶם, מָה אַתֶּם מְבַקְשִׁים?
אָמְרוּ לוֹ, ה׳ אֱ־לֹהֵי הָעִבְרִים שְׁלָחָנוּ אֵלֶיךָ וְאָמַר לָנוּ שֶׁנֹּאמַר לְךָ, שַׁלַּח אֶת עַמִּי וְיָחֹגּוּ לִי
בַּמִּדְבָּר (שמות ה א). אָמַר לָהֶם, מִי ה׳ אֲשֶׁר אֶשְׁמַע בְּקֹלוֹ? (שם ב). וְלֹא הָיָה יוֹדֵעַ לִשְׁלוֹחַ לִי
עֲטָרָה מִשֶּׁלּוֹ, אֶלָּא בִּדְבָרִים בָּא אֵלָי? מִי ה׳ אֲשֶׁר אֶשְׁמַע בְּקֹלוֹ? אָמַר ר׳ לֵוִי: בְּאוֹתָהּ
שָׁעָה הוֹצִיא דִיפְּתְּרָא שֶׁל אֱלוֹהוּת וְקָרָא, אֱלוֹהֵי אֱדוֹם מוֹאָב וְצִידוֹן. אָמַר לָהֶם, הֲרֵי
קָרָאתִי וְאֵינִי מוֹצֵא מַה שֶּׁאַתֶּם אוֹמְרִים. אָמַר ר׳ לֵוִי: לְמָה הַדָּבָר דּוֹמֶה, לְכֹהֵן שֶׁהָיָה לוֹ
עֶבֶד. יָצָא הַכֹּהֵן מִן הַמְּדִינָה, הָלַךְ עַבְדּוֹ לְבַקְּשׁוֹ בֵּין הַקְּבָרוֹת, הִתְחִיל צוֹוֵחַ, אֲדוֹנִי,
אֲדוֹנִי! אָמְרוּ לוֹ, מִי הוּא אֲדוֹנֶךָ? אָמַר לָהֶם, פְּלוֹנִי כֹּהֵן. אָמְרוּ לוֹ, שׁוֹטֶה שֶׁבָּעוֹלָם, כֹּהֵן
אַתָּה מְבַקֵּשׁ בְּבֵית הַקְּבָרוֹת? כָּךְ אָמַר פַּרְעֹה לְמֹשֶׁה, מִי ה׳? הוֹצֵאתִי דִיפְּתְּרָא שֶׁל אֱלוֹהוּת
וּבִקַּשְׁתִּיו בְּתוֹכָהּ, וְלֹא מְצָאתִיו. אָמַר לֵיהּ, שׁוֹטֶה שֶׁבָּעוֹלָם, הָאֱלוֹהוֹת שֶׁבְּיָדְךָ מֵתִים הֵם,
אֲבָל אֱ־לֹהֵינוּ חַי וְקַיָּם הוּא.... (תנחומא הקדום, וארא ב; ילקוט שמעוני ח״א קע״א)

Said R. Ḥiyya b. Abba: It was Pharaoh's day to receive royal ambassadors,
and all the kings came and crowned him, as he was a world ruler; and
Moses and Aaron were standing at the palace entrance. [His servants] went

in to Pharaoh and told him, "Two elders are standing at your palace door."

"Do they have crowns in their hands?" he asked them. "No," they replied. Finally he said, "Let them enter." They came in to Pharaoh, and he asked them, "What do you want?" They replied, "The Lord, God of the Hebrews, sent us to you, and he bade us tell you, *Let My people go, that they may hold a celebration to Me in the wilderness*" (Exodus 5:1). Said he to them, "*Who is the Lord, that I should hearken to His voice?* (ibid. 2). Did He not know enough to send me a crown of His, but instead He comes to me with words? Who is the Lord, that I should hearken to His voice?"

Said R. Levi: He then took out a parchment roll [with the names] of the deities, and he read: the gods of Edom, Moab, Sidon... Said he, "Here I have read [the whole list] and I have not found the one you named."

Said R. Levi: To what can it be compared? — to a kohen who had a servant; the kohen left the country, whereupon his servant went looking for him among the graves [in the cemetery]. He began calling out, "My master, my master!" So people asked him, "Who is your master?" "So-and-so the kohen," he replied. "You absolute fool!" they berated him. "You are looking for a kohen in the cemetery?" Similarly Pharaoh asked Moses, "Who is the Lord? I took out a parchment roll listing the gods, and I searched for Him there, and did not find him." He answered him, "You absolute fool! The gods that you have there [on the list] are dead, whereas our God lives and endures."... (*Early Tanḥuma, va' éra* 2; *Yalkut Shimoni* I § 175.)[52]

If a political commentator on a national television network were to sum up this first encounter between Moses (and Aaron) and Pharaoh, he would probably note what a poor beginning Moses made in his Divine mission to get the Hebrews out.

Egypt was "the dominion of two lands" (the Hebrew for Egypt means literally two lands). Pharaoh ruled successfully over Upper and Lower Egypt, and his sovereign power extended far and wide in the Mediterranean world. Once a year there was a ceremony of enthroning him anew as supreme ruler of the known world of the Middle East. The king of every city or province, tributary to him, would send an ambassador with a crown as a gift. And Pharaoh would sit on his elegant throne, receiving one crown after another on his sweet little head.

One such day the kings all came themselves, to show him even greater homage. And *davka* (specifically) on that day Moses and Aaron showed up, with not the smallest, cheapest crown between them. They had nothing but a message, when finally, out of curiosity, Pharaoh admitted them to his presence: *Let My people go!*

Pharaoh laughed outright. Who was this God of the Hebrews who gave the message? He had a complete list of the gods of the Middle Eastern world; he checked it carefully; and this Deity was not there. It was all stuff and nonsense, he snorted; not worth paying any heed to Moses and Aaron. And so ended round one in their encounter with Pharaoh.

When the Zionist movement began stirring, there were some who saw a kind of Moses in Theodor Herzl (may the good Lord preserve us). After all, he too looked very dignified, austere and dedicated. *Nu*, he too went to royal palaces. He dashed and rushed about, hatching plans. Above all, he concentrated on the Sublime Porte, the magnificent palatial head-quarters of the Turkish sultan and his corrupt, decaying government. Herzl evidently made a simple calculation: Turkey ruled Palestine, so its sultan had the power to allow a sizable Jewish settlement there, perhaps even a national home worthy the name. On the other hand, Turkey was "the sick man of Europe," ridden and haunted by debts. All he had to do was offer the sultan a vast sum of money, raise it among Jewish bankers, and the deed was done.

Turkey was a world power, somewhat like ancient Egypt. The sultan ruled in splendor (at least so he could fondly imagine), like Pharaoh of old. And as ancient Egypt enslaved the Hebrews, so Turkey ruled Palestine. But if anyone thought Theodor Herzl was a second Moses, at the gate of the Sublime Porte the resemblance faded to a ghostly shadow. Herzl spoke not a word about God, to anyone. In Egypt it was Pharaoh who knew nothing about Him; here it was our Theodor who knew nothing of Him. He brought no clear message from Mount Ḥoreb or Scripture. Instead, a great deal of bribery was dispensed among palace officials (standard palace procedure); and as one main god or source of power in nineteenth century Europe was money, there were delicate, guarded, protracted discussions about a huge sum for the sultan's coffers in return for ... perhaps ... a charter for Jewish settlement in Palestine? Yes?

The discussions came to nothing and led nowhere, except to Herzl's early death. Unlike Moses, Herzl had never been to Mount Ḥoreb; nor did he accept the Torah as God's word. His incentive came from seeing

Captain Dreyfus in Paris fall victim to anti-semitism. So he tried to bring a crown to the great and mighty ruler, and to speak in the name of a known, acceptable god: money. And he failed abominably.

Chaim Weizmann also reminded some people of Moses.[53] He too came to a royal court of pomp and majesty and power: the government of England. Yet neither did he ever know or acknowledge the God of Israel (although he might quote Scripture occasionally to reverent non-Jews, to suit his purpose). So he tried to play ball in the royal court on its own terms. He came as an ambassador, representing (supposedly) the masses of Jewry spread across the earth. Moreover, he could offer a kind of crown: He was a chemist, and in the critical period of the First World War he produced acetone, an artificial rubber, which England needed desperately. In addition he offered the good will of all Jewry; and for his crown he was rewarded: the Balfour Declaration was declared.

He lived to see England and the Jewish people locked in implacable hostility, when there was no further point in his talking to anyone at the head of the British empire. Whatever resemblance to Moses he may ever have seemed to possess, this "distinguished ambassador" of Jewry to the English court had no destination left to which to lead his people.

There was, alas, precious little resemblance between either Herzl or Weizmann and Moses. Yet in their way they sought to make a home where the tempest-tossed and persecuted Jews of the world could find safety. In their way they sought to bring Jews back to the Promised Land. To this extent, gainsay it as we may, there was a spark of resemblance. So there was an element of resemblance in the results.

Moses' first encounter with Pharaoh was a débacle, a "complete flop." Things became worse for the Hebrews in Egypt. Yet it was the beginning of a process. A ferment of events followed. Egypt was stricken by plagues, until at last it was only too glad to see the Hebrews go (Exodus 12:31–33). Herzl tried to get a charter from the sultan of Turkey for a Jewish settlement in Palestine. He saw the kaiser of Germany, since that monarch could influence the sultan if he wished. With both he got exactly nowhere. Came the First World War, and Germany and Turkey suffered the plagues of defeat. Palestine was freed from the sultan's grip.

While Britain ruled the holy land under a mandate from the League of Nations, Chaim Weizmann worked to prevail on the Britishers to allow a proper Jewish settlement there, a desperately needed homeland. He too got exactly nowhere. Yet Britain found itself plagued by a divisive, muddle-headed shilly-shallying program in the holy land which turned world opinion fiercely against it and goaded a multitude of Jews in the land into sworn enmity in an organized underground resistance movement. By 1948 Britain was only too glad to relinquish control, and we had an independent homeland again, after 2,000 years.

Consider these amazingly prophetic words by R. Naḥman of Bratzlav, the profound innovative ḥassidic leader, spoken perhaps a century before Herzl made his dramatic appearance before the first Zionist congress:

וְאַף־עַל־פִּי שֶׁאָנוּ צוֹעֲקִים וּמִתְחַנְּנִים כָּל־כַּךְ שָׁנִים לָשׁוּב לְאֶרֶץ יִשְׂרָאֵל וַעֲדַיִן אָנוּ רְחוֹקִים מִשָּׁם, אַף־עַל־פִּי־כֵן אֵין שׁוּם תְּפִלָּה וּצְעָקָה נֶאֱבֶדֶת, וַאֲפִילוּ שֶׁל הַפָּחוּת שֶׁבַּפְּחוּתִים, כִּי בְּכָל צְעָקָה וּתְפִלָּה כּוֹבְשִׁים אֵיזֶה חֵלֶק אוֹ נְקֻדָּה מֵאֶרֶץ יִשְׂרָאֵל, עַד שֶׁבְּעֵתָּה יְחִישֶׁנָּה שֶׁיִּתְקַבְּצוּ כָּל הַנְּקֻדּוֹת שֶׁכְּבַשְׁנוּ בִּתְפִלָּתֵנוּ וְנָשׁוּב לְאֶרֶץ יִשְׂרָאֵל.... אַף־עַל־פִּי שֶׁהֵם גָּזְלוּ מֵאִתָּנוּ אֶרֶץ יִשְׂרָאֵל שֶׁהִיא אַרְצֵנוּ וְנַחֲלָתֵנוּ וְאֵין בָּנוּ כֹּחַ לְהוֹצִיאָהּ מֵאִתָּם, מֵחֲמַת פְּגַם מַעֲשֵׂינוּ הָרָעִים, אַף־עַל־פִּי־כֵן מִתְפַּלְּלִים וְצוֹעֲקִים בְּכָל פַּעַם ... שֶׁאֶרֶץ יִשְׂרָאֵל הִיא שֶׁלָּנוּ, כִּי הִיא נַחֲלָתֵנוּ, וּבָזֶה אָנוּ עוֹשִׂים בְּחִינַת מְחָאָה לַסִּיטְרָא אַחְרָא, שֶׁלֹּא יִטְעוּ שֶׁאֶרֶץ יִשְׂרָאֵל תִּשָּׁאֵר כְּבוּשָׁה בְּיָדָם חַס־וְשָׁלוֹם, כִּי אֵין חֲזָקָתָם חֲזָקָה כְּלָל. כִּי אָנוּ מוֹחִים בָּהֶם עַל־יְדֵי שֶׁאָנוּ צוֹעֲקִים וּמְפַרְסְמִים בְּכָל פַּעַם ... שֶׁאֶרֶץ יִשְׂרָאֵל הִיא שֶׁלָּנוּ מֵאֲבוֹתֵינוּ, וְסוֹף כָּל סוֹף נוֹצִיא אוֹתָהּ מִידֵיהֶם.

Although we have been crying out and imploring for so many years to return to the land of Israel, and we are still so distant from it, nevertheless, no prayer or outcry whatever gets lost in oblivion — even that of the most inferior of lowly persons. For with every outcry and prayer some part or point of the land of Israel is conquered, until He will "hasten it in its time" (Isaiah 60:22), as all the points we have conquered by our prayer will flow together, and we shall return to the land of Israel. ... Although they [the nations] robbed us of the land of Israel, our country and our heritage, and we have not the strength to take it away from them, because of the blemish of our bad deeds, we nonetheless pray and cry out all the time ... that the land of Israel is ours, being our heritage; and by this we create a kind of protest against the "other side" [darkness and evil among the nations], so that they should not make the mistake of thinking that the land of Israel will remain captive in their possession (Heaven forbid): for their hold [on it] is no rightful tenure at all. For we repudiate them by exclaiming and proclaiming all the time ... that the land of Israel is ours, bequeathed by our Patriarchs. And in the end we shall finally get it out of their hands.[54]

However they may have failed, Herzl and Weizmann did create a massive cry and shout from our people that the land was ours by right and had to be returned to us. This was their only real achievement: that they mobilized a mass movement among our people; and its voice of protest and demand could not be stilled. Religious Jewry continued praying for it; and the cumulative effect was independence in 1948.

So in a way the prophet's words have proven true: *As in the days of your emergence from the land of Egypt, I will show him marvels* (Micah 7:15). And the pattern has continued. Ever since the Balfour Declaration, our spokesmen have had to keep "playing in the royal courts" of the world powers. They had to come before the League of Nations and the United Nations. They had to deal and negotiate, discuss and request, at every major capital in the Western world. And always, as in ancient Egypt, the underlying question was: *What crown did you bring?* What have you to offer to enhance the prestige and splendor of the nations?

Our people spoke of honor, justice and glory. They mentioned Scripture and morality. They dwelt on Jewry's blood-drenched history, six million dead, the need for the homeland. True to his name, such a silver-tongued orator as Abba Hillel Silver offered visions of silvered radiance. In thundering, passionate rhetoric he called on the world, with England in the lead, to grant Jewry its haven, its bit of Promised Land — in the name of common humanity.

Echoing Pharaoh of old, the underlying response was: Why do you come with nothing but words? What kind of unseen, unknown God have you that sends us only words? Even if they were winged words of silver, the Arabs offered gold — the black gold of oil — riches enough to provide a hundred royal crowns. The Western nations had valuable oil interests in the Arab world. In the ears of America's Department of State, the gurgle of oil flowing into the tankers of a colossus like Standard Oil Company of New Jersey drowned out the oratory of Stephen Wise, Abba Hillel Silver and all the lesser Zionist spokesmen combined. American (and European) business interests owned the rich oil fields in the Middle East, and paid the Arab heads of state a pittance for all the profits they reaped. England ruled territory in the Middle East. It was a major power there, on friendly terms with the Arabs. English generals, captivated by "the romantic East," even trained the Arabs into fighting units. It would never do for the British to lose control and influence and power by offending the Arabs. The Arabs added to the splendor of their crown of empire, while the Jews brought nothing but words, words, words — even if they *were* occasionally from sacred Scripture. You had to be practical, said John Bull.

As the homeland struggled to be born and survive, the encounters of its spokesmen with sovereign heads of state were every bit as dismaying as Moses' chat with Pharaoh. Yet afterward, true to pattern, events moved in a ferment, and plagues came. The Arab countries nationalized their oil fields. Standard Oil of New Jersey and all the rest were booted out. And Arab armies which the British had trained helped oust Britain from the whole Middle East. Gone up in smoke were all the great advantages in power and profit for which the Western nations were so ready to sacrifice the Jews of Israel. And Israel surged ahead. The gods that the nations worshipped — profit and power, political gain and prestige — proved to be dead as a doornail. Our God was as flourishing as ever.

It may not have been an immaculate conception, but Israel was born.

Since 1948 it has been more of the same. The Jewish state sends ambassadors to the Western countries, especially Washington, explaining its position, its right to live, its need for security, meaning defensible borders — all honest, ringing, heartfelt words — yet no more than words. However splendid the throne of a head of state may be, when a sharp winter threatens he finds the thought of Arab oil a more warming consideration than all of Israel's words. And the Arab spokesmen offer another crown: influence. If their desires are too frustrated by America, they can become the friend of the Soviets instead. Hurry, Uncle Sam, and get our crown of political influence for *your* head. . . . Israel has no such crown to offer.

Among the gods that the Western world worships, the God of Israel is not listed. At the United Nations, He has no credentials to present, to be accredited. He remains unknown, unrecognized, unacknowledged. Yet let us remember that after Moses' "failure" in his visit to Pharaoh, things worked out quite well for the Hebrews eventually.

So time and again Henry Kissinger paraded about the Middle East on his famous shuttle (perhaps his own version of *hakafoth* ?), exerting "no pressure" on anyone, and Israel was pushed to compromise and yield and give up territory, endangering its security. When our ancestors left Egypt, they also retreated and endangered their security. Instead of marching on, straight away from Egypt, they doubled back toward the Red Sea; and when the Egyptians came in fierce pursuit, they were in great peril. Yet it turned out well. Then regarding the Middle East, let us bear in mind: *As in the days of your emergence from the land of Egypt, I will show him marvels.*

302

# ≈ DAVID'S DIPLOMACY

So Israel is on the map, thank God, as the world spins on its axis. Life goes on in the land, seemingly as in other lands. People eat and sleep and work; they marry, have children, and die. They have thieves and policemen, judges and laws. They have a government with a Ministry of the Interior and a Foreign Ministry; and unfortunately, they also have a Ministry of Religious Affairs, taking care of all three faiths to which the land is holy.

The Torah tells us clearly that Israel is no ordinary land, but literally "God's own country": *a land which the Lord your God cares for; the eyes of the Lord your God are always upon it* (Deuteronomy 11:12). Israel cannot get along on just any system of government. *And what comes up in your mind, shall never be — that which you say: We will be like the nations, like the families of the countries* (Ezekiel 20:32). The Torah was not meant to be relegated to one department in the Ministry of Religious Affairs. It was meant to be the guide and blueprint for every section and detail of Israel's life and government.

Yet what can we do? An international survey done about 1975 showed that among the developed nations, Israel's students ranked lowest in reading comprehension. This may not be so surprising when we consider that our Written Torah is included in Israel's national curriculum; it is taught in every government school; but the children also learn (from the attitude of their elders) to read it with a blind eye. For them it is beautiful literature, ancient religious writings, an interesting vestige from antiquity — anything but the living, compelling word of God, for us today. With the Hebrew Bible they are taught to read and not comprehend. *Hear indeed, but do not understand; see indeed, but do not perceive* (Isaiah 6:9). And so the youngsters grow up and become the country's men and leaders.

It is bad enough that the laws of the Torah are dismayingly ignored. They learn nothing even from the narratives of the Bible, from the simple record of events. Take for example this incident in the reign of David, as Scripture tells it:

303

And it happened after this that the king of the people of Ammon died, and Ḥanun his son reigned in his stead. And David said, "Let me do a kindness for Ḥanun the son of Naḥash, as his father did a kindness for me." So David sent by the hand of his servants [a message] to comfort him about his father; and David's servants came into the land of the people of Ammon. But the princes of the Ammonites said to Ḥanun their lord, "Do you think that David is honoring your father, since he has sent comforters to you? Has not David sent his servants to you to search the city, and to spy it out, and to overthrow it?" So Ḥanun took David's servants and shaved off half their beards, and cut off their garments in the middle, up to their buttocks, and sent them away. When it was told David, he sent to meet them, for the men were greatly ashamed. And the king said, "Remain at Jericho until your beards have grown, and then return" (II Samuel 10:1–5).

What was the upshot? Knowing that David was highly offended, the people of Ammon hired twenty thousand Syrian soldiers and thirteen thousand others, expecting trouble. Since an army of this size certainly meant trouble, David sent his general, Joab, and his army to take care of it. And Israel had to fight a full-fledged war.

Seemingly, fate was unjust to David here. He was simply being friendly. Ammon was a neighboring country, and its king, who had once treated David kindly, had died. Surely it was only common courtesy to send court servants to pay a condolence call on the king's son, who now sat on the throne of Ammon. Why was he repaid with a cruel insult to his servants that led to war? Was this Divine justice?

The Midrash has the answer:

אַתְּ מוֹצֵא בְּמִי שֶׁבָּא עִמָּהֶם בְּמִדַּת רַחֲמִים לַסּוֹף בָּא לִידֵי בִזָּיוֹן, מִלְחָמוֹת וְצָרוֹת. וְאֵיזֶה, זֶה דָוִד, שֶׁנֶּאֱמַר, וַיֹּאמֶר דָּוִד אֶעֱשֶׂה חֶסֶד עִם חָנוּן בֶּן נָחָשׁ (שמואל ב, י ב). אָמַר לוֹ הַקָּדוֹשׁ־בָּרוּךְ־הוּא: אַתָּה תַּעֲבֹר עַל דְּבָרָי? אֲנִי כָּתַבְתִּי, לֹא תִדְרֹשׁ שְׁלֹמָם וְטֹבָתָם (דברים כג ז), וְאַתָּה תַּעֲשֶׂה עִמָּם גְּמִילוּת חָסֶד? אַל תְּהִי צַדִּיק הַרְבֵּה (קהלת ז טז) – שֶׁלֹּא יְהֵא אָדָם מְוַתֵּר עַל הַתּוֹרָה – וְזֶה שׁוֹלֵחַ לְנַחֵם (בְּנֵי) [מֶלֶךְ] עַמּוֹן וְלַעֲשׂוֹת עִמּוֹ חֶסֶד וְטוֹבָה. סוֹף בָּא לִידֵי בִזָּיוֹן: וַיִּקַּח חָנוּן אֶת עַבְדֵי דָוִד וַיְגַלַּח אֶת חֲצִי זְקָנָם וַיִּכְרֹת אֶת מַדְוֵיהֶם בַּחֵצִי עַד שְׁתוֹתֵיהֶם וַיְשַׁלְּחֵם (שמואל ב, י ד). וּבָא לִידֵי מִלְחָמָה עִם אֲרַם נַהֲרַיִם וּמַלְכֵי צוֹבָה וּמַלְכֵי מַעֲכָה וְעִם בְּנֵי עַמּוֹן, אַרְבַּע אֻמּוֹת; וּכְתִיב, וַיַּרְא יוֹאָב כִּי הָיְתָה אֵלָיו פְּנֵי הַמִּלְחָמָה מִפָּנִים וּמֵאָחוֹר (שם ט). מִי גָרַם לְדָוִד כָּךְ? שֶׁבִּקֵּשׁ לַעֲשׂוֹת טוֹבָה עִם מִי שֶׁאָמַר הַקָּדוֹשׁ־בָּרוּךְ־הוּא, לֹא תִדְרֹשׁ שְׁלֹמָם וְטֹבָתָם. (במדבר רבה כא ה; תנחומא, פנחס ג)

You find that one who came to them with the quality of mercy eventually bore disgrace, battles and tribulations. Who was that? — David; as Scripture states, *And David said, "Let me do kindness with Ḥanun the son of Naḥash"* (II Samuel 10:2). Said the Holy, Blessed One to him, "I wrote, *You shall not seek their peace or their prosperity* (Deuteronomy 23:7), and you would treat them with acts of kindness? *Do not be exceedingly righteous* (Ecclesiastes 7:16); a man should not tolerantly ignore the Torah; and he sends a message to console the king of Ammon and treats him with kindness and favor!" In the end he underwent disgrace: *Ḥanun took David's servants and shaved off half their beards, and cut off their garments in the middle, up to their buttocks, and sent them away* (II Samuel 10:4). And he underwent battle with Aram-naharaim, the kings of Zobah, the kings of Maacah, and the people of Ammon — four nations; and it is written, *Then Joab saw that the battle was set against him both in front and in the rear* (ibid. 9). What brought this on David? — his wish to treat with favor someone about whom the Holy, Blessed One said, *You shall not seek their peace or their prosperity* (*Be-midbar Rabbah* 21, 5; *Tanḥuma, pinḥas* 3).[55]

Whatever David may have thought, however much he wanted to play the gentleman and show common or international courtesy, the Torah's law was clear: It was forbidden to take any interest in the welfare of any member of the people of Ammon. It was forbidden to treat them with favor. Even if for ten generations a family line of Ammonites kept converting to Judaism, they were forbidden to marry into the Jewish people.

Why is the Torah so harsh toward them? — *because they did not meet you with bread and with water on the way, when you came forth out of Egypt* (Deuteronomy 23:5). The Ammonites were related to the Israelites: The father of Ammon, their founding ancestor, was Lot, Abraham's nephew. And when Lot found himself captured by hostile kings, Abraham waged war against them to set him free (Genesis 14:12–16). When Abraham's descendants came journeying through the wilderness, on their way from Egypt to the Promised Land, by common courtesy the Ammonites should have given them a friendly welcome, with a bit of bread and a drink of water, to let them rest and refresh themselves. With no capacity for gratitude (for Abraham's kindness) they had nothing but a stare of hostility for our people in the wilderness.

Of course, it might be argued that the Ammonites could not afford any bread or water for our people. So the Torah continues its reason for

305

ordering us to treat them as outcasts: *and because they hired against you Balaam the son of Beor from Pethor ... to curse you* (Deuteronomy 23:5). It they could not afford bread and water, how could they afford Balaam, whose fees for fancy curses were high?[56]

So the Torah set the law for us: In the wilderness the Israelites were not to attack the people of Ammon. They were relatives. As far as personal relations, however, or marital ties — absolutely no. We were not even allowed to wish them good morning or to ask them, "How are you?" If Abraham could face war to save Lot from captivity, and Lot's descendants felt no gratitude, to show some simple human kindness to Abraham's descendants, this was what they deserved. As the Sages put it, there is nothing worse in the sight of the Holy, Blessed One than ingratitude.[57]

Now, David could not very well plead ignorance of the law. The Torah itself ordains for a king: *And it shall be, when he sits on the throne of his kingdom, that he shall write for himself a copy of this Torah ... and he shall read in it all the days of his life* (Deuteronomy 17:18). Still he sent his servants to Ammon on the condolence call. Evidently he decided that in this case the Torah had to be temporarily overlooked. He had to maintain friendly international relations. He was a king in the Mediterranean world. There were standards of courtesy. Besides, the dead Ammonite king had once done him a great favor (see II Samuel 10:2) — which is not recorded in Scripture but is related in the Midrash:

When Saul was king of Israel, he was determined to kill David; and in his paranoid enmity Saul decided to kill David's family too. David found asylum for them with the king of Moab (I Samuel 22:3-4) — only, that treacherous enemy killed them himself, except for one brother of David's, who escaped — and Naḥash kept him safe.[58] Surely that made him a true friend?

The Torah says, however, that the Ammonites were a bunch of ingrates, incapable of true hospitality, kindness or loyalty. Had Naḥash meant to befriend David dependably, his son Ḥanun would have known it, and he would have welcomed David's words of condolence. However, when Naḥash saved David's surviving brother, it was not out of love of David. It was out of hatred for Saul. In I Samuel 11 we read how Saul waged his very first battle, after becoming Israel's king, against Naḥash king of Ammon — and Saul won. Evidently Naḥash kept David's brother safe because it was a way of thwarting the wishes of an old enemy whom he would not forget or forgive.

What happened then, when David's men arrived at the court of Naḥash's son Ḥanun? Let us turn again to the Midrash cited above:

כֵּיוָן שֶׁבָּאוּ שְׁלוּחָיו שֶׁל דָּוִד אֵצֶל חָנוּן, אָמְרוּ לוֹ שָׂרֵי בְּנֵי עַמּוֹן: מַהוּ כָּךְ? הַמְכַבֵּד דָּוִד אֶת אָבִיךָ בְּעֵינֶיךָ? אַל תַּאֲמֵן בְּדָוִד. לָמָה? שֶׁהַקָּדוֹשׁ־בָּרוּךְ־הוּא כָּתַב בְּתוֹרָתוֹ, לֹא יָבֹא עַמּוֹנִי וּמוֹאָבִי בִּקְהַל ה', וּכְתִיב, לֹא תִדְרֹשׁ שְׁלוֹמָם וְטוֹבָתָם. הַקָּדוֹשׁ־בָּרוּךְ־הוּא מַזְהִירוֹ בִּשְׁבִילֵנוּ, וְהוּא מְבַטֵּל דִּבְרֵי אֱלֹהָיו? הֲלֹא בַעֲבוּר חֲקוֹר אֶת הָעִיר. מִיַּד, וַיִּקַּח חָנוּן אֶת עַבְדֵי דָוִד וַיְגַלַּח, וגו'.

When David's emissaries reached Ḥanun, the princes of the Ammonites said to him, "What is this? Do you imagine David is honoring your father? Do not believe David. Why? — because the Holy, Blessed One wrote in His Torah, *No Ammonite or Moabite shall enter the assembly of the Lord* (Deuteronomy 23:4); and it is written, *You shall not seek their peace or their prosperity* (*ibid.* 7). The Holy One warns him about us, and he ignores the words of his God? It must surely be in order to search and spy out the city." Immediately Ḥanun took David's servants and shaved off half their beards, etc.[58]

The Midrash makes a plain point. Incapable themselves of gratitude, friendship or loyalty, the Ammonite princes could not imagine such qualities in David. To their simple, malformed minds it was out of the question that David was violating a point in the Torah to show gratitude for a past favor. So of course they had their own way of understanding David's act, and they reacted accordingly.

(If we may add a footnote to Biblical history, let us note that in the land of Israel under the British mandate, some peppery Jews of the Revisionist persuasion once seized some British officers and similarly cut away half their clothing, leaving their buttocks exposed. If we accept the teaching of the Zohar that there is reincarnation, that people are born into the world more than once, it is tempting to think that those Revisionists had been David's messengers in a previous lifetime, and the British officers the Ammonite officers; and so the score was settled.)

At any rate, there is certainly food for thought here, especially if Israel's Foreign Office might wish to curry international ties and friendships. Especially is the lesson sharp if we contrast David's behavior with the decision of Abraham, David's ancestor, in dealing with Lot, the king of Ammon's ancestor. When the two became so wealthy in livestock and property that they could not stay comfortably together, Abraham told his nephew Lot, *Pray separate yourself from me. If you take the left hand, then I will go to the right; or if you take the right hand, then I will go to the left* (Genesis 13 :9). He was not afraid to go it alone. He must have seen enough of Lot to know that his nephew was a type that would like to live in Sodom, among evil, wicked sinners — as he afterward did. So he told him in effect, "Please go away." For better or worse he would find his way in life without Lot's company. And thus Abraham set a precedent that Israel should not be afraid to follow. *Behold, it is a people that dwells alone, and is not to be reckoned among the nations* (Numbers 23 :9).

(In a lighter vein, we might see another meaning in Abraham's words: "If you take the left hand" — if you turn "liberal," becoming a Reform Jew and beginning to move away from authentic observant Judaism, "I will go to the right": I will be Orthodox, without your influence. But "if you take the right hand" — if wanting to retain your Judaism you open synagogues and temples, seminaries and schools, then "I will go to the left": Your influence will harm and spoil me; you will make me turn "liberal" and move away from the true Judaism of the Torah. So just go away.)

This lesson from the Bible is clear enough. Yet who in Israel's government has ever pondered it and learned anything from it? The country's foreign policy was long pursued as if a Torah had never been given us — and the country has suffered for it.

A wise old Jew in Jerusalem once wrote, in our time: "There are those for whom the Torah is the content of their life. The Jewish religion and faith is their life-purpose — to build the edifice of Jewry on the foundations of the Written and Oral Torah. Then there are those who acknowledge Jewry's past and look forward to its future. They are bound to the Jewish community and strive to defend the Torah, though they themselves do not observe it. They speak splendidly in praise of Jewry. Their way is called nationalism. Yet they ought to realize that you cannot separate the flame from the wick ... There are also those, however, for whom the 'new ideals' [of our 'modern times'] are the main thing, and they have no share whatever in the Torah of Israel. To them every religious sentiment is alien, and every coarse common feeling is holy. Their way is full of thorns and brambles. ..."[59]

And so it is that as Israel's foreign policy has rolled not too merrily along, without any influence or wisdom of the Torah in it, Jews everywhere have felt the thorns and the brambles.

EVERYONE KNOWS Israel is the land of milk and honey; the Torah calls it that many times.[60] It is a pleasant name, conjuring up tasty, comforting visions of sustenance and security. It is so pleasant, in fact, that when a romantic (shmaltzy) musical, set in Israel, reached Broadway some years ago, it was titled simply "Milk and Honey."

Let us stop and think about it, though: Is the Torah's metaphor for the holy land altogether fitting? Has it really been a land of milk and honey, either in the far past or in our contemporary history? From ancient times to the present, Israel was a bloodied battlefield, over and over again. By Divine command, our people battled seven nations to take the land. Ever since, they faced invasion and attack, massacre and defeat. There were few peaceful decades in Israel's ancient history. And for good measure there was even tragic dissension within, that split the Hebrew kingdom into two: Israel and Judah — until the ten tribes in the kingdom of Israel were exiled, to vanish into oblivion; and only the tribes of Judah and Benjamin remained.

The Second Commonwealth, that began with the return under Ezra from Babylon, and the rebuilding of the holy Temple, felt the savage force of the Seleucid empire of Greek Syria and the vicious tyranny of Rome. Later centuries witnessed their own gory battles in the holy land, as warriors of conflicting religions vied for supremacy, each army in the name of its own "true faith"; and whatever Jews lived there were trodden underfoot, to subsist in misery and fear.

In contemporary times our people began their return to the Promised Land with bluster and defiance enough. There was sufficient horn-blowing and braggadocio to arouse a passionate Arab "nationalism" that had never existed before. So the ruling British measured the land's "economic absorptive capacity" and, conveniently for the Arabs, they decided that the land could tolerate very little Jewish immigration. (It is told that one day Lord Peel came to see Weizmann at his quarters in Reḥovoth, and he found him measuring something carefully in a test-tube. "Whatever are you doing?" asked the British lord. "I am creating economic absorptive capacity," came the sardonic reply.) While Hitler was busy with his "final solution" for them, Europe's Jews found the gates of the holy land shut tight against them. Talk to old-timers in Israel, and they will tell you how the British attitude and activities goaded and forced them into underground fighting movements, impelled to use violence in their frustration. The land of Israel knew conflict and bloodshed again.

When the UN imposed partition, giving Israel only a small part of the land that God promised to Abraham, we accepted it. Came the Arabs and forced Israel into war for sheer survival, three times in a quarter of a century; and each time, against its will, Israel's territory increased — but again, at the cost of violence, bloodshed and sudden death.

Surely we are entitled to shake our heads a little dubiously, a little sadly, and ask,"What kind of land of milk and honey is this? With such a history, it flows with milk and honey?"

The question is a strong one; but the answer lies in the very nature of milk and honey. Neither of them grows of itself. Each comes from a living creature — milk from cows, honey from bees. And truth to tell, this very fact bothered the Sages of the Talmud: If milk comes from a cow, a living animal, surely it should be prohibited like any part of an animal taken while it is alive? If a Jew cuts himself a ribsteak out of a living cow and broils it, the Torah absolutely forbids him to eat it. סלקא דעתך אמינא הואיל וליכא מידי דאתי מחי ושרייה רחמנא, והאי חלב כי אבר מן החי הוא "We might have thought that since there is nothing which comes from a living creature that the merciful God permits, and milk is comparable to a part of a living creature," etc. (TB *B'choroth* 6b).

Nor can we dismiss this point so easily by arguing that "of course milk is different" because it is not a vital part of the cow; the animal suffers no pain upon losing it; on the contrary, a milch cow must be milked regularly for its own relief. There is a view in the Talmud that a cow produces its milk from its blood supply: blood is decomposed and converted into milk. Then it should perhaps be forbidden as a form of blood? No, says the Talmud: the Torah specifically permits us to drink it. In 1 Samuel 17:18, Jesse tells David, *and carry these cheeses to the captain of their thousand,* as food for the Israelite soldiers. The prophet proclaims, *come buy wine and milk without money and without price* (Isaiah 55:1). And of course, there is Scripture's description of Israel as *a land flowing with milk and honey.* "If

[milk] were not permitted, would the Writ have praised [the land] to us by something not fit [to be eaten]?" (TB *B'choroth* 6b).

Again, honey comes from bees, which are themselves forbidden as food. But the honey is something external and apart from them; they merely produce it from the nectar they gather from flowers, to serve them as food through the winter. At no point does it form or contain any part of the bees themselves.[61]

By a Divine wisdom beyond our understanding, there are laws of nature in the world that require destruction in order to lead to new construction, the creation of something that could not exist before. Thus, to produce its milk, the cow must chew grass; and chewing too is a destructive process. In the Torah we read, כי יבער איש שדה או כרם ושלח את בעלה ובער בשדה אחר which means literally, *If a man makes a field or vineyard be consumed, letting his "consumer" go, and it consumes in another man's field . . .* (Exodus 22:4). The Hebrew verb *bi'ér* can refer to the action of either a fire or a grazing animal. Both "consume"; both destroy. Yet from the cow's grazing, milk results. Bees swarm far and wide to gather their nectar. If anyone interferes or annoys them, they will sting him painfully. But the result is the sweetness of honey.

For a very long time seven Canaanite nations had possession of our Promised Land. As archaeological evidence attests, they were amoral and evil; and by a wisdom beyond ours, the Almighty decreed their removal from the world. There had to be the destruction that battle and conquest leave in their wake, to make the land the rightful home of the Israelites. Yet it was "a land of milk and honey" — separate and apart from its Canaanite origin. It was never really Canaan's land but God's; and it could provide sweet sustenance for the Israelites — if they would be God's people. This is what Israel is "all about": Despite its origins in destructiveness, in the stings of fate and adversity, it is a holy land destined for a holy people. And for them it will flow with milk and honey.

In our era, in the Zionist resettlement of the Jewish homeland, there was also internal violence and destruction enough — not only physically but spiritually. The early *halutzim* who came to build the homeland against all obstacles, battling malaria and the lack of water, showed little interest in our spiritual heritage, and largely ignored the laws of our sacred faith.

Yet R. Abraham Isaac Kook of blessed memory, the profoundly religious first chief rabbi of the holy land, was able to see them in a different light.

The prophet foresees a glorious day for Israel: *Rejoice greatly, O daughter of Zion! Shout, O daughter of Jerusalem! Behold, your king comes to you; righteous and victorious is he,* עָנִי וְרֹכֵב עַל חֲמוֹר *lowly and riding on a donkey* (Zechariah 9:9). As tradition teaches,[62] this refers to the arrival of our righteous royal Messiah.

Now, the word עָנִי (lowly, humble) means literally a poor man. A poor man, said R. Abraham Isaac Kook, goes in tattered clothing and rags. Unkempt and dirty, he is an appalling sight. Yet in one important respect he is superior to a man of wealth. An old Yiddish proverb goes, דער זאַטער גלויבט נישט דעם הונגעריקן "A well-fed man does not believe a hungry person" (that he is really hungry).[63] When someone has a satisfied stomach, mind and bank account, he has room in his heart for himself alone. The plight of others hardly touches him. He is like a man in a car, comfortably encased in his sleek upholstered high-powered vehicle, speeding along the sunlit road, with never a care in the world for a poor pedestrian trudging along the sun-baked dusty path. When a man is himself hungry, however, he has room in his heart to be aware of the next man also — that the next man too may be hungry, or may be laden with other woes. The wealthy man may present a flashing, gold-plated exterior; but within, if you could see it, his heart may well be a terrible sight. On the other hand, a poor man's outward appearance may be a frightening spectacle; but within him beats a heart of gold.

The *ḥalutzim* who came to settle the land were often rambunctiously irreligious. Yet they had the saving grace of the poor. They were ready to word hard without lordly airs. They were ready to build their communal life by honest toil, without exploiting others. And they were willing to share their bread and their land with others. The doors of Israel have always been open to Jews of the Diaspora, rich and poor alike.

A donkey (continued R. Kook) has not one of the signs of a kosher animal. It neither chews its cud nor has cloven hooves. So it is an unclean animal. Yet it was singled out for a mitzvah, a particular religious commandment: וְכָל פֶּטֶר חֲמֹר תִּפְדֶּה בְשֶׂה *And every firstling donkey you shall redeem with a lamb* (Exodus 13:13). Unclean, unkosher though it is, the first donkey born to its mother has a certain holiness, because it is the first. So it may not be used until it is redeemed (exchanged) for a lamb, which becomes holy instead and must be given to a kohen.[64]

Well, the Talmud asks a logical question: Why, of out all the non-kosher animals, was only the donkey singled out for this law? Why not horses and camels also, for example? The answer, says the Talmud, is that when the Israelites left ancient Egypt, the land of their enslavement, they had only donkeys to help them carry all the goods and possessions with which they went laden (TB *B'choroth* 5b).

With a touch of homiletic license, may we not apply this to the rebuilding of our homeland? The camel is a large, grand animal that looks out at the world from its eminence with an expression of lofty disdain. Well, there were people enough (including ardent Zionist orators) who felt too proud and stately to go themselves to the malaria-ridden swamps of Palestine and reclaim the land. They had a comfortable, dignified existence where they were. (Remember the "standard definition" of a Zionist: a man who prevailed on a second man to give money so that a third man could go to Palestine.)

The horse is a swift, graceful animal, capable of great speed. Many were too busy speeding toward goals of their own, such as "making it" in America. They could not be bothered to go to Israel to plow the land, dig ditches and pave roads.

Only the donkey is the common, lowly, dependable beast of burden in the Middle East. So the *halutzim* were there through the early decades of our century, patiently carrying the burden of building a homeland for a new exodus, a new series of migrations from countries of exile and oppression.

So this (said R. Kook) is the symbol of the arrival of the Messiah: a lowly poor man on a donkey. You look at them, and you see not a single outward sign of holiness; it is just a man in tattered rags, looking sad, forlorn and hungry, riding an unclean beast of burden. Yet they are a sure sign of the Messiah's advent. The achievement of the *halutzim* is a milestone in our unmistakable progress toward the Messianic era.

How R. Abraham Isaac Kook felt about the early builders of our homeland, with their deplorable attitude toward the Torah, is perhaps best revealed by this little anecdote:

It is told that an American Jew visiting Israel once complained about the situation to R. Kook, since he was the chief rabbi of the holy land. "It just hurts me," said the visitor, "to see such flagrant violation of the Torah in our homeland. So many people everywhere violate the Sabbath openly, and do not keep the laws of *kashruth*! I just don't understand it. This is the holy land?"

313

"Tell me," said R. Kook: "what part of America do you come from?"
"I'm from Denver, Colorado."

"Denver?" said the chief rabbi. "That must be a miserable city, with a terrible sickly climate. So many people there suffer from tuberculosis."

"Oh no," the visitor protested. "It is just the opposite: Denver has such a dry healthy climate that people with tuberculosis are sent there from every part of the United States, and from all over the world, to get well there."

"*Nu,*" said R. Kook gently, "it is the same thing here . . ."

The profoundly religious chief rabbi believed firmly that the holiness of the land was bound to have its effect with the passage of time, to correct the illusions and aberrations of Israel's irreligious Jews. The very atmosphere of the land would do its healing work, slowly but surely. As the Sages taught,[65] "the air of the land of Israel imparts wisdom."

Well, if the air of the country isn't doing it, the tumultuous array of events in the short history of the State of Israel has certainly been educating the citizens of the land. In ancient Greece it was already noted that "wisdom comes by suffering"; "for he who has much suffered, much will know."[66] In the words of an English poet, "Sorrows are our best educators. A man can see further through a tear than a telescope."[67]

The troubles of the young small state have kept coming thick and fast. In fact, things reached such a point that Ephraim Kishon (Israel's foremost humorist, who *nebbach* often has to give up trying to be funny) wrote once in his newspaper column that the only people to whom living in Israel still makes sense are the religious ones — the observant Jews.

For the pious Jew knows that whatever adversity or trouble comes along, Heaven has decreed it; and he looks for the reason and meaning of the trouble accordingly. A glimmer of this idea is starting to get through to others in Israel; and hopefully the point may penetrate into governmental circles some day. But it is slow, uphill going.

One man who surveyed the entire course of man's ongoing development once wrote, "Human history becomes more and more a race between education and catastrophe."[68] However much this may be true for the rest of the world, it applies most strongly to the State of Israel. It is in desperate need of learning the Almighty's ways and His immutable laws — because Israel is simply different, as the famed *maggid* (preacher) of Dubno (R. Jacob Krantz) once explained with a telling parable.

314

He began with a question: as we look through history, we find something strange: When other nations sinned to such an extent that by Heaven's decree they were conquered, they always remained in their own lands. Occasionally, in ancient times, they may have been resettled in other areas, to keep them under the conqueror's heel; but they always stayed on their own territory. Poland was carved up and recarved. At one time it was divided up among Austria, Germany and Russia. Often the Russians alone were in control. Yet the Poles always remained in Poland. Germany lost two world wars, whereupon the British had a sector and the Americans had a sector. Today it is divided into two countries, but the Germans are still there, as much as ever. In its own crushing way, the Soviet Union affirmed its control of Hungary and Czechoslovakia—but there was never a question of exile for their citizens.

The Hebrews in ancient Israel sinned twice to such an extent that they were defeated and conquered by mighty neighboring powers — and both times they were exiled. They were driven from their land, the first time for seventy years, the second time until our century — and Jewish life in the Diaspora is still far from over. If, as we firmly believe, the Almighty's will shapes human destiny and human history, why was Israel alone — the Jewish people alone — singled out for this special treatment?

The *maggid* of Dubno answered with a simple story: Once a wealthy man married off his daughter, and he made a tremendous wedding feast. There were no professional caterers at the time, but sparing no expense he hired enough help to prepare food aplenty. In all, he prepared three types of meals: For the rich (who, he assumed, would have good taste and cultured palates) he offered the delicacy of stuffed squab. For the ordinary ("middle income") people there was solid roast beef. And for the poor there was herring with onions, coupled with black bread, which they were sure to consider a delicacy.

The wedding went off splendidly, amid much gaiety and great enjoyment; and then the guests headed for the laden tables to enjoy the feast. Among them all, the happy father of the bride noticed one man who had only recently become rich. Not well acquainted with the "old timers" in his income bracket, this man was uncertain where to sit. The father of the bride, though, wished to honor him properly, and he seated him firmly among the rich.

The man looked at his stuffed squab, and was at a loss as to what to do. Ordinarily he would have tried picking it up in his hand and starting

315

with a good solid bite. But everyone else was working with a knife and fork, with delicacy and finesse. Never in his life had he treated a stuffed squab with finesse. What should he do?

Suddenly the breeze wafted the aroma of herring and onions to his nostrils. He looked across to another table, and sure enough, it was set with elegant plates of herring and onions. At last he knew what to do. Rising, he went to the other table, took a plate of fine schmaltz-herring with rings of onion, and returned with it to his seat. It never occurred to him that the smell would offend his rich neighbors and spoil their delicate, cultured taste for squab. The host, however, realized it, and he came over at once. "Yankel," he said, "what are you doing? I thought that having become wealthy, you were now a man of refinement, at least a bit of a gourmet. So I seated you here to enjoy the squab. If you insist on herring and onions, you have to go over there."

Israel is a land of spiritual refinement and high standards. It cannot long tolerate any from of idol-worship, whether the idol be called Dagan or socialism or Zionism. It is a land where Jews can live only with the pure, cleansing words of the Torah, observing its laws to let the people rest every seventh day and let the land rest every seventh year. It is a land fit only for the spiritually refined menu of strictly kosher food, and a life style that includes family purity. Those who want herring, however, must move to the herring table.

For those who wanted to worship the idols of Babylon, living in Babylon could be just as good. For those who wanted pure Zionism, as Herzl formulated it, Uganda would have been just as good (until the nightmares of Idi Amin would have cured them of their rosy dreams). For those who want kibbutz life and socialism, and nothing more, other lands can do as well. If you want to live in Israel French-style, you can do it better in Paris. If your ideal in life is fervent Communism, go to the Soviet Union.

Spiritually, Israel was, is, and will be a land of refinement and nobility. It cannot long tolerate the gross, the coarse and the vile. So our people of old were warned, in immortal words that remain forever in force, *But you shall keep My statutes and My ordinances, and do none of these abominations, either the native or the stranger who sojourns among you — for all these abominations, the men of the land did who were before you, and the land became defiled — so that land shall not vomit you out, when you defile it, as it vomited out the nation that was before you* (Leviticus 18:26–28).

316

When the Almighty prepared to give our people the Torah, He ordered Moses to tell them, *and you shall be to Me a kingdom of* kohanim *and a holy nation* (Exodus 19:6). With the Torah we can all become His holy ministering servants, a spiritual nobility or aristocracy. And then we will belong in His holy land, that will indeed flow with milk and honey.

# *Notes* TO PART FOUR

1. See David Zaretsky, *The Ḥafétz Ḥayyim on the Siddur*, § 227.

2. Séder Olam 2; TB M'gillah 17a; B'réshith Rabbah 78, 16; and Rashi on the verse.

3. So TB Bava Bathra 100a, TJ Kiddushin i 3; B'réshith Rabbah 41, 17 end.

4. Tanḥuma, *mattoth* 2; Be-midbar Rabbah 22, 9; so also *Lekaḥ Tov*.

5. Cited also in Yalkut Shimoni II on Ezekiel 37; readings from both these sources and *Dikduké Sof'rim* on the Talmud have been used here.

6. Séder Olam 3; Pirké d'R. Eliezer 48: Rashi to Exodus 12:40.

7. So Targum (R. Joseph) to I Chronicles 7:21, and Rashi and *Yad Ramah* to TB Sanhedrin 92b.

8. According to Midrash T'hillim (81 end) no descendants of Joseph were subjected to the enslavement in Egypt (since he had been the country's viceroy); so the Ephraimites kept apart from the other Hebrews, neither working nor eating with them, but spent their time bearing armor and learning warfare; hence we read in Psalms 78:9, *The children of Ephraim, armed, handling the bow.*

9. Pirké d'R. Eliezer 48; Targum, Psalms 78:9 and I Chronicles 7:21.

10. Thus B'réshith Rabbah 44, 21: "that your progeny will be alien" — from the time that progeny of yours will appear.

11. *Yad Ramah* to Sanhedrin 92b. The tradition about the Ephraimites is also mentioned in Targum Jonathan, Exodus 13:17 and Psalms 78:9; Mechilta *b'shallaḥ, p'thiḥta* and *shirah* 9; Sh'moth Rabbah 20:11; P'sikta d'R. Kahana 10 (85a-b); and Midrash Va-yosha, Exodus 15:14.

12. R. Naḥman of Bratzlav, *Likkuté Moharan*, § 9.

13. Phrase recorded in Naḥum Stutchkoff, *Thesaurus of the Yiddish Language*, § 599, p. 695b. It evidently derives from the use by the Talmud of the single, composite term, *n'veyloth ut'reyfoth sh'katzim ur'masim,* for vile and detestable forbidden food (Mishnah, Sh'vi'ith vii 3, N'darim ii 1, Sanhedrin viii 2, Makkoth iii 2, Sh'vu'oth iii 4; Tosefta, Bava M'tzi'a iii 25, Horayoth i 5; TB Yoma 73b, Yevamoth 114a, Bava M'tzi'a 58b, Sanhedrin 70b, Makkoth 16b, Sh'vu'oth 21b, 22b, 23b, 24a, Horayoth 11a, B'choroth 37a).

14. See TB Sukkah 30a, and *Tosafoth Yom Tov* to Mishnah, Sukkah iii 1, s.v. *ha-gazul.*

15. This has been well noted by at least one veteran observer and historian of the history of contemporary Jewry. In a book dated 1969 he wrote: "The Middle East war of June 1967 was only six days' fighting in a limited area, but its repercussions will continue for a long time in every part of the world. For it resulted not only in the almost instantaneous victory of a small nation against an alliance of thirteen adversaries but also in the victory of Israel over 13 million Jews dispersed across the continents. . . . Jews everywhere found that the nation whose existence they had grown to take for granted was too important to be allowed to disappear. . . . When [Israel] seemed about to be destroyed a spontaneous movement was born among the Jews of the world to come to Israel's aid. . . . Demonstrations of support attracted many thousands.

318

Letters on behalf of Israel's cause appeared in the world's press from intellectuals who hitherto would not complicate their lives with Jewish preoccupations. . . . Money flowed towards Israel in torrents . . . " (Barnet Litvinoff, *A Peculiar People*, London [1969] pp. 1–2). It need but be added that the Yom Kippur War evoked the same phenomenon of fervent response from Jewry the world over, only more so.

16. The phrase derives from TB Shabbath 119b: Résh Lakish said in the name of R. Judah haNassi: The world endures for nothing else but the sake of the children in the schools [learning Torah]. R. Papa asked Abbaye, "But what of your [Torah study] and mine?" He answered him, "There is no comparison between the breath [of a mouth] tinged with sin and the breath [of mouths] free of sin."

17. R. Naḥman of Bratzlav, *Likkuté Etzoth*, s.v. *eretz yisraél*, § 7.

18. *Ibid.* § 17.

19. TJ Yoma v 3 (42c); High Holyday Prayer Book, ed. Birnbaum, p. 825.

20. TB Sotah 44a.

21. Similarly, all of Jewry is conceived as one human body, in the writings of R. Jonathan Eybeschütz, *Yaaroth D'vash*, I first sermon, s.v. *r'faénu;* and R. David Sh'lomo Eybeschütz, *Arvey Naḥal*, sermon on *Rosh haShanah*.

22. TB Sanhedrin 106b, version of Rashi.

23. R. Sh'néor Zalman of Liady, *Tanya, iggereth ha-kodesh*, chapter 14 beginning (cited in Joel Diskin, *Mishnath Yoél*, p. 38).

24. B'réshith Rabbah 54, 2 (see commentary in ed. Mirkin).

25. So Tosefta, Sotah iii 12; Sifre, Deut. § 43; Mechilta, *shirah* 2; TB Sanhedrin 109a-b; Pirké d'R. Eliezer 25.

26. B'réshith Rabbah 52, 1.

27. Midrash haGadol, Genesis 21:23 (342).

28. B'réshith Rabbah 54, 1.

29. R. Israel Berger, *Séfer Yismaḥ Yisraél*, Piotrkov 1910, p. 15; a different version is to be found in R.Yoétz Kim Kaddish, *Si-aḥ Sarfé Kodesh*, I (Lodz 1928), pp. 23d-24a; see also Buber, *Or haGanuz*, pp. 422-23.

30. How strongly Jewry tried to find unity with England in the Zionist aspirations after 1917, and how often it failed miserably, may be read in such a book as N. A. Rose, *The Gentile Zionists*, London 1973. Time and again the British government announced its pious intentions and firm resolve to further Jewish aims and needs in the holy land, only to back down in the face of Arab protest and pressure, and pro-Arab feelings among its own officers. Chaim Weizmann found himself continually chiding, berating or imploring the British heads of state, and threatening to resign as head of the Jewish Agency (and thus as the official liaison man between Jewry and England).

There is yet another fascinating parallel: Here it was Abimelech's servants who seized Abraham's well. Under the British mandate it was generally the Colonial Office and the English officials in Palestine who followed a pro-Arab, anti-Jewish policy, especially in regard to Jewish purchase of land, and often without the full knowledge or consent of the men who headed the government.

31. B'réshith Rabbah 54, 5.

32. TB Sanhedrin 56a.

33. Midrash T'hillim §110; B'réshith Rabbah 54, 6.

34.  *The Complete Diaries of Theodor Herzl,* ed. Patai, II p. 581, entry for September 3, 1897.

35.  Onkelos; Ramban and R. Joseph H. Hertz, commentaries on Genesis 26:1.

36.  This is how the Midrash understands the verse. The usual translation, based on the Targumim, is: Go away from us, for you are much mightier than we.

37.  B. Yeushzon, *Fun unzer alten oytzer,* I p. 60 (2nd ed., Jerusalem 1955, p. 137).

38.  So *Lekaḥ Tov* to Genesis 26:17. Another homiletic work of an earlier age points out that if Isaac came to Gerar because of a famine in Canaan, conditions could not have been too good there either. Then Isaac's neighbors should have been happy at his bumper crop of wheat (see Genesis 26:12). It could relieve their economic distress. Yet because Isaac was a Hebrew, they found it a reason to hate him and drive him out (B. Yeushzon, *Fun unzer alten oytzer,* I p. 60; 2nd ed. p. 139).

39.  *Fables of Aesop,* trans. S. A. Handsford, Penguin Books [1954], § 29; *Aesop's Fables,* Peter Pauper Press, Mt Vernon [1941], p. 23. In Aesop's version, the wolf tells the heron (or crane) something like, "Is it not reward enough to have put your head into a wolf's mouth and taken it out safe and sound?"

40.  P'sikta d'R. Kahana 9 (78b); Va-yikra Rabbah 27, 11; Tanḥuma, *emor* 13; Early Tanḥuma, 18; Esther Rabbah 7, 23; Midrash T'hillim ii 4; Aggadath B'réshith ii 2; Aggadath Esther iii 13; Yalkut Shimoni I § 116, II §§ 583 and 1155. Bracketed additions from Midrash T'hillim.

41.  Sh'moth Rabbah 1, 18.

42.  Midrash Tanna'im, Deut. 32:9 (190); Pirké d'R. Eliezer 24; see also Targum Yerushalmi, Genesis 11:8, Deuteronomy 32:8-9.

43.  With a bit of license we might see an indication of this perhaps in the fact that the first Soviet cosmonaut, who flew successfully in outer space, was Yuri Gagarin: The first part of his name is strikingly similar to Gog; and he reported brashly that while in outer space he looked through his wndow for God, and could not see Him anywhere. One could almost imagine him at the window of his spacecraft cocking a snoot and saying, "God, I came to see you; so where are you?" — which in a way sums up the Soviet attitude.

44.  TB B'rachoth 7b; Midrash T'hillim ii 2.

45.  Yigal Allon, Introduction to: Devora and Menaḥem Hacohen, *One People, the Story of the Eastern Jews,* New York [1969] p. 6.

46.  Va-yikra Rabbah 20, 2; Koheleth Rabbah 9:7—1; Koheleth Zuta 9:7 (121); and sources in next note.

47.  Midrash haGadol, Genesis 22:3 (351-52); Pirké d'R. Eliezer 31; Midrash Va-yosha (from which the bracketed additions).

48.  Old English proverb, found in Richard Taverner, *Proverbs or adagies . . .* (1545).

49.  Mishnah, Yadayim iv 4: Said R. Joshua to him, "Are the Ammonites and Moabites then in their original native locations? Long ago Sennacherib, king of Assyria, came up and scrambled all the nations . . . " Replied R. Gamliel, "Yet Scripture says, *But afterward I will bring back the returning people of Ammon* (Jeremiah 49:6), and so they have already returned." Said R. Joshua to him, "Scripture says, *And I will bring back My returning people Israel* (Amos 9:14), and they have not yet returned." In Tosefta, Yadayim ii 17 (ed. Zuckermandel) the ending reads, "and just as *these* have not returned, so have *they* not returned." Tosefta, Kiddushin v 4: Said R. Akiva to him, "Minyamin, you are in error. The normative ruling is that Sennacherib

king of Assyria came up in the past and jumbled up all the peoples. The Ammonites and Moabites are not in their original locations, nor are the Egyptians and Edomites in *their* original locations . . . "

Rambam, *Mishneh Torah, hilchoth issuré bi'ah,* xii 25: When Sennacherib king of Assyria arose, he jumbled up all the peoples and commingled them with one another, exiling them from their native locations. The Egyptians in the land of Egypt are now other people, and so the Edomites in the plain of Edom.

50. If any "inside" evidence is needed on the pronounced enmity of the British to the Jews in Palestine in the years of the mandate, consider these sentences by Alice Ivy Hay, Orde Wingate's mother-in-law (both non-Jews), in *There was a Man of Genius,* London 1963, p. 61: In those days, it was not easy to have a pleasant association with most of our fellow countrymen for any length of time. One had to watch one's step and keep all reference to "Jews" out of the conversation unless one was willing either to hear or to say oneself something unpleasant about them. Some of our compatriots, both in Britain and in Palestine, were extremely unfriendly to all three of us [Mrs Hay, her daughter, and Orde Wingate] when they realised that we were willing actually to like or admire Jews. I remember a dinner party in Jerusalem where there was a young officer newly arrived from home. He had just visited one of the settlements in Galilee and was heard to remark that he thought the Jews had done a fine job of work there  A disapproving silence fell on the assembled company and the poor fellow looked round bewildered before realising his mistake. He was one of those who would not make it again and who would soon join the majority who had nothing good to say about the Jewish population.

(Of course, the case of Orde Wingate himself tells volumes: Because he admired the Jews in Palestine and did much to train them in armed self-defense, this British army officer was booted out of the country by his commanding officer in May 1939 and was never allowed to set foot in the land again. No British officer, such as John Glubb, was ever criticized for giving military training to Arabs.)

51. *Siddur Otzar haT'filloth,* p. 648.

52. There are more elaborate versions in Sh'moth Rabbah 5, 14, and Midrash haGadol, Exodus 5:1 (82).

53. Thus for example Alice Ivy Hay, *There was a Man of Genius,* London 1963, p. 50: "To me he always seemed like a figure from the Old Testament. His dignity, wisdom, vision and patience reminded me of what I imagined Moses to be like . . . "

54. R. Naḥman of Bratzlav, *Likkuté Halachoth, ḥoshen mishpat, hilchoth ḥezkath m'talt'lin* v 12 (Jerusalem 1957, p. 140d); partly cited, with changes, in Eliezer Steinman, *Kithvé R. Naḥman,* p. 194.

55. It should be noted that, judging from later times, the beard was always regarded with reverence by the Orientals, as a sacrosanct mark of dignity. Cf. the Moslem practice of swearing "by the beard of the prophets."

56. So R. Jonathan Eybeschütz, cited in B. Yeushzon, *Fun unzer alten oytzer* (first edition, II pp. 115-16).

57. Mishnath R. Eliezer, p. 134.

58. Yalkut Shimoni II § 147; Early Tanḥuma, *va-yéra* 25.

59. R. Aryeh Levin, in Simḥa Raz, *Ish Tzaddik Hayah,* pp. 284-85.

60. Exodus 3:8,17; 13:5; 33:3; Leviticus 20:24; Numbers 13:27; 14:8; 16:13–14; Deut. 6:3; 11:9; 26:9,15; 27:3; 31:20; Joshua 5:6; Jeremiah 11:5; 32:22; Ezekiel 20:6,15.

61. TB B'choroth 7b and Rashi there; s.v. *shemachnisoth*; Rambam, *Mishneh Torah, hilchoth maachaloth asuroth* iii 3.

62. R. Abraham ibn Ezra and R. David Kimḥi (Radak) on the verse; Yalkut Shimoni *ad loc.,* etc.

63. Ignacz Bernstein, אידישע שפריכווערטער און רעדענסארטען p. 95, s.v. זאַטער.

64. Mishnah, Ḥallah iv 9 and B'choroth i 3-4.

65. TB Bava Bathra 158b.

66. Aeschylus, *Agamemnon*, line 177; Homer, *Odyssey*, book xv line 436 (trans. Pope).

67. Lord Byron, cited in *Useful Quotations*, ed. Tryon Edwards (New York 1933), p. 607a.

68. H. G. Wells, *The Outline of History*, chapter 15.

# 5

## Of war and human conflict

*. . . and they shall beat their swords into plowshares, and their
spears into pruning-hooks; nation shall not lift up sword
against nation, neither shall they learn war any more*

(Isaiah 2 :4)

T HE HUMAN BEING developed many abilities on earth. He
learned to hunt and plant, raise sheep and build cities. He learned to dance
and sing. And he learned to make war. First with primitive tools, then with
ever more sophisticated weapons, men learned that they could kill their
fellow-men, or capture and enslave them.[1] Victory brought territory, power
and wealth.

In the words of a foremost historian, "Our predecessors began to go to
war with each other as soon as they had learned to produce a surplus
beyond the provision for the bare necessities of life."[2] Already in 2500 BCE
a king of Egypt recorded an important message for his people: "Train up
the young men to be soldiers."[3] And war became a constant feature of human
history.

From 1496 BCE to the year 1860, in over three thousand years, there
were exactly 227 years of peace: less than seven percent of the time. From
the rise of ancient Greece to the birth of the League of Nations there was
an average period of exactly two years between wars in the world.[4] It seems
to have been characteristic that while many were still mourning their dead
or nursing their wounds from one savage conflict, the bugles and trumpets
already sounded to call up new soldier-boys to their dreams of heroism
and glory. . . . Such has been the sad, sick story of man's progress on
earth.

In the 19th century, an American thinker wrote, "War, to sane men
at the present day, begins to look like an epidemic insanity, breaking out
here and there like cholera or influenza, infecting men's brains. . . ."[5]

Yet sickness or sport, carnival or catastrophe — what are the causes of war? What has impelled people since time immemorial to rush into battle against other human beings? ... One thing is certain: It is not a simple question. Entire library shelves are filled with books and studies on the subject.

For *his* basic answers, however, the authentic Jew turns to the Torah, the written Word of God, with the great body of wisdom and lore by the Sages. Well, there is much about war in our sacred Scripture; but for its underlying root causes, let us turn to the very first mortal conflict recorded in the Torah.

In its moving, imperishable words, the Bible tells of a fatal clash at the very dawn of human history. We might well call it the first civil war: it was a conflict between two brothers. Yet in truth all armed battle everywhere has really been between brothers. Long ago a prophet of ours cried out, *Have we not all one Father? Has not one God created us?* (Malachi 2:10). Out of his own realization a British poet wrote of a soldier slain in war:[6] "Another's sword has laid him low — / another's and another's; / and every hand that dealt the blow, / aye me! it was a brother's!"

This first lethal conflict in our Bible could also be called the earliest world war: because after their father, the two antagonists were the only men on earth. Von Clausewitz, the German theoretician of war who studied it clinically, wrote that "war is nothing but a duel on a large scale."[7] So the fatal encounter in the early pages of our Written Torah gives us a microcosm, a small-scale model, of all brutal conflict.

We read, then, that Adam (the first man on earth) had two sons: Cain and Abel; *and Abel was a keeper of sheep, while Cain was a tiller of the soil* (Genesis 4:2). Each found his own peaceful occupation: Abel as a shepherd, and Cain as a farmer. *And it happened in the course of time that Cain brought of the fruit of the soil an offering to the Lord. And Abel — he too brought of the firstlings of his flock and of their fat (choice) portions (ibid. 3–4).* Each brought an offering, in worship of the Creator, from what he raised. *And the Lord responded to Abel and his offering, but to Cain and his offering He did not respond; so Cain was very wrathful, and his countenance fell (ibid. 4–5).*

Cain was angry and vexed. But as the Midrash points out, the Almighty had good reason for His two different reactions: Cain merely brought "from the fruit of the soil"—some poor, miserable things for which he had no use.[8] He thought just anything would do. Abel, however, brought the choice of his flock: fine fat sheep;[9] he did his best to please his Maker. So fire came

326

down from heaven, says the Midrash,[10] and consumed Abel's offering; but no fire descended for Cain's miserable gift. And Cain felt disgraced — rejected and dejected.

The Almighty chided Cain: *Why have you grown wrathful, and why has your countenance fallen? If you improve, will you not be accepted? and if you do not improve, sin crouches at the door; its craving is unto you, but you can be master over it* (Genesis 4:6–7). Cain had only himself to blame for his rejection; it was up to him alone to improve matters. Yet what do we read further? *Then Cain spoke to his brother Abel; and it was when they were in the field that Cain rose up against his brother Abel and killed him* (ibid. 8).

Thus Scripture tells of the first murder — the first bit of war in the world. For as a French philosopher wrote in the 16th century, "The same reasons that make us quarrel with a neighbor cause war between princes."[11] Well, when a major war embroils whole nations, the situation is described as "a world gone mad." What made Cain "go mad"? What went on in his beclouded brain, in his fateful encounter with Abel?

In the words of Scripture, ויאמר קין אל הבל אחיו *Then Cain spoke to his brother Abel*. What he said, though, does not appear in our Written Torah. The Midrash gives details:

עַל מֶה הָיוּ מְדַיְּנִים? אָמְרוּ, בּוֹא וְנַחֲלִק אֶת הָעוֹלָם. אֶחָד נָטַל אֶת הַקַּרְקָעוֹת וְאֶחָד נָטַל
הַמְּטַלְטְלִין. דֵּין אָמַר, אַרְעָא דְּאַתְּ קָאֵם עֲלֵהּ דִּידִי הוּא; וְדֵין אָמַר, מַה דְּאַתְּ לָבֵשׁ דִּידִי
הוּא. דֵּין אָמַר חֲלֹץ, וְדֵין אָמַר פְּרַח. מִתּוֹךְ כָּךְ, וַיָּקָם קַיִן אֶל הֶבֶל אָחִיו וַיַּהַרְגֵהוּ. רַ׳
יְהוֹשֻׁעַ דְּסִכְנִין בְּשֵׁם רַ׳ לֵוִי אָמַר: שְׁנֵיהֶם נָטְלוּ אֶת הַקַּרְקָעוֹת וּשְׁנֵיהֶם נָטְלוּ הַמְּטַלְטְלִין;
וְעַל מֶה הָיוּ מְדַיְּנִין? זֶה אוֹמֵר, בִּתְחוּמִי בֵּית הַמִּקְדָּשׁ נִבְנֶה; וְזֶה אוֹמֵר, בִּתְחוּמִי. שֶׁנֶּאֱמַר,
וַיְהִי בִּהְיוֹתָם בַּשָּׂדֶה, וְאֵין שָׂדֶה אֶלָּא בֵּית הַמִּקְדָּשׁ, הֵיךְ מַה דְּאַתְּ אָמַר, צִיּוֹן שָׂדֶה תֵחָרֵשׁ
(מיכה ג יב). וּמִתּוֹךְ כָּךְ, וַיָּקָם קַיִן אֶל הֶבֶל אָחִיו וַיַּהַרְגֵהוּ.... אָמַר רַ׳ הוּנָא: תְּאוֹמָה יְתֵרָה
נוֹלְדָה עִם הֶבֶל; זֶה אוֹמֵר, אֲנִי נוֹטְלָה, וְזֶה אוֹמֵר אֲנִי נוֹטְלָה. זֶה אוֹמֵר אֲנִי נוֹטְלָה, שֶׁאֲנִי
הַבְּכוֹר; וְזֶה אוֹמֵר אֲנִי נוֹטְלָה, שֶׁנּוֹלְדָה עִמִּי. וּמִתּוֹךְ כָּךְ, וַיָּקָם קַיִן אֶל הֶבֶל אָחִיו וַיַּהַרְגֵהוּ.
(בראשית רבה כב ז)

About what were they arguing? They said, "Come, let us divide up the world between us." One took the lands, and one took the movable property. Then this one said, "The ground you are standing on is mine"; and the other said, "What you are wearing is mine." The one said, "Undress!" and the other retorted, "Fly off!" As a result, *Cain rose up against his brother Abel and killed him.*

R. Joshua of Sichnin said in the name of R. Lévi: Both took possession of the lands, and both took the movable property. Then what were they quarreling about? This one said, "On my territory shall the holy Temple be built"; and that one said, "On *my* territory": For Scripture states, *and it was when they were in the field,* and "field" denotes nothing other than the Sanctuary, in keeping with the verse, *Zion* [the Temple] *shall be plowed as a field* (Micah 3:12). As a result, *Cain rose up against Abel his brother and killed him. . . .*

Said R. Huna: An extra twin girl was born with Abel. This one said, "I am taking her," and that one said, "I am taking her." This one [Cain] said, "I am taking her, because I am the firstborn son"; and that one [Abel] asserted, "I am taking her, because she was born with me." The result was that *Cain rose up against his brother Abel and killed him* (*B'réshith Rabbah* 22, 7).

Evidently the brothers lived amicably at first. They had the whole world before them (no overcrowding). In fact, the Midrash tells[12] that each gave the other food out of what they raised. Once they brought their offerings, however, and Cain faced God's rejection, everything changed.[13] Jealous of Abel, he turned surly and irascible; the veneer of civilized amiability was stripped away.

A new thought possessed him: 'You depended on the Almighty's favor to be safe and well in this frightening uncertain world; and He could reject you, so that you faced failure. Then by golly, you had to look after yourself! Only fools could be easygoing and share everything, without a care.'

He struck up a conversation with Abel, until (says the Midrash) they agreed to divide up the world. "Let us decide," said Cain in effect, "what is mine and what is yours. A man has to know where he stands in the world. I won't go on depending on God to accept my offerings!"

This, the Midrash teaches, led to the first civil war — between brothers; and it led to the first world war — between the only two young men on earth. They divided up their world: All land would belong to Cain; all movable property, to Abel.[14] At first the two might have thought it a satisfactory arrangement. Then complications set in. It suddenly bothered Cain (as another Midrash notes)[15] that Abel's sheep were grazing on *his* land, and he began chasing his brother and the flock over hills and valleys — until they confronted each other. "Fly off!" Cain ordered. For all he cared, Abel and the sheep could go to the moon. He wanted them off his earth.

Yet Abel also had a powerful argument. They made their clothing then from the wool and skins of sheep. So everything Cain wore belonged to Abel. "Strip!" he exclaimed. For all he cared, Cain could wear his birthday suit. . . . In the grip of his overheated emotions, Cain settled the argument by murder.

In sum, as we learn from the Midrash, the basic cause of mankind's bloody conflicts is economic. In our time, at least one popular book[16] has made the point that the human male (like many animals) has a "territorial imperative": A man must stake out some area in the world as his own; then he feels adequate and secure. Thus the world has known countless battles over disputed territory.

Many a reader may still remember Adolf Hitler's shrill demoniac ranting as he demanded *lebensraum* (room to live in) for his "beloved Germans" who lived as minorities in other countries. He always needed more and more territory for his poor little people, till he had to start the Second World War.

From early in the 19th century, the Socialists (headed by Karl Marx) preached a gospel of the economic factor in the human (class) struggle and the outbreak of armed conflict. Economic facts and laws, said they, made war in the capitalist countries inevitable. Thus it was later claimed, quite convincingly, that the First World War erupted because Germany and Turkey wanted to join forces and build a road to Baghdad, with which they could capture the markets of the world. This was also the purported basic reason (it was said) behind the intensive missionary activity through earlier centuries in Africa and Eastern Asia, China and the Far East — to conquer and develop new markets for the growing commerce and industry in the Western world. This activity too produced enough armed clashes and battles.

As the world grew more complex, there was good reason to believe that in time, the munition-makers and their dealers did *their* bit to foment war — for their own economic motive: It was "good for business."

However, behind all the bloody battles and conflicts over territory and economic rights and advantages, lies a primary search for security in an insecure world. Man knows he is vulnerable. He can suddenly be left, through circumstances, without food for his next meal. In some of its words, the Hebrew language carries clues to this very point. "War" in Hebrew is מלחמה *milḥamah*; the word for bread is לחם *leḥem* (which apparently meant food in general, originally).[17] The word זין *zayyin* denotes weaponry or

329

fighting equipment (*k'lé zayyin* means weapons, the tools of battle); how similar is the word זָן *zan* (root: *zun*), meaning to feed or provide with food. A sword in Hebrew is חרב *ḥerev*; a dry crust is פת חרבה *path ḥarévah*. The standard Hebrew term for food is אוכל *ochel*; מאכלת *ma'acheleth* denotes a large knife, which can be used to end a creature's or a human's life. . . . Evidently, somewhere in the recesses of the Hebrew mind, the core-concern over food was linked with a need or readiness to give battle for it.

When Cain found his offering to the Almighty spurned, he became angry and aggrieved. Feeling insecure and threatened, he wanted the power of territory and economic certainty, so that fear could no longer touch him. He wanted this so strongly that he murdered his brother. How well the Midrash puts it: "Hence it is written, *A man of evil eye hastens after wealth* (Proverbs 28:22). This applies to Cain, who became in a rush to possess the world . . . whose eye turned evil against his brother" (*Sh'moth Rabbah* 31, 17).

Here is our first conclusion in the study of the basic causes of war: the economic factor — which, in short, leads man on from fear to simple greed, and from there to organized murder. Over 1900 years ago, a Jewish philosopher in ancient Alexandria noted, "The wars of the Greeks and the barbarians . . . have all flowed from one source: greed, the desire for money, glory or pleasure — for it is on these that the human race goes mad." A Roman historian, living in the most militant and conquering empire of the ancient world, wrote of "gold and riches, the chief causes of war."[18]

In the aftermath of the First World War, people in the United States heard these memorable words from President Woodrow Wilson (who could certainly speak with authority): "Is there any man here or any woman — let me say, is there any child — who does not know that the seed of war in the modern world is industrial and commercial rivalry?"[19]

How valid, then, is this lesson in the Midrash. From Cain at the dawn of human history down to our day, when the world lives in a shivering palsy under the shadow of atomic weaponry, the economic factor has loomed large in the nightmares of man's activities of aggression.

This is only one view, however, in the Midrash on Cain and Abel. R. Lévi disagrees: The brothers could not have been so naive as to have one take all

330

the land, and the other all the movable property. Obviously it was impractical. They must have shared everything reasonably, to exist. Then what did they quarrel about? Said R. Lévi: Each insisted that the holy Temple must be built on his territory.

Taken at face value, this is puzzling. The Temple was built several thousand years later by King Solomon. What did Cain and Abel know about a Temple?

Well, this seems to be R. Lévi's way of expressing in metaphor a basic point that emerges from other passages in the Midrashim. When Cain saw that the Almighty accepted Abel's offering and rejected his, he evidently decided that the key to the problem was the location: Abel had simply found the right spot for his offering. So the Midrash relates:

וַיֹּאמֶר קַיִן אֶל הֶבֶל אָחִיו: מַה אָמַר לוֹ? נְחַלֵק הָעוֹלָם, וַאֲנִי הַבְּכוֹר, וְאֶטֹּל פִּי שְׁנָיִם. אָמַר לוֹ הֶבֶל, אֶפְשָׁר. אָמַר לוֹ קַיִן, אִם כֵּן אֲנִי נוֹטֵל יֶתֶר חֵלֶק עַל חֶלְקִי מְקוֹם שֶׁנִּתְקַבֵּל בּוֹ קָרְבָּנֶךָ. אָמַר לוֹ הֶבֶל, לֹא תִטֹּל. וְעַל דָּבָר זֶה נָפְלָה קְטָטָה בֵּינֵיהֶם... (תנחומא, בראשית ט)

*Then Cain spoke to his brother Abel*: What did he say to him? "Let us divide up the world. I am the firstborn, so I will take a double share." Replied Abel, "It can be done." Said Cain, "Then I am taking as my extra share the spot where your offering was accepted." Retorted Abel, "You will not take that"; and over this question a quarrel broke out between them... (*Tanḥuma, b'réshith* 9).

As a firstborn son, Cain was entitled to a double share of inheritance, as though he were two sons (see Deuteronomy 21:17). For his second share, Cain insisted on the area where Abel had presented his offering to God. Why did Abel refuse to give it up? By Divine grace he had hit on the exact location where the sacred altar in the holy Temple would stand one day.[20] He knew it was hallowed ground, and he would not let Cain have it.

The Almighty had told Cain, *If you improve, will you not be accepted?* Let him become worthy of God's favor, and his offering would be welcome wherever he brought it. He had no need of owning that plot of ground. (In fact, according to some Midrashic sources,[20] Cain had presented his offering at the same place as Abel.) Cain's mind was made up, however, and he could not be bothered by facts and details. Apparently he thought that once he owned the plot of ground, he alone would bring offerings there, and God would then *have* to accept him and grant him what he wanted, whether he was worthy or not. .... So when Abel told him in effect, "You will get this spot only over my dead body," Cain decided that this could be arranged. He removed the obstacle in his way — Abel.

Here then is another basic motive for war, for organized wholesale murder: conflicts concerning religion. "There is only one religion," wrote George Bernard Shaw, "but a hundred versions of it."[21] With a bit more salt Mark Twain observed that man "is the only animal that loves his neighbor as himself, and cuts his throat if his theology isn't straight. He has made a graveyard of the globe in trying his honest best to smooth his brother's path to happiness and heaven."[22]

Over two thousand years ago a Roman poet mused, "Too often in times past, religion has brought forth criminal and shameful actions." In the 17th century an Englishman noted, "Men have lost their reason in nothing so much as in their religion."[23] And in our time a philosophic writer has put it so: "The crimes of a Caligula shrink to insignificance compared to the havoc wrought by Torquemada [the notorious head of the Spanish Inquisition in the 15th century]. The number of victims of robbers, high-waymen, rapers, gangsters and other criminals at any period of history is negligible compared to the massive number of those cheerfully slain in the name of the true religion, just policy, or correct ideology."[24]

Can any doubt remain that R. Lévi put his finger on a basic raw nerve in the human being that can bring out the killer in him? It was clear to him that people can find a noble, holy reason for their vilest actions. Cain ostensibly killed Abel because he wanted religion: He wanted to be more pious and devout, bringing his offerings at the holiest place. In man's bloody course through history, even where a war was not fought directly over a question of religion, each party to the conflict assured itself that the Almighty was on its side. During the American Civil War, some people visited President Lincoln to discuss a possible truce. Before they left, their spokesman said, "We trust, sir, that God is on our side." Somberly the president replied, "It is more important to know that we are on God's side."

In 1939 there was a news dispatch that "the Pope gave his apostolic benediction to a group of Spanish generals from Madrid." They were generals of the Nationalist (authoritarian) side in the Spanish Civil War — Franco's side, aided by Hitler and Mussolini, which had produced frightful massacres in the city of Badajoz and the town of Guernica, wiping out thousands of innocent men, women and children. Having read this news item, an American poet was moved to write:[25] "Behold, the Bishop of Rome . . . / he speaketh to urb and orb. The generals / are blessed. The sword is blessed . . . . / Blessing, the Bishop of Rome / lays, for a healing unction, balm and oil / on bombed Guernica and on Badajoz. / Here is another twilight . . . / and silence, shaken only where / speaking to urb and orb / a voice goes seeking, calling: / 'Cain, Cain, Cain! Where is your brother Abel? / Abel, your brother — where is Abel, Cain?' / in bombed Guernica and in Badajoz / calling among the ruins of those stones."

No matter how "religious" the cause, no matter how strongly God is joined to a cause by main force, making Him its honorary chairman — the Cains of this world do not escape the mark of Cain.

As the times became more "modern," however, formal religion and its disputes "went out of style." Nothing really changed, though. In a hot or cold war, a world power still had to justify its foreign policy as noble and pious. So ideology took the place of religion.

Till August 1914, Belgium and its neighbors felt quite safe. Kaiser Wilhelm of Germany made a treaty with Belgium, solemnly promising not to invade it. Then he declared war, and his troops marched through Belgium, leaving ruin and misery behind them. How could it happen? How could the emperor of Germany break his word? He blithely carried on the war, leaving it to his advisors and philosophers to find good reasons, that would make first-rate propaganda. So Europe became embroiled in the First World War.

In the United States, President Wilson decided that America should have no part of it. In his 1916 election campaign he promised to keep the country out. The next year, however, he joined the United States to the Allied Powers, and General Pershing sailed for Europe to head the American army. "The world must be made safe for democracy," Wilson told the American Congress in sincere belief. The war was fought and won — and the world did not become safe for democracy.

In the 1930's Hitler had to keep seizing territory: his dear little country-men (the Germans — although he came from Austria) needed *lebensraum* in the neighboring countries: room in which to live a little. When he invaded Poland in 1939, he knew this claim would not cover it. But he left it to his propaganda chief, good old Goebbels, to provide a good explanation — something like this: The "Aryan super-race" of Germany was to bring a glorious new order into the world, in a dazzling reign of a thousand years.

333

They were "the wave of the future." They were on a holy crusade, in their march of triumph, in spiked boots, across the face of Europe.

Even the program that killed six million Jews so efficiently had its splendid ideological reason: to rid the world of its "basic scourge, the pathogenic source of all its ills: the Jews." Obviously the devil himself could preach a good religious line if he wished.

In recent decades the Soviet colossus has spread its influence abroad like a mammoth menacing sea-monster swimming in the waters of international relations, seeing what may be swallowed silently and profitably. This too is justified by a kind of religion: Soviet ideology. They want to bring other countries and areas of the world the blessings of communism, the sure road to utopia. They want to save everyone from the terrible, reactionary, counter-revolutionary disease of aggressive and exploitative capitalism. They have to slaughter and massacre now and then; they have to rule by tyranny and terror — to bring the world the magic elixir of Marx's and Lenin's communism.

Today Arab terrorists take the lead in a campaign to move Israel to a new location: somewhere out in the Mediterranean Sea, where they would like Israel to settle. The Arabs find many friends and backers in the world. Some are virulently or moderately anti-Jewish, and others need oil. But they too must have a "holy cause"; so they present the perennial, undying tableau of the "pathetic need" of Palestinian refugees to return to their "beloved land" — a claim that no one dares examine rationally for its intrinsic truth (if any).

Cain and Abel, said R. Lévi, were embroiled in the world's first conflict over religious causes. No one knows how many more "religious" conflicts the world is yet to see. . . . And that, as the saying goes, is the way the world spins.

R. Huna gives a different explanation. Perhaps he thought Cain and Abel were too early in human history to disagree over a matter of religion. They were only the second generation of mankind. Their argument must have been on a more primitive level. Besides, violent arguments over religion are generally only rationalizations — excuses or "covers" to convince everyone (including oneself) of being nobly in the right. Something else must have been the real cause of Cain's rage.

Well, the Sages teach that with Cain, and again with Abel, a twin sister was born; and each girl became her twin brother's wife. For if this did not

334

happen (although the Bible tells nothing of it) how could there have been any third generation of mankind? Necessarily, they had twin sisters, and the Torah's later ban on incest was not imposed as yet.[26]

Yet, says R. Huna, there was a complication. With Abel a second girl had been born. Eve had not given birth to twins then, but to triplets. So there was an extra young lady, when they all grew up; and about her the brothers clashed. Since the Torah grants a firstborn son a double share of inheritance (as though he were two sons) Cain claimed the girl for a second wife. But, Abel argued, the girl had been born with him: It was a sign from heaven that she should be his. So Cain picked up a stone and let fly, and he settled the argument.

Another Midrash tells a simpler tale: Only one twin sister was born with each brother, but Abel's twin was much prettier than Cain's — which decided Cain that he must have her.[27] Either way, the result was a heavy stone aimed at Abel's forehead.[27]

Here then is the third motive in the Midrash for brutality among men: quarrel and conflict over a woman. The Divine order in the world is clear: for every Adam there is an Eve. "Forty days before the formation of an embryo," says the Talmud,[28] "a heavenly voice emanates and declares: The daughter of so-and-so is for so-and-so." Yet men have always been gifted at snarling up Divine plans; and from earliest times, passions and lusts have led to fights over women.

Some 3,000 years ago Homer gave the world the *Iliad*, an epic poem about a long hard war between the Greek and Trojan armies, that finally destroyed Troy. What caused the war? Paris, a prince of Troy, had kidnapped Helen, the wife of a Greek nobleman, to make her *his* wife.

There is the familiar phrase (supposedly originated by a French minister of police under Napoleon), *Cherchez la femme*, "Look for the woman" — as the cause behind every trouble. A Britisher later put it in rhyme: "In all the woes that curse our race / there is a lady in the case."[29] Over 1800 years ago it was already noted in Rome, "There never was a case in which the quarrel was not started by a woman."[30] Perhaps, however, an English proverb from the 13th century put it best of all: "Woman is the confusion of man."[31]

Even where it is not lust and passion that has driven men into battle, it certainly comes to possess men once they are embarked on war. In physical combat, the animal forces are unleashed. (In fact, Ethiopia's king Haile Selassie, who styled himself "the lion of Judah," used to feed his soldiers

335

lion's flesh, believing it would make them fearless warriors — fiercer animals. Evidently he believed that, literally, "a man is what he eats.")[32] In ancient times, Israel won a stunning victory over Sisera, the star general of the king of Ḥatzor; and Deborah the prophetess sang a hymn of victory. She pictured Sisera's mother waiting for him to come home in triumph (while he lay dead in Yael's tent, with a tent-pole driven through his brains). Deborah imagined this Canaanite mother worrying as the hours slid by and her Sisera failed to appear: *"Why is his chariot so long in coming? Why are the beats of his chariots delayed?" The wisest of her princesses answer her; indeed she rejoins the answer for herself: "They are surely finding, dividing the booty — a wench, two wenches to every man..."* (Judges 5:28–30). And Rashi explains: The large amount of booty (loot) taken in the war must be delaying Sisera's men; and they are raping the beautiful women of Israel, each one having a few at his disposal. . . . This was the expected behavior of victorious soldiers after a battle.

It may be added that through history large armies of long duration invariably had "camp followers" (harlots) fairly close by, knowing they would be needed. Since armed combat began, war and lust have gone together. Or, you might say, the lust to kill always links up with the lust of the passions.

In sum, then, the Midrash gives three causes of savage conflict: One is economic and one ideological; and the third points to man's animal drives. Which of the three is correct? Beyond any doubt, all three are right. In every war there are impassioned militarists, blazing with an animal desire to attack and inflict defeat — and enjoy the lusty triumphs and rewards of victory. When philosophers, clergymen and ideologists call for war, it is on "noble" ideological grounds. Bankers, merchants and captains of industry can want a splendid war for the profits in it.

Get them all together, and you have a good chance for a blazing world war.

# OUR MILITANT DEVELOPMENT

O<small>UR SAGES GAVE THREE CAUSES OF WAR</small> — but perhaps beneath them all lurks a sheer animal passion to let go and have at an antagonist, to revel in using a prowess that can inflict injury and defeat. There is a satanic thrill, a fiendish delight in throwing off restraint, to create havoc and carnage in a never-ending gamble for the "glory" of victory. Whatever the official reasons or causes, battles and wars have gone on endlessly since man's earliest beginnings.[33]

Somehow, though, among the Israelite and Jewish people, the satanic glories of army life and militancy never really caught on.

From the earliest times of our ancient history, our people knew the taste and meaning of war. In fact, they were quite good at it originally. Consider our first Patriarch, Abraham. The Torah tells of a battle of four kings against five, where the four were victorious (Genesis 14:1–11). Clearly they and their men were superior warriors. Well, they captured Abraham's nephew Lot, with all his possessions (*ibid.* 12). When Abraham learned of this, he took *his* men, all 318 of them, and went after the four kings — and he defeated them roundly, and set his nephew free (*ibid.* 14–16). Obviously he could wage war with a vengeance when he had to.

Shechem the son of Ḥamor treated Jacob's daughter shamefully, then sought to marry her. Her brothers Shimon and Lévi were so incensed, not only at him but at his townspeople for accepting such outrageous behavior, that they slew everyone in the town (Genesis 34). Clearly they too knew how to wield a sword.

Over two centuries went by, and our people left Egypt after genera-tions of enslavement. They journeyed through the wilderness, and the people of Amalek fell upon them in a vicious attack. Without panic or hysteria, Moses bid Joshua pick men to lead in a counter-attack; and with Moses' unflagging encouragement giving them faith, the Hebrews were victorious (Exodus 17:8–13). So at the very start of their history as a free nation, our people tasted the heady wine of success on the battlefield. They knew how it felt to fight and win.

337

The next generation was to know even greater military success, as it met and vanquished enemies in the Transjordan, then went on under Joshua to conquer the land of Canaan. In the course of time, the dangerous foes who still menaced and troubled Israel were defeated by David. The victories of the Maccabees many centuries later were equally impressive.

*Yet our people's way of development was not mainly military.*

If in our very earliest history, Abraham and his trained men knew the exhilaration of victory (Genesis 14:15), he had fought only to free his captured nephew Lot (*ibid.* 12, 14, 16). Shimon and Lévi slew the people of Shechem only because the town's young prince had treated their sister disgracefully, unforgivably, and the town had condoned it (Genesis 34). Then, when our people in the wilderness had a superb army of valor, they were put under the restraint of Divine command and religious law.[34]

The battles they fought were *milhemeth mitzvah*, war by Divine commandment — for example, against Amalek, a people that chose to be a bitter enemy, for no reason; and against the seven nations in Canaan. As Rambam notes, these nations "were the very essence and focal center of idol-worship, its first root and foundation." Scripture made it clear that they had to be eradicated "so that we should not learn any of their heresy."[35] And evidently, as we learn in the Torah, in their idolatry they had practiced every kind of immoral intimacy and perversion: *For all those abominations, the people of the land that were before you did, and the land became defiled; then let the land not vomit you out also, because you are defiling it, as it vomited out the nation that was before you* (Leviticus 18:27–28).

Yet even going to war with these morally rotten people (writes Rambam) the Israelites had to offer them peace first. If they but accepted the seven commandments that the Torah imposes on all mankind, they were to be left alive, as a subject people under Israel's rule.[36] For any other war (*milhemeth r'shuth*) the Hebrews had to have the consent of the *sanhedrin* (the supreme court — Israel's seventy-one finest elders and scholars); then the women and children had to be spared, and a way left open for the men to escape.[37] As the Almighty's own people, we were not encouraged to become brutal and bloodthirsty.

At the Red Sea our people under Moses were overwhelmed with relief and gratitude when, having crossed safely on dry land, they saw the pursuing Egyptians drowned in the returning waves of the rushing waters. So moved were the Israelites at their final escape from these cruel oppressors, that with Moses they sang a hymn of praise to the Almighty (Exodus 15:1–

19). Says the Talmud:[38] The angels also wanted to sing His glory, but He silenced them: "The creations of My hands are drowning in the sea, and you would utter praise-song?"

For the Hebrews it was only natural to sing, in their boundless gratitude to God, now that they were fully safe. But from a higher point of view, as angels in heaven may see human conflict and victory, there was no reason for joyous song. In every splendid triumph, every "happy ending" to a war, God's creatures have suffered and perished. (How well an old German proverb put it: A great war leaves a country with three armies: an army of cripples, an army of mourners, and an army of thieves.)

The Sages teach that our ancestor Jacob already realized this tragic truth. When he knew Esau was coming with 400 men to attack him, what do we read: *Then Jacob was greatly afraid and distressed* (Genesis 32:7-8). The Midrash then asks: Why the double expression? Surely "afraid" and "distressed" denote the same thing? And the Sages reply: He was greatly afraid that he might be killed, and he was distressed that he might commit murder. He thought, 'If he [Esau] prevails against me, he will kill me; and if I prevail against him, I will kill him.'[39] Either way, he faced anguish.

In our time our people have known no victory more dazzling than the outcome of the Six-Day War. In six days Israel went from the prospect of annihilation to a total defeat of its bitter enemies, regaining parts of the Promised Land which had been held by this unyielding enemy for nineteen years.

What was the lasting reaction in Israel? Did the Jews there crow in gleeful triumph? Did they have pictures taken with one foot on the enemy's neck, to record the glorious victory for posterity?

Not quite. In a book on the reactions of the soldiers,[40] it was noted that those who faced the onslaught of the fighting returned dazed by the range of their victory and, no less, shocked by the discovery of what war actually was. This was a book originally published privately — not for public consumption — by "young members of the kibbutz movement," non-religious *kibbutznikim* trying to make "a spiritual reckoning" of the war. Time and again they dwelt on their fear of the brutalizing effects of war, the danger of losing the *tzelem elokim*, the Divine self-image of man, and turning into a killing animal.

As the book's English editor wrote, the great majority would admit to no real hatred of the enemy. One man recalled an enemy soldier fleeing. The Israeli soldiers shot at him, but he escaped. The Israeli commented, "I couldn't really say I had any pangs of conscience [about their shooting at him] but I was glad he got away."

The soldiers knew what their enemy was like. They had no illusions. "You won't get peace flowering up out of humane acts," said one; ". . . the Arabs really hate us. Look: a bunch of Arabs who had never seen a Jew in their lives grabbed a [captured] Israeli pilot and butchered him — even before the war had really begun. . . . Just because you didn't kill them, you haven't made them love you any better. As a matter of fact, there were a lot of cases where enemy soldiers surrendered with their hands up, and when our boys turned their backs for a minute, those Egyptians whipped out guns and shot soldiers who had spared their lives! That's how it is — because that's the Arab mentality."

The young men of the kibbutzim had been raised without Torah. They knew little of our age-old faith. Yet they were Jews, descendants of Abraham the Patriarch. "There are three characteristic signs of this people," say the Sages: "They are compassionate and modest, and given to acts of kindness." And the Sages taught: Whoever takes pity on human beings is for certain a descendant of our father Abraham; and anyone who does not. . . is quite certainly not. . . .[41]

"A lot of Egyptians were roaming around among the dunes," a kibbutznik recalled after the Six-Day War. "We had almost no water left. Still, our boys gave the Egyptians, who were almost dying of thirst, water to drink from their canteens. They'd been wandering around . . . since the first day of the war, and they were almost completely fagged out. . . . I remember: we were going along this road to Kantara, and we saw an older woman walking with a little girl in her arms, together with her husband and a small boy. We were traveling with the unit's reconaissance squad, which had suffered a lot of casualties in the fighting. . . . Well, we rode along in our jeeps, and as we passed this couple and the kids, there was a feeling in me that maybe we should take them along. . . . The first jeep stopped, backed up, and took the woman and her child aboard. Then I saw that everybody had been debating it in their minds. There wasn't much room in the jeep. It was really loaded up with stuff. Still, we took the woman and her little girl, and the husband and the boy. We all got out candies and gave them to the kids. . . ."[42]

Above all, when it was over, despite the immense gains that the victory had brought, at least one soldier (most certainly speaking for many) felt only regret over the fighting: "It seems to me that if on June 4 [1967, a day before

340

the war broke out] Nasser had announced that all his guns had been sunk and his tanks had gone up in flames (without any outside help) — and it was certain that we weren't just hearing more lies from Radio Cairo; and if on June 4, Hussein had tried to make a true peace settlement with us, and the Syrians had immediately gone along with him on it — I am convinced that in spite of our wish to return to the territory of our forefathers, we would have preferred not to go to war — not out of any fear of the UN, but by our own honest decision."

So much for the rampant militancy and the blustering love of war and its glories among our people, either in ancient times or in the present.

In the aftermath of the Yom Kippur War, when Golda Meir was still Israel's prime minister, she asked in dismay how the Arabs could look with pride, arrogance and ambition on such brutal encounters and the dubious gains that they might bring. Didn't Arab mothers (she asked) weep as bitterly when *their* sons were killed or maimed? Alas, there was not an echo of a response from Israel's kill-happy neighbors. *They have ears, but they hear not* (Psalms 115:6). All they have are *haughty eyes, a lying tongue, and hands that shed innocent blood; a heart that devises wicked thoughts, feet swift in running to evil* (Proverbs 6:17–18).

## ❧ STRUCTURES OF STONE

LONG AGO, FACING AN ARMED CLASH WITH HIS BROTHER ESAU, Jacob the Patriarch knew that, win or lose, in a battle you come out a loser. You become either a corpse or a killer. At the Red Sea the Israelites were overjoyed beyond their wildest dreams to find themselves forever safe from the Egyptians. Yet the Almighty told the angels that for them there was no reason to sing for joy. He had saved the Hebrews, but at the cost of human death. People, God's creatures, had drowned.

However unavoidable human conflict has been, whatever the gains that have come from it, God could not be expected to like it.

341

By all accounts, King David was a brilliant warrior, military strategist and tactician. Under his command, the Hebrew army finally broke enemies that had long plagued and harassed Israel; and at last the people could live secure, as a feared and respected nation. Yet, say the Sages, David was not a happy man, revelling in his exploits and conquests. All his years, declares the Talmud, David never once had a good, happy dream. His military triumphs inevitably left a trail of bloodshed and murder, desolation and ruin — and these, the Zohar explains, came by night to trouble his sleep.[43] In short, with all his triumphs, the man knew not happiness but nightmare.

He had a dream by day, though: a hope and ambition that he longed with all his heart to achieve. Scripture tells *how he swore to the Lord* . . . *"I will not enter the tent of my house nor get into the bed prepared for me; I will give neither sleep to my eyes nor slumber to my eyelids — until I find a place for the Lord, a dwelling-place for the Mighty One of Jacob"* (Psalms 132:2–5). As soon as he found a respite from battles and wars, he wanted to make his dream a reality. We read in the Bible: *Now, when the king dwelt in his house, the Lord having given him rest from all his enemies round about, the king said to Nathan the prophet, "See now, I dwell in a house of cedar, and the ark of God dwells in a tent"* (II Samuel 7:1–2).

As the Midrash conveys, the Almighty knew just what David had in mind, and that very night He bade Nathan bring David His answer. The Holy, Blessed One (says the Midrash) told Nathan the prophet, "Nathan, the man to whom I am sending you is given to acting swiftly. Before he hires workers, go and tell him, 'Not you shall build Me a house' — so that he should have no complaint against Me [afterward]."[44]

David, then, was ready to go into action the very next day, to build the Sanctuary in Jerusalem, the House of God. Nathan the prophet had to hurry to him and tell him, *Thus says the Lord: Would you build Me a house to dwell in? . . . When your days are fulfilled . . . I will raise up your son after you. . . . He shall build a house for My name* (ibid. 5, 12–13).

Not David would be allowed to build the Sanctuary, but his son Solomon. Why? Elsewhere in the Bible we find the answer: *And David said to Solomon, "My son, I had it in my heart to build a house to the name of the Lord my God. But the word of the Lord came to me, saying: You have shed blood in abundance and have waged great wars; you shall not build a house to My name* . . . (I Chronicles 22:7–8). Again we read: *Then David the king stood up on his feet and said, "Hear me, my brethren and my people. I had it in my heart to build a house of rest for the ark of the covenant of the Lord, and for the footstool*

*of our God; and I made preparations for building. But God said to me: You shall
not build a house for My name, because you are a man of war and have shed
blood"* (*ibid.* 28:2–3).

However necessary warfare may have been (waged even by Divine
order and sanction) to let the Israelites receive the Promised Land and live
there in safety, no trace or shadow of human conflict, bloodshed and
murder was to touch the Sanctuary itself, the holy House of God.

Actually, the point was already made clearly enough in the wilderness,
when the Almighty gave our people instructions about building an altar of
stones. In the *mishkan*, the portable temporary Sanctuary in the wilderness,
the altar was of earth in a box-shaped case of copper. In the great permanent
Sanctuary of Jerusalem, however, it was to be built of stones. There animal
offerings would be brought, to bring atonement and Divine protection.
Well, about a sacred object like that the Torah was specific: *And if you make
an altar of stone, you shall not build it of hewn stones; for if you lift up your cutting
tool upon it, you have profaned it* (Exodus 20:22).

There was another altar for which the instructions were quite the same.
On the eastern shore of the Jordan, Moses commanded his people what to
do once they crossed the river: *And there you shall build an altar to the Lord
your God, an altar of stones; you shall lift no iron tool upon them; of whole
stones* (sh'lémoth) *shall you build the altar of the Lord your God* (Deuteronomy
27:5–6).

While the instructions are evidently the same in both cases, there are
differences. In the first instance, the Hebrew for "cutting tool" is *ḥerev*,
which literally means a sword. So the Midrash makes a memorable point:[45]

מִכְּלָל שֶׁנֶּאֱמַר, כִּי חַרְבְּךָ הֵנַפְתָּ עָלֶיהָ וַתְּחַלְלֶיהָ, יָכוֹל לֹא יְהוּ פְסוּלוֹת אֶלָּא אִם כֵּן
נִתְגַּזְּזוּ בְחֶרֶב; תַּלְמוּד לוֹמַר, לֹא תָנִיף עֲלֵיהֶם בַּרְזֶל: הֲרֵי בַּרְזֶל כְּחֶרֶב. אִם סוֹפֵנוּ לַעֲשׂוֹת
בַּרְזֶל כְּחֶרֶב, מַה תַּלְמוּד לוֹמַר, כִּי חַרְבְּךָ? זוֹ הִיא שֶׁרַבָּן יוֹחָנָן בֶּן זַכַּאי אוֹמֵר: מַה רָאָה
בַרְזֶל לְפָּסֵל מִכָּל מִינֵי מַתָּכוֹת כֻּלָּן? מִפְּנֵי שֶׁהַחֶרֶב נַעֲשֵׂת מִמֶּנּוּ, וְחֶרֶב סִימָן פּוּרְעָנוּת,
וּמִזְבֵּחַ סִימָן כַּפָּרָה. מַעֲבִירִין דָּבָר שֶׁהוּא סִימָן פּוּרְעָנוּת מִפְּנֵי דָּבָר שֶׁהוּא סִימָן כַּפָּרָה.

(מכילתא דרשב״י, שמות כ כב)

Since it is written, *for if you lift up your ḥerev, your sword, upon it, you have
profaned it,* I might think that [stones] do not become disqualified unless
hewn with a sword? — hence Scripture states, *you shall lift up no iron tool
upon them.* Thus anything of iron is like a sword [under the law]. But then,
if we finally rule all iron tools to be like a sword [equally disqualifying], why

343

did Scripture say, "if you lift up your sword"? It drives home what Rabban Yoḥanan b. Zakkai said: Why was it seen fit to single out iron from among all the metals for disqualification? — because the sword is made from it, and the sword symbolizes calamity, while the altar symbolizes atonement. The symbol of calamity is to be removed from the presence of the symbol of atonement.

Even more moving is this passage: [46]

כִּי חַרְבְּךָ הֵנַפְתָּ עָלֶיהָ וַתְּחַלְלֶיהָ: מִכָּאן הָיָה רַבִּי שִׁמְעוֹן בֶּן אֶלְעָזָר אוֹמֵר: הַמִּזְבֵּחַ נִבְרָא לְהַאֲרִיךְ שְׁנוֹתָיו שֶׁל אָדָם, וְהַבַּרְזֶל נִבְרָא לְקַצֵּר שְׁנוֹתָיו שֶׁל אָדָם. אֵינוֹ רַשַּׁאי לְהָנִיף הַמְקַצֵּר עַל הַמַּאֲרִיךְ. רַבָּן יוֹחָנָן בֶּן זַכַּאי אוֹמֵר: הֲרֵי הוּא אוֹמֵר: אֲבָנִים שְׁלֵמוֹת תִּבְנֶה: אֲבָנִים שֶׁמַּטִּילוֹת שָׁלוֹם. (מכילתא, שם)

*For if you lift up your sword,* etc.: Hence R. Shimon b. Elazar used to say: The altar was created to lengthen a man's life, while iron was created to shorten a man's life. It is not permissible to lift up the 'shortener' over the 'lengthener.' Rabban Yoḥanan b. Zakkai said: Here Scripture states, *you shall build the altar . . .* of sh'lémoth, *whole stones* — stones that make *shalom,* peace!

Man has done much with his tools and weapons of iron and steel. His achievements have been dazzling — and deadly. In ancient times, whoever discovered or developed a harder, more durable metal became a better warrior, a more resplendent conqueror. They developed skills with sword and lance, rapier and spear. They learned to joust and fence superbly. Even when real wars with those weapons went out of style, movie cameras went on filming scenes of splendid heroic virtuosity with such weapons by Hollywood's most dashing actors. Which red-blooded American youngster has not thrilled to watch a movie (or television) hero use sword or lance or fencing foil for mighty deeds of derring-do?

The altars that our ancestors built, and the sacrifices they offered there, never became a matter of spell-binding interest in the movies. There seems nothing spectacular about them, to bedazzle the eye. The immense power of holiness in religious devotion cannot be photographed in brilliant color. It took the insight of the Sages to appreciate the timeless, enduring lesson of the Torah: Man's weapons of iron, steel and gunmetal shorten human life. One thrust, one gasp of pain, and a human being lives no more. But the altar lengthened life. It brought a man forgiveness and inner peace. It brought Divine grace and protection to Israel.

344

So it was not only war and human conflict that God could not really accept with any joy. It was not only murder, individual or *en masse*, that He necessarily found reprehensible. Where man would worship Him, there was to be not the slightest touch, not the least influence or reminder, of the means and materials for murder.

An altar, though, was not the only structure of stone that our forefathers built in their relationship to the Almighty. We read: *Then Jacob rose up early in the morning, and he took the stone that he had put under his head, and set it up as a* matzéva *(pillar), and poured oil on the top of it* (Genesis 28:18). Years later, again, *Jacob set up a* matzéva *at the site where He had spoken to him, a* matzéva *(pillar) of stone, and he poured a libation on it, and poured oil on it* (Gensis 35:14). Though translated pillar, the word has more the sense of a small monument. What was Jacob's purpose in setting up such a monument twice? Both times, we read immediately afterward that *he called the name of the site* béth él, *the house of God* (Genesis 28:19, 35:15). His *matzéva* was evidently for much the same purpose as an altar: in essence it was a focal point, to worship the Almighty there.

There were two other times when Jacob set up a *matzéva*. Knowing that his father-in-law, Laban, would never let him leave peacefully with his family and possessions, the Patriarch fled with them when Laban was away. His father-in-law learned of his flight, however, and he set off in pursuit. When he caught up with him, the two confronted each other; and after some harsh words they reached a friendly settlement (thanks to a dream Laban had the night before, in which the Almighty warned him not to dare harm Jacob). The Patriarch was to be allowed to return to his own land in peace, with his family and his wealth. *Then Jacob took up a stone and set it up for a* matzéva (Genesis 31:45). This was a small monument to peace between them, as Laban declared (*ibid.* 52): neither was to come to the other for any hostile purpose.

Finally, when his wife Rachel died, Jacob buried her *by the way to Efrath, which is Bethlehem; and Jacob set up a* matzéva *on her grave; this is the* matzéva *of Rachel's grave to this day* (Genesis 35:19–20). This monument was a grave-marker, a tombstone.

Why did he put it there? Years later, Jacob told his son Joseph, *Now, as I came from Paddan, Rachel died, to my sorrow, in the land of Canaan on the way, when there was still some way to go to Efrath; and I buried her there, by the way to Efrath* (Genesis 48:7). Says the Midrash:[47] Why there? It was by

345

the Almighty's word of command. For what reason? — because it was foreseen and revealed before Him that the holy Temple was destined to be destroyed, and his [Jacob's] descendants would have to depart into exile. They would then go to the Patriarchs and beg them to pray for them, but they would be of no help to the exiles. When they would go on the road, however, they would come over and embrace the tomb of Rachel; whereupon she would arise and implore mercy from the Holy, Blessed One, pleading with Him, "O Master of the world, hear the sound of my weeping and take pity on my children." ... And the Holy, Blessed One would hearken at once to the sound of her prayer. How do we know this? — because so is it written: [*A voice is heard in Ramah*] *lamentation and weeping, Rachel weeping for her children* (Jeremiah 31:15); and it is written, *There is hope for your future, says the Lord, and your children shall come back to their own country* (*ibid.* 17).

So we learn from the Midrash that, like the *matzéva* that Jacob set up when he made a peace pact with Laban, this stone too was placed as a marker or landmark. It would show where Rachel lay buried — so that the Israelites, banished into exile when the Sanctuary was destroyed, would know to stop there to pray[48] and seek her help, her intervention in heaven — and she would indeed pray for them.

Such, then, were the small, simple stone structures and monuments that our ancestors built: an altar of whole stones, untouched by sword or iron blade, to bring God's forgiveness, peace and life; and the *matzéva*, a single stone[49] — as a focal point for man's worship of the Almighty; as a permanent marker designating peace among human beings; and as a landmark to indicate the grave of a Matriarch, a mother of our people, so that our people in distress might turn to her, and she would pray for them before the Divine throne of glory.

It did not remain, however, only a practice of the Hebrews to set up a *matzéva*. The heathen erected them also, as focal centers for their idol-worship. They simply decided that a stone somehow embodied some holy spirit, and to that they bowed down and prostrated themselves, stretching out on the ground in worshipful self-abasement.

Toward a *matzéva* of this kind the Torah's attitude was implacable: *you shall break their pillars* (matzévoth) *to bits* (Exodus 23:24); *and smash their pillars* (Exodus 34:13); *and their pillars you shall smash* (Deuteronomy 7:5). Idolatry was a vile thing that cruelly misled people in the spiritual realm.

346

And because the *matzéva* (pillar) came to be used so widely for idol-worship, the Almighty forbade it to the Israelites, even for worshipping *Him*. As Rashi explains (Deuteronomy 16:22): He commanded an altar of earth or stones to be made, but these [pillars] He hated, beacuse it became the set way [for worship] of the Canaanites; and although it was beloved to Him in the days of the Patriarchs [see Genesis 31:13] now He detested it, as it had become the rule in idolatry.

One thing is certain, though: The heathen did not stop at a simple modest pillar of a single stone. They went on to large, elaborate constructions for their idolatry. Rambam (Maimonides) describes their *matzéva* as a large structure where all would gather to worship.[50] And of course, for their "great" emperors and kings the dividing line faded away between monuments to a god of theirs and monuments to themselves. As often as not, they regarded themselves as living embodiments of the spirits of gods. So they set up large, even colossal monuments and statues of their charming selves.

Between the archaeologists and the museums of the world, a sizable collection of such remainders of the past have been unearthed and amassed, mostly in the form of ruins and relics. One theme runs through them all: vainglory and boasting: "Look at me! See what I achieved. Behold what I built!"

Jacob set up a simple stone for a *matzéva*, as a marker of peace between men. They set up obelisks, steles and statues with inscriptions, to boast of the wars they fought and won. In the words of Julius Caesar,[51] "Monuments are made for victories over strangers." The "great" men of the ancient world needed their constructions of marble and stone to flaunt their achievements and their magnificence in the face of posterity.

When Tiberius ruled in Rome, an immense statue of him rose up in Israel, in the city of Caesaria (a name derived from *Caesar*, the standard title of the Roman emperor). When Titus finished the destruction of our second Temple in the year 70, he went parading proudly with his men through the city of Rome, in the traditional march of triumph upon return from a successful war. On an arch of triumph that stands to this day, a sculptor depicted it all, including the sacred *menorah* from the Sanctuary being carried as a trophy, and countless captured Jews dragged along toward a life of slavery. The boast had to be made permanent.

Jacob reverently placed a *matzéva* on Rachel's grave so that his descendants could know where to turn to obtain Heaven's help in their time of trouble. Not one marker or landmark did the heathen ever erect to help them, through prayer to the Almighty, in a day of misfortune. When calamity came, they were finished. They disappeared from the scene (or, in the bright lingo of our time, they no longer made the scene). They perpetuated their exploits and fame in stone; and the monuments crumbled; from their statues limbs and parts broke off. The statue of Tiberius in Caesaria stands today shorter by a head. . . . Above all, the stone they used to make themselves and their glories remembered was a heavy, lifeless material. So *the deeps covered them; they went down into the depths like stone* (Exodus 15:5). In the seas of time they sank to the bottom. In the sands of time they were covered completely.

Early in the last century a noted British poet expressed the thought in memorable metaphor:[52]

> I met a traveller from an antique land
> who said: Two vast and trunkless legs of stone
> stand in the desert . . . Near them, on the sand,
> half sunk, a shattered visage lies, whose frown
> and wrinkled lip and sneer of cold command
> tell that its sculptor well those passions read
> which yet survive, stamped on those lifeless things,
> the hand that mocked them, and the heart that fed;
> and on the pedestal these words appear:
> "My name is Ozymandias, king of kings.
> Look on my works, ye mighty, and despair!"
> Nothing beside remains. Round the decay
> of that colossal wreck, boundless and bare,
> the lone and level sands stretch far away.

With the Jews and their monuments of stone, it has been an utterly different story. Stone is actually a valuable material. It is hard and durable. Well, long ago a Western Wall was built at the Temple Mount, as part of a structure to protect the Sanctuary and enhance its prestige. When the Temple itself was demolished, this wall remained. Our Sages teach that as long as the Sanctuary stood, the *shechinah* (the Divine Presence) was there. When that was destroyed, the *shechinah* nevertheless remained at the site, lodged at the *kothel maaravi*, the Western Wall; and from there it has never budged.[53]

The *kothel* can certainly be called a monument, if you will. It is certainly visited by as many tourists as any ancient monument in the world.

Two things, though, are different about it: First, it has remained standing there, all these many moons. Fierce battles took place in the area through the centuries since we lost the Sanctuary. Time and again earthquakes occurred in the region, not too far away. The Wall is only a pile of massive stones set carefully on one another. No cement or mortar binds them. Yet there it has stood, through the expanse of time.

Of course, there are those who say that the stones are held in place today by the innumerable pieces of paper that people have folded up small and pushed into the crevices, with their names and words of prayer written on them. But that cannot really be called a likely theory. More to the point is the teaching of the Midrash[54] that the Almighty vowed that the Western Wall would never be destroyed.

The second difference is that the *kothel* is no mere dead relic of a forgotten past. It is a timeless center of ceaseless prayer. Through the centuries Jews have ever gathered there to pray; and this is still going on, a very thriving "business at the old stand." How accurate is the designation of our Sages for the Temple site, where the *kothel* stands: "*talpiyoth* — the mound (*tel*) to which all mouths (*piyoth*) turn: the mound toward which all mouths pray."[55]

When the heathen built their stone structures and monuments for their purposes — the purposes did not last. The people vanished, and the purposes went with the wind. When our ancestors and our people set up their monuments in stone for *their* reasons, the purposes endured. Jacob erected a *matzéva* to form a focal point for Divine worship. To this day we gather regularly in our synagogues and pray — to the same abiding Creator and Protector. He set a *matzéva* as a testimonial to peace with Laban. To this day we do our utmost to find peace and make it last. When we say hello and goodbye in Hebrew, it is a blessing of peace: *shalom*. (Unfortunately, in the Middle East we don't get too much cooperation in this direction.)

Jacob placed a tombstone at Rachel's grave, so that our people would know where to turn, to pray and seek God's help. To this day the Tomb of Rachel stands, on the road to Bethlehem. It is second only to the Western Wall as a magnet or focal center for Jews from all over the world, to come there and pour out their hearts in prayer. This was actually a promise implied in Scripture: for when Rachel died, we read in the Torah, *Then Jacob set up a* matzéva *upon her grave; this is the* matzéva *of Rachel's grave to this day* (Genesis 35:20). And the Zohar (I 175a) adds: Said R. Yosé: What is the reason [for these added words in the verse]? It means that that ϡite will never become concealed [lost to sight] until "this day" when the Holy, Blessed One is destined to bring the dead back to life. . . .

What is our secret? By what "Jewish mystique" have these purposes of ours, expressed in small, simple monuments of stone, lasted through the centuries? The clue to the answer lies in the Hebrew word for stone: אבן *e-ven*. When Jacob blessed his twelve sons on his deathbed, to Joseph he spoke in poetic imagery of Joseph's triumph over adversity, by the Almighty's aid. Then Jacob added, משם רועה אבן ישראל (Genesis 49:24), which Onkelos renders, "from there [as a result of that, you became] the shepherd [the provider, sustaining] the *e-ven* of Israel"; and what does *e-ven* mean? — it is a combined or condensed form of *av* and *ben*, "father and son." (In other words, it was granted Joseph to maintain his father and brothers — and their families — during the years of famine.)

So the word *e-ven* (stone) connotes a combination of father and son. This is our secret: the inner core of our history lies in the link and cooperation of father and son.

Early one morning Abraham and Isaac went off together, because the Almighty had bidden Abraham offer up this only son of his as a sacrifice to Him. Then Abraham sighted the place for the sacrifice afar off. The two left the servants behind, and father and son continued alone; Scripture recounts simply, *and they went on, the two of them, together* (Genesis 22:6). Knowing nothing of his father's plans, Isaac asked him, *Here are the fire and the wood, but where is the lamb for a burnt-offering? And Abraham said: God will see about a lamb for a burnt-offering, my son* (ibid. 7-8).

The Gaon of Vilna notes that the accent (*trop*) marks indicate a slight pause after the word "lamb", indicating that Abraham meant to hint, "God will see about the lamb; for a burnt-offering — my son!" Rashi cites the Midrash[56] that he thus implied, "God will see about a lamb; and if there is no lamb for a burnt-offering, then it will be — my son." But another view in the Midrash[57] is that he told him the truth outright, point-blank — and Isaac accepted it; he took it without flinching, panicking or rebelling; and Scripture continues, *and they went on, the two of them, together*.

Our people did not go in for carving in stone impressive inscriptions of glorious achievements. They incised in their hearts a determination and dedication to serve the Almighty. *Keep My mitzvoth and live*, He told us, *and My Torah like the apple of your eye. Bind them about your fingers, write them on the tablet of your heart* (Proverbs 7:2-3). This dedication every father taught his son, every tutor his pupil, through the long odyssey of our age-old faith. And whatever the cost, whatever the sacrifices required, whatever pain and tragedy came from a hostile irrational world about, that knew how to persecute, pillage and burn, *they went on, the two of them, together — e-ven*, father and son. From father to son, the Torah lived on. And thus our faith endures today.

As Jacob put a *matzéva* on Rachel's grave, Jewry has made this its normal practice, to set a tombstone on the grave of a parent who has departed this world. We might believe that it is to perpetuate the departed parent's memory — but that cannot be its exact purpose. What is not memorable about a human being will not be kept in mind, beyond the covering sands of time, by any tombstone or monument. As the Sages teach,[58] from the Creation it was Heaven's wish that the dead should be forgotten by the heart. What is all too human about a person's life — the trivial and ephemeral, the shoddy and the banal; all the small change arising from the frailty and weakness of human nature — must vanish with a person's departure and be mercifully forgotten.

For this, no monument can help. For splendid stone creations can be made even for evil lives. Some 2,000 years ago, a thoughtful Greek observed, "Do not, good sir, judge the dead by his monument. The stone is senseless, and can cover vile corpses as well as any other."[59] Only, as a Roman poet in the 4th century noted wisely, "Death comes even to the monumental stones and the names inscribed on them."[60]

On the other hand, what *is* memorable in a person's life needs no monument. How truly our Sages taught, אֵין עוֹשִׂין נְפָשׁוֹת לַצַּדִּיקִים; דִּבְרֵיהֶם; הֵן הֵן זִכְרוֹנָן Tombstones cannot [really] be made for righteous men of piety; their words are their [lasting] memorial.[61] The words of Torah that they learned and taught, accompanied by their actions that spoke yet louder than words, must leave their own imperishable impact. With their thoughts and acts of piety and kindness they leave an enduring influence on those who knew them. This is their true memorial.

For the true memorial to a parent's life is implied by the significance inherent in the Hebrew word for stone: *e-ven* — a combination of *av* and *ben*, father and son. The lasting element in a man's life lies in the link he forged between the generations. For decades it has been fashionable in the world at large to speak of a generation gap — the unbridgeable chasm between the old and the young. It has been fashionable to say glibly, "My parents don't understand me." The clue to the supple strength and healthy

351

life of authentic Judaism has been *e-ven*, *av* and *ben*, father and son — not the generation gap, but the generation link!

Through the course of our history, the young have understood the vital, essential enduring values of the Torah, the age-old faith that gave dignity and meaning to their parents' lives. And they have continued in the same Heaven-blessed path. וילכו שניהם יחדיו *They went on, the two of them, together* — whatever the sacrifices it might require.

The true memorial to a parent can emerge only in the life-style of the child, grown to adulthood with his own life to live. There it should be perceived, as a hallowing influence and a benison. When a son has learned to value his departed parent's religiosity and devotion to *yiddishkeit*, and he determines to continue on this path, that is the only structure of permanence which he can erect to commemorate his parent's life.

How beautiful beyond price it has always been when down through the ages, in unbroken tradition, a family line has kept faith with authentic Judaism, observing the Sabbath and the laws of kosher food, attending the synagogue, and making certain that the children receive a sound Torah education.

Now, when Jacob set a tombstone on Rachel's grave, it became a landmark, where his descendants could seek Heaven's help against calamity and misfortune, through the channels of prayer. This has remained the purpose of every tombstone erected for a dear relative who is gone. In a time of deep trouble, when one's own inner resources fail, a Jew has traditionally gone to the hallowed burial-ground, to the tombs of beloved kin and the graves of men of piety and learning — knowing that there his prayer would ascend to Heaven, and the spirit of the departed would invoke Divine mercy for him.

When children, grown to the years of adulthood, sometimes strayed from the Torah's pathway, and crisis and disaster broke in on them, how often it was the *matzéva* on a parent's grave, like the Tomb of Rachel, that gently, silently reminded them to turn back in prayer to their Father in heaven.

Thus, in life as in death, we built the mosaic of our enduring, imperishable way of faith — out of our unique durable "stone": *e-ven, av* and *ben*, father and son, going on together. Out of this link of the generations have come the modest monuments, markers and *matzévoth* of our Jewish life. With stone and with faith we have formed our permanance.

We might well recall another point from the teaching of our Sages. Ordinarily stone is a heavy material. We still marvel at the feats of ancient peoples in moving the massive blocks to erect their impressive structures, left as lifeless memorials to a dead past. For us, the burden of our structures of stone has been light — because it has been a burden of *e-ven*, *av* and *ben*, father and son, linked in faith across the spans of time.

The Ten Commandments too were of stone: *He gave Moses . . . the two tablets of the testimony, tablets of stone, written with the finger of God* (Exodus 31:18). They were large blocks of heavy sapphire stone, say the Sages, measuring forty *se'ah* in volume (18.5 cubic feet; 528,884 cubic centimeters).[62] Yet Moses handled them with the greatest of ease: they carried themselves, as it were; they were weightless. Only when he came down Mount Sinai and saw the people dancing madly in idol-worship around the Golden Calf — only then was there a drastic change. He saw the letters, that God had incised into the stone, flying off. Blank meaningless tablets were left, with no people in view to keep the Commandments. Suddenly, say the Sages,[63] Moses felt their full crushing weight: *he saw the calf and the dancing, and Moses' anger flared, and he smashed them at the foot of the mountain* (Exodus 32:19).

Without a living faith, monuments of stone are so much burdensome dead weight. They might as well be smashed. When we learn and obey the Divine letters of the Torah, then we build our life of faith out of *e-ven, av* and *ben*: the durable stone of the link between father and son, the bond that spans the generations. And to this, every *matzéva* erected to a good Jew, every tombstone to a life of value that ended, makes its imperishable contribution.

## ❧ TOLERANCE IN UNIFORM

By a pond near Concord, Massachusettus, a thoughtful American wrote in the 19th century,[64] "The mass of men live lives of quiet desperation. . . . A stereotyped but unconscious despair is concealed even under what are called the games and amusements of mankind." Life had a way of becoming humdrum, turning into an endless round or grind of routine work and insipid social activities. There was a wish for adventure, a yearning for a life of bravery, with some glory shining in it. So men thought it a fine thing to serve as soldiers, in peace or in war. It was so tempting and alluring. "Glory is the soldier's prize," wrote a Scottish poet;[65] "the soldier's wealth is honor."

It looked splendid to dress up in a striking uniform and go marching in rank to "all the delusive seduction of martial music."[66] The profession became so widespread that in the 19th century an Englishman wryly observed,[67] "Man is a military animal — glories in gunpower and loves parades." After all, just about every country in Europe had to have a standing army. A sardonic French author put it this way:[68] "Beyond some rare exceptions . . . man may be defined as an animal with a musket. Give him a fine uniform with the hope of fighting, and he will be happy. Also, we make the military calling the noblest, which is true in a sense: for it is the oldest calling, as the oldest of mankind made war."

Wasn't it obviously a glorious profession, bespeaking valor, bravery, courage and such? Who else could appear as such a bold he-man? No wonder Samuel Johnson, pontificating from his seat of learning in 18th century London, grunted, "Every man thinks meanly of himself for not having been a soldier. . . ."[69] They looked so handsome and dashing. In 1907 George M. Cohan (Irish, not Jewish, despite the interesting name) wrote and sang a song on the Broadway stage, that began, "There's something about a uniform." In one of Dickens' novels, a character confidently asserts that "a good uniform must work its way with the women, sooner or later." Another author asked, "What female heart can withstand a redcoat?" And with his own caustic wit George Bernard Shaw declared, "When the military man approaches, the world locks up its spoons and packs off its womankind."[70]

Would you doubt the allure of a uniform and military parades? Consider the history of the Grand Army of the Republic, the organization of veterans of the American Civil War. What did they have to celebrate? — their share in a miserable corrosive internal war that left America scarred for decades? a war in which brother had to fight against brother? Yet every year there was a magnificent reunion, where they all put on their old uniforms and marched again to the spirited army bands. When time retired them from this annual rite, the veterans of the two world wars took over, under the name of the American Legion, and *they* marched splendidly.

Well, the French author cited above wrote that "with rare exceptions . . . man may be defined as an animal with a musket," etc.[68] Unknown to him perhaps, those "rare exceptions" include the ranks of observant Jewry through the centuries of our history. Whatever dreams of glory beckoned others to a military life, our people failed to share those dreams. With the insight of our Sages to guide them, for our people the soldier's way remained a road not taken.

The tractate *Shabbath* in the Mishnah begins with the rule that on the Sabbath it is forbidden to carry anything from a private into a public domain, or vice versa. The sixth chapter makes it clear, though, that ornaments (e.g. women's jewelry) may generally be worn as part of one's dress, unless the Sages had a reason for banning them.

Now, in the time of the Mishnah there were no military uniforms, but there were pieces of armor that a warrior put on, and there were weapons and arms that he buckled on or carried. So in the second *mishnah* (paragraph) of this sixth chapter of *Shabbath* we find an interesting law: If a man wore a piece of armor on the Sabbath, such as a metal helmet, a coat-of-arms, or iron footwear reaching to the knees (greaves), by the law of the Torah it could not be forbidden. He was wearing it as clothing. Yet the Sages banned it! Such things were worn for battle. They had no place in the spirit of the Sabbath. It never entered the minds of the Sages to permit wearing such items because they made a man look handsome and dashing.

What of actual weapons and arms, though? Surely, if a woman might wear jewerly and finery pinned to her clothes, a man should be permitted, for instance, to buckle on his sword in its shining decorative scabbard? About this, opinion was divided. We read in the fourth *mishnah*: A man is not to go out [on the Sabbath] with a sword, a bow, a shield, a lance[71] or a spear. . . . R. Eliezer said: They are ornaments for him [and so he may wear them]. But the Sages said: They are nothing but disgraceful — for Scripture states, *and they shall beat their swords into plowshares and their spears into pruning-hooks; nation shall not lift up sword against nation, neither shall they learn war any more* (Isaiah 2:4).

The reasoning of the Sages is simple: If in the ultimate future, when the world will be as the Almighty wants, armor and arms will have no place in it, they cannot be considered ornamental for a Jew on the Sabbath, because obviously the Almighty really wants no part of them.

What of R. Eliezer, though? Why did he permit wearing arms on the Sabbath? Did he believe they made a man so handsome and dashing that they might be worn like any diamond-studded tiepin? In the Talmud,[72] Abbaye explained: What is R. Eliezer's reason . . . ? — because it is written in Scripture, *Gird your sword on your thigh, O mighty one, your glory and your majesty* (Psalms 45:4). The Torah is our supreme authority, and it called the sword a man's "glory and majesty." R. Kahana asked R. Huna, however, "But this was written about the words of the Torah!" The reply was: A verse of Scripture cannot be divested of its plain meaning.

R. Eliezer would seem to have a powerful argument. If a sword girded on a man's thigh is his glory and majesty, it is clearly ornamental, no? Yet the Sages were not swayed by this. To them it was inconceivable that the Torah really meant to glorify an armed warrior. As far as they were concerned, the verse is a metaphor, plainly telling a person to gird and arm himself for life with the Torah's immortal teachings. The Almighty could not have meant us to understand anything else by it. So the Zohar (I 240b) notes: "Is *this* glory and majesty, to buckle on weapons and thus become attired? When a person engages in Torah study and wages the Torah's battle, girding himself about with it — that is praisewrothy; that is glory and majesty!"

Thus the Midrash[73] applies the verse (about girding on the sword) to Moses, "who attained the Torah, that is likened to a sword." As the Sages taught, because he went up Mount Sinai and brought down the Torah, Scripture terms him a conqueror: *You ascended on high and seized capture; you took gifts for men* (Psalms 68:19).[74]

After Moses it has remained the task of every student and scholar to "ascend on high and capture the Torah" anew, to make it again and again "a gift for men," by weaving it into their everyday activities and into Jewish community life. This, for the Sages, is the plain meaning of Scripture's call to "gird on your sword": to become imbued and fortified with the Torah, as weapon and armor.[75]

What of the ordinary Jew, though, who lacks the time or the training for regular Torah study? The verse applies equally, says the Zohar (I 28b), to *Sh'ma yisraél*, the mighty affirmation of our faith and loyalty to God, which we recite in our prayers morning and night. Of this affirmation of faith, continues the Zohar, Scripture states, *The high praises of God are in their throat, and a two-edged sword in their hand* (Psalms 149:6).

With the constant, concentrated study of the Torah, and the unswerving loyalty to our Maker that the observant Jew renews every day, we wield our sword in the world: the two-edged weapon of moral discipline and religious growth, to free man from his enslavement to his passions. It is this battle which must be fought and won, if mankind is to find its way out of its moral morass, where it is forever threatened by its own propensity and itch for mutual self-destruction, with *its* dazzling, incredible weapons of "glory and majesty."

Of the world at large it was well observed that "the mass of men live lives of quiet desperation."[64] Of the ranks of devout Jewry in general, and our Torah scholars in particular, it may be well observed that they have always lived lives of quiet heroism.

The world about was ever a source of storm and stress for our people. We have been subject to decimation and dispersal, extortion and expulsion, pillage and pogrom — yet when did Torah study and *Sh'ma yisraél* ever stop sounding forth, loud and clear? Wherever we traveled, with or without a visa, we took the Torah with us, and our prayer-books, too. Whatever homes we built, we also built our houses of prayer and study. The age-old words of *Sh'ma yisraél* continued to throb and pulse with life. The words of the Torah ever lit up heart and mind, from generation to generation.

In a stage-play by a 19th-century dramatist, a character quotes a supposed proverb, "The man-at-war is the only man"[76] (or, in Americanese, there's a real he-man for you, dear paleface). At the Red Sea, after their miraculous rescue from the Egyptians, our people sang, *The Lord is a man of war!* (Exodus 15:3). As our people realized from the Torah's words and from experience, war is God's business. At times armed conflict was necessary and inevitable in our people's past — but only by the sanction of His word and the Torah's law. "Even though wars are recorded in the Torah," says the Midrash,[77] "the wars too were written down only for the purpose of peace." The battles Israel fought were vitally necessary to establish peace in its world; their description in the Torah gave our people no sanction for any militant approach in life. Not that way lay glory for us. . . . So the Sages banned wearing weapons and armor on the Sabbath, to look handsome and heroic.

The Torah bids the Jew to "gird on your sword, O mighty one." The Jew was born to give battle. But our battlefield is the *béth midrash*; our weapons, the Divine word of law; and our enemies are ignorance and illusion, man's bestial nature and venal capacity for corruption and evil.

Around the year 1200 a devout Jew in France wrote for his people to read:[78] "If hostile persons fell upon you to wrest you from the Torah of your reverent faith, you would have given your life [in resistance; as Scripture says] *Indeed for Thy sake are we slain all the day long* (Psalms 44:23). How much they [our people] suffered at the time of forced conversion and martyrdom. So now, should a sickening attack of the evil impulse befall you, you must [resist and] triumph over it — because it is harder to recover from that than from the most difficult illness. Therefore, if you overcome it, you deserve ample reward, recompense according to the pain; for it is a great achievement to win the battle over one's vile evil inclination."

Thus born to give battle, the observant Jew goes garbed in *his* uniform: a four-cornered garment with a special tassel at each corner, called *tzitzith*. Why do we wear it? — so that *you shall see it and remember all the commandments of the Lord, and do them; and you shall not go straying after your own heart and your own eyes* (Numbers 15:39).

His uniform on, the observant Jew armors himself well: Each morning he puts on a pair of *t'fillin* (phylactereies) in preparation for prayer: on his forehead, close to his mind, and on the biceps of his left arm, close to his heart.

To us the *t'fillin* may not look very formidable. Our Sages knew better. "How do we know," asks the Talmud,[79] "that *t'fillin* are a source of might for Jewry? — because it is written, *Then all the peoples of the earth shall see that the name of the Lord is pronounced over you, and they shall be afraid of you* (Deuteronomy 28:10); and it was taught: R. Eliezer said: This means [on account of] the *t'fillin* of the head." (As *tosafoth* points out, this is prominently visible on the forehead, whereas the phylactery of the arm is traditionally covered.)

"The soldier should be fear-inspiring," wrote a Roman historian some 2,000 years ago.[80] This the Jewish "soldier of God" has ever been, not by buckling on a flashing sword and gnashing his teeth ferociously, but by leading the onslaught, patiently and steadily, on depravity and evil in the world. Into the consciousness of mankind the image of the Jew in his *t'fillin*, worshipping the Almighty in devotion, has impressed itself. Casting awe by his religiosity, the observant Jew has continually instilled an indelible concept into the awareness of humanity: that to survive and grow spiritually, man must live in accord with Divine law.

Such has been the Jew's way of warfare, and such his "awesome armor," making him an object of awe in the perception of the world, as he endures past the disappearance of mighty nations and empires.

Interestingly enough, Scripture tells that Moses sent 12,000 Hebrews to battle Midian (Numbers 31:5), and not one failed to return safely (*ibid*. 49). The Midrash notes that R. Huna said:[81] Not one of them put on the *t'fillin* of the head before the *t'fillin* of the hand (in violation of the law); for had one of them put on his *t'fillin* in reverse order, Moses would not have praised them, and they would not have come out of it unharmed.

Even when our people had to wage war literally, it was the *t'fillin* (say the Sages) that made the Hebrews mighty warriors who could strike terror and emerge from battle safely — because they observed this mitzvah strictly. In the Talmud there is a related teaching. By the law of the Torah, when the Israelites formed ranks for *milḥemeth r'shuth*, a voluntary permitted war, whoever was *afraid and faint-hearted* (Deuteronomy 20:8) was to leave the lines and go home. In the Talmud we read:[82] It was taught: If someone chatted between putting on the *t'fillin* of the hand and the *t'fillin* of the head, it is a sin in his heavenly account, and because of it he is to turn back from the army ranks (TB *Sotah* 44b).

The slightest defect in observing the mitzvah of *t'fillin* would endanger a soldier's life in battle. For the Israelite always depended not on his own strength and might, but on Divine aid. Small wonder, then, that by the standing order of the present *rebbe* (ḥassidic spiritual leader) of Lubavitch, his *ḥassidim* in Israel go out several times a year to the Israeli army posts and try to get every single soldier in Israel's defense forces to put on *t'fillin*.

Well, whether they had to fight a physical enemy or not, every day since time immemorial our people have put on *tzitzith* as their uniform, and *t'fillin* as their Divine armor. The soldiers of the world have always had their uniforms, weaponry and duties; and observant Jewry, the Almighty's soldiers, have always had theirs. *These come with chariots, and those with horses; but we speak the name of the Lord our God* (Psalms 20:8). Others put on their uniforms and went strutting in perfect formation. As Shakespeare put it,[82] they went

> all furnished, all in arms,
> all plumed like estridges that wing the wind,
> bated like eagles having lately bathed;
> glittering in golden coats, like images;
> as full of spirit as the month of May,
> and gorgeous as the sun at midsummer.

They fancied themselves real men, brave and true. Yet how rightly Einstein observed, "The man who enjoys marching in line and file to the strains of martial music falls beneath my contempt: He received his great brain by mistake; the spinal cord would have been amply sufficient."[83]

We took a different line of development, using very much the mind — in the intensive study of the Torah. There has our battleground been, and there our lasting victories and achievements. How rightly an illustrious rabbi of Prague wrote in the 18th century:[84] "O my sons, my brethren . . . idle chatter and tales of wars — who will triumph and who will be defeated . . . to view the parades of those who bear bows and shields and devices of war . . . such things are fitting for high officers and their lieutenants; but what have we to do with that, thus to waste our time?"

*I am for peace,* hymned the psalmist, *but when I speak, they are for war* (Psalms 120:7). We have gone our tranquil way with the Torah, and the people of the world have taken their road of belligerence and bellicosity. Between their love of a good fight and their love of uniforms and parades, they could not give up their enjoyment of jousting and scrapping, and having a rousing little battle once in a while.

Yet alas, war and conflict left a charnel-house behind. Human beings were left miserable and woebegone, and frightened of their own destructiveness. In sheer self-defense they had to find an alternative to their natural belligerence — and at last, of necessity, they developed something called tolerance.

First on the neighborly level, among individuals, then on the community level, and so through city, state and country, and finally between countries, the civilized people on this earth developed an approach called tolerance: live and let live. It even appears in the Preamble of the United Nations' Charter, as one of the aims of the member nations: "to practice tolerance and live together . . . as good neighbors. . . ."

This has been the world's answer to its own aggression, that has proved so costly and so deadly. Yet what does tolerance mean? When you boil away the vapors and smoke-screens of effulgent oratory, what is left is essentially this: "Look: I do not like you. I am really sorry you are here. In fact, truth to tell, I cannot stand you. I dearly wish you were elsewhere — say, on another planet. But since you will not conveniently go away and disappear, I will tolerate you." The basic meaning of the word is to endure something and put up with it. Its origin is a Greek and Latin root meaning to bear a burden. How aptly tolerance has been defined as "the lowest form of human cooperation . . . the drab, uncomfortable halfway house between hate and charity."[85]

If you do not perceive this sense in the word on the local level, consider the international level. Since both the United States and the Soviet Union have atomic weaponry enough to change each other's appearance on the map quite significantly, of necessity these two world powers developed a policy called détente (you shouldn't know from it). Détente is tolerance on a global scale; and there it is quite obvious that each world power would dearly like the other to drop dead or do something equally refreshing; but since such a spectacular thing is not likely to happen, each has to abide the other's presence somehow. That is tolerance.

Of what real worth is it then, on the international, national, state or city level, or even in a neighborhood or a city block or an apartment building? Is this how human beings are to live together in harmony? with a thin veneer of politeness over a lurking cordial detestation? Scratch the surface of tolerance, and the hostility underneath flares out.

The observant, authentic Jew is not tolerant. He knows nothing of tolerance. *O Lord*, he is given to praying, *deliver my soul from lying lips, from a deceitful tougue* (Psalms 120:2). He is merely clear on what he accepts and what he does not. In his worship of God he knows only one way: the path of the Torah. With every fiber of his being he knows there can be no other way. (In fact, you don't have to be Jewish to realize that in religion there can be no true tolerance. Early in the 17th century a Puritan minister in colonial America wrote, "He that is willing to tolerate any religion, or discrepant way of religion, beside his own . . . either doubts his own or is not sincere in it." Late in the 19th century the supreme head of Catholicism was shorter and snappier: "The equal toleration of all religions . . . is the same thing as atheism."[86])

What then is an observant Jew's attitude toward a neighbor? — not tolerance but love, the unalloyed affection of a brother — a far cry from tolerance. We have the Torah's golden rule: *you shall love your neighbor as yourself* (Leviticus 19:18).

But, you might say, this is easy. It applies to other observant Jews — as it were, members of the same club. Consider, then, a *gér*, a convert to Judaism — a man born into a different people, a different faith, a different culture. Somehow he has decided, despite the enormous difficulties and hardships it will mean, to become Jewish and observe the 613 *mitzvoth* of the Torah faithfully.

Obviously we should accept him fully and extend to him the love and

361

affection that we owe every observant Jew. He is now included in the command, *you shall love your neighbor as yourself.* The Torah was not so sure of us, however. It is easy enough to like a fellow-Jew, from your own kind of people and background. The *gér* may be practicing your religion very commendably; but the original, basic meaning of *gér* is stranger, alien; and that he certainly is. He probably cannot say the Hebrew prayers and benedictions with the same fluency and right accent as you. His mannerisms of speech and behavior are most likely different too, and tend to jar you. You probably won't feel comfortable with him; and your natural, instinctive reaction will be to look down on him from an attitude of comfortable superiority.

So the Almighty (as it were) took no chances. He added an extra commandment: *And you shall love the* gér, *the proselyte stranger* (Deuteronomy 10:19). Similarly, as the anonymous author of *Séfer haḤinnuch* noted in the 13th century,[87] the Torah added an extra warning not to hurt a *gér*, either in business matters or in ordinary social conversation — although there are already laws of the Torah forbidding us to wrong or hurt any fellow-Jew. For you see (this anonymous author writes) it is much easier to mistreat a *gér* than an ordinary Jew. An ordinary man always has friends and *mishpocheh* (relatives) to stand up for him and defend his rights. A *gér*, though, as the Talmud noted so insightfully,[88] is like a newborn child. For a long time he surely feels lost between two worlds. He has cut himself off from his roots, from the milieu into which he was born; and he comes groping and aching to find himself in a new milieu — among Jews. He needs the soil of genuine acceptance and friendship to strike roots and start flourishing anew.

Well, the Torah does not command us to tolerate him. Over and above the general precept to "love your neighbor as yourself" it gives us a special order: *you shall love the* gér. And as Rambam notes,[89] this term "love" is not to be taken lightly. "In most of the Midrashim," he writes, "it was pointed out that the Lord gave us the same order about a *gér* as He gave about Himself (be He exalted). He stated, *you shall love the Lord your God* (Deuteronomy 6:5); and He stated, *you shall love the* gér."[90]

This charts the path that the observant Jew has taken through the ages, a path which has nothing to do with tolerance. Once a human being joins us in our system of faith, whatever his make-up, whatever his nature and personality, we have to love him in the same way as our Maker.

Yet behind this norm and practice in our life of faith lies a further concept. The original meaning of *gér* in Scripture is not a convert to Judaism (*he* is called a *gér tzedek*, a righteous proselyte, in Rabbinic literature). The original meaning is a stranger, an alien. Moses named his first son Gershom (denoting *gér*, an alien, *sham*, there) *because, he said, I was a gér in a foreign land* (Exodus 18:3). In peril for his life, he had fled from Egypt to Midian, where he married and became the father of two sons. He was never a convert in Midian, but an alien, feeling all the poignant loneliness and insecurity of an outsider.

In fact, Scripture makes it clear directly that the line is not to be drawn at proselytes: *And you shall love the* gér, *because you were* gérim *in the land of Egypt* (Deuteronomy 10:19). We certainly never became converts to any Egyptian religion. In our earliest period as a people we experienced the racking pain of alienation, of being strangers, outsiders, in a foreign land. So we are commanded to bear love, understanding and compassion for others who must suffer this plight — be they Jewish or not. Every human being is God's creation, in His image, living on earth by His express will. We have no sanction to overlook his pain or ignore his anguish if he is an "outsider" in our midst. As we must love God, so must we love His human beings.

Indeed, can the two requirements be split apart? Seven centuries ago, the illustrious sage Ramban (Naḥmanides) taught:[91] "Bestowing love is a positive commandment, as it is written, *and you shall love the Lord your God;* and this includes loving one's neighbor, which is thus [also] a positive commandment: *you shall love your neighbor as yourself* (Leviticus 19:18) — as we find in Midrash *B'réshith Rabbah* (24 end): This [to love one's neighbor as oneself] is a yet greater rule ... so you should not say: Since I have suffered disgrace, let my neighbor suffer disgrace with me. Said R. Tanḥuma: If you act like that, know Whom you are putting to shame — *in God's image He made him* (Genesis 1:27).

So to mistreat a human being is tantamount to mistreating the Almighty Himself. And how obviously right the Maharal of Prague is when he writes:[92] "... loving people is [in effect] loving the blessed God as well. For when one person bears another affection, he loves all the other's handiwork, that the other has wrought and formed. Therefore, when a person loves the blessed Lord, he cannot possibly fail to love His human beings; and if he hates people, he cannot possibly love the blessed Lord who created them. So too must the honor of his neighbor, created in God's image, be valued equally with the honor of God."

363

Over nineteen centuries ago a Jewish philosopher in Alexandria wrote,[93] "The nature which is pious is also kindly; and in the same person both qualities will be evident: holiness toward God and fairness toward man."

The point is echoed by the sages and scholars of *ḥassiduth*. In one volume[94] we find: We can take as an illustration two friends who bear each other great affection. Then each loves the other's children as he loves his own ... and he rejoices in the happiness of his friend's children as in the happiness of his own child; while his friend's distress seems to him literally like his own. Well, past any doubt we are the children of the blessed Lord (Deuteronomy 14:1). ...

In another volume of ḥassidic learning[95] it is noted, "If you do not know where, so to speak, the Almighty abides, there is a fully explicit verse in our holy Torah: *you shall love your neighbor as yourself; I am the Lord* (Leviticus 19:18). When you really love your neighbor as yourself, you will want him too to have all his needs. In that situation, *I am the Lord*: there, so to speak, you can find Me."

Another work of ḥassidic wisdom[96] interprets the verse this way: *you shall love your neighbor,* for as you relate to your neighbor in friendship and affection, כָּמוֹךָ אֲנִי ה' *like you, I am the Lord*. As a man acts toward his neighbor and acquaintance here below, with friendliness and good qualities of character, so the Divine King on high will relate to him.

This, then, is what the Torah requires of the Jewish people: mutual friendship, affection and concern. (Indeed, one ḥassidic teaching makes a strong point: *You shall love your neighbor as yourself.* If a man knows something bad and deplorable about himself, he will hate this evil quality or element; he knows it needs to be corrected or eliminated. But normally he does not hate himself on account of it. This is the attitude he is required to take toward a neighbor — because all Jewry is one body.)[97]

Above all, if we know the Torah, we know that all human beings are God's creatures. By the Torah's teaching, Adam was the first man on earth, created by the Almighty himself; so he is the ancestor of all mankind. And Adam was neither Hebrew nor Israelite nor Jew. He was simply a man. The Mishnah (*Sanhedrin* iv 5) makes the point clearly: "For this reason man was created as a single individual [the Almighty did not bring several into being] ... for the sake of peace among humankind — so that no one could ever say to another: My earliest forefather was greater than yours."

If all people on earth are descended from one primordial man, we are all ultimately of one family, and all equally human. Every person is entitled to equal status and consideration on this planet. Telling us that the Almighty created but one man as the ancestor of all is the Torah's way of teaching that in regard to basic rights, all men are created equal.

The Midrash makes the point yet more forcefully:[98]

הִתְחִיל לְקַבֵּץ אֶת עֲפָרוֹ שֶׁל אָדָם הָרִאשׁוֹן מֵאַרְבַּע פִּנּוֹת הָעוֹלָם, אָדוֹם שָׁחוֹר לָבָן יְרַקְרַק. אָדוֹם זֶה הַדָּם, שָׁחוֹר אֵלּוּ הַקְּרָבַיִם, לָבָן אֵלּוּ עֲצָמוֹת וְגִידִים, יְרַקְרַק זֶה הַגּוּף. וְלָמָּה מֵאַרְבַּע פִּנּוֹת הָעוֹלָם? שֶׁאָמַר הַקָּדוֹשׁ־בָּרוּךְ־הוּא: אִם יָבוֹא אָדָם מִמִּזְרָח לְמַעֲרָב אוֹ מִמַּעֲרָב לְמִזְרָח, אוֹ לְכָל מָקוֹם שֶׁיֵּלֵךְ, וְיַגִּיעַ קִצּוֹ לְהִפָּטֵר מִן הָעוֹלָם, שֶׁלֹּא תֹאמַר הָאָרֶץ, "אֵין עֲפַר גּוּפְךָ מִשֶּׁלִּי; חֲזוֹר לַמָּקוֹם שֶׁנִּבְרֵאתָ מִשָּׁם". אֶלָּא לְלַמֶּדְךָ שֶׁבְּכָל מָקוֹם שֶׁאָדָם הוֹלֵךְ וּבָא קִצּוֹ לְהִפָּטֵר מִן הָעוֹלָם, מִשָּׁם הוּא עֲפַר גּוּפוֹ וּלְשָׁם הוּא חוֹזֵר. (פרקי דר׳ אליעזר, כא)

[The Almighty] began to gather the dust [earth] for the first man from the four corners of the world: red, black, white, pale green. The red became the blood; the black, the innards; the white became the bones and sinews; and the pale green, the body. Why from the four corners of the world? — Said the Holy, Blessed One: If a man should come from the east to the west or from the west to the east, or wherever he may go, and his time comes to leave this world, let the earth not say, "The dust of your body is not mine. Go back to the location from which you were created." Let this rather teach you that wherever a man goes and his time comes to take his leave of this world, from there the dust of his body came, and there it is to return.

How bright and quick human beings have been, since time immemorial, at establishing basic reasons — axioms beyond question — why they are superior to others. Once it was realized that humans came in various colors (so to speak), that became an "obvious" basis for feelings of superiority. For lo and behold, you could find people in sundry shades and tints of white, yellow, red and brown....

Surely there is more than a hint in the Midrash that the idea of superiority by color is pure hogwash (or, expressed more delightfully, it is a pigment of the imagination).[99] The raw material that formed man, says the Midrash, was multi-colored. No man is all of one color, better or worse than another's. All human blood is red (although aristocrats used to like

365

the phrase "blue-blood"); all sinews and bones are white; and in the viscera there is always blackness. The processes of digestion and elimination are certainly the same for all. Then, if Adam's skin had a pale green tinge, surely in another sense all humans can be of several colors: Everyone can be green with envy, red with rage, or white with fear. Under certain psychological conditions, anyone might be "yellow" in the American slang sense of being cowardly. And many a white man has been justly called black-hearted. Moreover, who could not become *farshvartzt* — blackened with the grime and toil of the workaday world, the difficulties of dealing with obligations and cares? In the *Song of Songs* (1:5) we read, *I am black but comely*; and the Midrash applies the words to Jewry: "I am black all the days of the week, but comely on the Sabbath. I am black all the days of the year, but comely on *Yom Kippur*, the Day of Atonement."[100]

Jewry itself has been a living disproof of any theory of superiority by color. Our people have tended to acquire the physical characteristics of every kind of population among whom they lived. You can find Jews who look Hungarian or Turkish, Indian or Negro; and once there were even Chinese Jews, complete with pigtail. Yet all were and are of one people, stemming from a common ancestry.

Prejudice, however, is little affected by visible facts. People see what they want to see, and believe what they find comfortable. The "colorful" ideas of superiority have survived to our day; and of course, long ago they led to a "logical" and inevitable development: the "theory" of racial superiority. Only a few decades ago this reached its zenith or nadir (depending on how you look at it) when the Nazis preached with a hysterical intensity their doctrine that their obese, pudgy countrymen (brilliantly caricatured by the late Arthur Szyk) were members of the Aryan "master race," typified by blond, blue-eyed Norsemen; while all Jews were of a terribly inferior racial stock, a virtual disease among mankind.

The Midrash continues, however. If people will not accept that all humans are equal regardless of color, let them contemplate death. In the grave all are certainly equal; death is the great leveller. And for this, says the Midrash, there is a reason. Physically, all human beings are of the same raw material. Like the earth itself, the human body is composed of the same ninety-two elements that make up all matter on our planet. For Scripture tells that man was created from the dust of the earth; and, says the Midrash, when the time came to create him, the Almighty gathered the raw material from the four corners of the earth.

The earth of our planet is not the same everywhere. Some parts have rich, fertile soil, with plenty of water for irrigation; other parts are desert land. There are areas with oil fields or gold mines or diamond mines. There are sites that yield copper, tin, aluminum, uranium, or what-have-you. People have become rich or poor by the kind of land they have gotten.

The same is not true about humans. Short or tall, fat or thin, all human bodies are worth about as much; all are made from the same ingredients, from the common stuff of mankind. No patch of earth, says the Midrash, has the right to refuse a man burial because, supposedly, it is superior to him in its physical nature. As an English proverb puts it, the cemetery is the place which receives all without asking questions.[101]

Did the Midrash mean to make this point only about the dead — that in death all are equal, and entitled to a resting-place? Or, if the Almighty made this rule implicit in His creation, that for his final repose the earth anywhere will accept any man, did He mean to teach the people on this earth a profound lesson on how to relate to other *living* people?

The American poet Robert Frost wrote an unforgettable poem called *The Death of the Hired Man*. Out of his vision and compassion he conjured up a scene of an old man coming back to a Vermont farm where he had come intermittently over many years to work as a hired hand. The farmer's wife found him "huddled against the barn-door fast asleep, / a miserable sight, and frightening too." She dragged him into the house, where he was asleep by the stove when her husband came home.

The farmer was annoyed to learn that the man was there. This hired hand had never been dependable, disappearing when he was needed most and coming only, as it seemed, when he had no other place to go to. At last, as the farmer went on talking with his wife about it, "Warren," she said, "he has come home to die...". Her husband responded, "It all depends on what you mean by home. / Of course, he's nothing to us, any more / than was the hound that came a stranger to us / out of the woods, worn out upon the trail."

His wife's simple reply is perhaps the most touching thing in the poem: "*Home is the place where, when you have to go there, / they have to let you in.*" (As the poem continues, the farmer becomes reconciled to accepting his visitor, only to go inside and find the man dead.)

The Midrash began the lesson that man must learn: that when a human being is worn out, this earth of ours must give him a place of final rest wherever he has come, wherever he is. In his dramatic tableau of a Vermont farmhouse, in his local New England scene with a meaning for all mankind, Robert Frost as it were took the lesson further: Not only the dead, silent earth must accept everyone. It is a moral obligation for living people too.

The Jewish people learned this lesson long before Frost wrote his memorable poem. We had the Torah's imperishable account of the creation of Adam, one man, as the ancestor of all. It was enough for us to have a prophet exclaim, *Have we not all one father? Did not one God create us?* (Malachi 2:10). It has ever been our task to make His will our own; and whatever people He has seen fit to bring into being, it has been for us to accept them, as His creatures, formed in His image.

No, we did not learn tolerance. We did not grant recognition, equal status or equal time to any way of life but the way of the Torah. We could never accept darkness as equal to light; we could never accept blindness as equal to vision. Our intolerance, however, has applied only to the darkness and blindness in which so many have been content (even happy) to live, but not to the human beings themselves.

There is a charming anecdote told by *hassidim*[102] of a time when the noted *rebbe* R. Moshe Leyb of Sassov sat at his table at night, deeply immersed in his recondite Torah study. The hours flowed by, until, about midnight, he heard a knock at the window. Pulled by surprise out of his realm of profound contemplation, he looked up; and there, outside, stood an old (non-Jewish) reprobate from the neighborhood, thoroughly drunk, and motioning for the *rebbe* to let him in, so that he could sleep off the load of alcohol that he was carrying.

The *rebbe*'s first reaction was a flare of rage: How offensive it was for that old reprobate to disrupt his holy study so completely. His entire beautiful train of mystic thought was now gone, vanished. How dare the man come knocking here, at the *rebbe*'s window, to ask for a place to sleep?

Then R. Moshe Leyb of Sassov calmed down; and he thought, 'Nu, if the good Lord can bear to have him in this world of His, he probably needs to be here. (There must be a good reason for his existence here and now.) In that case, I will bear with him too.' He opened the door, and the old souse was soon fast asleep.

We have had little love, and less tolerance, for the spiritual blindness and darkness in which people have lived. But the Almighty told Adam, *dust you are, and to dust you shall return* (Genesis 3:19). Whatever man is given existence by Heaven's will, it is his fate to live in a body created from the same elements as the earth, until death returns that body to the earth, to revert to the basic elements of its composition. And between birth and death a man is entitled to his place on earth. Being of earth, a human being belongs on it as long as he lives.

All we have ever asked is that people not impose their blindness on us, nor impair our vision with their darkness. In ancient Israel, by the Torah's rule, if an alien accepted the seven laws which the Torah imposed on all mankind (e.g. not to practice idol-worship or rob or steal) he could live peacefully among our people as a *gér toshav*, an "alien settler." Under the guidance of our Sages, we did not impose on outsiders the benefits and obligations of our religion, by ramming it down their throats. (On the contrary, one Midrash teaches: *the Lord loves tzaddikim* (Psalms 146:8) — if a man wants to be a *tzaddik*, a righteous person of piety, even if he is a non-Jew he can do so. In another Midrash, Elijah the prophet avows, "I call Heaven and earth to witness that whether one is a non-Jew or Jew, man or woman, or a male or female bondservant, it is entirely according to his behavior that the sacred Divine spirit may abide upon him."[103])

We kept our way of faith, content to teach by example, and let the rest of the world go spinning merrily on its way. Alas, when we entered the decades and centuries of our odyssey in exile, this courtesy was not reciprocated. We found ourselves not merely in an alien milieu but in a hostile world. When you live exposed to plaguing attacks and demands, even for the sake of your immortal soul, to help you get straight to heaven in a clear column of smoke from the fire beneath you, there is a strong temptation, surely, to wish your unfriendly neighbors dead, so that you can find a little peace. Yet observant Jewry never developed such an approach or policy in its communal life.

There is the known story in the Talmud (TB *B'rachoth* 10a) of some roughnecks or ruffians in R. Meir's neighborhood who caused him a great deal of distress. As our grandfathers might have phrased it, they made him *tzores*. Well, R. Meir took to praying about them, that they should leave this world, so that he could have some peace. His wife B'ruryah asked him, however, "What do you think? [Prayer like that is permitted] because it is written, *Let sinners cease from the earth* (Psalms 104:35)? Is it then written *hot'im*, sinners? It is written *hatta'im*, sins! Furthermore, look at the end of the verse: *and the wicked shall be no more*. Once sins will cease, there will be no more wicked people! Then pray rather for them that they should repent. Once they have returned to the good path, there will be no more wicked

369

men there." He prayed for them (says the Talmud) and they changed through repentance.

Our way is to entreat Heaven, knowing that prayer can change things. For all human beings are God's creatures. We cannot serve Him by wishing them ill or doing them harm (unless they are actual murderers).

Our people went into exile, into the countries of Europe, and found themselves actually cursed and damned, not only by ignorant common persons filled with superstition, but by clerical spokesmen of a "religion of love." Around the year 1200, for instance, this message of "love" appeared in a papal letter: "The Jews, like Cain, are doomed to wander the earth as fugitives and vagabonds, and their faces are covered with shame." (To paraphrase a popular saying, such people were always ready to help us out. They only wanted to know which way we had come in.) Echoing centuries of such hatred and vituperation, a brilliant English dramatist of the 16th century, who had probably never seen a Jew in his life, wrote in one of his plays, "To undo a Jew is charity, and not sin."[104] A Ukrainian proverb sharpened the point considerably: "It lifts forty sins from the soul to kill a Jew."

In response, the sages and scholars of Jewry gave their people instructions like these: Beware of wronging people, whether in money matters or by words. Do not raise your hand against your fellow-man. Do not be resentful over trifles against any man, lest you gather enemies for nothing. Be trustworthy for every man. Do not be lazy to offer a friendly greeting to any and every man, including a non-Jew, for the sake of peace.[105]

Deriving from Spain in the early decades of the 14th century, these directives concerned behavior toward all people, whether Jewish or not. Over a century earlier, at about the same time that the papal letter cited above was written, a pious scholar in Germany wrote instructions like these:[106] It is forbidden to deceive any man, including a non-Jew; and those who curse non-Jews while giving them a [supposedly] friendly greeting, so that the non-Jew thinks the other has told him something good, commit a sin: for there can be no greater deceitfulness than this.... If a non-Jew conscientiously observes the seven commandments given to Noah's descendants [all mankind], beware of misleading him, for it is forbidden. Return him any found object that he has lost. Do not humiliate him, but rather treat him with greater respect than a Jew who does not busy himself with Torah study.... Just as you must act in good faith toward a Jew, so also toward a non-Jew.... If a Jew is in charge of tax-

370

collection and it has been settled that so much is to be taken [from a person], if he takes more from a non-Jew, in the end he will lose his possessions. . . . Know that although it was taught that one may deviate from the strict truth for the sake of peace, if a non-Jew or Jew comes and asks someone, "Lend me money," and the man will not willingly give him the loan because he fears the other may not repay him, he has no right to say [falsely] "I have no money.". . . If a Jew and non-Jew are together and the latter asks the former, "I want to go to this-and-this place; there are Jews there, and I am afraid they may swindle me. Tell me who is trust-worthy there and who is not" — that Jew should tell him, "Do not have any dealings with so-and-so and so-and-so" [etc. if they are unreliable]. . . . If a man sees a non-Jew committing a sin, let him deter him if he can; for the Holy, Blessed One sent Jonah to Nineveh [a city of non-Jews] to turn them back to the good path. . . .

These teachings were not wholly new and original. They were based on Talmudic dictums given centuries before. Thus the Sages teach that "the non-Jewish poor are to be sustained along with the Jewish mendicants; the non-Jewish sick are to be visited along with the Jewish; and the non-Jewish dead, buried along with deceased Jews — for the sake of peace. The same care is to be taken with a non-Jew's domestic animal as with a Jew's. Robbing a non-Jew is a more serious crime than robbing a Jew. If someone steals from a non-Jew, swears falsely to him, or falsely denies an obligation to him, ultimately he will treat a Jew in the same way." So too, the law that forbids deceiving a non-Jew is Talmudic.[107]

The astonishing thing, though, is that despite the conditions in which medieval Jewry existed, such laws continued to be formulated, taught and learned, to be practiced in daily life. Close to our time, a scholarly British authority on Jews and Judaism was moved to write, "When it is re-membered what were the outward conditions under which the Jews for the most part lived . . . the attitude of the Jewish mind toward the Christian tormentors is truly remarkable. Over and over again the Jewish moralists teach the lesson of charity and forbearance, of strictly honorable and truthful conduct, of kindly and helpful service a Christian as well as Jew. The hymns in the synagogue uttered the grief and the longing for the deliverance of tortured Israel, but seldom if ever a note of hatred against the oppressor. . . . And in controversial writings, or in books intended for the instruction of Jews in their religion, the difference in tone between Jewish and Christian polemics is as the difference between day and night."

371

Elsewhere this scholar wrote, "Criticism and dissent were of course to be found in Jewish writings, but not the excecration which filled so many Christian pages."[108]

The world at large heaved and puffed and struggled, and developed an approach called tolerance. Observant Jewry developed with the teachings of the Torah, guided by its scholars and sages. The Torah commanded, ואהבתם את הגר *you shall love the stranger, the alien, the outsider* (Deuteronomy 10:19). Our heritage taught us that one God created all humanity, from one common ancestor. Our bodies are all of the common material of the earth, and to the earth they are to return. In death, our bodies must find acceptance in the ground wherever we are. Then we should find a right to exist *on* the earth while we live, wherever we go.

So we hoped and wished; but in the world's reality, things were different. The people in the world about us developed tolerance; and as we might say, our people responded with a "tolerance" of their own. Heinrich Heine put it well: "A brotherly forbearance / has united us for ages: / You tolerate my breathing / and I tolerate your rages!"[109]

Of course, the peoples among whom Jewry lived spoke not only of tolerance. There was also love. In contrast to our "stern and vengeful old testament" they had a "new testament" filled with teachings of kindly affection. And with all that love, nation after nation locked its doors to our people.

How poignantly true the words of Robert Frost ring: *Home is the place where, when you have to go there, they have to take you in.* Driven from our homeland into exile, we went traveling across the face of Europe in search of a home, a base to build a life on. And we found less than a simple welcome. "The Jews themselves, and all that is theirs, belong to the king." So read the law of Edward the Confessor, sovereign of England in the middle of the 11th century. Some three centuries later a king of France made the condition of our people even clearer: "Jews have no country or place of their own in all Christendom where they can live and move and have their being, except by the purely voluntary permission and good will of the lord or lords under whom they wish to settle to dwell under them as their subjects, and who are willing to receive them and accept them to this end."[110]

Clear, no? Our people were given a home sometimes, somewhere, by the good will or whim of a monarch or a local ruling nobleman; which meant that our forefathers could stay put as long as they were useful (profitable) to their ruler, or until some impulse of so-called religious zeal and piety moved him to expel them, in order to gain favor in Rome.

In 1290 the Jews (some 16,000) were cordially invited to leave England; and none resettled there until 1650. France had expulsions from most of its territory in 1306 and 1394, which kept Jews out until 1789. The mass evictions from Spain in 1492 and from Portugal several years later (involving at least 100,000 Jews) are well known. When the plague of the Black Death struck Europe (in 1348–50), the Jews were blamed (they were supposed to have poisoned the wells, just for fun or something); and many local expulsions of whole communities followed, especially in Germany.

In 1569 a papal decree ordered the Jews in all lands owned or ruled by the papacy, kicked out within three months. And so it went in Europe, wherever our people tried to build some semblance of a home life. This, however, is only half the story. It was once well said that the world was divided into two groups of nations: those that wanted to expel the Jews, and those that did not want to receive them. Thus, from the 15th century to 1772, Jews were absolutely forbidden to step foot into Russia. Then the country "acquired" Jews because it annexed other lands, where they were already living. But certain territories (including Moscow) remained forbidden for our people, "beyond the pale."

As late as 1851, this appeared in the Law of the Canton of Basle, Switzerland: "No Jew, without exception, is permitted to settle or carry on commerce, trade, or any handicraft in the canton. Any citizen who admits a Jew into his house, be it for commercial purposes, as clerk or servant, or in any other capacity, or for whatsoever other purpose, is liable to a fine of 300 francs." Such were the bitter conditions that our people faced, harried and driven by the "civilized" countries of Europe with their religion of love. Too much to bear in silence, the troubles spilled over into our people's songs. Who has not heard the refrain, with its tones of pathos,

וווי אַהין זאָל איך גיין,

ווער קען ענטפערן מיר?

וווי אַהין זאָל איך גיין,

אַז פאַרשלאָסן איז יעדער טיר?

(Tell me, where can I go? / who can answer my prayer? / Tell me, where can I go, / when the doors are locked everywhere?)

373

At last, however, there seemed to be a heaven-sent answer on the shores of America. Here was a land of immigrants, with a guarantee of freedom and equality for all, written into its Constitution. It was a big country, with room for all who came. A bastion of democracy, with its open, welcoming doors it became a symbol of hope for the world. So in 1881 a Frenchman named Fréderic Auguste Bartholdi mounted a huge statue in Paris, that he called *Liberty enlightening the world*. It was part of a dream that he had nursed for twenty years. In 1885, as his dream continued to be realized, the statue was presented to the United States of America, where it was set on a massive pedestal on Bedloes Island, out in the New York harbor. On October 28, 1886 it was dedicated; and since then it has been known as the Statue of Liberty.

In 1903 a tablet was affixed to the pedestal, with a poem engraved on it. It was a sonnet that a Jewish poet, Emma Lazarus, had written back in 1883, knowing what the sculptor Bartholdi was making in France, and knowing that it was meant to be presented to America. These are the last six lines of the poem, about the famous "lady with the torch" in the harbor:

> "Keep, ancient lands, your storied pomp!" cries she
> with silent lips. "Give me your tired, your poor,
> your huddled masses yearning to breath free,
> the wretched refuse of your teeming shore.
> Send these, the homeless, tempest-tossed to me.
> I lift my lamp beside the golden door."

There the lady stands today, her torch aflame, symbolizing America's welcome to all who want to enter and settle in this New World. And for millions of Jews the land was a haven indeed, as the mass immigration from Central and Eastern Europe went on for decades around the turn of the century. *Home is the place where, when you have to go there, they have to take you in.* This was America for our people — till the Nazis rose to power in Germany, and the Jews there needed a place of refuge with desperate urgency. The Nazis were determined to get rid of every Jew who failed to get out. And no country, not even America, opened its doors and said, "Come. Here you will be safe."

One incident especially remains in the craw of our collective memory.[111] In May 1939 the Hamburg-Amerika liner *St Louis* sailed for Cuba with some 900 passengers aboard, bearing a hope that was to be cruelly betrayed. As the Jews in Germany were in a panic to get out, travel agencies and employees at the consulates sold them phony documents, quite certainly with the full knowledge and approval of the Nazi authorities. For in that year of 1939 the Nazis had themselves cynically decided on a "solution to the Jewish problem" by export: they would simply send their Jews out to other lands, whether the poor souls were wanted there or not. Thousands were given bogus visas and sent off to Latin America aboard German ships.

On May 27, 1939 the Hamburg-Amerika liner *St Louis* arrived at Havana, and was refused permission to land. The people aboard pleaded with Cuba's president to let them in; but the man would not yield. Somehow he could not let his precious Cuban soil tolerate those German Jews.

As the ship took to sea again, with no choice but to return "home" to Hitler, it passed within ninety miles from the American shore. Good swimmers among the 900 passengers would be able to dive overboard and make it to the coast of Florida. But our own dear, beloved President Roosevelt took care of that contingency. He sent out the Coast Guard to keep watch. It was not enough that, like Cuba, the United States had also refused those 900 souls entry. Roosevelt had to be sure that none of them sneaked in the back way. And no one stopped to wonder why the lady with the torch still held the flame aloft in the New York harbor.

The *St Louis* had to sail back to Germany with its human cargo. In June 1939 those 900 souls were sent to a concentration camp in Holland, to face extermination.

There was also, of course, the land of Israel. Surely the Promised Land should have become a haven for the Jews of Germany, who faced internment and death if they stayed? But the holy land was under British rule then and, with all the fine colonial arrogance of its empire days, Britain assumed the right to keep even the Jewish homeland shut to our people in Germany.

When the Second World War was finally over, Harry S. Truman, the president of the United States, pleaded personally with Ernest Bevin, Emgland's tough foreign secretary, to let 100,000 Jews leave their dehumanizing life in the "displaced person" camps of Europe and settle in Palestine. The answer was a vehement *No*!

Government leaders came, and government leaders went — and the Jew could only go on singing his pathetic refrain: *Tell me, where can I go? / Who can answer my prayer? / Tell me, where can I go, / when the doors are locked everywhere?*

How many centuries ago the Sages of the Midrash gave this simple metaphoric teaching: Man was created out of earth of many colors mixed together, out of soil gathered from the four corners of the world. Wherever he goes, a man has an affinity, a natural bond, with the earth beneath his feet. Whatever his nationality or color, religion or race, he has a primordial right to be there. It is for others to welcome him, like the earth, and make him a part of them, in pure humanity.

The world talks of tolerance and preaches a religion of love. Yet it has not learned this simple lesson of the Midrash. And we bear the scars, gathered in the course of our long, ongoing history.

Thank Heaven, the Jew has his own homeland today, where he belongs; and Israel's *ḥok ha-sh'vuth*, "Law of Return," keeps the doors open to everyone in Jewry who wants to settle there.

## ∾ TWO ALONE IN THE WORLD

We BEGAN THIS ESSAY with a study of Cain and Abel: two people in conflict, alone for all the world, with no one to help or hinder them. It was a study of antagonism and aggression on a small scale, war in miniature.

Let us close with two other instances of this kind: two people utterly alone, who confront each other, with their survival at stake. One instance is in the Talmud, the other in what is elegantly called English literature. To begin with the second case first, this is from a poem by Sir William Schwenk Gilbert (the famous partner in the team of Gilbert and Sullivan):

### THE YARN OF THE "NANCY BELL"

'Twas on the shore that round our coast
from Deal to Ramsgate span
that I found alone on a piece of stone
an elderly naval man.

His hair was weedy, his beard was long,
    and weedy and long was he,
and I heard this wight on the shore recite
    in a singular minor key:

"Oh, I am a cook and a captain bold,
    and the mate of the *Nancy* brig,
and a bo'sun tight, and a midshipmite,
    and the crew of the captain's gig."

The man listening to him is bewildered: How could this "elderly naval man" have been cook and captain, mate, bo'sun and midshipman, and so forth? So this bizarre individual replies:

" 'Twas in the good ship *Nancy Bell*
    that we sailed to the Indian sea,
and there on a reef we came to grief,
    which has often occurred to me.

And pretty nigh all o' the crew was drowned
    (there was seventy-seven o' soul),
and only ten of the *Nancy*'s men
    said 'Here!' to the muster-roll.

There was me and the cook and the captain bold,
    and the mate of the *Nancy* brig,
and the bo'sun tight, and a midshipmite,
    and the crew of the captain's gig.

For a month we'd neither wittles nor drink,
    till a-hungry we did feel;
so we drawed a lot, and accordin' shot
    the captain for our meal.

The next lot fell to the *Nancy*'s mate,
    and a delicate dish he made;
then our appetite with the midshipmite
    we seven survivors stayed.

And then we murdered the bo'sun tight,
    and he much resembled pig;

377

then we whittled free, did the cook and me,
    of the crew of the captain's gig.

Then only the cook and me was left,
    and the delicate question, 'Which
of us two goes to the kettle?' arose
    and we argued it out as sich.

For I loved the cook as a brother, I did,
    and the cook he worshipped me;
but we'd both be blowed if we'd either be stowed
    in the other chap's hold, you see.

'I'll be eat if you dines off me,' says Tom.
    'Yes, that,' says I, 'you'll be' —
'I'm boiled if I die, my friend,' quoth I,
    and 'Exactly so,' quoth he.

Says he, 'Dear James, to murder me
    were a foolish thing to do,
for don't you see that you can't cook me.
    while I can — and will — cook *you*!'

So he boils the water, and takes the salt
    and the pepper in portions true
(which he never forgot), and some chopped shallot,
    and some sage and parsley too.

'Come here,' says he, with a proper pride,
    which his smiling features tell.
''Twill soothing be if I let you see
    how extremely nice you'll smell.'

And he stirred it round and round and round,
    and he sniffed at the foaming froth,
when I ups with his heels and smothers his squeals
    in the scum of the boiling broth.

And I eat that cook in a week or less,
    and as I eating be
the last of his chops, why, I almost drops,
    for a wessel in sight I see!

And I never grin, and I never smile,
    and I never larf nor play,
but I sit and croak, and a single joke
    I have — which is to say:

Oh, I am a cook and a captain bold,
    and the mate of the *Nancy* brig,
*and* a bo'sun tight, *and* a midshipmite,
    *and* the crew of the captain's gig!"

The man called it a joke. Is it funny? Of course, you might say, it depends on your sense of humor. . . . W.S. Gilbert offered the poem first to England's famous magazine of humor, *Punch*; and it was refused. The editor felt it was "too cannibalistic" for his readers.[112] But it was eventually printed (1869), as the first of a whole series of "fun" poems, gathered under the name of *Bab Ballads*. The book became and remained a great success. The poems were supposed to be jokes, and if some people found many in bad taste,[113] the public at large enjoyed them immensely. It was all so jovial and rollicking, *ho ho ho*. So devilishly gifted a versifier was Gilbert that people memorized and quoted tidbits from the *Bab Ballads* at all possible occasions (even in the House of Lords).[112]

Humor is quite certainly a personal thing, and there is no accounting for tastes. Yet perhaps, to understand *this* sense of fun, we might recall that since time out of mind, the British have greatly enjoyed fox-hunting: A group of rich, idle, "cultured gentlemen" would dress up in special (expensive) clothes, and "with a yoicks and a tally-ho," would go "riding to hounds." They would mount their horses and go galloping off with a pack of large, healthy, well-fed dogs, to track down some poor bedraggled fox with very little chance to escape in their private (enclosed) hunting grounds. The animal was often literally hounded to death.

That was called sport. *The Yarn of the Nancy Bell* was called humor. It has gained its place in England's "immortal" literature, and has been taught in schools to pupils learning this literature. (One is only moved to wonder: When the fine minds of England's government decided that "Palestine has no economic absorptive capacity," and they locked the gates of the holy land against the Jews of the Holocaust — when the alternative for the Jews was to remain in the Nazi hell — was that English sport or English humor?)

379

At any rate, here is one hypothetical, imaginary case of two people abysmally alone, with not another soul in sight, where one can survive only with the death of the other — a "gem" of English literature. Let us contrast it with a passage in the Talmud:

...לְכִדְתַּנְיָא: שְׁנַיִם שֶׁהָיוּ מְהַלְּכִים בַּדֶּרֶךְ [בַּמִּדְבָּר] וּבְיַד אֶחָד מֵהֶם קִיתוֹן שֶׁל מַיִם: אִם יִשְׁתּוּ שְׁנֵיהֶם, [שְׁנֵיהֶם] יָמוּתוּ ; וְאִם יִשְׁתֶּה אֶחָד מֵהֶם, יַגִּיעַ לְיִשּׁוּב. [כֵּיצַד יַעֲשֶׂה ?] דָּרַשׁ בֶּן פְּטוֹרֵי, מוּטָב שֶׁיִּשְׁתּוּ שְׁנֵיהֶם וְיָמוּתוּ, וְאַל יִרְאֶה אֶחָד בְּמִיתָתוֹ שֶׁל חֲבֵרוֹ — עַד שֶׁבָּא רַבִּי עֲקִיבָא וְלָמֵד, "וְחֵי אָחִיךָ עִמָּךְ" (ויקרא כה לו): חַיֶּיךָ קוֹדְמִים לְחַיֵּי חֲבֵרֶךָ (בבלי, בבא מציעא סב ע"א, נוסח כי"י בד"ס)

...It was taught: [Let us imagine] two who have been traveling on a journey [in the wilderness][114] and one has a pitcher of water in his hand: If both drink, they will [both][114] die; but if [only] one of them drinks, he can reach a human settlement. [How should he act?][115] Ben (the son of) P'turé expounded: It is better that the two of them drink and die, and let not one of them witness his companion's death — until R. Akiva came and taught: [Scripture states, *Now, if your brother grows poor, and his means fail while with you, then you shall uphold him . . .*] *so that your brother may live, along with you* (Leviticus 25:35–36): Your life takes precedence over your companion's (TB *Bava M'tzia* 62a).[116]

The contrast between our two cases is startling. There is simply no spirit of fun here — no fresh, good (or grisly, or ghastly) humor to make anyone split his sides with laughter. To borrow a leaf from Freud (who wrote a whole book on the relation of humor to the unconscious) no one in the Torah academy seemed to have any repressed aggression, cruelty or cannibalism, that he needed to express safely in the form (disguise) of jolly great humor.

A question of life and death was considered, with the fate of human beings at stake: Two men are out alone somewhere, far from any outposts of civilization. One of them has a pitcher of water (a small quantity); the other has none. They know how long they have gone since their last drink of water. They know how far they still are from some place of human habitation, where they could get food and drink, and survive. But by careful calculation they realize that the water in the pitcher is just enough to let *one* last till he reaches civilization. If they share the water, neither will make it. Both will perish out there. *What should be done?*

Calmly the Sages brought their minds to bear on the question, seeking to decide what would be the Creator's will in this situation, insofar as the answer might be gauged from the Torah.

There was no *hubris* here, no sense of superior high spirits. The Sages could not play about with human life, even in a wholly imagined situation, with any carnival spirits or high-jinks. Even in theoretic discussion they could never take the imperious attitude of certain contemporary surgeons, who, only too ready to play God with their dazzling medical skill, feel free to shorten one person's life (by some small amount of time) in order to lengthen another's (who knows by how long) by transplanting a fresh, palpitating heart. Human life is the most precious creation and gift of the Master of the world. How can anyone smile or cry *Bravo!* at the thought of one person willfully terminating another's existence? Only the Torah, God's immutable word to man, can guide us in such a matter.[117] Without animal spirits or animal passions, the Sages considered their case.

Said Ben P'turé: Let both drink the water, sharing it equally — although it belongs only to one of them — and let them meet death together. This too has value, says the *Maharsha* (commentary by R. Sh'muel Edels, 16th–17th-century Talmudist): It will enable two human beings to live a while longer. For as Ben P'turé implies, how is it conceivable that the Torah would let one man act deliberately to ensure his own survival, when he knows that his companion cannot survive with him? when he knows that because he has finished the water now, the other will suffer a little sooner the torture of unslakable thirst, till death comes as a Divine mercy? In fact, in the Midrash *Sifra* (*b'har, parashah* 5) Ben P'utré gives as his reason the very same phrase of Scripture as R. Akiva: וחי אחיך עמך *and let your brother live, along with you.* To him it means that you should go on living only as long as your brother can live too. When you can keep just yourself alive but must leave him to die, it is better to share death with him. To survive alone and accept his demise — no matter what your conscious mind will say, it will have a brutalizing effect — as if somehow, in some degree, you participated in a murder.

The distinguishing characteristics of a Jew, says the Talmud (TB *Yevamoth* 79a), are that he is bashful (modest), compassionate, and given to acts of kindness. Could the Almighty possibly want a man to deaden any of these characteristics in his nature, merely to live longer? Far better to die sooner, but in a finer spiritual condition, as a good (Jewish) human being.

331

This decision by Ben P'turé was accepted, says the Talmud, until R. Akiva came along and disagreed. True, said he, when a person's situation turns bad and his very subsistence is threatened, the Torah commands us to do our utmost to help him survive and endure; Scripture states וחי אחיך *so that your brother may live*; but then the Torah adds a word: עמך *along with you*. The commandment applies only as long as you yourself have the means to subsist, and with the help you give him both of you can survive. Once helping him means ending your own life, says R. Akiva, the Torah no longer puts this demand on you. To require a person to deliberately help another man survive at the cost of his own life — is to tell him to be super-human; and this the Torah does not do. It was given to human beings to keep, not to angels.[118] We cannot tell this man with the pitcher of water to share it with his companion, whereupon both will perish. If he owns and has the means to survive, the Torah give him the right to live. No obligation lies on him to help the other man.

(If he succumbs afterward to a crushing sense of guilt, at having been a factor — however helplessly — in the other's death, he can pray Heaven for pardon and forgiveness. There is a rule in the Oral Torah — TB *Bava Kamma* 25b — that אונס רחמנא פטריה when a man has acted under duress or been involved in some pure accident — where he had no real choice — the merciful God leaves him free of blame. Then too, he can seek atonement by helping the living kin of his dead companion.)

A noted master of *ḥassiduth*, R. Simḥah Bunem of P'shis-cha, adds an important point:[119] R. Akiva gives the man only the right to drink the water and live, but not to laugh in triumph and cavort in glee, like the sailor in *The Yarn of the Nancy Bell*. As a present-day scholar of *ḥassiduth* notes,[120] Ben P'turé reached his decision (that both should face death together) by the simple compassionate approach toward human life that the Torah always takes. Past any doubt R. Akiva longed to agree with him. No Sage of the Talmud would ever sanction a course of action that left another human being to die, if he saw an alternative. And emotionally, from a purely human view (this scholar notes) it were far better to follow Ben P'turé.[120] No man would ever be altogether the same if (Heaven forbid) he found himself in this situation with the pitcher of water, and had to follow R. Akiva's ruling.

So, until R. Akiva's unassailable logic showed otherwise, the Sages fully accepted Ben P'turé's view. Therefore, said R. Simḥah Bunem of P'shis-cha, *this* is what a Jew must really want in his heart. He may obey

R. Akiva only with the greatest reluctance, at the point of heartbreak, and and solely because the Torah has directed him so. But he should feel in his heart that had Ben P'turé's decision remained, he would gladly share the water and die with his companion.

Two approaches were taken to hypothetic situations, drawn from the imagination. A century ago an Englishman conjured up a ship at sea with two survivors, only one of whom can go on living — by eating the other one. And this clever brilliant versifier said, "Let's think about it and laugh. Told in snappy rhyme, scintillating rhyme, it's a matter for jingling jollity and rollicking, frolicking fun." Generations of his countrymen agreed, accepting with the same equanimity the "fun" of hunting and an imperious colonialism. They found they could laugh right merrily at the whole thing. Ho ho ho, jolly good show.

So *The Yarn of the Nancy Bell* became, if you will, a forerunner of a fundamental attitude toward cruelty "as entertainment," toward senseless brutality and savagery "just for fun." It led logically to the "children" of this *Yarn*, successors to this form of "pleasure," that you can see in every animated cartoon about rabbits and cats, parrots and hounds and what-have-you, ever made for the movies and/or television, "to delight the kiddies."

Ask any honest child psychologist who is aware of the problem, who has no vested interest (financial benefit, directly or otherwise, from the glamor-world of entertainment) to distort his vision, and he will tell you what the enormous cumulative effect of this "entertainment" has been: a massive deadening of sensitivity in the young viewers to any pain or suffering in people, even when they are treated brutally. The "happy" characters in the animated cartoons undergo impossible punishments, and recover instantly, as if nothing happened. So the children assume in wide-eyed innocence, "Doesn't everybody?"

The weekly "dramatic" installments of violence shown on television to adults (adults in body if not in mind) have done the same for grown-ups. Here the emphasis is not on jolly good fun, *ho ho ho, ha ha ha*, but on thrilling, breathtaking excitement. The viewer must be kept glued to his set, so that he won't miss the commercials. And the result is the same. Violence, brutality by one man toward another, becomes regarded with indifference, as part of the impersonal world of entertainment — out there, beyond the screen — with no real, integral relation to oneself.

So the newspapers of America have reported cases of people in an apartment building hearing someone in the hall being robbed, raped, or stabbed to death — and not only would no one open his door (which could endanger his life). No one even lifted a telephone to call the police! All violence, on television or in the hall, had become part of some impersonal, dissociated world of entertainment.

A human being is born with a natural capacity for empathy, for feeling immediately what another is experiencing if he but sees the other person tortured or in danger of death. With any decent moral training, this capacity becomes part of one's character. לֹא תַעֲמֹד עַל דַּם רֵעֶךָ says the Torah: *Do not stand idly by when your neighbor's blood is spilled* (Leviticus 19:16). When our children learn this in schools they say, "Of course!" Not so the countless numbers who have been "entertained" by *The Yarn of the Nancy Bell* and an endless stream of animated cartoons and nightly "stupendous, thrilling" episodes of excitement. For the sake of so-called fun and amusement, "cliff-hanging" suspense and dramatic tension — to bring millions into the pockets of the advertising and entertainment industries — this basic human response of empathy with a person in anguish has been put to death, as surely as the cook of the *Nancy Bell*.

The passage in the Talmud also left its mark. It too had its effect, casting an influence in the consciousness of devout, observant Jewry. This case of two people in the wilderness was considered purely hypothetical, too improbable and unlikely to ever occur in real life; and in our great codes of religious law, no need was seen to record R. Akiva's ruling, for people to remember and follow. Yet it was remembered. It did its share to instill in our people a sense of responsibility for the life of others when their fate depends on us — a responsibility to the limits of human endurance and capacity.

It did its share in the year 1656 to make a man in Moravia (part of the present Czechoslovakia) bring a burning, tormenting question to his rabbi. He had been through a harrowing experience, which bore hardly the slightest resemblance to the case in the Talmud; but there too an answer was sorely needed to the same kind of question: How much did one person have to do to protect and save another? The man had a haunting need to know: Was he in any way guilty? Had he been at all to blame?

In the annals of rabbinic learning treasured by our people, the story is recorded in a volume of responsa (*she'éloth ut'shuvoth*, answers to questions that arose in religious law) by the chief rabbi of Moravia in the mid-17th century[121] — told by the rabbi himself:

". . . Here the estimable Yaakov b. Naftali Katz has come to me to relate what happened to him with a [non-Jewish] lad who was his servant, [to ascertain] if (Heaven forbid) any guilt for willful negligence in the boy's death lies upon him. He is willing to accept whatever way of repentance the instructors of Torah may give him: by fasting, and by severe, bitter physical punishments; perhaps he will thus avoid worse afflictions. He raised his voice in weeping [as he spoke]. These are the events, stinging as bees:

". . . On Thursday, 4 Adar I, 1656, he went with his servant-lad to the town of Lob, from here [the town of Nikolsburg — Mikulov] to there being two parsa'oth [some 9 kilometers or 5½ miles]. The next day, Friday, they ate breakfast and set out on the journey to return here . . . till they reached a village located between Lob and Nikolsburg, being about one parsa either way [some 4½ kilometers, less than 3 miles]. There they sat down to rest and relax, and ate there, and afterward continued their way. Then the wind was not yet storming up against them, because it was windy high up, not below, and neither was it so strong — till they came to a certain village about an hour-and-a-half's journey from here [Nikolsburg] when it is feasible to walk. It was then about one in the afternoon.

"Then they saw that the wind was getting stronger and turning stormy, with enough force to hurl a person to the ground. A certain non-Jewish smith who knew him called out, 'Here, Yaakov, come into my house. You're cold, so you'll warm up.' He went with the lad into the house, and they sat down to rest and relax. Said the blacksmith, 'It would be best for both of you to stay here'; and he added to the lad, 'If you want to stay here, you can and you may.' But the boy added as a joke, 'It would be better for me to go, and eat some of that round pudding [the kugel] that they make as a Sabbath dish.'

"So they stayed there about a quarter of an hour. Then the smith spoke up again, 'If you listen to me, you will remain here. That wind is getting stronger, and it's mighty stormy!' Said he [Yaakov] to the lad, 'Look: I don't want to stay here, because I want to be in my own home on the Sabbath. But you can stay on. You're not as strong as I am, to be able to walk as well and keep up with me. If we go, we'll have to walk all the way, and not stop any more in the village.' The boy replied, 'If you don't want to stay here, I don't either. Wherever you go, I'll go.' So he told the lad, 'In that case, you'll have to pick up your feet and muster your strength on the way.'

"The blacksmith gave the lad a Hungarian-style hat of his to tie around his head, so that the wind should not carry it off, and a pair of his gloves as well; and they set off on their journey. The wind kept growing stronger, a d snow was swirling from above and below, covering all the paths. On their way they came upon a pillar painted red, which served as a marker, so that they could recognize their course. He showed it to the lad. 'Do you see that?' he said. 'It means we're going the right way.' After that, again they could not recognize their way, till they came to a white pillar. 'Do you see that pillar?' he asked the lad. 'We are going the right way!'

"The boy sat down to rest and catch his breath, letting the pillar shield his eyes from the wind. Then they continued. There was a steep declivity somewhere about, with a bridge spanning it, but the snow simply covered both. So he told the lad, 'Look out, and follow me, so that you should not fall into the sharp drop.' He kept touching the ground with his pole, to guide himself to the bridge, and the youngster followed. But then the boy's feet slipped against the bridge, and he fell into the declivity. Yaakov now toiled and rescued him, but they were both freezing. He rubbed the lad's body, and gave the boy one of his gloves, so that he could warm his hands. It helped him only a little, though; and from then on the boy became tired and could not walk well. At times he dropped to his knees.

"Then the boy said, 'Look: you walk on this side, where the wind is blowing, and I'll walk here beside you' [to go sheltered]. They continued walking like that, but the boy had no strength to go on. He took him under his arm to help him walk, sheltering him from the wind. So he struggled along with him, till at last the boy said, 'I just cannot go on any more at all.' Replied Yaakov, 'Look! There is the town and the fortress, right before you. Why should you lose heart now? There is such a short road yet to go till the town.' Said the lad, 'I don't see the town and the fortress, but I seem to see a hill with a crucified figure standing on it.' They resumed walking a bit, till they came within a half-hour's distance from the town, or less.

"Now the boy grew very weak, till he could not walk further at all. Yaakov gave him one of the round hollow loaves which they [the non-Jews] bake during their days of penitence [Lent], but he did not have enough control to break it into pieces, since his hands had become frozen and had even changed color. The boy then said to him, 'Look, I'll stay here, and you go on into town, and please send me a horse-and-wagon, to bring me in.' So Yaakov went off swiftly to the town, the wind getting stormier, and he also tired, with his ears icy cold.

"With great difficulty and hardship he managed to reach a certain non-Jew's house, his life-spirit almost gone from him. He had not the strength to stand. The householder and his family came and made him sit by the fire. They put whiskey into his mouth to restore him, then asked him who he was. He told them to whom he was married, and where he had his home. Then he told them that his servant-boy was lying out there, all frozen through, and he was afraid the lad would die.

"The non-Jew made the matter known in the Jews' street, whereupon Yaakov's wife and the rest of the Jews gathered about him and went running off at once to the road leading into town from Lob, to rescue the lad. They were in such a hurry, however, that they never gave thought to ask Yaakov himself just where he had left him. For they reckoned they would find the boy right on the road. Neither did he bring it to mind, on account of his fatigue, to tell them, but [said] only that he had left him close to the town, near the first river.

"Well, they did not find him, and returned to town. Then, at dusk, they took a wagon with horses, and rode to that place to rescue the boy. The wind was ferocious, blinding the eyes, and the snow stung and hurt like a needle in living flesh. It grew all dark and black as they kept searching on that road. And they did not find him till the next day, on the Sabbath. As the morning light rose, people went and found him lying dead at that place which Mr Katz had specified. Only, he was lying about six cubits off to the side, not directly on the road. Hence they had not seen him the day before."

This is the simple tragic story, perhaps only to be expected in a region with severe long-lasting winters that bring ferocious stormwinds and treacherous snowfalls, where in tolerable weather long journeys were made on foot as a matter of course. This boy was certainly not the only one who ever lost his life to the freezing storms of Central Europe. It was, in sum, the kind of accident that was bound to happen sometimes.

Suppose this tale had been told to Sir William Schwenk Gilbert, perhaps as he was finishing a good dinner, licking his chops over an excellent chop and lighting a fine cigar. What would *his* response have been? Very likely he would have exclaimed, "Fiddlesticks! Put the whole thing out of your mind. Unfortunate of course . . . yes . . . but the lad isn't worth a second thought. Why, you couldn't even make a jolly bouncy jingle out of it. . . ."

Yaakov Katz of Nikolsburg didn't ask W. S. Gilbert, however. He went to his rabbi, racked by doubt and guilt, and he wept as he told the story. What had been the limits of his obligation in such a case? How much more strength and care should he have spent, to save the boy? What was the extent of his responsibility? Had he done enough?

The man he spoke to was both the rabbi of Nikolsburg and the chief rabbi of Moravia. Over four columns (two pages) of small, close-set type give the thread of his thoughts, as his mind sifted every point of the tragedy through the fine mesh of immense Talmudic knowledge. He seems to have overlooked nothing.

He begins with a general statement that, according to *tosafoth*, acting with discretion a man can avoid injury by severely cold, inclement weather, etc. Hence Yaakov Katz should be fully blamed for the boy's death, since he did not watch him properly and took him on a bad road. Yet here, the chief rabbi concludes, this rule from *tosafoth* cannot apply: "Truth to tell, we know nothing specific of which to accuse him . . ."

In setting out with the boy Friday morning to return to Nikolsburg (writes the rabbi) the man was certainly not at fault. The weather posed no danger then for anyone warmly dressed; and in fact, on Thursday they had reached Lob in perfect order. Moreover, Friday morning before starting out, they had eaten breakfast — a good defense against the dangers of cold weather. . . . So, although it was a frosty winter day, Yaakov had done nothing wrong in taking off with the boy. Later on, when the stormwind became so strong as to be blinding, that was an act of God, a condition of accident, which could not be foreseen and prepared for, even with extra clothing.

This principle applies, says the chief rabbi of Moravia, to any man setting out when it is not so very cold, and later, when he is out on the terrain, it storms up so much that he loses his way and his life is no longer safe. It is all beyond human agency or control, and rather in the nature of accident. Blame can attach only if a man sets out from home deliberately when the weather is already dangerous. . . . Nor could we demand of a person starting his journey in passable weather that he should consider how conditions might change unexpectedly [bear in mind too that the science of weather-forecasting was yet unknown]: for then there would be no

TWO ALONE IN THE WORLD

limit to the caution he ought to show. . . . He would hardly ever dare leave home . . . [all this with analyses of relevant passages from Talmudic commentaries and authorities].

Still, when they reached the blacksmith's village the wind was already stormy and getting worse, hurling people to the ground. Perhaps Yaakov can be condemned for not staying on at the smith's house? *Here too he was not at fault*: He gave the boy full permission to remain. The boy refused, and insisted on accompanying him home. Being a lad of sense, he obviously believed himself able to get through safely.

Now the rabbi of Nikolsburg reaches a critical point: When the boy could no longer walk, and Yaakov left him all alone on the terrain, had he stayed with him perhaps he could have restored him somewhat and saved him? *This too is out of the question.* Yaakov was himself wet and frozen through; his own life was then in serious danger; he had to save himself! Had he stayed, they would probably have perished together. Hence whatever strength Yaakov had left *can be likened exactly to the water in the pitcher* in the case of the Talmud that we cited (about the two alone in the wilderness).

Thus, with R. Akiva's ruling to guide him, the chief rabbi of Moravia concludes that even had Yaakov Katz left the boy deliberately and knowingly to die (perish the thought) he would bear no blame, having had the need and the right to rescue himself. How much less blameworthy was he then, when he had run the last part of the way, into the town, with the intent of sending out a rescue group immediately.

This is how a major rabbi in Jewry, thoroughly versed in Talmudic literature, lifted a burden from a Jew's heart: The man was in no way a murderer, not in the slightest degree.

*And yet,* added the rabbi, *the man should not go off scot-free*: He could have decided to remain at the blacksmith's till after the Sabbath, and the lad would have stayed too. Perhaps he should have realized that the boy would not want to stay behind alone, yet might lack the stamina to reach their home town in that weather. . . . Moreover, he had met his death in the course of his duties as servant lad. So as the employer Yaakov bore a general degree of responsibility. Had the youth not been his servant, the tragedy would not have occurred.

There must be some atonement.

The rabbi proposed two ways of penance: Let Yaakov Katz go with three worthy, reliable persons to the boy's grave, and beg his forgiveness.

Then let him fast forty days in a row, eating only at night, and then with no meat or wine in the meals. For a full year after that, let him fast every Monday and Thursday, etc.

Where in the literature of the world, in any language, will you find anything remotely like this — fact or fiction? Which author, even a Nobel-prize-winner, would ever expect his readers to believe that a man thus involved in his servant-lad's death (the boy being of another faith) would come in tears to know if he was at all to blame, and what atonement he could make — and he would receive an answer of authority?

Here you can feel a Jewish heart pulsing with a basic concern over a human life, needing to know the limits of the strength that should have been spent, the care that should have been taken, to save that life. And here you can see a Jewish mind answering.

In ancient Rome the senate loved to have philosophers and wise men appear and hold forth, to show the fruits of their wisdom.[122] It made such a pleasant change from the dreary business of making laws, changing laws, and debating the affairs of empire.

One day a noted Greek philosopher named Carneades (213–129 BCE) appeared. The head of the New Academy, perhaps he was eager to display his scintillating intellect. He undertook to show that in real life (outside the schools with their theoretical discussions) there was no such thing as natural justice, charity or virtue.

Suppose (he said) that a ship at sea founders on a rock, smashes up and goes under. Swimming about, a virtuous man sees another ex-passenger clinging to a log, which can keep one man — but not two — afloat till he reaches the safety of the shore. The virtuous one looks all around, and sees not another soul in sight; none but these two have survived till now; and he (the virtuous man) is stronger than the man on the log. No one else is there to bear witness to what he does. . . .

This is the scene Carneades pictured for the senators of ancient Rome. Then he continued, perhaps as follows: "Noble senators, what should that virtuous man do? — leave the log to the other man because he seized it, and let himself meet death in a watery grave? What an utter fool he would be. He is stronger. If he is wise, it will be but the work of a minute to dislodge the other from the log and take it. Should he choose death instead, he is a man of virtue — yes, noble senators, of virtue indeed — but an

390

absolute fool!" So this proved (he concluded in triumph) that there is no such thing on this earth as natural, innate justice or virtue.[123]

It needs no acute Talmudic reasoning to see how Carneades would have decided our case in the Talmud. Two people are out in the wilderness, and one of them has a pitcher with only enough water for one to survive? Let the stronger of the two take it and drink. Let him not be a fool!

How right our Sages were when they said ‏יש חכמה בגוים, תאמין; יש‎ ‏תורה בגוים, אל תאמין‎ [If you are told] "The nations have wisdom," you can believe it; "The nations have Torah" — do not believe it (Echah Rabbathi ii 17).

Certainly there was a kind of wisdom in Carneades' conclusion. Why bother with problems of ethics? If you are stronger, consider man an animal (and nothing more) and may the best man win. It was especially bright and clever of him to make this point before the senate of Rome. This is exactly the approach that the Romans had taken. They were stronger than all their neighbors. So they seized and took everything in reach, and thus became the mighty empire that ruled the Mediterranean world. How the senators must have nodded happily in agreement with this philosopher.

The Torah, however, offers a profounder level of truth: Might does not make right. If you survive unjustly at another's expense, you are simply a murderer — and Heaven has its own ways of carrying out justice.[124] Don't expect any heathen in ancient Rome to accept such a truth, however. "There is Torah among the goyim (meaning nations, but also ancient non-Jews)? — Don't believe it." It is not for nothing that our forefathers designated their type of mind as a goyishe kopp.

Well now, a Stoic philosopher named Hecaton (2nd century BCE) could not accept Carneades' crass approach. It was all too vulgar. With Greek refinement he posed the problem differently: What if the survivor on the log is a fool, and the other one is a wise man? Does he then have the right to wrest the log away from his companion? Hecaton decides that he does not. Then he goes further: What if the man without the log is the owner of the ship that foundered? Does he then have the right to wrench the log away from the other one? (After all, it could be argued that as the ship belonged to him, so does the log.) Again Hecaton decides that he does not. But now he has a third question: What if both find themselves holding on to the log, and both are wise men — and unless one lets go and agrees to forfeit his life, neither will survive? Here Hecaton's decision is that if the

391

life of one of them is worth less, either inherently or to the state, he has a duty to let go.[125]

Here we find some genuine wisdom. When a ship smashes up at sea, a log floating in the water is no longer the ship-owner's property. It is *hefker*, ownerless; and whoever seizes it becomes its new owner. Then too, wisdom does not give a wise man more of a right to survive than a fool. If the fool survives, he may have children far wiser than his companion at sea. It is not wisdom but selfish arrogance for a learned man to decide that his "great mind" gives him the right to live at another man's expense.

But then Hecaton comes to the question of the worth of human beings and the importance of the state, and there is the end of *his* wisdom. In general, he believes, the lives of human beings can be evaluated, to decide which of two lives is more precious and important — and especially, which is of greater value to the state.

No one would dispute that society values a research scientist far above a garbage collector. Yet can we be so sure that the scientist's life is really more valuable? Perhaps the lowly worker is a better neighbor than the other, always ready to help people in distress. Maybe a grandchild of his (who will come into the world if he survives now) will be of far greater value to mankind than the scientist. And as for judging people by their importance to the state, why take it for granted that a state or country is so fine and splendid a thing that we should consider *its* welfare above everything else? Sodom was also a fine little country with a fine little government. Only (as the Sages relate)[126] it had a system of law that made it right for a native to mistreat a visiting stranger to the point of death. The Soviet Union is a world power today, rivaling the United States in technology. Yet it has a satanic need for a dreaded secret police that must have a regular quota of victims. This seems to be a centuries-old tradition, from the dark days of the tsars. So great is the need there for a policy of suppression and terror that the heads of government spoke out in angry protest if a president of the United States raised too often the delicate question of basic human rights in the USSR — so conspicuous by their absence.

When two persons face death and only one can be given a way to survive, should one of the two have the right to live because he is of greater value to *such* a state?

In Hecaton's question two have hold of the log, and one can survive if the other lets go and drowns. It would have its parallel in the Talmud's case

392

if the two persons in the wilderness equally own the pitcher of water that can enable one of them to survive till he reaches civilization. In such an instance, says one of our learned authorities,[127] they should cast lots. Somehow or other they must let Heaven decide which of them will live. This is our way, beyond human wisdom or cleverness: In questions of life and death we abide by the Torah, the word of God; and if we find no clear answer there, we simply leave it to Him.

There was another fine mind in the non-Jewish world who gave this problem the benefit of his intellect. In the writings of a 10th-century Moslem philosopher we find the Talmud's case precisely: ". . . or for example, two people happen to be in a wilderness where there is no water, and one of them has enough water to save himself but not his companion. Under these circumstances the water should best be given to the one of the two whose life brings greater benefit to people or mankind; and so likewise in any similar situation."[128]

"There is wisdom among the nations? — you can believe it." This could be considered a wise answer. "There is Torah among the nations? — do not believe it." The Torah indicates that it is not for us to measure the respective worth of human beings, whether to the state or the neighbors, to society or mankind. Every person is precious to the Creator who gave him life; and He alone may determine who is to live. There is a haughty arrogance in the thought that we can measure who is of greater value, and who therefore has a greater right to survive. When we presume to decide that, we are playing God. Long ago a one-eyed heathen soothsayer-prophet cried out, אוֹי מִי יִחְיֶה מִשֻּׂמוֹ אֵל *Woe, who can live by making himself a god!* (Numbers 24:23).[129]

With this chapter on "two alone in the world," two pitted against the elements and forces of nature, we bring our book to a close. We began with the famous William S. Gilbert and his *Yarn of the Nancy Bell*, and went on to the Talmud's problem of two in the wilderness, one of them owning a pitcher of water.

Two attitudes were shown, in sharp contrast. One could treat murder and cannibalism as a "joke"; the other sought the Torah's guidance to know if a man might drink water *that belonged to him*, when it meant that his companion would perish, since the water was not enough for both to survive.

Two attitudes emerged: one flippant and chortling over savage murder,

393

the other reverent toward human life and human rights, and obedient to God's word. And here we can discern the whole difference and uniqueness of the Torah's attitude to war and human conflict.

From the dawn of civilization of our day, clans and peoples, nations and countries have been only too ready, willing and happy to accept (and revel in) their savagery and make war, believing the gains (if they won) worth the cost. Enough has happened, over and over, to make the world know better. Weaponry has developed so splendidly that at last the major powers know there must be no more major war. It may send our planet out of existence. Yet on the local level, on limited scales, the business of war has continued merrily.

The Arabs have remained only too ready to threaten Israel with armed attack (a) if they thought they had a chance of winning; and then they would generally go ahead and attack; or (b) if they thought it would be advantageous politically.

Behind it all is a sickening attitude of contempt for human life — not one's own, of course, but another's.[130] Consider the meaning of the Arab boast that ultimately they must defeat Israel, because their population is so much greater. It means they are ready to let millions of their own men die (like flies)[131] for the sake of (Heaven forbid) killing an immensely smaller number of Israelis and perhaps gaining a bit of territory that they could live without, if their brains ever cooled.

So many attitudes toward human life exist in the world. So many — like the philosophers we cited — are ready to play God and decide, each in his own way, who should live and who not, in any given situation. The authentic Jew shudders equally at the thought of killing or being killed. For him there is only One who may decide the fateful question of life and death. Since time beyond memory, in his perennial prayer on the *yamim nora'im* (Days of Awe) he affirms that "on Rosh haShanah," in God's own tribunal, "it is written, and on the fast day of Yom Kippur it is sealed — who shall live and who shall die."

When it comes to war, armed aggression, or any conflict, authentic Jewry has only one purpose and one hope in the world. Physically — in numbers, military power, political strength or what-have-you — we are no match for the sheer irrational hatred that surrounds us in the world. We are still "one lamb among seventy wolves."[132] We can only keep trying, as for centuries in the past, to make mankind appreciate the immense value of a human being (another person too, not just oneself).

Perhaps some day others too will realize that if they see themselves in a situation of (supposed) struggle for survival, where (supposedly) "it's either them or us," there is a better way to solve it than by reaching for their guns, or clubs, or brass knuckles. As the world seeks in vain for some kind of protection against atomic radiation — the ultimate side-effect of ultimate war — perhaps mankind will be willing to join us under the umbrella of Divine law: the Torah. Perhaps they will join us in letting only the Almighty "play God" and decide "who shall live and who shall die." Then the day may come when mankind realizes it is really just one family on earth, created by one Father, with space and provisions for all — if none come with arrogance or greed.

Then it might be only natural, even inevitable, that *many peoples will arrive and say, "Come, let us go up to the mountain of the Lord, to the House of the God of Jacob; and He will teach us about His ways, so that we will walk in His paths." For out of Zion shall the Torah issue, and the word of the Lord from Jerusalem. And He shall judge between the nations, and show truth to many peoples. Then they shall beat their swords into plowshares, and their spears into pruning-hooks. Nations shall not lift up sword against nation, neither shall they learn war any more* (Isaiah 2:3–4).

May we live to see that day.

# *Notes* TO PART FIVE

1.   The point is well (and ironically) made by Phyllis McGinley in her poem *The Conquerors,* which begins: "It seems vainglorious and proud / of Atom-man to boast aloud / his prowess homicidal / when one remembers how for years, / with their rude stones and humble spears, / our sires, at wiping out their peers, / were almost never idle." And the poem ends: "Though doubtless now our shrewd machines / can blow the world to smithereens / more tidily and so on, / let's give our ancestors their due. / Their ways were coarse, their weapons few. / But ah! how wondrously they slew / with what they had to go on." (Phyllis McGinley, *Times Three,* pp. 3–4)

2.   Arnold Toynbee, *Surviving the Future,* London 1971, p. 110.

3.   Khati I, king of Egypt, *Teaching how to live,* no. xiv.

4.   *Collier's Encyclopedia,* 1960, XIX, p. 256b.

5.   Ralph Waldo Emerson (1803–1882), *Miscellanies: War.* How well John Locke stated some two centuries earlier, "All the talk of history is of almost nothing but fighting and killing, and the honor and renown which are bestowed on conquerors, who for the most part are mere butchers of mankind and mislead growing youth, who by these means come to think slaughter the most laudable business of mankind and the most heroic of virtues" (*Useful Quotations,* ed. Tryon Edwards, New York 1933, p. 689).

6.   Thomas Campbell (1777–1844), *O'Conner's Child,* stanza 10.

7.   Karl von Clausewitz, *Vom Kriege,* I (1832).

8.   Tanḥuma, *b'réshith* 9; Pirké d'R. Eliezer 21; Midrash haGadol, Genesis 4:4 (114); Midrash Aggadah and Rashi, Genesis 4:4.

9.   TJ M'gillah i 11; Midrash Aggadah, Genesis 4:5.

10.   Midrash haGadol, Genesis 4:5 (115); Lekaḥ Tov, Midrash Aggadah, and Rashi, on Genesis 4:4.

11.   Michel de Montaigne, *Essays,* II (1580).

12.   Pirké d'R. Eliezer 21.

13.   Midrash Aggadah (Genesis 4:8) relates that when Cain realized that his wretched offering had not been accepted, he took to blaspheming and cursing. In the commentaries, R. Joseph B'chor Shor and R. Joseph Kara (in *Daath Z'kénim*) add that Abel grew so frightened of his brother that he kept away from him at first. Then Cain told Abel what the Almighty had said to him (Genesis 4:6–7), and Abel thought his brother had calmed down.

14.   As another passage in the Midrash (Tanḥuma, *b'réshith* 9) indicates, it was only a natural outcome of their occupations: Cain worked the land, so the ground would be his. Abel raised sheep, which were certainly movable property; so that would be under his ownership.

15.   Tanḥuma, *b'réshith* 9.

16.   Robert Ardrey, *The Territorial Imperative,* New York 1967.

17.   See e.g. Daniel 5:1.

18.   Philo (ca. 20 BCE–50 CE), *Decalogue,* 28; Tacitus (c. 55–120), *History,* book iv section 74.

19.   Woodrow Wislon, *Speech in St Louis,* September 5, 1919. Early in the 19th century, America's third president, Jefferson, wrote balefully, "Their seducers have wished war . . . for the loaves and fishes which arise out of war expenses" (Thomas Jefferson, *Writings,* IV, p. 300).

20.   This is indicated in Targum (Ps) Jonathan, Genesis 8:20, and Pirké d'R. Eliezer 23 and 30, which write of Noah's altar that Cain and Abel had brought their offerings on it long before; and B'réshith Rabbah 34, 9 states that Noah used "the great altar in Jerusalem, where Adam, the first man, had brought his offerings." Rambam (Maimonides) thereupon declares that this was on the very site of the Temple altar (*Mishneh Torah, hilchoth béth ha-b'ḥirah* ii 2).

21.   George Bernard Shaw, *Plays Pleasant and Unpleasant* [1898], II, preface.

22.   Mark Twain, "The Damned Human Race," in his *Letters from the Earth,* p. 227.

23.   Sir Thomas Browne, *Urn Burial,* chapter 4. Over 2,000 years ago a Roman poet wrote, "Too often in times past, religion has brought forth criminal and shameful actions." A bit later he noted,"Such evil deeds could religion prompt" (Lucretius, *De Rerum Natura,* book 1, lines 84, 101).

24.   Arthur Koestler, *The Ghost in the Machine,* p. 234. It might be further noted that when R. Lévi depicted Cain and Abel's "religious" quarrel as a conflict over the Temple site, it was no idle metaphor. That site has been the focal point of bitter and bloody conflicts through the course of history. Twice our Sanctuary was destroyed there. When Christians ruled the region, a church was erected there. When Moslems gained control of the holy land, a mosque arose on the spot. . . Now certain gentlemen in the world nervously watch every move that the Jews in Israel might make around the Temple Mount. Every bit of archaeological excavation around there is scrutinized with gimlet eyes, and condemnations are ready to come from the United Nations at the drop of a spade. The bloody massacres of the past cast their shadow over the site, leaving a haunting fear in certain places in the world that the question of "inheritance" may yet find its original, Divinely ordained solution.

25.   Maurice English, *The Benediction* (in *Where Steel Winds Blow,* ed. Robert Cromie, pp. 37–38. On April 14, 1936 the fortified city of Badajoz fell to the Nationalists (Franco's side) and thousands were then killed out. An American reporter there "was horrified by a style of warfare no American had seen in the 20th century; and his report of mass shootings in the bull ring electrified world opinion" (Gabriel Jackson, *The Spanish Republic and the Civil War,* 1931 –39, Princeton 1965, p. 269). On April 26, 1937 German aviators fighting on Franco's side chose a market day in Guernica,"a town without defenses, a town without military objectives . . . and dropped high-explosive bombs, then practiced machine-gunning the civilians fleeing from the town, and finally set it afire with incendiary bombs" (*ibid.,* p. 381). In intense emotional reaction, Pablo Picasso painted an unforgettable mural, titled simply *Guernica,* as a graphic, vivid memorial to the town and the horror of its people's fate. New York's Museum of Modern Art took the mural, to keep it in trust for the people in Spain, to whom Picasso left it, to be given them when their land would be free. The time came when Franco asked the museum for the mural, supposedly in keeping with the late artist's wishes; but the museum politely declined. One might almost hear a paraphrased echo of the Almighty's thundering outcry to King Aḥab (I Kings 21:9), הרצחת וגם ירשת "You have killed, and you would also inherit?"

26.   Pirké d'R. Eliezer 21; Midrash haGadol, Genesis 4:2 (113); B'réshith Rabbah 22, 7.

27.   Pirké d'R. Eliezer 21. According to Tikkuné Zohar §69 (113a), he seduced her, then decided to kill her husband.

28.   TB Mo'éd Katan 18b; Sotah 2a; Sanhedrin 22a.

29. William S. Gilbert (1836–1911), *Fallen Fairies.*
30. Juvenal (40–125), *Satires,* vi line 242.
31. *Oxford Dictionary of English Proverbs,* 3rd edition, p. 908b.
32. *Der mensch ist was er isst*: Ludwig A. Feuerbach, in *Blaetter fuer literarische Unterhaltung,* November 12, 1850.

33. Ancient inscriptions in the Middle East, discovered by archaeologists and deciphered by scholars, generally boast of the "great" military exploits and triumphs of kings. Yet what a hollow, dismal sound it all has now (as Percy Bysshe Shelley expressed in his poem *Ozymandias*— cited below in this chapter). The glory has long since evaporated over the centuries. All that remains is evidence of men's brutal, irrational will.

Armed clashes brought stark misery, yet the disease continued in the world, as kings and generals remained eager for the "pride, pomp and circumstance" of glorious war (as Shakespeare expressed it in *Othello,* act iii scene 3, line 354). "War should be the only study of a prince," wrote the cold, cynical Niccolo Machiavelli (1469–1527; *The Prince*). "He should consider peace only as a breathing time, which gives him leisure to devise, and furnishes the ability to execute, military plans." Some three centuries later, the German poet Goethe exclaimed, "War is the key word — Conquer! It clangs on and on" (*Faust,* part 2). It certainly did. His countrymen became quite rabid about it:

"War is a biological necessity of the first importance, a regulative element in the life of mankind, which cannot be dispensed with." So declared one German writer on military matters (Friedrich A.J. von Bernhardi, 1849–1930, *Germany and the Next War,* chapter 1). Ruminating further on war, he added, "But it is not only a biological law but a moral obligation, and as such an indispensable factor in civilization." A bit later he added, "The inevitablility, the idealism and the blessing of war, as an indispensable and stimulating law of development, must be repeatedly emphasized" (*ibid.*). In the words of another fine German mind, by war "the ethical health of a people is preserved. Just as the movement of the ocean prevents the corruption which would be the result of perpetual calm, so by war people escape the corruption which would be occasioned by a continuous or eternal peace" (George W. F. Hegel, 1770–1831, *Grundlinien in der Philosophie des Rechts,* English ed. London 1896, p. 331). There was also the famous (or infamous) Nietzsche (1844–1900), who went insane in his later years, but was unfortunately thought sane before that. He wrote such sweet nothings as these: "Your enemy shall you seek; your war shall you wage . . . You shall love peace as a means to new wars, and the short peace more than the long. You I advise not to work but to fight. You I advise not to peace but to victory. Let your work be a fight; let your peace be a victory!" At another point he blared forth, "You say a good cause will hallow even war? I say to you a good war hallows every cause. War and courage have done more great things than charity" (Friedrich Nietzsche, *Thus Spake Zarathustra,* x: *Of war and warriors*; ed. Modern Library, pp. 62–63).

With standing armies a permanent feature in the Western world, a military career became a fine, attractive thing among the nations, promising a carefree glamorous life. "Ah," wrote a Frenchman in the 19th century, "what a delight to be a soldier!" (Eugène Scribe, *Dame Blanche,* 1823).

Needless to say, however, the armies did not attract the gentlest types. "Men who have nice notions of religion," said the famed British general, the Duke of Wellington, "have no business to be soldiers" (cited in *Useful Quotations,* ed. Tryon Edwards, p. 689a). Napoleon (it is said) put it more plainly: "The worse the man, the better the soldier." A thoughtful Englishman summed it up well: "A soldier is a man whose business it is to kill those who have bever offended him. . . . It seems impossible that the soldier should not be a depraved and unnatural thing" (William Godwin in *The Enquirer*, v, 1797). Again, though, Napoleon was more succinct: "War is the business of barbarians" (*Useful Quotations, loc. cit.*).

A French writer used his own brand of irony: "I have noticed that the profession most natural to man is that of a soldier. It is the one to which he is drawn most easily by his instincts and his tastes, which are not always good" (Anatole France, *The Opinions of Jérome Coignard*, London 1913, p. 122). An American thinker put it this way: "War gratifies . . . the combative instinct of mankind, but it gratifies also the love of plunder, destruction . . . and arbitrary power" (Charles W. Eliot, 1834–1926, *Five American Contributions to Civilization*).

In the Middle Ages, when printing was unknown and all books were handwritten, some scribes with artistic ability produced Passover Haggadahs with handsome colorful illustrations; and a number of them remain today, as the treasures of great libraries and private collectors. In many of them we find a curious thing: Shortly after the beginning, the Haggadah text relates that "the Torah spoke in reference to four sons: one wise, one wicked," etc. To illustrate the "second son," the artist-scribes had to draw some figure that typified wickedness. So they pictured a soldier. That, they knew, meant wickedness. The same kind of illustrations (in woodcuts) appeared later in printed Haggadahs (see Charles Wengrov, *Haggadah and Woodcut*, p. 43a). It was a silent commentary on the nature of Europe's soldiery, from the Middle Ages onward, drawn from life (as one might say) by members of a people that were often the victims of those "gallant men."

34. When the journey from Egypt through the wilderness was almost over, and the generation of the Exodus had almost died out, an army of the second generation fought the people of Midian by God's order. With Pin'has at their head, they faced an alliance of five kings, and won brilliantly (Numbers 31:1–10).

There, east of the Jordan, our people's army became a fighting force to reckon with. *This day*, the Almighty told them, *I will begin to put the dread and fear of you upon the peoples . . . who, hearing a report of you, shall tremble and be in anguish because of you* (Deuteronomy 2:25).

On the banks of the Jordan our people knew their fighting strength. They could have scored many conquests, mopping up one adversary after another. But then they received a few Divine commands: *You are to pass through the borders of your brethren the people of Esau . . . and they will be afraid of you. So take great care: do not contend with them, for I will not give you any of their land* (Deuteronomy 2:4–5). A bit later the people were told, *Do not harass Moab, nor contend with them in battle; for I will not give you any of their land for a possession* (ibid. 9). Then there was a third order: *And when you approach the frontier of the people of Ammon, do not harass them, nor contend with them; for I will not give you any of the land of Ammon for a possession* (ibid. 19)

Three times they were warned to keep hands off some choice morsels or easy targets that might tempt them into a lively, rousing little war. Well, R. Samson Raphael Hirsch, the renowned battler for authentic Judaism, saw in this a profound meaning, as he wrote in his noted commentary on the Torah:

The Hebrew for "contend," *tithgareh* (he wrote) really means to incite. The Israelites were to do nothing to stir up those three peoples or upset them, to goad them into war. Why? At that particular period, the Israelites were endowed with great military powress, because it was their Divine destiny to take possession of the Promised Land — but only of that and nothing more. Just as the Almighty assigned them their land, so had He allocated territories to other

399

nations. Hence when any nation was on its proper land, it was there in accord with the Divine will and under His providence. And the Israelites, soon to take their place as a nation on *their* soil, would have to learn to accept and respect this.

Some people believe that the way to go through life is to swing hard and wide, till you hit something solid. This was not to be the way of the Israelites. There were to be no rampant, unbridled military conquests for them, whatever their fighting strength and skill. Only the Promised Land was to be theirs, no more; and its borders were clearly stated (Numbers 34:1–12).

This basic thought was already stated late in the 15th century, by Don Isaac Abarbanel. In his Bible commentary he wrote: Since the Israelites felt confident enough of their own strength to battle the Amorites and drive them out . . . in order to curb their bold temperament it was the blessed Lord's wish to forbid them three times to make war . . . and then He ordered them to battle Siḥon and Og and take their lands — to let them know, and make the point sink in, that not by their own strength would they win the land, nor would their own arm give them victory . . . [See Psalms 44:4.]

35.  Rambam, *Séfer haMitzvoth*, positive precept § 187.

36.  Rambam, *Mishneh Torah, hilchoth m'lachim* vi 1.

37.  *Ibid.* 4 and 7; v 1–2 and commentaries.

38.  TB M'gillah 10b; Sanhedrin 39b.

39.  B'réshith Rabbah 76, 2; Midrash haGadol, Genesis 32:8 (564). The two terms are interpreted in reverse fashion in Tanḥuma, *b'shallaḥ* 4; Ginzé Schechter I p. 60; and Lekaḥ Tov *ad loc.*

40.  *The Seventh Day: soldiers' talk about the Six-day War* [ed. English edition, Henry Near]. The passages cited or referred to below occur respectively in the New York (Scribner) edition on pp. 1, 9, 112–13, 115–16, 268. In the Penguin edition: pp. 13, 21, 144, 147, 309. As given here, however, the passages have been translated anew from the Hebrew original, *Si-aḥ Loḥamim,* which appeared in Israel in 1967; the passages (excluding the first) are there on pp. 108, 113, 272. One other passage (on the first of the pages listed) is worth nothing: Reminiscing after the war, there was a soldier who wrote, "This form of flesh [dead human beings] which was always taboo for you — you had learned, *Thou shalt not kill* — now lies around you piled high, as lifeless as the burnt-out vehicles, as the very stones; and you cannot absorb such horror."

41.  TB Yevamoth 79a; Bétzah 32b.

42.  Even when it came to booty and loot, the spoils of war, this remained a Jewish army. "Let me tell you a curious incident," said a kibbutznik, "about loot: In my company we had a religious commanding officer from Kibbutz Tirat Tz'vi . . . After we passed through Jenin, we . . . found all the Arabs had gone. . . . When we reached the company's base, we found the quartermasters and cooks . . . absolutely rolling in what they had looted from the village — draped in carpets and women's jewelry. It was an awful sight . . . The commanding officer got the whole company together, positioned them nicely all around, and stuck those quarter-masters and cooks right in the middle, with all their loot. Then he started throwing the Book at them: verses from the Bible — *You shall not plunder! You shall not* this; *you shall not* that. It really made an impact. One of the quartermasters got up, though, and asked him, 'But look here: In the Bible it's written [that Mordecai sent out a royal decree *that the king permitted the Jews . . . to defend their lives . . . and annihilate any armed force that might attack them . . .*] *and to take their goods as booty* (Esther 8:11). How would you explain that?' So the commanding officer explained: Rashi on the verse says that it indicates that a conquering army may take what it

really needs while the battle is on. Thus, if they have no food and they have to survive, they may take whatever they need to live on — but nothing else, that they don't need; no property. Well (concluded the kibbutznik) I stood in a corner and thought to myself: What a funny army this is, standing there and listening to all this.... After that scene, though, in our company there was no more looting. No one touched any booty" (ed. Scribner, pp. 126–27; Penguin, pp. 158–59; Si-aḥ Loḥamim, p. 122).

(Possibly the commanding officer's memory was garbled, but more likely, I fear, the mix-up occurred in the memory of the man recalling the incident. Rashi on the verse merely states that in actuality the Jews took no plunder or booty — as attested by Esther 9:10, 15–16 — to show that they fought only for their lives, not for wealth. Malbim notes that Mordecai put the phrase into his royal epistle to the Jews only because Haman had written the same thing in his royal epistle to the gentiles, and Mordecai's draft message was meant to counteract it. In *Mishneh Torah, hilchoth m'lachim* viii 1, Rambam gives the law that soldiers conquering enemy territory, etc. may eat any food they find there, even hog's meat (absolutely non-kosher), if the alternative is going hungry. In *ibid.* iv 9 he gives the law for dividing the spoils of war between the king, the fighting men, and those who manned the home front — from which it is clear that soldiers are not free to take booty privately, individually. The English edition, *The Seventh Day*, inaccurately cites II Chronicles 20:25 as the verse in the soldier's question — which does not apply, as that concerns booty taken by the entire army, led by the king, and not private looting.)

Another member of a kibbutz recalled being among the first soldiers to enter the Arab village of Sebastia. The whole place was simply stunned at the sight of the Israeli soldiers. The village notables, *et al.* came over and invited the men into a restaurant: "Take something . . . have something to drink. Take picture postcards, all you want!" The soldiers had one reply: "Fine; we'll be glad to; but on one condition: that you let us pay for everything, the full price." And they paid (ed. Scribner, p. 128; Penguin, p. 160; Si-aḥ Loḥamim, p. 123).

How many thousands of years had passed since the Almighty told the Hebrews in the wilderness, as they came close to the people of Esau, *You shall purchase food from them for money, that you may eat; and water also shall you buy from them for money, that you may drink* (Deuteronomy 2:6). Unlearned in the Torah though they were, this principle arose in the consciousness of a group of soldiers in Israel, in June 1967. Where fighting was neither indicated nor justified, no lives or loot might be taken willfully, for nothing.

43.   TB B'rachoth 55b; Zohar I 200a.

44.   Midrash Sh'muél 26, 1. Rashi on II Samuel 7:2 and Radak on verse 4, evidently citing a lost Midrash, give the reason that he might go and vow to take no food or drink till he built the Sanctuary, and thus he would come to grief.

45.   Mechilta of R. Shim'on b. Yoḥai, Exodus 20:22 (157); Midrash haGadol *ibid.* (445); see also Tosefta, Bava Kamma vii 6.

46.   Mechilta, Exodus 20:22 (244); see also Mishnah, Middoth iii 4; Tosefta, Bava Kamma vii 7; Sifra, *k'doshim* 10, 9 (92d); Tanḥuma, *yithro* 17.

47.   P'sikta Rabbathi 3 (11b).

48.   In a manuscript Midrash named Ḥem'ath haḤemdah, the reason given is: "in order that they should sit and weep at her grave" (Torah Shelemah, *va-yiggash* p. 1359, §85 note).

49.   So Rashi defines the *matzéva* used for sacrifice and worship: as an altar of a single stone (Rashi to Deuteronomy 5:7, 12:3, 16:22).

50.   Rambam, *Mishneh Torah, hilchoth avodah zarah* vi 6.

51. After the Battle of Pharsalia, in which he defeated his rival (internal enemy) Pompey.

52. Percy Bysshe Shelley, *Ozymandias* (1817).

53. Sh'moth Rabbah 2, 2; Early Tanḥuma, *sh'moth* 10; Midrash T'hillim 11, 3.

54. Shir haShirim Rabbah 2:9 — 4; Yalkut Shim'oni, *shir ha-shirim* § 986.

55. TB B'rachoth 30a; P'sikta Rabbathi 33, beginning (149b); TJ B'rachoth iv 5 (8c); Early Tanḥuma, *va-yishlaḥ* 21; Shir haShirim Rabbah 4:4 — 6.

56. B'réshith Rabbah 56, 4; B'réshith Rabbathi p. 90.

57. Tanḥuma, *va-yéra* 23; Midrash MS in Mann, *The Bible as Read . . .* I p. 66; P'sikta Rabbathi 40 (170b); Avoth d'R. Nathan, in Torah Shelemah, Genesis 22, §92 (p. 886); Pirké d'R. Eliezer 31 (70b).

58. TB P'saḥim 54b.

59. Crinagoras (fl. c. 45 BCE), *Epitaphs* (Greek Anthology, book vii no. 380).

60. Decimus Magnus Ausonius (fl. 310–394), *Epitaphs*, no. 32 line 10.

61. TJ Sh'kalim ii 5 (45a); B'réshith Rabbah 82, 10. Similar thoughts are to be found among other peoples: "The monuments of noble men are their virtues" (Euripides, 480–406 BCE, *Herakles Mainomenos*, line 357); "It is superfluous to raise a monument. If our lives deserve it, our memories will endure" (Pliny the Younger, ca. 62–113, *Letters*, ix).

62. According to the value of the *se'ah* in *Kitzur Shulḥan Aruch,* ed. R. David Feldman II p. 205. By two current views, it would be respectively 11.7 cubic feet (331,760 cubic centimeters), or 20.2 cubic feet (573,320 cubic centimeters).

63. Tanḥuma, *ki thissa* 26; Pirké d'R. Eliezer 45 (107b–108a); TJ Ta'anith iv 7 (66c).

64. Henry David Thoreau (1817–62), *Walden*, chapter 1.

65. Robert Burns, *The Sodger's Return*, line 59.

66. Fanny Burney (1752–1840), *Diary, Ce 4 florial, 1802.*

67. P.J. Bailey (1816–1902), *Festus: a Metropolis.*

68. Anatole France, *The Opinions of Jérome Coignard*, London 1913, p. 122.

69. James Boswell, *Life of Samuel Johnson*, April 10, 1778.

70. Sam Weller, in Charles Dickens, *Pickwick Papers,* chapter 37; Sidney Smith, *Lady Holland's Memoir,* I p. 313; George Bernard Shaw, *Man and Superman.*

71. So the *Aruch* explains the Hebrew term in the Mishnah (or perhaps a mace — Levy, *Woerterbuch*; or a leather strap with an iron point; see M. Jastrow, *Dictionary*, s.v. קולפא. Rambam explains it as a circular shield, taking the preceding term (*t'ris*) to denote a triangular shield. That these laws had their effect on Jewry in later centuries can be seen from this responsum (answer to a question on religious law) from the time of the *ge'onim*: "Now, you have asked: There is one location where all the coats are like those in which people go into war. Not one of them has fewer than three belts; and some of those belts are of leather. The rich put discs of gold and silver on the head [front end] of a belt, while the poor use brass and iron — buckling the strap with them. On their heads [they wear headgear of] silver discs; and this [material] they [also] attach to the boots below the knee; while their cape is that of cavalrymen, on which there are some who sew precious stones. What is the law about going out in articles like these?

"Thus we see the matter: Since such is their attire regularly and this is their usual way, it is permissible to go out in them on the Sabbath into the public domain . . ." (*T'shuvoth Ge'oné Mizraḥ uMa'arav,* ed. Joel Miller, §69). Thus clothes of a military character were permitted here only because they were the norm, and there was no real alternative.

402

72. TB Shabbath 63b.

73. Midrash T'hillim 45, 6 (271).

74. So Midrash T'hillim on the verse; TB Shabbath 89a; Tanḥuma, *va-yikra* 4; Early Tan. 6; Sh'moth Rabbah 28, 1.

75. Looking ahead to the Messianic era, one of our prophets declared, *On that day the Lord of hosts will be . . . a strength to those who turn back the battle at the gate* (Isaiah 28:5–6). "Those who turn back the battle," says the Talmud, means those who engage in the give-and-take of the battle of the Torah [to understand and establish the proper observance of its timeless laws]; "at the gate" implies the scholars who, early and late, are within the gates of our houses of prayer and study (TB M'gillah 15b). In the simple words of the Midrash, the *tzaddikim*, our righteous men of piety, can properly be called our "weapons of war" (Midrash Sh'muel 25, 4 — 124).

76. Henrik Ibsen (1828–1906), *Lady Inger*, act 1.

77. Tanḥuma, *tzav* 3; Early Tan. 5.

78. R. El'azar b. Judah of Worms, *Séfer Roké-aḥ, hilchoth ḥassiduth, shoresh z'chiyoth arum b'yir'ah.*

79. TB B'rachoth 6a.

80. Livy, *History*, book ix section 40.

81. Shir haShirim Rabbah 4:4 — 43.

82. William Shakespeare, *I Henry IV*, act iv scene 1 line 97.

83. Albert Einstein, cited in *Useful Quotations*, ed. Tryon Edwards, p. 690a.

84. R. Jonathan Eybeschuetz, *Ya'aroth D'vash*, Karlsruhe 1779, p. 29a.

85. Robert I. Gannon, in *Dictionary of Quotable Definitions*, ed. E. E. Brussell, p. 575a. On the origins of the word "tolerance" see Ernest Klein, *Comprehensive Etymological Dictionary* . . . s.v. *tolerate*.

86. Nathaniel Ward, *The Simple Cobbler of Aggawam* (1646); Pope Leo XIII, *Immortale Dei, November* 1, 1885.

87. *Séfer haḤinnuch*, ed. Chavel, §§ 63, 64, 429 (pp. 115–16, 553–54).

88. TB Yevamoth 22a; B'choroth 47a.

89. Rambam, *Séfer haMitzvoth*, positive § 207; see also his *Mishneh Torah, hilchoth dé'oth* vi 4.

90. Among the extant Midrashim this is found only in the Yemenite Midrash haGadol, Deuteronomy 10:19 (194–95) and *Ma'or ha'Afélah*, p. 501. They, however, may well have derived it from Rambam. Cf. though, Midrash haGadol, *ibid.* 18 (193), from Mechilta, Exodus 22:20, and Mishnath R. Eliezer p. 300, etc.

91. Ramban, *The 613 Mitzvoth* (in *Kithvé Rabbénu Moshe b. Naḥman*, ed. Chavel, II p. 522).

92. R. Judah Livva b. Beẓalel (Maharal of Prague), *Nethivoth Olam, nethiv ahavath ré'o* (Zhitomir 1867, p. 135b).

93. Philo Judaeus, *On Abraham*, xxxvii, § 208 (ed. Loeb, VI p. 103).

94. R. Yitzḥak of Radvil, *Or Yitzḥak*, Jerusalem 1961, p. 132.

95. R. Me'ir Shalom of Parisov, *Nehar Shalom*, Warsaw 1904 (Jerusalem 1959), p. 34b.

96. R. Yitzḥak Yehuda Yeḥiel Safrin (of Kamarna), *Otzar haḤayyim*, Leviticus 19:18 (ed. Pentateuch, III p. 172d).

97. R. Menaḥem Naḥum of Chernobyl, *Me'or Ena'yim, ḥukkath* (Warsaw 1881, p. 105b).

403

98. Pirké d'R. Eliezer 11 (27b); Yalkut Shim'oni I § 13; Midrash haGadol, Genesis 1:26 (57).

99. Sandra Griffiths, in *Dictionary of Quotable Definitions,* ed. E. E. Brussell, p. 476.

100. Shir haShirim Rabbah 1:5 — 2.

101. *Op. cit.* in note 99, p. 68b.

102. R. Dov Ber Ehrmann, *D'varim Arévim,* I p. 31a; cf. Buber, *Or haGanuz,* p. 296.

103. Be-midbar Rabbah 8, 2; Séder Eliyahu Rabbah (9) 10, beginning.

104. Pope Innocent III, *Letter to the Count de Nevers*; Christopher Marlowe, *The Jew of Malta,* act iv scene 6.

105 R. Ashér b. Yeḥiél (Rosh), *Orḥoth Ḥayyim,* as cited from two MSS in Israel Abrahams, *Hebrew Ethical Wills,* I pp. 119, 121–23.

106. R. Judah heḤassid, *Séfer Ḥassidim,* ed. Margulies, §§ 51, 358, 395, 425, 426, 1026, 1124.

107. The sources cited are respectively: TB Gittin 61a; Bava M'tzi'a 32b; Tosefta, Bava Kama x 15; Séder Eliyahu Rabbah (28) 26; TB Ḥullin 94a.

108. Robert Travers Herford, "The Influence of Judaism upon the Jews," in *The Legacy of Israel,* ed. Bevan and Singer, p. 124; idem, in *Menorah Journal,* 1919, volume 147.

109. Heinrich Heine, *To Edom* (Letter to Moses Moser, October 25, 1824), in his *Rabbi of Bacherach,* ed. Schocken, p. 72.

110. King John of France, *Charter,* 1361; cited in James Parkes, *Judaism and Christianity,* p. 125.

111. The story which follows can be found fully described and documented in Gordon Thomas and Max Morgan-Witts, *Voyage of the Damned,* London [1974] — which has since become the basis of a film.

112. Hesketh Pearson, *Gilbert: his Life and Strife,* London [1957], p. 21.

113. *Op. cit.* p. 22. It might be of interest to add that William S. Gilbert himself seemed to have a complete insensitivity to the feelings of others where his preening ego was concerned. In his early twenties, while working as a government clerk, he translated a song from the opera *Manon Lescaut.* A popular singer decided to render it at the Promenade Concerts, and he went to hear every performance. Imagining himself a grand success, he soon created the impression among his fellow-clerks that he somehow wielded control in the world of the theater. One man finally asked him if he could give him a signed note for tickets to a play. Gilbert gave him the note, and the poor fellow took his family to the theater, only to have to take them home again when the sole effect of the note was hearty laughter at the ticket office. When he complained bitterly to Gilbert, the "great versifier" replied, "You asked me whether I could write you an order [a note to the box-office for tickets] for the play. I replied that I could, and I did; but I never said that it would be of the least use to you" (*op. cit.* pp. 16–17). He remained throughout completely unruffled at the thought of the mortifying shame that he thus knowingly caused the man.

114. So in Sifra, *b'har, parasha* 5.

115. Phrase added in *Haggadoth haTalmud,* Constantinople 1511 (facsimile, Jerusalem 1961), p. 88b.

116. Version of MSS in *Dikduké Sof'rim.*

117. Nor is it conceivable that any Sage would take a "sporting" attitude to the question in the Talmud and say, "Let them toss for it. Or let them set the pitcher on a stone, and each one

move off ten paces. At a given signal they will make a dash for it, and whoever grabs the pitcher, bully for him: he drinks the water" — which is surely an answer we might get from W.S. Gilbert's "rollicking" approach in his dear Bab Ballad. The solution of a scenario-writer for screen or television can equally be visualized: We could picture the two men traveling on as the hours pass by and daylight yields to night. The other would keep a wary watch on the man with the pitcher, waiting to catch the first sign of drowsiness or the slacking of attention. If and when, weary with fatigue, the pitcher's owner let his eyelids droop and his head nod down, the other would spring like a tiger and snatch the pitcher away, with a huge animal laugh of sheer gleeful triumph. In such a situation, with two alone seeking survival, the world at large could probably consider only the law of the jungle ultimately relevant.

Not so Jewish religious law. If the decision is that the pitcher's owner uses the water, then, writes one early authority, "that man who has the water in his hand drinks it and saves his life, since his life takes precedence [for him] to save himself. If one of them [in a situation of more than two] snatches it from his companion and drinks it, and his companion dies on account of him, he is guilty and punishable by the laws of Heaven. So it would seem: for what makes him think that his blood is redder?" (*Ramach* — R. Moshe *ha-kohen* of Lunel — cited in *Shittah M'kubetzeth* to Bava M'tzia *ad loc.*). This last phrase is an idiom meaning: what gives one person the right to assume that he is superior, more precious than another, or of greater value to the world, and therefore more entitled to survive?

Thus the answer is clear: If the other man seizes the pitcher and drinks the water, he is guilty of plain, simple murder, since the water was not his. There are no witnesses to bring him to justice, but, says this early authority, Heaven has its own way of settling accounts.

118. So TB B'rachoth 25b. Let it be noted that when it is only a question of discomfort, not loss of life, the Torah may well require a man to do more for another than for himself. Thus *tosafoth* (TB Kiddushin 20a, s.v. *kol ha-koneh*) notes: If a man buys a Hebrew bondservant (to work for him for a period of six years) and he owns only one mattress, he may not sleep on it himself, leaving his servant in lesser comfort, nor may he leave it unused. He has no choice but to give it to his new servant, and use for himself whatever he can! Here, however, his own life is at stake, and he cannot be required to value the other man's life above his own, to give him the water. (He, or any man, may do nothing directly to the other person to shorten his life, in order to lengthen his own — as a doctor might do in a heart transplant — but no one can ask him to give up the means to survive, for the sake of the other man.

Another point is worth noting: A later authority states that if the pitcher belongs equally to both, they are to cast lots, and let Heaven thus decide who will live and who will die (R. Aryeh Léb Tzintz, *M'lo haRo'im, b'ḥukothai* — ed. London 1960, p. 228b). Even here the principle remains that it is better for one to survive, provided it is by the Almighty's will. (Incidentally, in the commentary *Etz Yosef* to *En Ya'akov ad loc.* this is cited differently: ". . . it is certainly permissible for them—the two in the Talmud's case—to agree that it should be decided by lot who will live and who will die." While this is not precisely what R. Aryeh Leb Tzintz wrote, it is a valid inference: Since a man may do as he likes with his property, the owner of the pitcher is certainly free to make his companion a partner in it; and then they have to cast lots. Thus, if a person in this stark situation does not wish to have his companion's fate sealed outright, he has this means of giving the other an even chance. R. Akiva's words make it clear, however, that he is under no obligation to do so. It is human to want to live, and he has the right to survive.)

119. R. Israel Berger, *Simḥath Yisra'él* (Piotrkov 1910), *ma'amaré simḥah*, § 87.

120. R. Moshe Shlomo Kasher, *P'rakim b'Torath haḤassiduth,* Jerusalem 1961, p. 6.

121. R. Menahem Mendl [Krochmal] of Nikolsburg, *She'éloth uT'shuvoth Tzemaḥ Tzedek,* Amsterdam 1675; 4th ed. Lemberg 1861; facsimile, Jerusalem 1968: responsum § 93.

122. It is apparently in keeping with this practice that R. Joshua b. Ḥananya and other Sages debated various questions with wise men of Rome and Athens while in Rome (TB Sanhedrin 90b; Avodah Zara 54b; B'choroth 8b; B'réshith Rabbah 20; etc.).

123. Cited in Cicero, *De Republica,* III 20, 30 (*Tarbitz,* XVI, 1945, p. 238). [The help of my friend Prof. Jonas C. Greenfield in locating this reference is gratefully acknowledged. — Ed.]

124. See the passage by Ramach (R. Moshe ha-kohen of Lunel) cited in note 117, second paragraph.

125. Cited in Cicero, *De Officiis,* III 23, 89–90 (*Tarbitz, loc. cit.*).

126. TB Sanhedrin 109a–b; Tosefta, Sotah 3, 12; Sifre, Deut. §43; Mechilta, *shirah* 2; Va-yikra Rabbah 4 and 5, 2; etc.

127. R. Aryeh Léb Tzintz (noted rabbi of Plotzk), cited in note 118, second paragraph.

128. Abi Bakr al-Razi, cited in *Tarbitz,* XVI, 1945, p. 239 [knowing no Arabic, I have necessarily rendered the passage from the Hebrew version given there]. S. Pines (there) is inclined to believe that this question of the two men in the wilderness originated as a hypothetical topic of discussion in the school of Hecaton (although no record of this has survived), and from there it found its way into the academy of the Talmudic Sages several centuries later, whereas some eight centuries afterward it came to the attention of the Moslem philosopher Abi Bakr (in an Arabic translation from the Greek). Be that as it may, only among the Sages did it evoke a respo nse from the wellsprings of the Torah rather than human fancy and speculation.

129. This translation follows Midrash Aggadah *ad loc.* — in keeping with the paraphrase of Resh Lakish in TB Sanhedrin 106a, as cited in Midrash haGa dol *ad loc.* (on Numbers, p. 432): "Woe to one who sustains himself (or perhaps: lets himself live well) in the name of a god" — i.e. posing as one; see the Midrash, ed. Fisch, II 195, note 53.

130. It may be interesting to note something further in this regard. In an article in the Israel newspaper *haTzofeh,* October 22, 1971, Abraham Bick cites the responsum of R. Menaḥem Mendl of Nikolsburg, about Yaakov Katz and the death of his servant-boy, which has been dealt with at length above. [It was this that brought the responsum to our attention, for which Mr Bick is to be thanked.] Afterward, in contrast, Abraham Bick cites two stories from the world's literature: In *The Burial of Roger Melvin,* the early American author Nathaniel Hawthorne (1804–1864) describes a young man returning from a battlefield with his father-in-law. The old man is on the verge of death, and they keep losing their way. Repeatedly he importunes and urges his son-in-law to leave him behind: His life will soon be over in any case; and without the burden of a dying man to impede him, the young man will quickly find the right road and reach home. The young man lets himself be persuaded, and returns to his home soon enou gh — only to find himself unable to open his mouth and tell about his father-in-law. How can he admit that he left the dying old man alone out there in the woods, a prey to the wild creatures of the forest? What will everyone think of him?... He decides to keep still and say nothing — and lives the rest of his life tormented by guilt.

Hawthorne was a master at understand ing and portraying the New England society of his time, with its cruelly inhuman puritanical standards. His story tells what could well happen to a young man in such a situation — because neither he nor his society had any Torah to guide them, but only the puritan conscience of New England that they had to live up to, or at least make an appearance (at all costs) of living up to it.

The second story is by the Russian novelist Leo Tolstoy (1828–1910), about a master and his worker who set out on a journey in the winter and found themselves caught in a snowstorm at night. Only the master had a fur-lined coat that could keep a person warm in such weather. If he wore it, the worker would soon freeze to death in his poor thin clothes. If the master gave him the coat, he himself would soon lose his life. Tolstoy was interested in preaching altruism, the need and value of loving another more than oneself. For him the best solution was to have the master give the other the coat. The alternative would be selfish and evil, corrupting the soul. . . .

Of course Tolstoy had a strong point to make. He found far too much unheeding selfishness in the world, especially in the tsarist Russia that he knew; and perhaps only the dedicated practice of altruism, to this extreme extent, could right the balance. Completely absent, however, is the blessed light of the Torah, teaching a person to help others live, always, in every way — only, not at the cost of his own life. With the Torah we have a balance between care for oneself and care for others. There is no need to flounder between the extremes of selfishness and altruism.

131. This is no mere armchair theorizing. In the Yom Kippur War, for example, the Syrian army had standing orders to bring only wounded *officers* to its hospitals for treatment. Ordinary soldiers were to be left to die. The Syrian high command did not think it wise or important to waste army fighting strength on too much rescue work, especially as not enough hospital facilities were prepared in the first place.

132. Esther Rabbah 10:11; Tanḥuma, *tol'doth* 5.

# Index to *p'sukim* (Scriptural passages)

410

411